YO-BZL-913

MINNEAPOLIS & ST. PAUL

TRICIA CORNELL

Contents

Maps

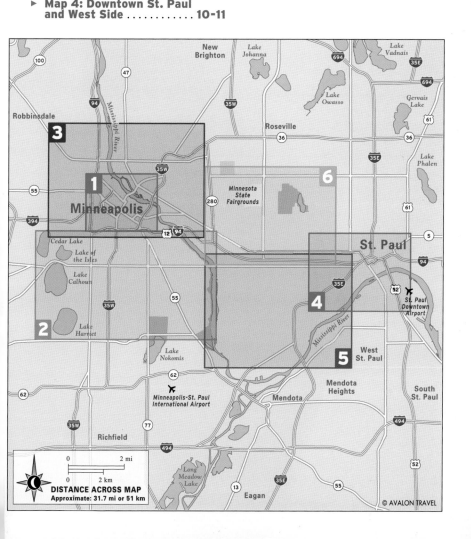

SIGHTS

8	HENNEPIN AVENUE BRIDGE	64	FOSHAY TOWER
13	ST. ANTHONY FALLS	67	BASILICA OF ST. MARY
16	STONE ARCH BRIDGE	73	NICOLLET MALL
34	MINNEAPOLIS CENTRAL LIBRARY	85	WALKER ART CENTER AND SCULPTURE GARDEN
38	MINNEAPOLIS CITY HALL AND HENNEPIN COUNTY COURTHOUSE		

RESTAURANTS

1	BE'WICHED	63	HELL'S KITCHEN
20	PIZZA LUCE	66	KEYS CAFÉ
23	CAFÉ BRENDA	69	BAR AND CAFÉ LURCAT
24	SAFFRON	70	NICK AND EDDIE
25	112 EATERY	71	JOE'S GARAGE
26	NAMI	72	BUCA DI BEPPO
30	D'AMICO CUCINA	76	VINCENT – A RESTAURANT
43	SPOONRIVER	77	MASA
51	MURRAY'S RESTAURANT AND COCKTAILS	86	20.21
54	SOLERA	87	LA BELLE VIE
62	ZELO		

SEE MAP 3

Mississippi River

NORTH LOOP

Minneapolis Central Library

DOWNTOWN WEST

Target Center

Minneapolis City Hall and Hennepin County Courthouse

Foshay Tower

Basilica of St. Mary

Loring Park

Nicollet Mall

To 83 Parade Ice Garden

Walker Art Center and Sculpture Garden

Loring Lake

LORING PARK

Franklin Steele Square

SEE MAP 3

SEE MAP 2

0   200 yds
0   200 m

DISTANCE ACROSS MAP
Approximate: 2.1 mi or 3.4 km

SEE MAP 3

Nicollet Island

Holmes Park

Chute Park

Hennepin Avenue Bridge

MARCY HOLMES

3RD AVE BRIDGE

Pillsbury Park

St. Anthony Falls

Hennepin Bluffs Park

Stone Arch Bridge

Lower Dam

Mill Ruins Park

WASHINGTON AVE S

Hubert H. Humphrey Metrodome

DOWNTOWN EAST

WASHINGTON AVE

Elliot Park

ELLIOT PARK

Currie Park

University of Minnesota

SEE MAP 3

CEDAR RIVERSIDE

SEE MAP 2

Augsburg College

Murphy Square Park

© AVALON TRAVEL

NIGHTLIFE

- 3 TOAST
- 4 BEV'S WINE BAR
- 6 MONTE CARLO
- 7 JETSET
- 10 NYE'S POLONAISE ROOM
- 19 THE LOUNGE
- 21 ENVY
- 22 FINE LINE MUSIC CAFÉ
- 28 FIRST AVENUE AND 7TH ST. ENTRY
- 31 BELLANOTTE
- 32 GAY 90S
- 33 SPIN
- 36 KIERAN'S IRISH PUB
- 56 THE SALOON
- 58 CHAMBERS ROOFTOP LOUNGE
- 68 BAR LURCAT
- 75 BRIT'S PUB
- 78 DAKOTA JAZZ CLUB AND RESTAURANT
- 79 THE LOCAL
- 88 19 BAR

ARTS AND LEISURE

- 2 PARADISE CHARTER CRUISES
- 5 HOUSE OF BALLS
- 11 ST. ANTHONY FALLS HERITAGE TRAIL
- 12 MAGICAL HISTORY TOURS
- 14 WATER POWER PARK
- 15 SOAP FACTORY
- 17 THE FIRM
- 27 LIFETIME FITNESS IN TARGET CENTER
- 27 MINNESOTA LYNX
- 27 MINNESOTA TIMBERWOLVES
- 27 TARGET CENTER
- 40 THE DEPOT
- 41 MILL CITY MUSEUM
- 41 MILL CITY MUSEUM TOURS
- 42 MILL RUINS PARK
- 45 GUTHRIE THEATER
- 47 GOLD MEDAL PARK
- 48 MINNESOTA CENTER FOR BOOK ARTS
- 50 MINNESOTA TWINS
- 50 MINNESOTA VIKINGS
- 50 ROLLER DOME
- 57 HENNEPIN THEATRE DISTRICT
- 74 YWCAS OF MINNEAPOLIS AND ST. PAUL
- 80 ORCHESTRA HALL
- 83 PARADE ICE GARDEN
- 84 LORING PARK

SHOPS

- 18 LYNDALE MARKET
- 35 FRIENDS OF THE MINNEAPOLIS PUBLIC LIBRARY BOOKSTORE
- 44 MILL CITY FARMERS MARKET
- 49 BIG BRAIN COMICS
- 52 FINNSTYLE
- 60 NICOLLET MALL MARKET

HOTELS

- 9 NICOLLET ISLAND INN
- 29 GRAVES 601
- 37 HOTEL MINNEAPOLIS
- 39 THE DEPOT
- 46 ALOFT
- 53 GRAND HOTEL MINNEAPOLIS
- 55 SALOON HOTEL
- 59 CHAMBERS MINNEAPOLIS
- 61 THE MARQUETTE HOTEL
- 65 W MINNEAPOLIS– THE FOSHAY
- 81 HILTON MINNEAPOLIS
- 82 HOTEL IVY

MAP 2

SOUTH MINNEAPOLIS

To **A** 1 Theodore Wirth Park

Chain of Lakes **2**

Cedar Lake

Lake of the Isles

W LAKE OF THE ISLES PKWY

W FRANKLIN AVE

W 21ST ST
W 22ND ST
W 24TH ST

PENN AVE S
LAKE PL
JAMES
IRVING AVE
HUMBOLT AVE S
GIRARD AVE S
HENNEPIN AVE

W 22ND ST
W 24TH ST
W 25TH ST
W 26TH ST
W 27TH ST
W 28TH ST

WHITTIER

SEE MAP 3

PLEASANT AVE S
NICOLLET AVE S
STEVENS AVE S
3RD AVE S
4TH AVE S
CLIFTON AVE S

35W

PHILLIPS

CEDAR LAKE BLVD
SUNSET BLVD

Lake St/Minnetonka Blvd

Lyndale Park

THE MALL
LAGOON AVE
W 29TH ST

W CALHOUN PKWY

CALHOUN AVE

Lake Calhoun

W 28TH ST
W 32ND ST
W 34TH ST
W 35TH ST
W 36TH ST

CARAG

LYNDALE

CENTRAL

HOLMES AVE S
HENNEPIN AVE S
FREMONT AVE S
EMERSON AVE S
COLFAX AVE S
BRYANT AVE S
ALDRICH AVE S
LYNDALE AVE S
GARFIELD AVE S
HARRIET AVE S
GRAND AVE S
NICOLLET AVE S
1ST AVE S
STEVENS AVE S
4TH AVE S
5TH AVE S
PORTLAND AVE S
OAKLAND AVE S
PARK AVE S

E 31ST ST
E 32ND ST
E 33RD ST
E 34TH ST

Lakewood Cemetery

Lakewood Cemetery Pond

RICHFIELD RD

W 37TH ST
W 38TH ST
W 39TH ST
W 40TH ST
W 41ST ST
W 42ND ST
W 43RD ST

LINDEN HILLS

BRYANT

CLINTON AVE S

Lyndale Park

ROSE WAY RD

Como-Harriet Streetcar

SHERIDAN AVE
LINDEN HILLS
QUEEN AVE S
W LAKE HARRIET PKWY

To **S** 61 France 44
S 62

Lake Harriet

E LAKE HARRIET PKWY

KINGS HWY

KING FIELD

35W

W 44TH ST
W 45TH ST
W 46TH ST
W 47TH ST
W 48TH ST
W 49TH ST
W 50TH ST
W 51ST ST

PLEASANT AVE S
PILLSBURY AVE S
WENTWORTH AVE S
BLAISDELL AVE S

E 47TH ST
E 48TH ST
E 49TH ST

OAKLAND AVE S
PARK AVE S

FIELD

CROWEN AVE S
BEARD AVE S
ABBOTT AVE S
ZENITH AVE S
YORK AVE S
XERXES AVE

WASHBURN AVE S
VINCENT AVE S
SHERIDAN AVE S
RUSSELL AVE S
QUEEN AVE S
PENN AVE S
OLIVER AVE S
NEWTON AVE S
MORGAN AVE S
LOGAN AVE S

GIRARD AVE S
FREMONT AVE S
EMERSON AVE S

TANGLETOWN

W 50TH ST
W 51ST ST
W 52ND ST

LYNNHURST

Pearl Park

FULTON

W 53RD ST
W 54TH ST
W 55TH ST
W 56TH ST

ROBBINS ST

KNOX AVE S
JAMES AVE S
IRVING AVE S
HUMBOLDT AVE S
GIRARD AVE S
FREMONT AVE S
EMERSON AVE S
COLFAX AVE S
ALDRICH AVE S

W MINNEHAHA PKWY

GRAND AVE S
PLEASANT AVE S
PILLSBURY AVE S
WENTWORTH AVE S
BLAISDELL AVE S
1ST AVE S
2ND AVE S
CLINTON AVE S

Diamond Lake

KENNY

W 65TH ST
W 66TH ST
W 67TH ST
W 68TH ST

To **R** 78 Shiraz Fire Roasted Cuisine

35W

0   0.5 mi
0   0.5 km

DISTANCE ACROSS MAP
Approximate: 6.2 mi or 9.9 km

© AVALON TRAVEL

SEE MAP 1

SEE MAP 6

SEE MAP 5

E FRANKLIN AVE

LONGFELLOW

EAST PHILLIPS

Midtown Exchange

CORCORAN

Powderhorn Lake

Powderhorn Park

Mississippi River

Mississippi Gorge

HOWE

BANCROFT

STANDISH

Minnehaha Falls

Minnehaha Park

⊙ ARTS AND LEISURE
1 THEODORE WIRTH PARK
4 LAKE OF THE ISLES
6 BRAVE NEW WORKSHOP
10 SOO VISUAL ARTS STUDIOS
17 ⬛ CHILDREN'S THEATRE COMPANY
17 ⬛ MINNEAPOLIS INSTITUTE OF ARTS
18 HENNEPIN HISTORY MUSEUM
20 OPEN EYE FIGURE THEATRE
21 AMERICAN SWEDISH INSTITUTE
22 FRANKLIN ART WORKS
25 NORTHERN CLAY CENTER
28 MIDTOWN GREENWAY
29 LAKE CALHOUN SAILING SCHOOL
29 WHEEL FUN RENTALS
30 CALHOUN RENTAL
35 UPTOWN THEATRE
41 BRYANT-LAKE BOWL
43 INTERMEDIA ARTS
44 JUNGLE THEATER
48 FREEWHEEL MIDTOWN BIKE CENTER
50 IN THE HEART OF THE BEAST PUPPET AND MASK THEATRE
55 THE BAKKEN
59 RIVERVIEW THEATER
68 LAKE HARRIET YACHT CLUB
69 LYNDALE PARK
75 ⬛ GRAND ROUNDS NATIONAL SCENIC BYWAY
76 MINNEHAHA FALLS
77 ⬛ THE MUSEUM OF RUSSIAN ART

✪ SIGHTS
2 ⬛ CHAIN OF LAKES
49 ⬛ MIDTOWN EXCHANGE
67 COMO–HARRIET STREETCAR

ⓡ RESTAURANTS
9 SEBASTIAN JOE'S
11 FRENCH MEADOW BAKERY AND CAFÉ
13 COMMON ROOTS
15 JASMINE DELI
15 QUANG
23 MARIA'S
24 SEWARD CAFÉ
26 TRUE THAI
27 BIRCHWOOD
31 ⬛ BARBETTE
32 ⬛ LUCIA'S
36 CHINO LATINO
40 BRYANT LAKE BOWL
45 FUJI YA
46 TAQUERIA LOS OCAMPO
52 MANNY'S TORTAS
53 TOWN TALK DINER
56 CREMA
57 VICTOR'S 1959 CAFÉ
64 THE ZUMBRO
71 BRODER'S PASTA BAR
72 HEIDI'S
73 BLACKBIRD
74 PUMPHOUSE CREAMERY
78 SHIRAZ FIRE ROASTED CUISINE

ⓝ NIGHTLIFE
12 ⬛ C.C. CLUB
37 FAMOUS DAVE'S
38 STELLA'S FISH CAFÉ & PRESTIGE OYSTER BAR
42 V.F.W. JAMES BALLENTINE POST NO. 246
58 CHATTERBOX
60 RIVERVIEW

Ⓗ HOTELS
16 HISTORIC KING INN AND MINNEAPOLIS HOSTEL

Ⓢ SHOPS
3 BIRCHBARK BOOKS
5 ⬛ VIA'S VINTAGE
7 ⬛ TWIN CITIES GREEN
8 PATINA
19 ELECTRIC FETUS
33 PAPER SOURCE
34 MAGERS AND QUINN
39 LOCAL MOTION
47 UNCLE EDGAR'S MYSTERY BOOKSTORE & UNCLE HUGO'S SCIENCE FICTION BOOKSTORE
51 ⬛ INGEBRETSEN'S
54 HYMIE'S VINTAGE RECORDS
61 ⬛ FRANCE 44
62 NEEDLEWORK UNLIMITED
63 ⬛ WONDERMENT
65 CREATIVE KIDSTUFF
66 ⬛ WILD RUMPUS
70 BIRCH

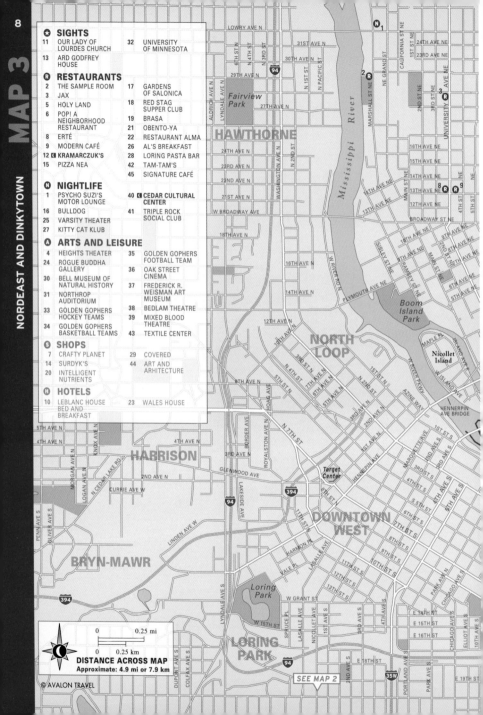

☺ SIGHTS
11 OUR LADY OF LOURDES CHURCH
13 ARD GODFREY HOUSE
32 UNIVERSITY OF MINNESOTA

☻ RESTAURANTS
2 THE SAMPLE ROOM
3 JAX
5 HOLY LAND
6 POPI A NEIGHBORHOOD RESTAURANT
8 ERTÉ
9 MODERN CAFÉ
12 KRAMARCZUK'S
15 PIZZA NEA
17 GARDENS OF SALONICA
18 RED STAG SUPPER CLUB
19 BRASA
21 OBENTO-YA
22 RESTAURANT ALMA
26 AL'S BREAKFAST
28 LORING PASTA BAR
42 TAM-TAM'S
45 SIGNATURE CAFÉ

☾ NIGHTLIFE
1 PSYCHO SUZI'S MOTOR LOUNGE
16 BULLDOG
25 VARSITY THEATER
27 KITTY CAT KLUB
40 CEDAR CULTURAL CENTER
41 TRIPLE ROCK SOCIAL CLUB

⬥ ARTS AND LEISURE
4 HEIGHTS THEATER
24 ROGUE BUDDHA GALLERY
30 BELL MUSEUM OF NATURAL HISTORY
31 NORTHROP AUDITORIUM
33 GOLDEN GOPHERS HOCKEY TEAMS
34 GOLDEN GOPHERS BASKETBALL TEAMS
35 GOLDEN GOPHERS FOOTBALL TEAM
36 OAK STREET CINEMA
37 FREDERICK R. WEISMAN ART MUSEUM
38 BEDLAM THEATRE
39 MIXED BLOOD THEATRE
43 TEXTILE CENTER

ⓢ SHOPS
7 CRAFTY PLANET
14 SURDYK'S
20 INTELLIGENT NUTRIENTS
29 COVERED
44 ART AND ARHITECTURE

ⓗ HOTELS
10 LEBLANC HOUSE BED AND BREAKFAST
23 WALES HOUSE

0   0.25 mi
0   0.25 km

DISTANCE ACROSS MAP
Approximate: 4.9 mi or 7.9 km

© AVALON TRAVEL

SEE MAP 2

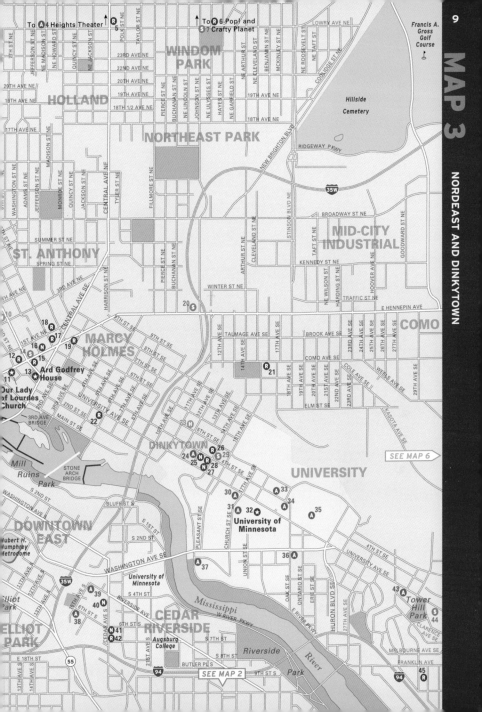

To 4 Heights Theater
To 6 Popl and 7 Crafty Planet

Francis A. Gross Golf Course

WINDOM PARK

HOLLAND

NORTHEAST PARK

Hillside Cemetery

RIDGEWAY PKWY

35W

ST. ANTHONY

Broadway St NE

MID-CITY INDUSTRIAL

KENNEDY ST NE

E Hennepin Ave

COMO

MARCY HOLMES

Talmage Ave SE

Brook Ave SE

Como Ave SE

Ard Godfrey House

Our Lady of Lourdes Church

SEE MAP 6

DINKYTOWN

UNIVERSITY

Mill Ruins Park

STONE ARCH BRIDGE

DOWNTOWN EAST

Hubert H. Humphrey Metrodome

University of Minnesota

University of Minnesota

35W

Mississippi

CEDAR RIVERSIDE

Augsburg College

Tower Hill Park

Riverside Park

River

55

SEE MAP 2

94

94

PAYNE-PHALEN

Swede Hollow Park

To 6 Vertical Endeavors

Metropolitan State University

DAYTON'S BLUFF

St. Paul Union Depot

LAFAYETTE BRIDGE

To 39 Indian Mounds Park

Navy Island

WEST SIDE

Prospect Terrace Park

Wabasha Street Caves

St. Paul Downtown Airport

SIGHTS

2	WESTERN SCULPTURE PARK
3	MINNESOTA STATE CAPITOL
10	CATHEDRAL OF ST. PAUL
11	MINNESOTA HISTORY CENTER
30	RICE PARK
32	JAMES J. HILL REFERENCE LIBRARY
35	ST. PAUL CITY HALL AND RAMSEY COUNTY COURTHOUSE
36	ST. PAUL UNION DEPOT
39	INDIAN MOUNDS PARK
44	WABASHA STREET CAVES

RESTAURANTS

1	MAI VILLAGE
5	STRIP CLUB
8	W.A. FROST AND COMPANY
12	BABANI'S KURDISH RESTAURANT
15	MANCINI'S CHAR HOUSE
17	FOREPAUGH'S
20	MICKEY'S DINER
23	MERITAGE
24	ST. PAUL GRILL
33	PAZZALUNA
34	SAKURA RESTAURANT & BAR
38	TANPOPO NOODLE SHOP
46	BOCA CHICA
47	EL BURRITO MERCADO

NIGHTLIFE

| 26 | ST. PAUL GRILL |
| 27 | ARTISTS' QUARTER |

ARTS AND LEISURE

4	GATEWAY TRAIL
6	VERTICAL ENDEAVORS
9	JAMES J. HILL HOUSE
13	MINNESOTA HISTORY THEATRE
14	FITZGERALD THEATER
16	ALEXANDER RAMSEY HOUSE
18	SCIENCE MUSEUM OF MINNESOTA
19	MINNESOTA WILD
19	XCEL ENERGY CENTER
21	MINNESOTA CHILDREN'S MUSEUM
22	PARK SQUARE THEATER
28	LANDMARK CENTER
29	ORDWAY CENTER FOR THE PERFORMING ARTS
31	WINTER CARNIVAL
31	LANDMARK CENTER RINK
40	HARRIET ISLAND REGIONAL PARK
41	CENTENNIAL SHOWBOAT
42	PADELFORD CRUISES
45	ST. PAUL GANGSTER TOURS

SHOPS

| 7 | COMMON GOOD BOOKS |
| 37 | ST. PAUL FARMERS' MARKET |

HOTELS

| 25 | ST. PAUL HOTEL |
| 43 | COVINGTON INN BED AND BREAKFAST |

0   250 yds
0   250 m

DISTANCE ACROSS MAP
Approximate: 3 mi or 4.8 km

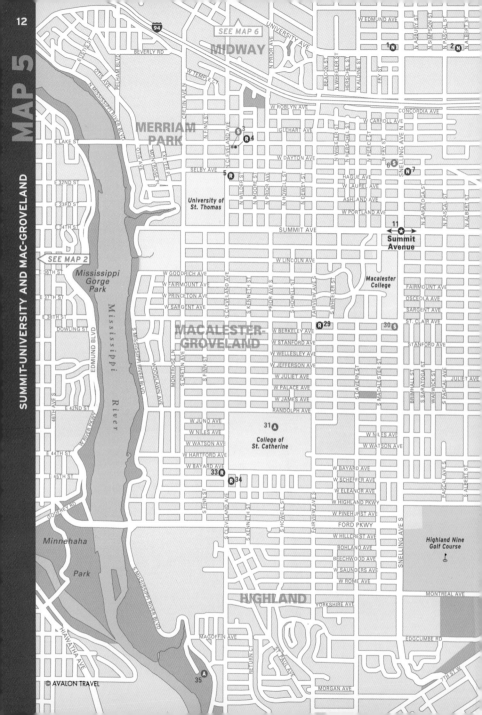

© AVALON TRAVEL

SEE MAP 6

DISTANCE ACROSS MAP
Approximate: 5.1 mi or 8.2 km

0   0.25 mi
0   0.25 km

SEE MAP 4

① SIGHTS
11 ◖ SUMMIT AVENUE

ℝ RESTAURANTS
4	IZZY'S ICE CREAM CAFÉ	27	BARBARY FIG
5	128 CAFÉ	29	HEARTLAND
10 ◖	MOSCOW ON THE HILL	32	CASPER & RUNYON'S NOOK
14	EVEREST ON GRAND	33	CECIL'S DELICATESSEN
22 ◖	CAFÉ LATTÉ	34	PUNCH PIZZA
26	GRAND OLE CREAMERY		

ℕ NIGHTLIFE
1	TURF CLUB	7	O'GARA'S BAR AND GRILL
2	TOWN HOUSE	9	HAPPY GNOME

ⓐ ARTS AND LEISURE
8	PENUMBRA THEATRE	31	THE O'SHAUGHNESSY
20	STEPPINGSTONE THEATRE	35	HIDDEN FALLS PARK
		36	CROSBY FARM PARK

ⓢ SHOPS
3	LEGACY CHOCOLATES	18	THE RED BALLOON BOOKSHOP
6	LULA'S VINTAGE WEAR	19 ◖	COOKS OF CROCUS HILL
12	TREADLE YARD GOODS	21	GARDEN OF EDEN
13	PICKY GIRL	23	QUINCE
13	SIJI KIDS	24	THE YARNERY
15	BABY GRAND	25	THE GOLDEN FIG
16	DANISH BOHEMIA	28	THE GRAND HAND
17 ◖	THE BIBELOT	30	PEAPODS

MAP 6

COMO AND ST. ANTHONY

U of M Golf Course
1 A
2 A
3 A

LARPENTEUR AVE W

FOLWELL AVE

W HOYT AVE

SEE MAP 3

W HENDON AVE

BUFORD AVE

RANDALL AVE

A 6

W VALENTINE AVE

Minnesota
State Fairgrounds

W DOSWELL AVE

4 S
5 R

COMMONWEALTH AVE

A 7

MINNESOTA AVE
CANFIELD AVE

COMMONWEALTH AVE

KNAPP ST
SCUDDER ST

JUDSON AVE

WHILLSIDE AVE

KASOTA AVE

ST. ANTHONY

ENERGY PARK DR

Midway
Field

13 A

ROBBINS ST

W PIERCE BUTLER RTE

MANVEL ST

CAPP RD

W TAYLOR AVE

280

W HAMPDEN AVE

HERSEY ST

HEWITT AVE

LONG AVE

W HUBBARD AVE

Hamline
University

VANDALIA ST

TRANSFER RD

ENGLEWOOD AVE

W TERRITORIAL RD

FRANKLIN AVE

CHARLES AVE

94

UNIVERSITY AVE

S 17

MYRTLE AVE

ST. ANTHONY AVE

WABASH AVE

CHARLES AVE

SEE MAP 2

MIDWAY

BEVERLY RD

R 19

PELHAM BLVD

18
R

94

ST. ANTHONY AVE

W TEMPLE AVE

GILBERT AVE

STINSON CT.

CONCORDIA AVE

W ROBLYN AVE

W CARROLL AVE

Mississippi

IGLEHART AVE

River

W DAYTON AVE

SELBY AVE

© AVALON TRAVEL

University of
St. Thomas

MERRIAM PARK

HAGUE AVE

SEE MAP 5

DISTANCE ACROSS MAP
Approximate: 4.6 mi or 7.4 km

0   0.25 mi
0   0.25 km

◎ SIGHTS
8	COMO TOWN	10	COMO PARK ZOO AND CONSERVATORY
9	CAFESJIAN'S CAROUSEL		

◎ RESTAURANTS
5	FINNISH BISTRO	19	FASIKA
18	RUSSIAN TEA HOUSE		

◎ NIGHTLIFE
16	HALF TIME REC

◎ ARTS AND LEISURE
1	LES BOLSTAD UNIVERSITY OF MINNESOTA GOLF CLUB	6	GOLDSTEIN MUSEUM
2	GIBBS MUSEUM OF PIONEER AND DAKOTAH LIFE	7	MINNESOTA STATE FAIR
3	MINNESOTA LIGHTNING	11	COMO PARK
		12	COMO SKI CENTER
		13	ST. PAUL SAINTS
		15	TWIN CITIES MODEL RAILROAD MUSEUM

◎ SHOPS
4	MICAWBER'S BOOKS	17	CHOCOLAT CELESTE

◎ HOTELS
14	BEST WESTERN BANDANA SQUARE

DISTANCE ACROSS MAP
Approximate: 31.7 mi or 51 km

0 — 2 mi
0 — 2 km

1 Ⓐ
101

To Ⓢ 2 Albertville
Premium Outlets

Ⓢ 3

694
94

4 Ⓐ 5
Ⓗ

6 Ⓐ

Brooklyn
Center

100

Eagle
Lake

494

169

55
Hamel

Bass
Lake

New Hope

Crystal

To Ⓐ 9 Baker National
Golf Course

Medicine
Lake

10 Ⓡ

Robbinsdale

94

Long
Lake

55

14 Ⓐ

Plymouth

Golden
Valley

55

Long Lake

146

494

394

12

15 Ⓐ 16 Ⓡ

17 Ⓐ 394

Lake of
the Isles

13 Ⓡ   Wayzata

12

Cedar
Lake

169

St. Louis
Park

18 Ⓡ

Lake
Calhoun

Lake
Minnetonka

Minnetonka

7

19 Ⓐ
20 Ⓢ

35W

Hopkins

25 Ⓐ 26 Ⓢ Ⓐ 27

Lake
Harriet

28 Ⓡ

Excelsior
Streetcar Line

21 Ⓐ
Ⓝ 22

23 ★

Shorewood

Christmas
Lake

7

29 Ⓢ Ⓝ 30
31 Ⓡ Ⓢ 32

Excelsior

To ★ 24 Minnesota
Landscape Arboretum

62

Bryant
Lake

62

Edina

35 Ⓡ

Lotus
Lake

169

36 Ⓢ

35W

100

37 Ⓝ

Richfield

Ⓡ 38

34 Ⓝ

312

Eden Prairie

212

43 Ⓝ

Anderson
Lakes
Park
Reserve

44 Ⓐ

Hyland-
Bush Lakes
Park

Bloomington

Lake
Riley

Staring
Lake

45 Ⓐ

212

46 Ⓐ

48 ★
Valleyfair

James W.
Wilkie
Regional Park

Minnesota River

101

Shakopee

47 Ⓐ
169

101

13

Burnsville

35W

© AVALON TRAVEL

Map labels:

To Ⓐ8 Minnesota Thunder
Fridley
7Ⓡ
New Brighton
694
47
35W
Turtle Lake
Arden Hills
10
Pleasant Lake
Shoreview
96
Birch Lake
White Bear Lake
35E
White Bear Lake
Lake Vadnais
61
Lake Johanna
Lake Owasso
694
Gervais Lake
Ⓝ11
12Ⓐ
Roseville
36
Maplewood
36
U of M Golf Course
35E
35W
280
Minnesota State Fairgrounds
Como Park
Lake Phalen
61
Oakdale
5
694
Minneapolis
12 94
St. Paul
94
94
55
Nokomis Hiawatha Park
Minnehaha Park
Lake Nokomis
62
Historic Fort Snelling 33✪
Minneapolis-St. Paul International Airport
77
Mississippi River
West St. Paul
Mendota
Mendota Heights
35E
55
35E
St. Paul Downtown Airport
52
61
10
To Ⓝ50 Afton House Inn
494
41
39 40
Ⓐ Ⓐ42
Mall of America
494
Long Meadow Lake
13
Eagan
Black Dog Lake
77
35E
Minnesota Zoo
49✪
Lebanon Hills Regional Park
52

Ⓐ ARTS AND LEISURE
1 RUSH CREEK GOLF CLUB
4 GRAND RIOS
6 KETTER CANOEING
8 MINNESOTA THUNDER
9 BAKER NATIONAL GOLF COURSE
12 GATEWAY CYCLE
14 LUCE LINE TRAIL
15 3RD LAIR SKATE PARK
19 PAVEK MUSEUM OF BROADCASTING
21 OLD LOG THEATRE
25 STAGES THEATER
27 SOUTHWEST REGIONAL LRT TRAIL
39 WATER PARK OF AMERICA
42 METROCONNECTIONS
44 HYLAND SKI AND SNOWBOARD CENTER
45 HYLAND LAKE PARK PRESERVE
46 THE LANDING
47 CANTERBURY PARK

Ⓢ SHOPS
2 ALBERTVILLE PREMIUM OUTLETS
3 THE SHOPPES AT ARBOR LAKES
20 KIDDYWAMPUS
26 HOPKINS ANTIQUE MALL
29 HOT MAMA
32 PREMIER CHEESE MARKET
36 THE GALLERIA

Ⓗ HOTELS
5 GRAND RIOS
22 BIRD HOUSE INN
34 CHANHASSEN INN
37Ⓒ MARRIOTT RESIDENCE INN, EDINBOROUGH
40 GRAND LODGE
43 CROWNE PLAZA BLOOMINGTON
50 AFTON HOUSE INN

✪ SIGHTS
23 EXCELSIOR STREETCAR LINE
24 MINNESOTA LANDSCAPE ARBORETUM
33 HISTORIC FORT SNELLING
41Ⓒ MALL OF AMERICA
48 VALLEYFAIR
49 MINNESOTA ZOO

Ⓡ RESTAURANTS
7 KING'S FINE KOREAN CUISINE
10 ST. PETERSBURG
13 PATRICK'S BISTRO
16Ⓒ GOOD DAY CAFÉ
17 TASTE OF INDIA
18 YUM!
28 CONVENTION GRILL
31 SALUT BAR AMERICAIN
35 PATRICK'S BAKERY AND CAFÉ
38Ⓒ JUN BO
30 BEAUJO'S

Ⓝ NIGHTLIFE
11 MYTH

Discover
Minneapolis & St. Paul

Let's just get this out of the way: Yes, it can get pretty cold here. Yes, both Minneapolis and St. Paul have "elevated sidewalk things" (skyways) connecting buildings downtown. And, yes, we've got the largest mall in the United States.

Those vague and vaguely dismissive impressions may be why people in the Twin Cities love hosting friends from out of town. There's a deep satisfaction – and yes, a little smugness – when we treat out-of-towners to an authentic Vietnamese meal or to dinner from a national award-winning chef. We love to wear guests out on the trails that wrap around the cities' 22 lakes. It feels good to pull out the paper and say, "Feel like going to the theater? There are more than 45 professional shows tonight." A proud local will view every satisfied visitor as a convert who will head back home and bust some Minnesota stereotypes: Mary Tyler Moore tossing her tam; Garrison Keillor's Norwegian bachelor farmers.

We're past that now. We're modern. We're hip. St. Paul is compact, pretty, and offers plenty in the way of sights and classic neighborhood bars. Minneapolis is the glitzy twin and the hub of the music scene where Prince, the Replacements, and Soul Asylum first rocked. Both cities are buzzing year-round. Far from hibernating, we embrace the winter. Joggers put on an extra layer, windsurfers transform into ice surfers, cyclists install winter tires, and skiers exult. And when temperatures climb back above freezing, the whole process rewinds; the lakefronts, river paths, and outdoor restaurants fill with people who enjoy spring more than anyone on earth.

Yes, it can get a little cold here. And we love it.

Planning Your Trip

► WHERE TO GO

Downtown Minneapolis

Raised indoor walkways, known as skyways, connect 70 downtown city blocks, creating an indoor network of offices, shops, restaurants, theaters, hotels, and condos. Outside, there's even more to discover: the **Mississippi riverfront**, the **Guthrie Theater**, the **Walker Art Center,** and **Nicollet Mall**, home to some of the best dining and bars in the Twin Cities. Three of the Twin Cities' four **major sports franchises**—the Twins, Vikings, and Timberwolves—have their homes downtown, too.

South Minneapolis

The leafy green neighborhoods of South Minneapolis, popular with families and young professionals alike, are home to the **Chain of Lakes**, the **Minneapolis Institute of Arts,** the **Children's Theatre Company,** and **The Museum of Russian Art**. Recent college grads gravitate to the Uptown neighborhood, at the intersection of Lake Street and Hennepin Avenue, for shopping and nightlife. The residents of South Minneapolis love to eat well and the area is packed with great dining options, including the multiethnic **Midtown Global Market.**

Nordeast and Dinkytown

Nordeast, or Northeast Minneapolis, was once home to a thriving community of Eastern European immigrants, still reflected in the area's landmarks: **Surdyk's** wine store, **Kramarczuk's** deli, and **Nye's Polonaise Room.** Today the area, still largely middle class, is also home to Somali, Middle Eastern, and Latin American communities. The area

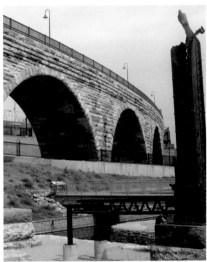
The Stone Arch Bridge curves gracefully across the Mississippi near downtown Minneapolis.

has also welcomed many of the artists forced out of the gentrified Warehouse District. Dinkytown, once Bob Dylan's haunt, is inseparable from **University of Minnesota** student life.

Downtown St. Paul and West Side

St. Paul is known as the slower-paced twin but has plenty to offer in terms of culture, including the **Ordway**, the **Science Museum of Minnesota,** and the **Minnesota Children's Museum.** The heart of Downtown is **Rice Park,** bordered by the architecturally stunning **Landmark Center.** West 7th Street, heading southwest from the **Xcel Energy Center,** is a great destination for a night on the town. St. Paul's West Side—southeast of downtown—is the home to St. Paul's deep-rooted Latino community, now rebranded as the **District del Sol.**

Summit-University and Mac-Groveland

The St. Paul neighborhoods west of downtown are home to five colleges and universities, with all the bookstores and coffee shops you expect. **Summit Avenue** is the historical seat of St. Paul's moneyed elite and still a wide, lovely boulevard for strolling. **Grand Avenue** is excellent for boutique shopping and people watching. Just north of I-94, which cuts St. Paul decisively into northern and southern halves, runs the more ethnically and economically diverse **University Avenue,** known for dive bars and great Vietnamese food.

Como and St. Anthony

The northern neighborhoods of St. Paul feel about as removed from urban bustle as you can get. **St. Anthony Park,** with its compact shopping and dining district, is almost like a separate small town, where you can have a light meal at the **Finnish Bistro** or browse the selection at **Micawber's Books.** The "garden district" of **Como Park** attracts people from around the Twin Cities who want to run, boat, fish, ski, golf, or enjoy the **Como Park Zoo and Conservatory.**

Greater Twin Cities

The older first-ring suburbs around Minneapolis and St. Paul are hard to distinguish from their gridded and green counterparts within the city limits. Once you hit the second ring and the exurbs, however, the streets start to curve and suddenly the buildings all seem newer and more spread out. There are plenty of good reasons to venture beyond the cities proper, including **Historic Fort Snelling,** the **Minnesota Zoo,** and the excellent **Minnesota Landscape Arboretum.** And how could you go home from Minnesota and tell your friends you missed the **Mall of America,** in the southern suburb of Bloomington?

▶ WHEN TO GO

Take a tip from Minnesota brides: **October,** not June, is the most popular month for weddings in Minnesota. That's when the Twin Cities are at their best—after the sticky summer and before the snow flies. **May and June** are a close second, although spring is an elusive thing here, lasting just a week or two. **Summer is high season,** when you'll see longer hours at venues, slightly higher hotel prices (except downtown), and venues packed with music and festivals. In late June, the sun sets around 9 P.M. and dusk lingers until around 10. But don't count out the **winter!** Yes, the snow and cold can add a bit of hassle, but these cities know how to deal with it, even how to revel in it (case in point: late January's Winter Carnival).

Fall is a favorite time of year for many Minnesotans.

Explore Minneapolis & St. Paul

► THE BEST OF THE TWIN CITIES

Divide and conquer is the best way to squeeze the best the Twin Cities has to offer into just two days. If you take it by foot, plan on three or four miles of walking a day.

Day 1

► Start your tour where Minneapolis began, on the Mississippi River. On a summer Saturday, grab a pastry, coffee, and even an early-morning bratwurst at the **Mill City Farmers Market.**

► There's plenty right on the riverfront to fill a morning: the **Guthrie Theater's** endless

bridge, the one-mile **St. Anthony Falls Heritage Trail,** the stunning **Stone Arch** and **Hennepin Avenue Bridges, Mill Ruins Park,** and the **Mill City Museum** (don't miss the film *Minneapolis in 19 Minutes Flat*).

► To get an even closer view of **St. Anthony Falls,** the only waterfall on the Mississippi, stop at **Water Power Park.**

► Spend the afternoon strolling down **Nicollet Mall.** Start at the **Minneapolis Central Library** and head southeast.

St. Anthony Falls has powered Minneapolis since the city's earliest days.

The IDS Tower is the tallest building in Minnesota.

Cathedral of St. Paul, downtown St. Paul

Along the way, see the **skyways** by ducking into just about any store or office building and following signs. On Thursdays between May and October, the **Lyndale Farmers Market** sets up along most of the mall. At 12th Street, head down the Loring Greenway—a park-like path between two high-rise condo buildings—to **Loring Park.**

▶ Directly across the park from the greenway is the yellow-and-blue Irene Hixon Whitney Bridge, which leads to the **Walker Art Center and Sculpture Garden,** home of the iconic *Spoonbridge and Cherry,* by Claes Oldenburg and Coosje van Bruggen, and, inside the **Cowles Conservatory,** Frank Gehry's *Standing Glass Fish.*

▶ Your evening options from here are great: Treat yourself to fine dining at Wolfgang Puck's **20.21** inside the Walker, or **La**

Belle Vie, across Hennepin Avenue. For less expensive ethnic fare, head to **Eat Street** (Nicollet Ave. between 13th and 29th Sts.).

▶ After dinner, if you don't have theater tickets, the **bars along 1st Avenue** are always hopping. Or unwind with lawn bowling on **Brit's Pub's** rooftop or a jazz show at the **Dakota Jazz Club and Restaurant.**

Day 2

▶ Start your day in St. Paul with a croissant and café au lait at **Meritage,** then step right outside and enjoy beautiful **Rice Park,** flanked by some of the city's most recognizable buildings. Spend a few minutes admiring the interior of the **Landmark Center** or spend an hour or so at one of the small museums inside. Before leaving the park, take a peek inside the **James J. Hill Reference Library,** find out what's showing at the **Ordway,** and snap a few pictures with F. Scott Fitzgerald and his friends the Peanuts characters, cast in bronze.

► Your next stop is the **Minnesota History Center,** which deserves as much time as you're able to give it (the gift shop is a great place to get souvenirs).

► The **Cathedral of St. Paul,** a short walk away, welcomes both the faithful and the respectfully curious.

► A little less than a mile away, the **Minnesota State Capitol** offers tours on the hour, or you can wander on your own. Leave a little time to explore the memorials on the grounds.

► For dinner and entertainment, head back to downtown St. Paul proper. The classic

BEST OUTDOOR ACTIVITIES

- Walk, run, bike, skate, paddle, or sail on or around the **Chain of Lakes.**
- Stroll St. Paul's **Summit Avenue.**
- Explore the **Minnesota Landscape Arboretum.**
- Shop the full length of **Grand Avenue.**
- Ice skate at **The Depot** or **Rice Park.**
- Snowtube at **Theodore Wirth Park.**
- Ski the easy hills at **Como Park** or the tougher slopes at **Hyland Ski and Snowboard Center.**
- Snowshoe at **Hyland Lake Park Preserve.**

American **St. Paul Grill** and the Japanese **Sakura Restaurant & Bar** are on Rice Park. For a less expensive meal, try the serene **Tanpopo Noodle Shop.**

► Most of the Twin Cities' livelier nightlife takes place in downtown Minneapolis, but the **Artists' Quarter** hosts live jazz nearly every night.

Day 3

If you've got an extra day in the Twin Cities and you've exhausted those rather ambitious itineraries for the first two days, it's time to head out of the two downtown cores.

► Get some fresh air on the walking paths around the **Chain of Lakes** in Minneapolis, or in St. Paul's sprawling **Como Park.** Take a short hike around **Minnehaha Falls,** which inspired Henry Wadsworth Longfellow's epic poem *The Song of Hiawatha.*

Minnesota State Capitol, St. Paul

▶ On warm days, you can get some of the best seafood in the Twin Cities at **Sea Salt** (in Minnehaha Falls Park) and **Tin Fish** (on the shore of Lake Calhoun, in the Chain of Lakes).

▶ If you're in the mood to shop, then St. Paul's **Grand Avenue** is your best bet. To venture any farther out of town, you'll need your own car. The only real exception to this is the **Mall of America,** which is a good option on a cold winter day.

▶ For some kid-friendly sightseeing, head west to the **Minnesota Landscape Arboretum** or south to the **Minnesota Zoo.**

The Chain of Lakes in South Minneapolis attracts hundreds of thousands of visitors a year.

ART AND ARCHITECTURE

The architecture surrounding downtown St. Paul's Rice Park is stunning.

Even in cities as young as Minneapolis and St. Paul, you'll find plenty of interesting architecture. Minneapolis has attracted a number of very impressive recent architectural designs, including the **Walker Art Center, Guthrie Theater, Minneapolis Central Library,** and Frank Gehry's **Weisman Art Museum.** A symbol of Gilded Age extravagance, the **Foshay Tower** was the cities' tallest building until the IDS Tower took over in 1971.

In St. Paul, start your architectural tour at **Rice Park** and the **Landmark Center,** then head for the art deco **St. Paul City Hall and Ramsey County Courthouse.** Native son Cass Gilbert's **Minnesota State Capitol** and the beaux arts **Cathedral of St. Paul** were both built as the young capital was on the rise. St. Paul's finest residential architecture dates to the Victorian era. Two excellently preserved homes from this period are open to the public: the **Alexander Ramsey House** and the **James J. Hill House.**

SIGHTS

When Minnesotans want to play or relax, they head for the water. Visitors who want to see the best of the Twin Cities should do the same. The Mississippi River and the lakes scattered throughout residential neighborhoods are intertwined with culture, history, and daily life here. Both Minneapolis and St. Paul grew up on the riverfront—driven by the river—and never turned their backs on it, as some cities did in the middle of the century. (The river, by the way, does separate the two cities for the most part, but the two downtowns do not lie directly across the water from each other at any point; Minneapolis is a few miles upstream from St. Paul.)

In Minneapolis, you can trace the history of the city on the riverfront, from the ruins of the earliest mills to the ultramodern Guthrie Theater. Once powered exclusively by the mighty Mississippi and St. Anthony Falls, many of the flour mills and silos that put Minnesota on the map still stand, converted into lofts, art galleries, and museums. They are joined by well-groomed and popular recreation areas and restaurants. The river creates the northern and eastern boundaries of Minneapolis's downtown zone, running downstream from the historic Warehouse District, under the Hennepin Avenue Bridge (the shortest suspension bridge in the country) and the historic Stone Arch Bridge, and passing the eastern edge of downtown at the Guthrie Theater and adjoining parkland. As the river travels south, winding its way past historic Fort Snelling and toward St. Paul, the river banks climb. St. Paul sits high above the river on bluffs, interlaced with

© BRUCE MANNING

HIGHLIGHTS

LOOK FOR 🌙 TO FIND RECOMMENDED SIGHTS.

🌙 **Best Places to Witness the Power of Hydroelectricity:** Minneapolis as we know it today got its start at **St. Anthony Falls,** the only waterfall on the Mississippi. You can also see the falls from the **Stone Arch Bridge** and easily fill a day with all there is to see and do on the riverfront (pages 30 and 31).

🌙 **Best Place to See Contemporary Art:** The **Walker Art Center and Sculpture Garden** brings leading artists and performers to the Twin Cities (page 32).

🌙 **Best Place to See Twin Citians in their Natural Environment:** In just about any weather, locals are drawn to the **Chain of Lakes** in South Minneapolis, to walk, bike, canoe, sail, and sit in the sun (page 33).

🌙 **Best Expression of the Twin Cities' Many Cultures:** With a Mexican grocery, a Middle Eastern buffet, a Scandinavian tchotchke shop, and more, the **Midtown Exchange** showcases the cities' many cultures better than any museum or exhibit could (page 34).

🌙 **Most Peaceful Cultural Landmark:** The **Cathedral of St. Paul** generously welcomes all visitors to enjoy it quietly as a place of worship, a stunning architectural design, and an important part of St. Paul's history (page 36).

🌙 **Most Enjoyable Way to Learn About Minnesota's History:** History becomes fun for the whole family at the very well-curated **Minnesota History Center** (page 38).

🌙 **Best Place to Start a Tour of St. Paul:** So much of downtown St. Paul's architectural beauty is arranged around tiny **Rice Park** that a thoroughly enjoyable tour can be had within a single block (page 39).

🌙 **Best Place to Aspire to the Life of a Railroad Baron:** St. Paul's toniest address has long been **Summit Avenue.** A stroll along the shady streets is a treat for history and architecture buffs (page 41).

🌙 **Best Place to Enjoy Consumer Escapism:** It's no surprise that the **Mall of America,** while popular year-round, is busiest on frigid winter days (page 44).

the Lake Harriet Bandshell on the Chain of Lakes

© TRICIA CORNELL

soaring bridges. Lined with parks, the river at this point is wider and calmer, inviting recreational use.

Getting oriented on foot in both downtowns is fairly easy and an enjoyable form of sightseeing in itself. See Minneapolis by strolling down Nicollet Mall, starting from rolling Loring Park and heading toward the Cesar Pelli–designed Minneapolis Central Library. The Hiawatha light rail line has one terminus at the new Twins Stadium and the other at the Mall of America, passing through downtown and in front of a classic city hall.

St. Paul, the older of the Twin Cities, is also laid out on a grid, albeit a somewhat cockeyed one. The stately Cathedral of St. Paul is perched on one hill to the west of downtown, facing the State Capitol, on another hill across the interstate. The central business district itself lies below these two domes and is centered on Rice Park.

Early leaders in both cities had the foresight to set aside lakefront land for public enjoyment. The Chain of Lakes in South Minneapolis and Como Lake in St. Paul are destinations in themselves, but seeking them out brings a bonus: a glimpse of the two cities' beautiful residential neighborhoods.

Downtown Minneapolis   Map 1

BASILICA OF ST. MARY

Hennepin Ave. and 17th St. N., Minneapolis,
612/333-1381, www.mary.org
HOURS: Mon.-Sun. 6:30 A.M.-5 P.M.; tours Tues.-Thurs.
2 P.M., Sun. after 9:30 and 11:30 A.M. masses
COST: Free

Many of the earliest European settlers in Minnesota were Catholic, including the Belgian priest Father Louis Hennepin, who was the first European to see St. Anthony Falls. In fact, the first Catholic church west of the Mississippi was built in Minneapolis in 1868, several blocks northeast of where the Basilica of St. Mary stands now.

Construction on the basilica began in 1908, at the same time as on the cathedral in St. Paul, and it served as a co-cathedral within the archdiocese. In 1926, it officially became the first basilica in the United States (there are now 58). The basilica, which is on the National Register of Historic Places and has been called one of the finest examples of beaux arts in the country, was designed by the principal architect of the 1904 St. Louis World's Fair, Emmanuel Masqueray. Look for the many symbols of Mary in the stonework and windows, including pomegranates, doves, and fleurs-de-lis.

When Highways 94 and 394 were built in the 1960s, the parish splintered and the congregation dwindled. By the 1980s, the building itself was seriously suffering. But, as downtown Minneapolis revived, so did the basilica; a full restoration was completed in the 1990s, along with a new dome. Today the basilica is known not only as a spiritual home, but also as the host of the rockingest block party in town, every July.

FOSHAY TOWER

821 Marquette Ave., Minneapolis

Funny story about the Foshay: It was meant to be an homage to the Washington Monument and an art deco shrine to its owner, Wilbur Foshay. Instead what people remember is this: the $20,000 check to John Philip Sousa that bounced. That's right, bounced. Real estate and utilities mogul Foshay went all out for the official opening of his new building in 1929, even commissioning the "Foshay Tower-Washington Memorial March" for the occasion. But, six weeks after the gala, Foshay lost his entire fortune and then spent 15 years in Leavenworth prison for fraud. Sousa, so the story goes, refused to allow the march to be played until his debt was repaid. In 1999, a group of Minnesotans paid back the composer's estate.

Minnesotans of several generations remember

© TRICIA CORNELL

For 50 years, the Foshay Tower was the tallest building in Minneapolis. Today, it is dwarfed by the office buildings around it.

the 32-story Foshay Tower as the tallest building in downtown Minneapolis, which it was until 1972, when the 55-story IDS Tower surpassed it. There are now 17 buildings in Minneapolis taller than the Foshay, but generations of families remember riding the elevator to the 31st-floor observation deck to look out over the city. In 2008, the W Hotel moved into the tower, preserving the observation deck and adding a layer of 21st-century opulence that would have made the bankrupt mogul proud. The observation deck is still open to visitors, and there is an $8 charge.

HENNEPIN AVENUE BRIDGE

Hennepin Ave. South and West River Pkwy., Minneapolis

The first bridge to cross the Mississippi River was completed right on this spot in 1854 and hailed at the time as the "Gateway to the West." The current bridge, completed in 1990, is the fourth in this location, an impressive art deco–influenced suspension bridge paying homage to the wooden suspension bridge the ambitious first engineers constructed, even though the site doesn't necessarily call for this expensive

type of construction (in fact, this is the shortest suspension bridge in the country). Underneath its six lanes of traffic, you can explore some remnants of the bridge's predecessors in **First Bridge Park,** including the original footings and the massive iron anchors for the cable suspension system. Interpretive signs include pictures of the bridge's predecessors. And kids can have fun counting the whimsical metal worms set in the pavement.

MINNEAPOLIS CENTRAL LIBRARY

300 Nicollet Mall, Minneapolis, 612/630-6000, www.hclib.org

HOURS: Tues. and Thurs. 10 A.M.-8 P.M., Wed. and Fri.-Sat. 10 A.M.-6 P.M., Sun. noon-5 P.M., Mon. closed

Even if you don't have any literary or reference needs during your visit to the Twin Cities, the Minneapolis Central Library is worth a look for the architecture and atmosphere alone. A four-story glass atrium joins two buildings: one with four floors of open stacks and sunny work spaces, the other with stacks, meeting rooms, and more secluded work spaces. The 350,000-square-foot building occupies a whole block and was designed by Argentine-born

MAIN STREET ON THE SECOND FLOOR: IN THE SKYWAYS

More than four decades ago, the business leaders of downtown Minneapolis realized they needed to compete with the expanding parking lots and indoor amenities of the suburbs (Southdale, the nation's first enclosed shopping mall, opened in Edina, Minnesota, in 1956). Their solution has become one of the Twin Cities' most recognizable traits: the skyway system. In Minneapolis, second-floor, enclosed walkways total seven miles and connect more than 80 blocks – nearly every building in downtown's central business district, including 4,000 hotel rooms. It's the nation's first and most extensive system of this kind. St. Paul's slightly smaller and less lively system totals about five miles.

Detractors say moving people up to the skyways kills street-level businesses. Others argue that you have to redefine "street-level": 200,000 pedestrians walk the skyways in Minneapolis alone every day, patronizing small shops, restaurants, and businesses of all kinds. Skyway maps are posted throughout each system and, for Minneapolis, are also available in the free biweekly newspaper the *Downtown Journal*.

© TRICIA CORNELL

The Twin Cities are known for their extensive skyway systems.

architect Cesar Pelli. It opened in 2006 to great excitement locally and around the country. Finding it is easy: Look for the massive metal wing floating out over Hennepin Avenue.

Teens and younger kids will each find their own space in the library: Teens can hang out and read in Emma B. Howe Teen Central, with wraparound bookshelves and all kinds of places to sit. The Children's Library on the ground floor has the largest public collection of children's books in the Midwest, including books in more than 30 languages. There's space for families to curl up with a book together and recharge and even room for little ones to get some wiggles out. Special collections on the fourth floor focus on genealogy as well as Minnesota and Minneapolis history. You don't need a library card to visit the library or browse, but

© BRUCE MANNING

The Minneapolis Central Library is a new architectural landmark on the north end of Nicollet Mall.

you do need one to check out materials or use one of the 300 computers available for free public use. There is one particularly modern feature of the library you'll probably never see: an 18,000-square-foot green roof planted with ground cover, reducing heating and cooling costs for the building.

MINNEAPOLIS CITY HALL AND HENNEPIN COUNTY COURTHOUSE

350 5th St. S., Minneapolis, 612/673-3000, www.ci.minneapolis.mn.us/government

When the Municipal Building, as it is also known, was completed in 1888, it boasted the biggest public clock in the world (beating out Big Ben by four inches). With a 345-foot tower, it also remained the tallest structure in Minneapolis for four decades. (The Foshay Tower topped it in 1929.) The building, with its romanesque gables and green copper roof, still houses the Minneapolis City Council offices and meeting rooms, but many of Hennepin County's court functions have moved across the street to the Hennepin County Government Center, built in 1977 (look for the twin towers placed so close to each other that together

they resemble a toaster). The main draw in the City Hall, and definitely worth a brief stop as you walk through downtown, is *Father of Waters,* the massive statue of a Neptune-like figure, representing Minneapolis's status as the City of Lakes. "Father of Waters" is also one of the many names for the Mississippi River. City Hall, for architectural reasons, was never connected to the downtown skyway system but can be accessed by tunnels from the Hennepin County Government Center.

NICOLLET MALL

Nicollet Ave. between 4th St. S. and 12th St. S., Minneapolis

HOURS: Store hours vary.

When Mary Tyler Moore tossed her tam o'shanter into the air, she was standing on Nicollet Mall in front of what was then Dayton's department store, a Minneapolis institution. Dayton's is now Macy's, but Mary is still there on Nicollet Mall—or at least a bronze representation of her is, erected by the TVLand network in 2002. And Nicollet Mall is still where Minneapolis gathers, especially in warm weather. The 11-block stretch was closed to most traffic in 1967 (buses and taxis still use it). Now outdoor cafés line the wide sidewalks; concerts and special events fill **Peavey Plaza,** in front of **Orchestra Hall;** and, every Thursday from May through October, a **farmers market** draws the office workers out of the skyways and into the fresh air. The **Minneapolis Central Library**—an impressive glass structure designed by renowned architect Cesar Pelli—anchors the north end of the mall, and the south end is connected by the **Loring Greenway**—a shady, park-like walkway—to **Loring Park.**

◖ ST. ANTHONY FALLS

West River Pkwy. between Hennepin Ave. S. and Portland Ave. S., Minneapolis, 612/333-5336

HOURS: Visitors center Apr.-Nov. daily 8 A.M.-6 P.M.

Right here, on the banks of the Mississippi, is where Minneapolis began. The only waterfall on the Mississippi River, St. Anthony Falls powered the city's birth and growth and continues

Minneapolis City Hall is an impressive example of neo-Gothic architecture.

to provide enough electricity for downtown Minneapolis. The falls originated nearly nine miles downriver, near what is now downtown St. Paul, and migrated upstream as the soft sandstone underlayer eroded and the limestone top layer collapsed. Had this erosion continued, the waterfall, which was moving a few feet to a hundred feet every year, would have disappeared altogether and Minneapolis wouldn't exist. But human industry intervened and today the waterfall flows over a concrete apron.

The Mdewakanton Dakota people, who dominated the area before the arrival of Europeans, called the falls Owamniyomni (whirlpool) and considered many locations in the area sacred, including the now-vanished Spirit Island.

Father Louis Hennepin, a Belgian priest, was the first European to see the falls in 1680, just three years after he was the first to set eyes on Niagara Falls. He sent home enthusiastic (perhaps overly so) descriptions of a 60-foot cataract, attracting explorers and a growing stream of settlers. The waterfall was first harnessed for industrial use in 1848, when the first sawmill

was built, and the logging industry drove rapid development until the 1880s, when flour milling took over. By that time, there were 25 flour mills on the river's banks, as well as the North Star Woolen Mill—which later became one of the first condo developments in downtown Minneapolis.

The best view of the falls is from **Hennepin Island,** home to Xcel Energy's hydroelectric plant and **Water Power Park,** where it almost feels like you could reach out and touch the foam from the observation platform. University of Minnesota scientists also use the island to study the falls at the **Saint Anthony Falls Laboratory,** home to the National Center for Earth-surface Dynamics.

You can also get a good look at the falls from the Stone Arch Bridge.

STONE ARCH BRIDGE
Portland Ave. S. and West River Pkwy., Minneapolis
When railroad baron James J. Hill completed the Stone Arch Bridge in 1883, the state's railway commissioner said the limestone structure had been "constructed for a thousand years."

More than a century and a quarter on, his prediction is holding true.

Built as the first rail connection from the industry on the east side of the Mississippi to the growing metropolitan hub on the west side, it led right to the Union Depot, now a hotel, ice rink, and water park. Its unique and impressive design was dictated by the location: Hill's Great Northern Railway needed to connect a point on the east bank below the falls to a point on the west bank above the falls. It couldn't cross the falls diagonally, and engineers feared that if the bridge sat entirely above St. Anthony, the falls would collapse. So it skirts the downstream edge of the falls for most of its length and then goes into a beautifully engineered and fairly sharp curve on the west side. The metal trusses were incorporated into the western end of the bridge in the 1960s to accommodate boats. The beloved Minneapolis landmark carried trains until 1978, then opened to pedestrians and bikes in 1994.

◖ WALKER ART CENTER AND SCULPTURE GARDEN

1750 Hennepin Ave., Minneapolis, 612/375-7600, www.walkerart.org

HOURS: Gallery Tues., Wed., Sat., and Sun. 11 A.M.–5 P.M., Thurs. and Fri. 11 A.M.–9 P.M.; garden daily 6 A.M.–midnight

COST: Gallery $10 adults, $6 students and teens, $8 seniors; garden free

Like a giant tinfoil marshmallow floating on the southeast corner of downtown, the Walker Art Center makes an impression. It's known as one of the best places to experience multidisciplinary contemporary art in the country, having built its reputation over nine decades. When it opened in 1927, it was the first public gallery of art in the Upper Midwest. Today it holds works by Pablo Picasso, Henry Moore, Alberto Giacometti, Claes Oldenburg, Chuck Close, Roy Lichtenstein, Yoko Ono, and Andy Warhol, and others in its permanent collection and hosts consistently forward-looking exhibitions combining visual arts, sound, and movement.

The 11-acre Minneapolis Sculpture

WHO CAN TURN THE WORLD ON WITH HER SMILE?

When that small-town girl with big dreams first saw the lights of the big city in TV's *Mary Tyler Moore Show,* she was heading into the Twin Cities, of course. The series, which ran from 1970 to 1977, was filmed on a soundstage in Studio City, California, but memorable parts of the opening credits were filmed on location in Minneapolis. Mary walks around Lake of the Isles in South Minneapolis and throws her hat in the air on downtown's Nicollet Mall, in front of what was then Dayton's department store. A statue, depicting the famous tam toss, now stands on that very spot in front of Macy's, at 7th Street and Nicollet Mall. Mary's house, which was shown from the outside in between scenes, was at 21st Street and Kenwood Parkway. The old Victorian, a private residence, has tripled in size and is now tan instead of white, but it's still there for old TV buffs to see.

Garden, a joint project of the Walker and the Minneapolis Park Board, opened in 1988 adjacent to the Walker itself. The highlight of the park, Oldenburg and Coosje van Bruggen's *Spoonbridge and Cherry,* has become a beloved symbol of Minneapolis, and locals find winter solace in the tropical **Cowles Conservatory** (Tues.–Sat. 10 A.M.–8 P.M., Sun. 10 A.M.–5 P.M., Mon. closed, free), where Frank Gehry's *Standing Glass Fish* is surrounded by palms and orange trees year-round.

The Irene Hixon Whitney Bridge—two linked yellow-and-blue arches—connects the sculpture garden to **Loring Park** across 16 lanes of traffic. You can read John Ashbery's specially commissioned untitled poem—"And now I cannot remember how I would have had it. It is not a conduit (confluence?)"—as you cross the bridge, to keep yourself from looking down.

South Minneapolis   Map 2

⬤ CHAIN OF LAKES

612/230-6400, www.minneapolisparks.org

One of the greatest gifts Minneapolis's early civic leaders secured for future generations is the treasured Chain of Lakes. Whereas in other cities, lakeshore trades hands privately, limiting enjoyment of the water to a few public-access beaches, in Minneapolis nearly every inch of land bordering the city's dozen lakes is public parkland. (The notorious exception is a short piece of private land on the east side of Cedar Lake.) The land was acquired piece by piece through market-rate purchases and private donations starting in the early 1880s by the Minneapolis Park Board. The jewel of this ambitious system is the Chain of Lakes, four interconnected bodies of water: Cedar Lake, Lake of the Isles, Lake Calhoun, and Lake Harriet.

Today, parkways encircle the lakes, along with more than 13 miles of walking and biking paths. Bike paths run one-way around each lake and are separated from the walking paths. Residents take advantage of the paths and parks year-round, but on especially beautiful days the heavy foot and wheel traffic can resemble a parade.

Lake Calhoun is the largest of the four, with just over three miles of paths surrounding it. The broad, unshaded swathes of grass—along with a couple of sand volleyball courts—attract a young and fit crowd. Small sand beaches on the south and east sides are popular with families, and canoes and paddleboats can be rented at the north end.

Lake Harriet is slightly smaller and shadier. During the summer, concerts are held daily at the bandshell on the north end. The Lake Harriet Yacht Club holds regattas and lessons. Children can hunt for the home of the Lake Harriet elf on the south end.

© TRICIA CORNELL

Free outdoor concerts, held every night during the summer at the Lake Harriet Bandshell on the Chain of Lakes, attract crowds.

Surrounded by marshy lowlands, **Lake of the Isles** (2.6 miles around) makes up for what it lacks in recreation opportunities with great bird-watching. **Cedar Lake,** the smallest at 1.7 miles, is the quietest but has two terrific beaches. No swimming is allowed outside of marked areas.

COMO-HARRIET STREETCAR

42nd St. and Queen Ave., Minneapolis, 952/922-1096, www.trolleyride.org

HOURS: Mid-May-Labor Day Mon.-Fri. 6:30 P.M.-dusk, Wed. 1-4 P.M., Sat.-Sun. 12:30 P.M.-dusk, holidays 9:30 A.M.-dusk; early May and Sept.-Thanksgiving Sat.-Sun. 12:30 P.M.-dusk

At its peak, the Twin Cities Rapid Transit company's streetcars traveled from Stillwater (east of St. Paul) to Excelsior (west of Minneapolis), well over 50 miles. Today, two portions of that track remain, lovingly and expertly tended to by the volunteers of the **Minnesota Transportation Museum,** and both are open for rides. One portion is in Excelsior, on the shores of Lake Minnetonka. The other runs here, between **Lake Harriet** and **Lake Calhoun** in Minneapolis. The mile-or-so roundtrip takes about 15 minutes. Trolleys board at the station (a faithful replica of one of the originals, rebuilt in 1990) and run through a glade of trees, under a historic stone bridge, and past **Lakewood Cemetery** until the track emerges opposite Lake Calhoun. Then the car backs up along the same single track and returns to the station. Along the way, a volunteer in a conductor's uniform tells the story of the Como–Harriet streetcar line, beloved in the Twin Cities for its scenic views and high speeds along dedicated rights of way. It was the last line to close when the streetcar system was dismantled in 1954. The current track—relaid by the train buffs themselves—follows the original line until it reaches the cemetery, which has since annexed part of the land where the trolley once ran.

Two cars run on the line: The all-wood No. 1300 is the car that started it all. In the 1960s, trolley enthusiasts formed a nonprofit organization to save the car—an organization that

© BRUCE MANNING

The Como-Harriet streetcar line, the last vestige of a once-extensive streetcar system, is open for pleasure rides.

later became the Minnesota Transportation Museum. One of only two of its type to survive (of 1,140 built by Twin Cities Rapid Transit), No. 1300 celebrated its 100th birthday in 2008. The No. 322 is an art deco beauty. The all-steel body with clean, modern lines was created in the 1930s and '40s to combat the streetcar's reputation as an outmoded form of transport and to compete with the sleek automobiles and buses of the day. Vintage ads line the insides of both cars.

◖ MIDTOWN EXCHANGE

Lake St. and 10th Ave., Minneapolis, 612/872-4041, www.midtownglobalmarket.org

HOURS: Mon.-Sat. 7 A.M.-8 P.M., Sun. 7 A.M.-6 P.M.

What to do with the second-largest building in the state (after the Mall of America)? The city of Minneapolis puzzled over this for more than 10 years, after the Sears, Roebuck Corporation closed its 1.2-million-square-foot catalog order–processing facility in 1994. The massive building, with its landmark 16-story tower, sat empty until 2006, when the **Midtown Global Market** opened on the ground floor. (Condos and office space occupy the rest of the building.) The lively market, the result of the joint effort of neighborhood groups, the African Development Center, and the Latino Economic Development Center, was modeled on successful community markets like Seattle's Pike Place. Today it houses a dozen specialty grocers (need tortillas, *dashi,* Finnish flatbread, or local, organic chicken?),

almost 20 restaurants, and dozens of booths selling jewelry, crafts, and art from all over the world. A central stage area sees frequent casual music concerts, and a small children's play area keeps restless little ones amused. You might be able to snag one of the popular chess tables, but you'll probably need your own pieces. Most shops open at 10 A.M., but you can get a cup of coffee and a pastry before that. The two sit-down restaurants (**A la Salsa,** 612/872-4140, and **Jade,** 612/886-1378) are both open until 10 P.M.

Nordeast and Dinkytown Map 3

ARD GODFREY HOUSE
50 University Ave. NE, Minneapolis, 612/870-8001, www.ardgodfreyhouse.com
HOURS: June-Sept. Fri.-Sun. noon-3:30 P.M.
COST: Free

Sitting on an improbable patch of green amid the rising condos just across the river from downtown Minneapolis is an improbable little yellow house. This is the Ard Godfrey House, the oldest surviving wood-frame house in Minneapolis. In 1949, millwright Ard Godfrey, who supervised the building of the timber mill at St. Anthony Falls, built this house—originally at Main Street and 2nd Avenue, a couple of blocks closer to the river—with the first lumber sawed at the mill. Today the Women's Club of Minneapolis operates the house as a museum, open in the summer and the holiday season. The one-and-a-half-story house is decorated with period furnishings and photos. One fact you'll be sure to learn is that gardeners of Minnesota have Ard's wife Harriet to thank for the humble dandelion. It seems she missed things like dandelion bread, tea, and wine and had seeds shipped from Maine. The small park surrounding the house, **Chute Square,** is where the University of Minnesota got its start in 1851, before moving a couple of miles east.

OUR LADY OF LOURDES CHURCH
1 Lourdes Pl., Minneapolis, 612/379-2259, www.ourladyoflourdes.com
HOURS: Mass Mon., Wed., and Fri. 12:05 P.M., Tues. and Thurs. 5:05 P.M., Sat. 5:30 P.M., and Sun. 9 A.M., 11 A.M., and 7 P.M.

The skinny spire poking up behind the restaurants and bars of St. Anthony Main, just across the Hennepin Avenue Bridge from downtown Minneapolis, is the oldest continuously operated church in Minneapolis, Our Lady of Lourdes Church. The building was built by the First Universalist Society in 1854 and later sold to the French Canadian Catholic community, which worships there today. The original part of the building, which faces the street, was built in the Greek temple style, and most of the stained-glass windows date to the early 1900s. The congregation's claim to fame is its *tourtierres,* French Canadian meat pies, which volunteers make in great quantities both to raise funds for the continued refurbishment of the church and to feed the hungry. Keep in mind that Our Lady of Lourdes is an active church, not a museum.

UNIVERSITY OF MINNESOTA
612/625-5000, www.umn.edu
The University of Minnesota was founded as a secondary school in 1851, seven years before

Minnesota became a state, and became a land-grant university in 1869. Today, with more than 50,000 students, it is the fourth largest university in the country.

The U of M—as it is known locally, or, sometimes, "the U,"—is divided between the St. Paul campus, where most of the agricultural disciplines are based, and the much larger and busier Minneapolis campus. The Minneapolis campus is further split by the Mississippi River into the West Bank, where the arts departments and law school are located, and the East Bank, the heart of the university. The U's answer to the classic quadrangle is **Northrop Mall,** designed by the legendary architect Cass Gilbert in 1908. The broad lawn is headed by the stately columns of Northrop Memorial Auditorium and lined by classic physics, chemistry, and administrative buildings. Directly across Washington Avenue, accessible by pedestrian bridge, is **Coffman Memorial Union,** the student activities center. A visitor who wanted to get a small taste of life at the U would do well to start here and combine that with a trip to the **Weisman Art Museum,** the shiny metal maze on the banks of the Mississippi. The Weisman sits on Washington Avenue, where the **Washington Avenue pedestrian bridge** crosses the river to the West Bank. Walking or biking across the double-decker bridge, one-fifth of a mile long, with a shelter running the length of the middle of it for pedestrians, is a daily part of university life for tens of thousands of students and faculty.

The U's oldest buildings are located in the Old Campus Historic District, known to most as **The Knoll,** north of Northrop Mall. While the U got its start in 1851 on a patch of land now known as **Chute Square,** a couple of miles to the west, it moved to the current location after the Civil War. Now 13 of the buildings in this part of campus, dating as far back as 1886, are listed on the National Register of Historic Places. **Pillsbury Hall** (310 Pillsbury Dr. SE), with its two-tone sandstone and artful mix of Romanesque, prairie school, and arts and crafts elements, is a particular favorite. The **Bell Museum of Natural History** is a worthwhile stop while you're exploring the Knoll.

Downtown St. Paul and West Side   Map 4

◖ CATHEDRAL OF ST. PAUL

239 Selby Ave., St. Paul, 651/228-1766,
www.cathedralsaintpaul.org

HOURS: Sun.-Fri. 7 A.M.-7 P.M., Sat. 7 A.M.-9 P.M.

Sitting on the highest point in downtown St. Paul, the Cathedral of St. Paul is the city's most visible and memorable landmark. The beaux arts building is an especially impressive sight at night, when it is illuminated on all sides with electric lights. The cathedral itself gave the city of St. Paul its name. When Father Lucien Galtier arrived in the unfortunately named riverside settlement of Pig's Eye, his first task was to build a log church, which he dedicated to St. Paul. It was Galtier who began writing "St. Paul" as the location on wedding certificates and other church documents. Three successively bigger cathedrals were built after that first humble building, on different sites. The current building was built concurrently with the **Basilica of St. Mary** in Minneapolis and completed in 1915. Both buildings were designed by Emmanuel Louis Masqueray.

The cathedral is built as a symmetrical cross and topped by a copper dome. The massive open interior seats 3,000 and was designed to give everyone in the congregation a clear view of the altar. The interior of the dome is entirely open to view from the floor. At 96 feet in diameter and 175 feet high, it dominates the sanctuary. In recognition of the many immigrant groups that have come to Minnesota since that first humble log church, the six shrines behind the sanctuary are dedicated to the patron saints of various countries: Saint Anthony of Padua (Italy), John the Baptist

The Cathedral of St. Paul gave the city its name.

(France and Canada), Saint Patrick (Ireland), Saint Boniface (Germany), Saints Cyril and Methodius (Slavic nations), and Saint Therese (protector of all missions).

More than 200,000 people a year take advantage of the free tours offered Mondays, Wednesdays, and Fridays at 1 P.M. (Call 651/228-1766 to arrange a private tour.) While the building is open to visitors every day, tourists are asked to stay out of the main sanctuary (unless they are there to worship) and refrain from flash photography during mass and other ceremonies. Daily schedules are posted in the entrance.

INDIAN MOUNDS PARK
10 Mounds Blvd., 651/632-5111, www.ci.stpaul.mn.us
HOURS: Daily dawn-11 P.M.

The first European explorers to come to this part of the Mississippi marveled at the mysterious symmetrical mounds they found high up on the bluff above overlooking the river. These burial mounds predate even the Dakota tribes, who had been living in the area since sometime before the 17th century, and may be as old as 2,000 years. Historians and archaeologists believe the mounds were built by the Native American tribes known collectively as the Hopewell culture, who traveled north up the Mississippi around that time. As many as 37 mounds in two locations were mapped out by 19th-century scientists, on what is now Dayton's Bluff and Indian Mounds Park. All of these were destroyed in the late 19th and early 20th centuries except for six, which are now the centerpiece of the park. Much of what we know about the mounds comes down from T. H. Lewis, who excavated the mounds, sometimes at breakneck speed, in the early 1880s. He found bones, masks, pottery, and other artifacts, as well as graves created in a variety of ways, indicating that the mounds had been in use over a very long period of time. Unfortunately, nearly all of these items have now disappeared.

The remaining mounds, the largest of which is 260 feet in circumference and 18 feet high, are fenced off but visible within the park, with a few interpretive signs nearby. The park is also a popular recreation area and offers fantastic views of the river and downtown St. Paul.

JAMES J. HILL REFERENCE LIBRARY
80 4th St. W., 651/265-5500, www.jjhill.org
HOURS: Mon. and Thurs. 9 A.M.-8 P.M.,
Tues.-Wed. and Fri. 9 A.M.-5:30 P.M., Sat.-Sun. closed

Railway baron James. J. Hill gave much to this area: a rail connection to both coasts that turned both cities into 19th-century boom towns, the magnificent Stone Arch Bridge in Minneapolis, and the James J. Hill Reference Library, one of the foremost collections of business literature in the country. Although Hill first envisioned it as a more general collection, the library decided to focus on business references in the 1970s as a tribute to Hill's legacy. The building, completed in 1921, has been called one of the finest examples of beaux arts architecture in Minnesota, and the striking Great Reading Room is a popular spot for weddings and receptions. Today, the library is heavily used by students, researchers, entrepreneurs, and others, but visitors are welcome to look around respectfully as well, free of charge.

MINNESOTA HISTORY CENTER

345 Kellogg Blvd. W., 651/251-3000, www.mnhs.org/
historycenter

HOURS: Mon.-Sat. 10 A.M.-5 P.M., Tues. till 8 P.M., Sun.
noon.-5 P.M.; Labor Day-Memorial Day closed Mon.

COST: $10 adults, $8 seniors and students, $5
children 5-17

The Minnesota Historical Society formed nine
years before the state of Minnesota itself, in
1949, but it moved into its impressive granite
and limestone home on the hill across from the
Minnesota State Capitol in 1992. The building houses the society's administrative offices,
massive collections, a research library, and a
museum that offers an excellent introduction
to Minnesota's past, from distant prehistoric
times to the recent development of the suburbs. The exhibits are designed to engage and
teach all generations: In Grainland, children
can climb through the kid-size model grain
elevator for what seems like hours. In Going
Places, they can pretend to launch a rocket or
drive a car. And in Weather Permitting they
can try on warm weather gear from previous eras or—the braver ones at least—sit in a
recreated Minnesota basement during a simu-
lated tornado. MN150, with multimedia exhibits more geared toward adults, celebrates
150 people, places, and products that help de-
fine the Minnesota experience, from Prince to
the 1980 Olympic hockey team.

The historical society's **library** (Tues.
noon–8 P.M., Wed.–Fri. 9 A.M.–5 P.M., Sat.
9 A.M.–4 P.M., Sun.–Mon. closed) houses over
half a million books and 45,000 cubic feet of
government records, along with maps, photographs, and more. The public is welcome to use
the library free of charge, and it is a popular
place to research family history.

MINNESOTA STATE CAPITOL

75 Rev. Dr. Martin Luther King Jr. Blvd., 651/296-2881,
www.mnhs.org

HOURS: Mon.-Fri. 9 A.M.-4 P.M., Sat. 10 A.M.-3 P.M.,
Sun. 1-4 P.M.

St. Paul's native son, architect Cass Gilbert,
wowed the local crowds and observers around
the country when the new State Capitol was
unveiled in 1905. The most remarkable feature
of St. Paul's capitol is its gleaming white dome,

© BRUCE MANNING

The Minnesota State Capitol was designed by local architect Cass Gilbert.

made from the Georgia marble Gilbert specified, invoking local ire. Local stone was used in the steps and interior, which is rich with carvings, portraits, and sculptures by some of the favorite artists of the early 20th century.

The building is open to the public, and people are free to visit the chambers of the State Senate and House of Representatives and to drop in on their legislators. The Minnesota Historical Society oversees preservation work at the capitol and leads free 45-minute tours on the hour when the building is open; last tour is one hour before closing. When the weather is nice, visitors can walk out on the roof to see the gold leaf–covered horses known as the quadriga. Although the quadriga and other exterior features got a much-needed sprucing up in 1995, parts of the interior are visibly crumbling and still awaiting a $65 million appropriation from the state legislature to restore.

There are several memorials worth visiting on the State Capitol grounds, including the **Minnesota Vietnam Veterans Memorial,** which opened in 1992. The memorial, just south of the capitol building itself and behind the Veterans Administration building, is called *Lakefront DMZ.* It includes elements evocative of home for all Minnesotans and a wall inscribed with the names of Minnesota's fallen fighters.

The **Minnesota Korean War Memorial** was added in 1998, with evocative twin sculptures of a young soldier and an empty silhouette. A spiral of obelisks memorializes local civil rights leader Roy Wilkins, who led the NAACP for 46 years. And a stark arch, the **Minnesota Peace Officers Memorial,** honors law enforcement officers who gave their lives in the line of duty.

◖ RICE PARK
4th St. and Market St.
HOURS: Daily dawn–11 P.M.

Though tiny, Rice Park offers a prime view of some of downtown St. Paul's most pleasing architecture and public art. The irregular park is surrounded by beautiful public buildings—**Saint Paul Hotel, Landmark Center,**

Ordway, and the **Central Library**—as well as some of St. Paul's finest restaurants. The centerpiece of the park is *The Source,* a fountain designed by the prolific Wisconsin-born sculptor Alonzo Hauser, who taught for a time at Carleton College in Northfield, Minnesota. A young woman cavorts in the center of the broad pool of water, invoking Minnesota's beloved summers on the lake. The park may be best known as the home of sculptures of Peanuts characters, who joined the bronze F. Scott Fitzgerald in 2004. While the sculptures (wisely treated with a heat-reducing coating, so they don't burn small, curious hands) are beloved by locals, it's worth noting that Peanuts creator Charles Schulz was never particularly fond of his hometown, St. Paul.

Adjacent to Rice Park (you may not even notice it's a separate tract of land) is **Landmark Plaza,** an elegant public art installation, where documents reproduced in the pathway ask visitors to consider some tough questions: "What are you willing to do for your country?" "What are the true costs of war?"

ST. PAUL CITY HALL AND RAMSEY COUNTY COURTHOUSE
15 Kellogg Blvd. W., 651/266-8266
HOURS: Mon.-Fri. 8 A.M.-4:30 P.M.

This stunning example of art deco architecture represents an unusual case of a city benefiting from the Great Depression. The money for the building was approved in 1928, before the 1929 Black Tuesday crash. Even though the costs of materials and labor dipped dramatically, the city let the original $4 million appropriation stand, ensuring a building that was, and remains, truly opulent inside and out. The strong vertical lines of the 21-story exterior stand out in a city that has very few examples of this style of architecture. Inside, the three-story Memorial Hall is an art deco marvel, rich with mirrors, inlaid wood, and black marble. The room is dedicated to Ramsey County soldiers who died in World Wars I and II, Korea, Vietnam, and Grenada. Their names are inscribed on the walls. The centerpiece of the hall is *Vision of Peace,* by

Carl Milles, the largest white onyx sculpture in the world. The massive sculpture depicting Native Americans smoking peace pipes (it was originally called *The Indian God of Peace*) rotates on its motorized base once every 2.5 hours. Visitors are welcome to take self-guided tours and view the distinctive details, right down to the elevator doors and the door handles. Ask at the front desk about drop-in guided tours or call 651/266-8000 to schedule a tour. Be sure not to miss the views from the 18th-floor law library of the Mississippi River, Cathedral of St. Paul, and capitol building.

ST. PAUL UNION DEPOT
214 4th St. E., www.uniondepot.org

Even though passenger rail service abandoned Union Depot in 1971, when Amtrak moved to a train station in St. Paul's Midway neighborhood, the neoclassical building has never been allowed to fall into disrepair. The United States Post Office uses the concourse area for mail handling, **Christo's** Greek restaurant (651/224-6000) occupies the center of the main lobby, and private offices and condos take up the rest of the building. This building, with its severe columns, was completed in 1923, after St. Paul's original Union Depot burned down and World War I delayed reconstruction. In its heyday, the depot's 18 tracks served 282 trains and 20,000 passengers a day. Visitors are welcome to view the ornate lobby, with its soaring ceiling. A coalition of St. Paul and Ramsey County transit leaders is floating plans to return the building to its original purpose as a passenger rail and transit hub.

WABASHA STREET CAVES
215 Wabasha St. S., 651/292-1220, www.wabashastreetcaves.com

This complex of caves on St. Paul's West Side has lived many lives: Originally silica mines, the caves have also housed a mushroom farm, a nightclub that saw figures famous in the jazz world and in the underworld, and, currently, an event space specializing in themed tours. The nightclub, Castle Royal, which opened in 1932 and closed in the 1960s, is reputed to have welcomed both Cab Calloway and John Dillinger. Today, swing-dancing parties on Thursday nights (6–10 P.M., $7) bring the big, hardwood dance floor back to life. Popular 45-minute cave tours ($5)—a little bit of history mixed with a little bit of sass—are offered Thursday at 5 P.M. and Saturday and Sunday at 11 A.M. The caves also host a number of holiday-themed events and offer a mobster-themed bus tour ($22) around St. Paul.

WESTERN SCULPTURE PARK
Marion St. and Fuller Ave., 651/290-0921, www.publicartstpaul.org
HOURS: Daily dawn–11 P.M.

The 4.5-acre park just west of the Minnesota State Capitol grounds is perhaps one of St. Paul's best-kept secrets. (This could be, in part, because the neighborhood is not the area's safest.) Shady, intertwining paths lead visitors to 20 large-scale sculptures, most of which were created by local sculptors, both established and emerging. Perhaps the most prominent are *Grace à Toi,* by Mark di Suvero, a tripod of leaning I-beams with eerily moving parts suspended overhead, and *Walking Warrior I,* by Melvin Smith, a solemn black metal human figure. Families have fun with *Frame,* by Shaun Cassidy, which is just what it sounds like—a large, cheeky white frame. Neighbors and visitors make use of the volleyball court and playground as much as they enjoy the art.

Summit-University and Mac-Groveland   Map 5

◖ SUMMIT AVENUE

For most of its 150-year history, Summit Avenue has been among St. Paul's most sought-after addresses. Even for those who can't quite afford one of the stately homes, a stroll or a jog along the broad, elm-lined boulevard in the center of the avenue is among the chief pleasures of living in or visiting St. Paul. The 4.5-mile avenue stretches from the edge of downtown St. Paul in the east to the Mississippi River in the west. The entire length is part of one of two National Historic Districts and includes fine examples of nearly every type of residential architecture from the past century.

The park-like divided boulevard begins at the intersection with Lexington Avenue and continues west. But the stretch of Summit Avenue east of Lexington is rich with interesting historic homes, especially as the street starts to curve and climb up tony Crocus Hill. This neighborhood remains largely as it was in the early 1900s. At 312 Summit Avenue,

the oldest extant house on the avenue and one of the oldest in St. Paul is the Stuart House. It, like most of the buildings, is a private residence. Other private buildings of interest include 516 Summit, where Minnesota author Sinclair Lewis lived for a time, and 599 Summit, where local boy F. Scott Fitzgerald wrote his first published novel, *This Side of Paradise.* The governor's residence—not open to the public—is at 1006 Summit, near the intersection with Lexington. You can tour the museum in the **James J. Hill House,** the largest single-family residence in Minnesota. You can also peek inside the **Germanic American Institute** (301 Summit Ave., 651/222-7027, www.gai-mn.org, Mon.–Fri. 10 A.M.–5 P.M.).

The only park along the length of Summit Avenue is **Lookout Park,** a long-neglected triangle of land at the intersection with Ramsey Avenue. Here you can enjoy views from the Mississippi River bluffs that once belonged to rail and timber barons.

Como and St. Anthony   Map 6

COMO PARK

The nearly 400-acre Como Park has been a center for recreation and family fun in St. Paul since the late 1800s. Today, more than 2.5 million people come to the park every year to picnic, walk, run, bike, ski, fish, and visit the attractions—the Como Park Zoo and Conservatory, Cafesjian's Carousel, and Como Town.

CAFESJIAN'S CAROUSEL

1245 Midway Pkwy., St. Paul, 651/489-4628, www.ourfaircarousel.org
HOURS: May-Aug. Tues.-Fri. 11 A.M.-4 P.M., Sat.-Sun. 11 A.M.-6 P.M.; Sept.-Oct. Sat.-Sun. 11 A.M.-4 P.M.; Memorial Day and Labor Day 11 A.M.-4 P.M.
COST: $1.50
Cafesjian's Carousel was built on the Minnesota

State Fairgrounds in 1914. In 1988, when owners unexpectedly announced plans to close the beloved annual attraction, a group of neighbors banded together to save it. The carousel operated for 10 years in downtown St. Paul and moved to Como Park in 2000. Gerard Cafesjian, for whom the carousel is named, donated $1.2 million to finance its restoration and move in the late 1990s. Its new home—a beautiful copper-roofed pavilion—has massive doors that can open on summer days and close to extend the season in the fall. Sixty-eight hand-carved horses in four rows ring the carousel, which is 50 feet in diameter. A restored Wurlitzer band organ, while not original to this carousel, sounds appropriately old-fashioned as it calls out across the park, playing paper rolls of classic carousel tunes.

SIGHTS

COMO PARK ZOO AND CONSERVATORY
1225 Estabrook Dr., 651/487-8200,
www.comozooconservatory.org
HOURS: Daily 10 A.M.-6 P.M.

COST: Free

The Como Zoo holds a treasured place in many Minnesotans' hearts—so much so that Apple Valley's larger Minnesota Zoo, built in 1978, is still occasionally referred to as "the new zoo." Como's history goes back much longer than that, all the way to 1897, and several of the buildings were built in the 1930s by the Works Progress Administration. Truth be told, nostalgia is kinder to some of the outdated exhibits than they actually deserve, with animals standing behind chain-link fences on concrete pads. But the zoo is working hard to change that, including opening a spacious and naturalistic home for the polar bears—Polar Bear Odyssey—in 2010. Other favorites include the outdoor harbor seals and the community of gorillas in the primate house. The Marjorie McNeely Conservatory's Tropical Encounter, on permanent exhibit, is an innovative collaboration with the zoo. Visitors see fish, birds, and other small animals interacting with the tropical plants almost as they would in the wild. A sloth even wanders freely, if slowly, throughout the "tropical forest."

COMO TOWN
1301 Midway Pkwy., 651/487-2121, www.comotown.com
HOURS: Jun.-Aug. Sun.-Thurs. 10 A.M.-7:30 P.M., Fri.-Sat. 10 A.M.-8 P.M.

COST: Free admission, rides $0.75-3

Como Town offers pint-sized excitement, with rides and play structures for toddlers through tweens, with one or two rides for adults to enjoy as well. Most rides are old-school, like the teacups, the swings, and the train, but all

THE GREAT INDOORS

Not everyone wants to revel in the cold. Even those who love a good snowstorm may need a break from the long gray stretches of winter or the rainy patches of summer. Smart locals know where to find a bit of the tropics right in the Twin Cities, and visitors can have a great time here even in the worst weather.

While much of the **Minnesota Zoo** is outside, the Tropics Trail and aquariums are all indoors, with hundreds of animals, birds, fish, and plants from warmer climes on display. You could skip the outdoor trails entirely and still spend a happy and full morning or afternoon at the zoo, especially if you catch a dolphin show or an IMAX film.

Likewise, the **Como Park Zoo and Conservatory** in St. Paul has a much smaller tropics display uniquely combining botanical and zoological exhibits. Keep your eye out for the sloth.

A perennial favorite of downtown Minneapolis office workers who need a midwinter boost is the **Cowles Conservatory** in the **Walker Sculpture Garden.** The greenhouse is small but packed with hibiscus, oranges, palms, and other tropical plants. Frank Gehry's *Standing Glass Fish* sculpture is oddly uplifting.

All of Minnesota's cultural institutions are, of course, indoors and are excellent ways to escape the elements. But if you like your escapism untainted by high culture, there is no better place to run away to than the **Mall of America.** Keep in mind that everyone else in the metro area is likely to hit upon this very idea when the mercury plunges, and the 13,000 on-site parking spaces have actually been known to fill up on the coldest days, forcing chilly shoppers into the 7,000 overflow spaces across the street. The mall opens at 7 A.M. every day of the week so mall walkers can get a few laps in before the stores open (one pass around the first level is 0.57 mile).

Thanks to Minneapolis and St. Paul's **skyways,** you can combine shopping, dining, and a little indoor exercise. St. Paul has five miles of indoor walkways and Minneapolis has seven. If you can bear to brave the elements for a single block, the **Minneapolis Central Library** is just off the skyway system and a worthwhile escape, especially if you have small children.

is not passive entertainment: Kids can climb, swing, explore, and dig in Hodge Podge Park. Como Town's size and energy level are well-suited to the littlest ones, who will be able to take it all in without getting overwhelmed. Opening hours are shorter in May and down to weekends only in September, after which the park closes for the winter.

Greater Twin Cities   Map 7

EXCELSIOR STREETCAR LINE

Water and George Sts., 952/922-1096,
www.trolleyride.org

HOURS: May-early Sept. Thurs. 2-6 P.M., Sat.
10 A.M.-4 P.M., Sun. 1-4 P.M.; Sept.-Oct. Thurs. 2-6 P.M.

COST: $2

On the shores of Lake Minnetonka, one of the vestiges of the Twin Cities' once-vast streetcar line still operates. The same volunteers who work tirelessly on the Como–Harriet Streetcar Line also run four trolleys on a short stretch of track in pretty downtown Excelsior. The conductor is sure to tell you stories about the days when everyone rode the trolleys and will give you a tour of the car barn where they keep and restore the trolleys if you ask. Combining a ride with a round-trip on the **Steamboat Minnehaha** (952/474-2115, www.steamboat-minnehaha.org, $10 adults, $5 children), which once ferried trolley commuters and vacationers across the lake and now docks near the Old Excelsior Road end of the trolley line, is a great way to spend a summer afternoon.

HISTORIC FORT SNELLING

Hwy. 5 and Hwy. 55, 612/726-1171, www.mnhs.org

HOURS: Memorial Day-Labor Day
Mon.-Sat. 10 A.M.-5 P.M., Sun. noon-5 P.M.; May and Sept.-Oct. Sat. 10 A.M.-5 P.M., Sun. noon-5 P.M.

COST: $10 adults, $8 seniors and students, $5 children 5-17

Fort Snelling marks the beginning of an important era in Minnesota's history. The U.S. military arrived here in 1819 to wrest control of the increasingly lucrative fur trade from the British. Construction on the fort at the confluence of the Mississippi and Minnesota Rivers began in 1820 and was completed in 1824. The soldiers themselves, far from the relative civilization of the East Coast, needed to be self-sufficient and so began much of the development that led to the establishment of Minneapolis at St. Anthony Falls, building mills and roads. The fort even played a bit part in American civil rights history, as the home of Dred and Harriet Scott while they lived in Minnesota, forming the base of their claim that they should be allowed to live as free citizens.

Fort Snelling continued to be an active military base, including housing the Military Intelligence Language School during World War II. It was decommissioned in 1946 and started to fall into disrepair, a process Minnesotans are still fighting to reverse. The National Trust for Historic Preservation has placed Fort Snelling's Upper Post on its list of America's Most Endangered Places.

Today, the fort sits within the Fort Snelling Unincorporated Area, bordered by both Minneapolis and St. Paul (as well as three suburbs) but inside neither city. The Minnesota Historical Society operates the fort as a living history center, where costumed guides help visitors imagine the year is 1827. The guides act out both military and everyday life, from musket drills to mending clothes, with plenty of hands-on activities for the whole family.

Fort Snelling Military Cemetery is adjacent to the fort and open to visitors. **Fort Snelling State Park** (www.dnr.state.mn.us/state_parks/fort_snelling), surrounding the fort, includes five miles of paved bicycle trails, 12 miles of groomed cross-country ski trails, a nine-hole golf course, and swimming, boating, and fishing opportunities on Snelling Lake.

SIGHTS

THE MEANING OF FREE SOIL: THE STORY OF DRED AND HARRIET SCOTT

One of the most infamous U.S. Supreme Court cases in history had its roots right here in Fort Snelling. In 1836, Dred Scott came to Minnesota with his owner, John Emerson, the fort's physician. There, he married Harriet, who was owned by the local Indian agent, Lawrence Taliaferro. Slavery was prohibited in the area that now includes Minnesota under the Northwest Ordinance of 1787 and the Missouri Compromise of 1820, but this law was often ignored. Emerson's family, along with Dred and Harriet Scott, later moved back to Missouri (a slave-owning state).

After Emerson died in 1843, the Scotts sued for their freedom on the grounds that they had lived in a free state. They won their first round, but Emerson's widow appealed and the case went all the way to the Supreme Court, which, in 1857, ruled against them seven to two. Dred Scott died the next year and Harriet died in 1876.

◖ MALL OF AMERICA
60 E. Broadway, Bloomington, 952/883-8800, www.mallofamerica.com
HOURS: Stores open Mon.-Sat. 10 A.M.-9:30 P.M., Sun. 11 A.M.-7 P.M.; mall opens daily at 7 A.M.

Visitors come to the Mall of America to gawk, to say they've seen the largest mall in the United States, and, yes, to shop. There's no reason to be intimidated by the mall's layout: Stores are arranged on three levels of an oval, with four large department stores anchoring the corners (Macy's, Nordstrom's, Sears, and Bloomingdales). The sides are all labeled north, south, east, or west, so if you know what side and what level you're on, there's no way to get lost. The **Nickelodeon Universe** theme park (952/883-8600, www.nickelodeonuniverse .com) occupies the center, with a full-size Ferris

wheel, rollercoaster, and log chute, as well as milder rides that thrill the little ones with references to Dora the Explorer and Diego, rather than by whipping them around.

While sheer density makes the mall a shopper's mecca, you won't necessarily find any particular deals or very many shops outside the usual mall standards. One exception is the **Lake Wobegon USA** store (E350, 952/854-3795, www.prettygoodgoods.org), a gift shop playing homage to (and benefiting) the *Prairie Home Companion* radio show and a good place to pick up souvenirs. There are some surprisingly good dining options at the mall, including **Napa Valley Grille** (W220, 952/858-9934), which serves high-end, white-tablecloth California cuisine with a "patio" overlooking the theme park and a quieter dining room "indoors." Even nonshoppers would enjoy combining a nice dinner with a movie on one of 14 screens at the **Theatres at Mall of America** (952/851-0074, www.theatresmoa .com) on the fourth floor.

If you see a large blue shark wandering the mall, it's advertising **Underwater Adventures** (952/883-0202, www.underwaterworld .com, Mon.–Thurs. 10 A.M.–8 P.M., Fri.–Sat. 9:30 A.M.–8:30 P.M., Sun. 10 A.M.–6:30 P.M., $18.95 ages 13 and up, $11.95 ages 2–13), a full-size aquarium located under the mall.

Keep in mind that after 4 P.M. on Fridays and Saturdays, everyone age 16 and under must be accompanied by an adult. Mall security guards aren't shy about asking for ID.

MINNESOTA LANDSCAPE ARBORETUM
3675 Arboretum Drive, Chaska, 952/443-1400, www.arboretum.edu
HOURS: 8 A.M.–8 P.M. or sunset, whichever comes first
COST: $7, children 15 and under free

The Minnesota Landscape Arboretum is the largest public garden in the Upper Midwest—a massive and varied collection of display gardens as well as cultivated and wild landscapes. And, beyond allowing visitors to wander beautiful paths among well-labeled flower beds, the arboretum curates innovative exhibits that combine gardening with sculptures, activities,

© TRICIA CORNELL

The Minnesota Landscape Arboretum has exhibits of interest to both adults and children.

mazes, and more. Nearly every exhibit includes a component to engage children. The arboretum was established as part of the University of Minnesota's horticultural department in 1907 and has produced such objects of Minnesotans' undying pride as the honeycrisp apple, a cold-hardy—and very tasty!—variety. Many visitors choose to wander the gardens nearest the welcome center on foot—the herb gardens, annual and perennial demonstration gardens, and Japanese gardens, for example, can all be easily taken in by walking a less-than-two-mile loop. But others drive a three-mile loop through prairies, woodlands, and marshes. (Guided tours are available for an additional fee.) While the grounds are open long hours every day except Christmas and Thanksgiving, the conservatory and welcome center, including the cafeteria and gift shop, are open Mon.–Sat. 8 A.M.–6 P.M., Sun. 10 A.M.–6 P.M. Summer Thursday evenings feature extended hours (until 8 P.M.) and free admission. In the winter, November–April, buildings close at 4:30 P.M. and Thursdays are free all day.

MINNESOTA ZOO

1300 Zoo Blvd., Apple Valley, 952/883-8600, www.mnzoo.com

HOURS: Daily 9 A.M.–4 P.M.; Labor Day-Memorial Day and weekends in May and Sept. 9 A.M.–6 P.M.

The Minnesota Zoo offers a wide variety of experiences for all sorts of animal lovers. In the outdoor exhibit the Northern Trail, the animals are all native to climates very similar to Minnesota's own, from the native moose to the Siberian tiger. Most have plenty of room to roam (and hide from visitors) in enclosures spread wide across the zoo's 500 acres. Inside the zoo building, you'll find the Tropics Trail, with a collection of very different animals, from the rare sun bear to ring-tailed lemurs from Madagascar. In Discovery Bay, a massive tank of sharks and other large fish stops kids cold and the zoo's family of dolphins put on 15-minute shows twice a day.

Two unique exhibits have opened in the past few years. In 2007, the zoo overhauled its Minnesota Trail, making the time-honored trip to see beavers, coyotes, wolves, lynxes, and even a bald eagle much more pleasant and exciting. In 2008, Russia's Grizzly Coast wowed the community when it opened, with 3.5 acres representing three distinct landscapes of Russia's far east: the Pacific coast, the volcanic Kamchatka Peninsula, and the taiga forests of Primorsky Krai. Visitors get an amazing up-close look at northern sea otters, brown bears, wild boars, and Amur leopards in a beautifully designed space.

When it's too cold to wander the grounds, or when you want to get a view from up high, the monorail is a fun choice. It operates Mon.–Fri. 10:30 A.M.–3 P.M., Sat.–Sun. 10:30 A.M.–3:30 P.M., with extended hours on summer weekends, and costs $4. One of the zoo's most eagerly awaited exhibits, Farm Babies draws tens of thousands of visitors each spring to see newborn chicks, cows, pigs, and more.

VALLEYFAIR

1 Valleyfair Dr., Shakopee, 952/445-6500, www.valleyfair.com

HOURS: Mid-May–early Sept. daily 10 A.M.–10 P.M.
COST: $37.99 anyone over 48 inches tall, $16.99 seniors and anyone under 48 inches, free for children 2 and younger

Valleyfair prides itself on being the largest amusement park in the Upper Midwest, with 75 rides on 90 acres. New and popular thrillers include the spinning RipTide, the Xtreme Swing (which launches riders into the air), and the wooden rollercoaster Renegade. Tickets include unlimited rides and as much time as you want to spend in the 3.5-acre Whitewater Country water park, with five water slides and plenty of other soaking wet fun. (Swimsuits are required; changing facilities and lockers are provided. Whitewater Country opens later and generally closes earlier than the rest of the park.) Challenge Park lets visitors indulge their competitive spirits with a zip-cord ride, mini golf, go-carts, and bumper boats, all for an additional fee. The park also puts on one of the area's most popular haunted houses, dubbed "Valleyscare." Note that Valleyfair's hours vary, with the park staying open until midnight a few weekends in late summer and closing between 5 and 10 P.M. or on weekdays at the beginning and end of the season. Call ahead or check the website.

RESTAURANTS

The Twin Cities are a fantastic place for people who love food. Throw out your images of meat-and-potatoes farm food and under-seasoned ghosts of Scandinavian fare. In fact, the Upper Midwest's connection to farming is serving eaters well.

With a dozen or so young chefs leading the way, "local," "seasonal," and "sustainable" have become more than buzzwords; knowing exactly where your vegetables, beef, chicken, and pork come from—and telling your diners—has become *de rigueur* for fine dining. And that benefits the pioneering small bistros and cafés that have been cooking and serving food this way for a couple of decades. Those same young chefs, by the way, regularly show up on the list of James Beard Award nominees—the food world equivalent of sending the hometown kids to the Oscars.

Diners in the Twin Cities also benefit from the robust Laotian, Vietnamese, and East African communities here. Spring rolls and *bánh mì* (Vietnamese stuffed baguettes) show up on menus all over town, even far away from the rows of Vietnamese holes-in-the-wall on University Avenue in St. Paul and Nicollet Avenue in Minneapolis. And the fragrant *phở* soup and noodle salads have become staples in the local cuisine.

The upshot of the new focus on chef-driven short menus is that, unless the chef herself is dedicated to a less-meat lifestyle (like local food leader Brenda Langton of

© TRICIA CORNELL

RESTAURANTS

HIGHLIGHTS

LOOK FOR ☾ TO FIND RECOMMENDED RESTAURANTS.

☾ **Best Sandwich in the Upper Midwest:** The tuna confit at **Be'wiched** is unbeatable. Don't like fish? Go for the house-cured pastrami (page 49).

☾ **Best Breakfast:** You may have to wait in line at **Hell's Kitchen** in Minneapolis, but you will understand why once your stack of ethereal lemon ricotta pancakes arrives (page 51).

☾ **Best Place for Vegetarians and Their Carnivore Friends:** Brenda Langton's two downtown Minneapolis restaurants, **Café Brenda** and **Spoonriver**, don't take a hard line against meat, they just make tasty, healthy food everyone can enjoy (page 54).

☾ **Best Local, Seasonal Fare:** Lucia Watson, the dynamo behind the Minneapolis institution **Lucia's,** has been garnering well-deserved attention for her sustainable take on cuisine for two decades (page 55).

☾ **Best Place to Live the Bistro Lifestyle:** On a leafy street in South Minneapolis, **Barbette** opens early to serve croissants and café au lait and serves perfect *pommes frites* into the wee hours (page 58).

☾ **Best Place to Taste Minnesota's Immigrant Past:** Links of Polish sausage and plates of butter-soaked *pelmeni* fueled Nordeast Minneapolis's Eastern European immigrant families, and at **Kramarczuk's** they keep hungry tourists and locals fed, too (page 63).

☾ **Best Afternoon Tea:** Grand Avenue's **Café Latté** offers shoppers the perfect afternoon respite: a classically English plate of finger sandwiches and cakes (page 68).

☾ **Best Place to Feast and Toast and Dance and Drink All Night Long:** Russians know how to keep the party going, and will be happy to show you at **Moscow on the Hill** (page 70).

☾ **Best Place to Keep a Crowd Happy:** When you're feeding a crowd for breakfast or lunch, you'll find options – and space – for everyone at **Good Day Café** (page 71).

☾ **Best Dim Sum:** **Jun Bo** doesn't look like much, but that's because they've put all their effort into the best dim sum in the metro area – served all day, every day (page 72).

Café Brenda and Spoonriver), vegetarians often get shortchanged with an afterthought pasta dish or salad. (Of course, it will likely be a salad of local butterleaf lettuces.)

Minnesotans eat early. Most restaurants open for dinner at 5 P.M. and the busiest seating is likely to be 6 P.M. That's good news for people who would rather eat around 8 but bad news for those who like to dine even later, because many kitchens close at 9 P.M. on weekdays and 10 P.M. on weekends. It's another vestige of the farming culture. You

could, of course, adapt by joining the crowds for breakfast and brunch, a Midwesterner's favorite meal.

PRICE KEY

- **$** Most entrées less than $10
- **$$** Most entrées $10-20
- **$$$** Most entrées more than $20

Downtown Minneapolis Map 1

RESTAURANTS

AMERICAN
BAR AND CAFÉ LURCAT ⑤⑤⑤
1624 Harmon Pl., Minneapolis, 612/486-5500,
www.damico.com

HOURS: Café Mon.-Thurs. 5-10 P.M., Fri.-Sat. 5-11 P.M.,
Sun. 5-9 P.M.; bar open until 1 A.M. on weekends

This is where you will find Minneapolis's
beautiful people, arranged artfully on Lurcat's
exquisite collection of couches and chaises
longues. The people-watching will provide
delightful entertainment while you eat. In the
bar, that means small plates, like rave-worthy
mini burgers and decadently golden fries. In
the café, you'll find creative contemporary
American fare with a touch of French influ-
ence—buckwheat crêpes, several cuts of steak,
butter-poached prawns, and foie gras.

⟨ BE'WICHED ⑤
800 Washington Ave. N., Minneapolis, 612/767-4330,
www.bewicheddeli.com

HOURS: Mon.-Fri. 8 A.M.-8 P.M., Sat. 10 A.M.-6 P.M.,
Sun. closed

At your typical sandwich shop you're lucky if
the person behind the counter can tell you what
day the pastrami came in. At Be'wiched, they
absolutely can tell you: They cured it themselves. They also smoked the turkey, braised
the pulled pork, made the tuna confit, and
even baked the bread. Chefs Matthew Bickford
and Mike Ryan, both refugees from fine dining, believe that all the classic flavor combinations and exquisite quality of haute cuisine can
be packaged between two slices of bread. By
the way, happy hour here is a bit of a surprise
and a very good deal: $2 tap beer and $4 wine,
accompanied by whatever tasty snacky things
they put together that day.

JOE'S GARAGE ⑤⑤
1610 Harmon Pl., Minneapolis, 612/904-1163,
www.joes-garage.com

HOURS: Mon.-Wed. 11 A.M.-10 P.M., Thurs.-Sat.
11 A.M.-11 P.M., Sun. 10 A.M.-10 P.M.

You never knew anyone could do so much with

EAT STREET

If you can't decide exactly what you want
for dinner and you're up for a bit of a culinary adventure, point your feet south
from downtown Minneapolis, along Nicollet Avenue. The stretch from the edge of
downtown proper – around 13th Street –
to around 28th Street is known as Eat
Street. That mile-or-so walk will take you
past Indian, Vietnamese, Chinese, and
Mexican restaurants – from holes-in-the-
wall to large and well-established places
like Quang. (Almost universally speaking,
what you find will be inexpensive, authentic, and tasty.

Eat Street is the place to go to
experience ethnic cuisine.

mashed potatoes. Humble spuds become gourmet meals when you stir in lamb meatballs,
smoky grilled ratatouille, or chipotle cream
sauce—or any combination of the two dozen
mix-ins and toppings. Burgers are also mul-
titaskers at Joe's Garage. Beyond beef, you'll
find spicy Asian pork, lamb with chèvre, and

a complex black bean and falafel mixture, among others. Right on Loring Park, Joe's has a fantastic third-story patio—a joy on summer evenings—and the bar is open until 1 A.M. on weekdays and until 2 A.M. on weekends.

KEYS CAFÉ $

114 S. 9th St., Minneapolis, 612/339-6399, www.keyscafe.com
HOURS: Mon.-Fri. 6:30 A.M.-10 P.M., Sat. 7 A.M.-10 P.M., Sun. 8 A.M.-10 P.M.

The downtown outpost of this sprawling network of restaurants (there are seven locations in the Twin Cities, all owned by the children and in-laws of the founder) is ideal for a homey, please-everyone, casual meal. The menu is classic (all-day breakfast, half-pound burgers, BLTs, and patty melts), and the name is practically a Twin Cities institution, but the new venue on the ground floor of the Foshay Tower is updated and urban. You might even consider this for happy hour or a relaxed business lunch. (Please note: This is classic Midwestern fare, so there will be grated orange cheese on your salad, but the walleye sandwich will be outstanding.)

LA BELLE VIE $$$

427 Groveland Ave., Minneapolis, 612/874-6440, www.labellevie.us
HOURS: Mon.-Thurs. 5-9 P.M., Fri.-Sat. 5-10 P.M., Sun. 5-9 P.M.

This is it, the top of the top, the finest of the fine dining in the Twin Cities—from the old-money elegance of the dining room to the award-winning cuisine (both *Gourmet* and *Food & Wine* have listed La Belle Vie among the top restaurants in the country). Chef Tim McKee has arguably the best culinary reputation in the area. While you can order à la carte, where he shines is in the tasting menus—five courses for $65 or seven for $80. And if you've got champagne taste on a beer budget, you can have a very fine dinner indeed in the comfortable lounge (which stays open an hour later than the dining room). Not-so-small small plates like foie gras with baguette, a lamb burger, and pappardelle with rabbit bolognese will fill you up for under $20.

NICK AND EDDIE $$

1612 Harmon Pl., Minneapolis, 612/486-5800, www.nickandeddie.com
HOURS: Brunch Sat.-Sun. 9 A.M.-3 P.M.; lunch Mon.-Fri. 11 A.M.-3 P.M.; dinner Mon.-Thurs.-10 P.M., Fri.-Sat. 5-11 P.M., Sun. 5-9 P.M.

Mix a little New York City deli (yes, that's a bialy with whitefish on the appetizer menu and the chicken liver is more popular than you might think in the Midwest), with a little French bistro (think plates of simple grilled meat and fish), with some classic Americana (the blue cheeseburger and Italian sausage sandwich on the bar menu hit the spot) and you've got Nick and Eddie. The too-cool-to-be-formal eatery facing Loring Park has attracted a certain segment of the Twin Cities hipster scene since it opened in 2007.

112 EATERY $$

112 N. 3rd St., Minneapolis, 612/343-7696, www.112eatery.com
HOURS: Mon.-Thurs. 5 P.M.-midnight, Fri.-Sat. 5 P.M.-1 A.M., Sun. 5-10 P.M.

What would a hungry cook or server want to eat after a long shift? Probably a hearty egg sandwich with tangy *harissa*. Meatballs made with foie gras. Duck pâté in the crusty Vietnamese sandwich known as a *bành mì*. Or a plateful of light-as-air parmesan gnocchi. They'd want the best ingredients served up in comforting dishes. That's what chef Isaac Becker set out to serve when he opened 112 Eatery in a tiny Warehouse District space in 2005. Since then, the tables have been full and the accolades have rolled in, including a James Beard nomination in 2008. (If you can't call well in advance for a table, your best bet is to accept an open 5 P.M. or 11 P.M. spot or take your chances at the bar.)

ASIAN
NAMI $$

251 1st Ave. N., Minneapolis, 612/333-1999, www.namisushi.com
HOURS: Mon.-Sat. 11:30 A.M.-10 P.M., Sun. closed

At big and stylish Nami, you can take your pick of environments when you walk in the door:

a table for two in a quiet corner, something closer to the rocking party going on at the bar, or right in front of the sushi chef. While Nami is known for some of the best sushi in the Twin Cities, you can also enjoy something comforting like a bowl of udon noodles, a tempura dinner, or a complex bento box.

20.21 $$$

1750 Hennepin Ave., Minneapolis, 612/253-3410,
www.wolfgangpuck.com

HOURS: Lunch Tues.-Sat. 11:30 A.M.-2 P.M.; brunch Sun. 10 A.M.-2:30 P.M.; dinner Tues.-Thurs. 5:30-10 P.M., Fri.-Sat. 5:30-11 P.M., Mon. closed

When it opened in 2005, the shiny new Walker Art Center building needed a restaurant that would make as much of an impression as its renowned collection of contemporary art. Enter Wolfgang Puck, with his brand of high-end Asian fusion you can't find elsewhere in the Twin Cities. "Asian" is broadly defined on the menu, from Mongolian lamb to Cantonese duck, to a Maine lobster with *shiso* and *yuzu*. The Sunday brunch buffet ($28) is unparalleled. Bear in mind that the dining room hangs right above busy Hennepin Avenue, with an iconic view of the Loring Park footbridge and the Basilica of St. Mary, as well as a congested tangle of highways (romantic at night when you can watch the lights but not particularly so during the day).

BREAKFAST AND BRUNCH
HELL'S KITCHEN $

80 S. 9th St., Minneapolis, 612/332-4700,
www.hellskitcheninc.com

HOURS: Mon.-Fri. 6:30 A.M.-10 P.M.,
Sat.-Sun. 7:30 A.M.-10 P.M.

This is the best breakfast in the Twin Cities, hands down (and it has repeatedly been recognized as such by the local press since opening in 2002). Here's why: ethereal lemon-ricotta pancakes, a plate of huevos rancheros as big as your head, local bacon cut seemingly a quarter-inch thick, and the popular wild rice porridge you won't find anywhere else. At 11 A.M.

the menu switches to lunch—hearty sandwiches and burgers, including bison—with a few hours of amnesty for the best breakfast items. Be sure to pick up a jar of their homemade peanut butter on the way out. Renowned road foodies Jane and Michael Stern can't get enough of it.

FRENCH
VINCENT – A RESTAURANT $$$

1100 Nicollet Mall, Minneapolis, 612/630-1189,
www.vincentarestaurant.com

HOURS: Mon.-Thurs. 11:30 A.M.-2 P.M. and 5:30-9 P.M., Fri. 11:30 A.M.-2 P.M. and 5:30-11 P.M., Sat. 5:30-11 P.M., Sun. closed

Vincent Françoual makes his grandmother's cabbage soup and a deceptively simple cookie-and-ice cream combination known as "Vincent's favorite childhood dessert," but don't be fooled. This chef's got serious fine-dining chops. Lunch is bistro fare: omelets, *steak frites,* buckwheat crêpes, and the fabulous

fine French dining on the sidewalk at Vincent – A Restaurant

RESTAURANTS

© TRICIA CORNELL

short-rib- and gruyère-infused Vincent burger. (Get your fix of bistro classics at the bar during the dinner hour.) Dinner brings out the classic French pan sauces and high-end cuts of meat.

ITALIAN
BUCA DI BEPPO $$

1204 Harmon Pl., Minneapolis, 612/288-0138, www.bucadibeppo.com

HOURS: Mon.-Thurs. 11 A.M.-10 P.M., Fri.-Sat. 11 A.M.-11 P.M., Sun. 11 A.M.-9 P.M.

Before there were 100 Buca outposts strung out across America, extended families and gangs of bachelorettes passed heaping family-sized platters of lasagna, antipasto salad, and chicken marsala, downed tumblers of wine, and laughed long into the night at the huge tables crammed into this rabbit warren of a Minneapolis basement. Okay, that was only 1993, but the patina of age has settled comfortably on this, the first of the Buca empire. For large gatherings and celebratory occasions, Buca hits the spot. Twin Citians in need of comfort swear by the garlic mashed potatoes.

D'AMICO CUCINA $$$

100 6th St. N., Minneapolis, 612/338-2401, www.damico.com

HOURS: Mon.-Thurs. 5:30-9 P.M., Fri.-Sat. 5:30-10 P.M., Sun. closed

When the mouths of Minnesota's bankers, lawyers, CEOs, and other expense-account types start to water, a good bet is they're thinking about D'Amico Cucina, an elegant, airy haven in downtown Minneapolis, where the best of fine Italian dining can be had with the wave of a platinum credit card. You can choose roasted scallops, ravioli with truffle butter, and Copper River salmon, but even better is to put yourself in your chef's hands with the $65 tasting menu. For a far more affordable taste of the D'Amico magic, visit one of the D'Amico and Sons locations. Two of our favorites are in Uptown (2210 Hennepin Ave. S., 612/374-1858) and Edina (3948 50th St. W., 952/926-1187).

PIZZA LUCE $

119 N. 4th St., Minneapolis, 612/333-7359, www.pizzaluce.com

HOURS: Sun.-Thurs. 11 A.M.-2:30 A.M., Fri.-Sat. 11 A.M.-3:30 A.M.

It's not polite to stare at the serving staff—even if facial tattoos and multiple piercings seem to be primary hiring criteria—so concentrate on the pizza instead. A little thicker, a little sweeter, a little breadier than your average pie, Pizza Luce's crust is in a category all its own. And the toppings blow attempts at categorization out of the water: Garlic mashed potatoes, black beans and pico de gallo, and mock duck and pineapple on barbecue sauce are just a few choices on the long menu. This is also a great place for hearty salads and pasta dishes. Vegans and vegetarians will love it here, as will any hungry souls wandering out after bars close at 2 A.M.

ZELO $$

831 Nicollet Mall, Minneapolis, 612/333-7000, www.zelomn.com

HOURS: Mon.-Thurs. 11 A.M.-11 P.M., Fri. 11 A.M.-midnight, Sat. 11:30 A.M.-midnight, Sun. 5-10 P.M.

Power-lunchers and anniversary-celebrators love the dark wood and rich ambiance at Zelo. The menu is primarily Italian, with touches of Asian flare (calamari *fritti* with lemon aioli, for example, lives comfortably next to ahi spring rolls with wasabi and soy). While the steak and veal entrées are understandably pricey, Zelo's tasty pastas and pizzas—as well as the lunch menu—are actually quite affordable. And you get the same great service. For Zelo taste on the go, head around the corner (same building, different entrance) to Zelino for takeout soups and sandwiches.

MEXICAN AND SPANISH
MASA $$$

1070 Nicollet Mall, Minneapolis, 612/338-6272, www.masa-restaurant.com

HOURS: Mon.-Thurs. 11 A.M.-2:30 P.M., 5-10 P.M., Fri. 11 A.M.-2:30 P.M., 5-11 P.M., Sat. 5-11 P.M., Sun. closed

Mexican food doesn't have to come out of a

Masa sets up a shady patio dining area in the summer.

taco truck to be authentic. Masa gives good old Mexican favorites the white-tablecloth treatment. Humble foods like tacos, *sopes,* and *pozole verde* still taste good when served by trained waiters on nice china. And then the kitchen stretches a bit to offer higher-end fare, like scallops marinated with chiles and mahimahi in *achiote* sauce. Don't skip their extensive, excellent cocktail menu; for a nonalcoholic kick, try La Vampira—a spicy tomato and citrus concoction. And you have to finish your meal with churros and a cup of butterscotch-thick chocolate for dipping. Enjoy happy hour at the bar weekdays 4–6 P.M.

SOLERA $$

900 Hennepin Ave., Minneapolis, 612/338-0062, www.solera-restaurant.com

HOURS: Mon.-Thurs. 4 P.M.-1 A.M., Fri. 4 P.M.-2 A.M., Sat. 5 P.M.-2 A.M., Sun. 5-11 P.M.

There are so many occasions that might draw you to Solera: a celebratory dinner for a crowd of friends, quiet cocktails for two, early-evening happy hour, late-night snacks. And, somewhere in this four-story complex,

you'll find just the right spot—a seat at the chef-staffed tapas bar, a banquette by the bar, a table under the stars on the roof (where you can also watch movies during the summer). Some of the best minds in the Twin Cities restaurant business compiled the tapas menu (with 50 kinds of tapas, including tasty marinated anchovies and shrimp croquettes) and heavily Spanish wine list. The vibe is youthful and the crowd is as beautiful as the Gaudi-inspired setting.

MIDDLE EASTERN
SAFFRON $$$

123 3rd St. N., Minneapolis, 612/746-5533, www.saffronmpls.com

HOURS: Mon.-Thurs. 5-10 P.M., Fri.-Sat. 5 P.M.-1 A.M., Sun. closed

Classic techniques meet Middle Eastern flavors. Chef Sameh Wadi once cooked at the upscale, French-inspired La Belle Vie, but his cousins own the homey Holy Land Deli. All that comes together in the white-linen dining room in surprising ways: lamb brains with tomato confit, for example, and carpaccio with crispy chickpeas. Happy hour specials (weekdays 4–6 P.M.

and weekends 11 P.M.–1 A.M.), served at low couches in the airy lounge, are a great way to fill up on hits of big flavor: kibbeh-inspired meatballs, *charmoula* burgers, French fries with feta dipping sauce, and even a classic fried egg with *harissa*.

STEAK HOUSE
MURRAY'S RESTAURANT AND COCKTAILS $$$

26 S. 6th St., Minneapolis, 612/339-0909, www.murraysrestaurant.com

HOURS: Mon.-Fri. 11 A.M.-2 P.M. and 5-10:30 P.M., Sat.-Sun. 5-10:30 P.M.

For more than 60 years, the Silver Butter Knife Steak at Murray's has been one of the classiest ways to say "I love you" to your meat-eating Minneapolis sweetheart. The Silver Butter Knife—you'll recognize it from the picture on the classic neon sign out front—is a 28-ounce cut of meat meant for two, so tender you barely need the titular carving implement. You can also choose among more than a dozen other cuts of meat and nearly as many luxurious seafood dishes. Vegetarians…well, the only things for vegetarians to enjoy at Murray's are the suave service and timeless setting.

VEGETARIAN
⟨ CAFÉ BRENDA $$

300 1st Ave. N., Minneapolis, 612/342-9230, www.cafebrenda.com

HOURS: Lunch Mon.-Fri. 11:30 A.M.-2 P.M.; dinner Mon.-Thurs. 5:30-9 P.M., Fri.-Sat. 5:30-10 P.M.; Sun. closed

You might think of Brenda Langton as the Twin Cities' own Alice Waters—a pioneer of fresh, local, healthy food. She opened her first restaurant in the 1970s, at the age of 21, offering only vegetarian food and seafood. Today, having found good local sources, she has added poultry and lamb dishes to the menu. But this is vegetarian food even meat eaters will love. The nut burger is hearty and the mock duck taco carries Latin flavor just as well as the original, but everyone raves about the fritters, always on the specials board. Brenda has a light hand with the oil and dairy, so visitors are sure to leave satisfied but not stuffed.

⟨ SPOONRIVER $$

750 2nd St. S., Minneapolis, 612/436-2236, www.spoonriverrestaurant.com

HOURS: Lunch Tues.-Fri. 11:30 A.M.-2 P.M.; brunch Sat.-Sun. 10 A.M.-2 P.M.; dinner Tues.-Thurs. 5:30-10 P.M., Fri.-Sat. 5:30-11 P.M., Sun. 5-10 P.M.; Mon. closed

Spoonriver is the elegant, urbane sister of Café Brenda, natural-food pioneer Brenda Langton's first restaurant. Right next to the Guthrie Theater, it's a popular choice for pre- or post-theater dining—something you should keep in mind if you're hoping to get a table in the long, slim dining room without a reservation. For pre-theater snacks, you can't beat the wild mushroom and pistachio terrine or the smoked chicken quesadilla with mango, which features Langton's signature savory/sweet, local/tropical combinations. For dinner, the seafood *okisuki* (Japanese noodles in broth) is a big bowl of comfort. But nothing is heavy enough to leave you snoring in the middle of the play. Weekend brunches (starting at 8 A.M. in the summer) are just a tiny bit more decadent, with omelets, French toast, and buckwheat crêpes.

South Minneapolis Map 2

AMERICAN
BLACKBIRD $$
815 50th St. W., Minneapolis, 612/823-4790,
www.blackbirdmpls.com
HOURS: Mon.-Fri. 11 A.M.-10 P.M., Sat. 8 A.M.-2 P.M. and
5-10 P.M., Sun. 8 A.M.-2 P.M.
What do crawfish casserole, Thai-flavored rabbit salad, and a Vietnamese-ish *bành mì* sandwich stuffed with liverwurst have in common? The only obvious answer is that's what owners Chris Stevens and Gail Mollner like to cook and eat. They've turned a former chain coffee shop into an expression of their own personal tastes, right down to the Japanese lanterns and the antlers on the wall. Weekend breakfasts are casual and kid-friendly. But keep in mind Blackbird doesn't take reservations and this is a town that loves its breakfast.

BRYANT LAKE BOWL $$
810 Lake St. W., Minneapolis, 612/825-3737,
www.bryantlakebowl.com
HOURS: Daily 8 A.M.-2 A.M.
There are a couple of reasons why it's so crowded in here: For starters, this popular establishment in the Uptown neighborhood is working on its second generation of hip regulars. More importantly, they cram a lot into a small space—a restaurant, bar, theater space, and, yes, a bowling alley. If you come for the food, you have to try the smoked trout quesadilla with chèvre and the carrot cake. Monday is cheap date night: dinner for two, bowling, and a bottle of wine for $25.

CHINO LATINO $$
2916 Hennepin Ave. S., Minneapolis, 612/824-7878,
www.chinolatino.com
HOURS: Sun.-Thurs. 4:30 P.M.-1 A.M., Fri.-Sat.
4:30 P.M.-2 A.M.
Big, bold, beautiful, and brassy—that's Chino Latino and most of its clientele. Once you get a table (reservations are recommended, but waiting to be seated is one of the most popular ways

to see and be seen in Uptown), choose "little plates to share" (appetizers) or "big plates to share" (mains that serve 3–5). The flavors—which look like a multiculti mishmash on the menu—will make sense once they hit your table: hot tastes from the hot parts of the world, like the calamari with jalapenos. Wash them down with selections from one of the longest and craziest cocktail menus in town.

HEIDI'S $$
819 50th St. W., Minneapolis, 612/354-3512,
www.heidismpls.com
HOURS: Tues.-Sun. 5-10 P.M., Mon. closed
Heidi, in this case, is Heidi Woodman, the restaurant's much-lauded pastry chef. Her husband and partner is chef Stewart Woodman, who has cooked at Lespinasse and Le Bernardin (to name just two) and graced the cover of *Food & Wine*'s Best New Chefs issue in 2006. Need we say more, or are you already making reservations? Since opening in 2007, Heidi's has been the hot reservation in town. Diners get to choose between about a half dozen appetizers and a similar number of entrées on the regularly changing menu, but all of them—perhaps a butter-poached lobster or a crispy chicken breast—are impeccably refined.

◖ LUCIA'S $$$
1432 31st St. W., Minneapolis, 612/825-1572,
www.lucias.com
HOURS: Lunch Tues.-Fri. 11:30 A.M.-2:30 P.M.; dinner
Tues.-Thurs. 5:30-9:30 P.M., Fri.-Sat. 5:30-10 P.M., Sun.
5:30-9 P.M.; brunch Sat.-Sun. 10 A.M.-2 P.M.; Mon. closed
Lucia's is a fixture in Uptown. Chef Lucia Watson, who has been nominated for a James Beard Award and counts *Gourmet*'s Ruth Reichl among her fans—posts her brief but tempting weekly menu online every Wednesday. If dinner's not in your plans, make time for a weekend brunch, little bites and sandwiches at the bar, or crêpes and salads at Lucia's Bakery next door (open Tues.-Fri. 7 A.M.–8 P.M.,

SEASONAL SEAFOOD

Yes, Minnesota is about as far from an ocean as one can get in the continental United States. But that doesn't mean people here don't enjoy the time-honored simple pleasure of sitting by a body of water and eating a fine piece of fish. The opening of two Minneapolis restaurants is an eagerly awaited sign of spring each year, and their closing each fall is a sad rite of passage into the colder, darker days.

Sea Salt (4825 Minnehaha Ave., Minneapolis, 612/721-8990, www.seasalteatery.com, April-Oct. Sun.-Mon. 11 A.M.-7 P.M., Tues.-Sat. 11 A.M.-8 P.M.) fills the pavilion at Minnehaha Falls with the scent of fish tacos and lines of eager eaters. The menu – from oysters on the half shell ($26/dozen) to crab cakes ($9.95) to fried fish sandwiches and fish tacos – is ideal for a picnic on a warm summer eating (be aware, though, that many, many other people know this is true. To beat the crowds get there earlier in the day or on a weekday. (Seating is in the open air or under the cover of the picnic pavilion.)

On Lake Calhoun, in the classic park building, is the equally eagerly awaited **Tin**

© BRUCE MANNING

Sea Salt's opening day is eagerly awaited at the start of every summer.

Fish (3000 Calhoun Pkwy. E., Minneapolis, 612/823-5840, www.thetinfish.net, late April-Memorial Day daily noon-8 P.M., Memorial Day-Labor Day daily 11 A.M.-9 P.M., Labor Day-Oct. daily noon-7:30 P.M.). The Tin Fish's specialty is the Mini Tin, a deceptively mammoth fried fish sandwich, but the shrimp tacos, the grilled mahimahi, the flavorful burgers – heck, all the things on the menu – are worth waiting for.

Sat. 8 A.M.–8 P.M., Sun. 8 A.M.–7 P.M.). Late-night bites are available on the bar menu (until midnight Tues.–Thurs. and Sun., until 1 A.M. Fri.–Sat.).

TOWN TALK DINER $$

2707½ Lake St. E., Minneapolis, 612/722-1312, www.towntalkdiner.com

HOURS: Lunch Tues.-Fri. 11 A.M.-2 P.M.; dinner Tues.-Thurs. 5-10 P.M., Fri.-Sat. 5-11 P.M.; brunch Sat.-Sun. 10 A.M.-3 P.M.; Mon. closed

This is food for reluctant grown-ups: baskets of batter-fried pickles and cheese curds, bacon-wrapped hot dogs, fried egg sandwiches, and alcoholic malts sprinkled with Trix. But don't mistake this reimagined Willy Wonka diner for a kiddie playground. The clientele here is the Twin Cities' young professional class, blowing off steam and looking for love at the loud, lively bar. The bar has later hours (Tues.–Thurs.

4 P.M.–midnight, Fri. 4 P.M.–2 A.M., Sat. 10 A.M.–3 P.M. and 4 P.M.–2 A.M.).

ASIAN
FUJI YA $$

600 Lake St. W., Minneapolis, 612/871-4055, www.fujiyasushi.com

HOURS: Tues.-Thurs. 5-10 P.M., Fri.-Sat. 5-10:30 P.M., Sun. 5-9 P.M.

Before you could get sushi in every grocery store, you could get it right here, at Fuji Ya. Well, not here exactly—the restaurant has moved a couple of times since it first shocked Minnesotans with raw fish—but from the same family. You'd never know Fuji Ya has five decades under its belt: It's still fresh and young and pulling in a hip crowd. On summer evenings, the secluded patio is a great place to score a seat, but your party may also request a tatami room for the most authentic experience. Fuji Ya is also in St. Paul (465 Wabasha St. N., 651/310-0111, lunch Mon.–Fri. 11:30 A.M.–2 P.M., dinner Mon.–Sat. 5–10 P.M., Sun. closed).

JASMINE DELI $

2532 Nicollet Ave. S., Minneapolis, 612/870-4700
HOURS: Tues.-Sat. 10 A.M.–8 P.M., Sun. 10 A.M.–6 P.M.

With just a half dozen tables and a spare, no-nonsense aesthetic, Jasmine Deli won't wow you until the food arrives: fragrant *phở* (Vietnamese noodle soup with a deep, rich broth), bright noodle salads, and perfectly sized *bành mì* (stuffed baguette sandwiches) are the things to order. Linger a little longer over a Vietnamese coffee—drip-brewed right at your table over sweetened condensed milk (iced in the summer).

QUANG $

2719 Nicollet Ave. S., Minneapolis, 612/870-4739, www.quangrestaurant.com
HOURS: Mon. and Wed.-Fri. 11 A.M.–9 P.M., Sat. 10 A.M.–9 P.M., Sun. 10 A.M.–8:30 P.M., Tues. closed

This is where big Southeast Asian families gather to celebrate and dine together. It's also popular with office workers looking for an inexpensive, healthy lunch, and with young Vietnamese couples on a date. Heck, just about everybody eventually comes to bright and friendly Quang for their first or their 4,000th bowl of *phở*. (If you've had enough *phở*, try the barbecue pork salad.) The line may stretch out the door, but you probably won't have to wait long. Service here is unbelievably fast.

TRUE THAI $

2627 Franklin Ave. E., Minneapolis, 612/375-9942, www.truethairestaurant.com
HOURS: Mon.-Thurs. 11 A.M.–9 P.M., Fri.-Sat. 11 A.M.–11 P.M., Sun. closed

Go beyond pad thai and *tom yum* soup (though those popular Thai dishes get very good reviews here). Try the Thai duck, a Minnesota bird that gets a spicy Asian treatment, or the pepper steak with pineapple. The long menu covers all the Thai classics and more (think

catfish salad) and is consistently mentioned as the Twin Cities' best Thai kitchen.

BREAKFAST AND BRUNCH

COMMON ROOTS $

2558 Lyndale Ave. S., Minneapolis, 612/871-2360, www.commonrootscafe.com
HOURS: Sun.-Thurs. 7 A.M.–10 P.M., Fri.-Sat. 7 A.M.–11 P.M.

When you move to a new town and can't find a decent bagel, what do you do? You make your own, or at least that's what Danny Schwartzman did. And he challenged himself along the way, to make and sell them in the most sustainable way possible. The café, new in 2007, was built using sustainable techniques and materials. And, at last count, 90 percent of their ingredients are local, fair trade, or organic. Get a bagel with cream cheese or lox or an egg scramble for breakfast. The dinner menu is brief—local chicken, local trout—but you can wash it down with one of the best Minnesota brews, a Surly beer.

FRENCH MEADOW BAKERY AND CAFÉ $$

2610 Lyndale Ave. S., Minneapolis, 612/870-7855, www.frenchmeadowcafe.com
HOURS: Sun.-Thurs. 6:30 A.M.–9 P.M., Fri.-Sat. 6:30 A.M.–11 P.M.

Founder and owner Lynn Gordon is the queen of organic, vegan, gluten-free, sprouted-grain, natural-yeast, low-glycemic baking. But you'd never know it, walking into this friendly, stylish café. The bakery case is filled with tasty treats and the tables are filled with diners enjoying breakfast burritos and platter-sized pancakes. While French Meadow has long lines at breakfast and lunch, it's something of a hidden gem for dinner, when the lights go down low and dates can moon at each other over free-range chicken, Midwest bison, and vegan stromboli.

THE ZUMBRO $

2803 43rd St. W., Minneapolis, 612/870-7855, www.thezumbro.com
HOURS: Tues.-Fri. 7 A.M.–2:30 P.M., Sat.-Sun. 7:30 A.M.–2:30 P.M., Mon. closed

Somehow this small breakfast-and-lunch place

feels sunny even in the winter. It may be all the blond wood, or it may be the happy diners and the always-cheery clatter of latte cups. The Zumbro has mastered the fine art of the frittata and serves a variety alongside tender potatoes and, if you choose, fantastic slices of thick-cut bacon. Keep in mind: It's small and popular, meaning this may not be the best choice for larger groups, active kids, or people in a hurry. (Those people should check out The Zumbro To Go, just around the corner.)

FRENCH
🄲 BARBETTE $$

1600 Lake St. W., Minneapolis, 612/827-5710, www.barbette.com

HOURS: Sun.-Thurs. 8 A.M.-1 A.M., Fri.-Sat. 8 A.M.-2 P.M.

The sign over the back door beckons: "French fries here." And many a wanderer has been lured into the rich, warm, lounge-like room for a big plate of *pommes frites* with béarnaise sauce or a frisée salad with poached egg and lardons or a filled buckwheat crêpe. Everything at Barbette is comforting, classically French, and frankly perfect, from breakfast right on through to late-night snacks. Save room for carrot cake.

ITALIAN
BRODER'S PASTA BAR $$

5000 Penn Ave. S., Minneapolis, 612/925-9202, www.broders.com

HOURS: Mon.-Thurs. 5-9:30 P.M., Fri. 5-10 P.M., Sat. 4:30-10 P.M., Sun. 5-9:30 P.M.

Housemade pasta cooked to order and tossed to order with individually composed sauces (nearly two dozen choices, as a matter of fact, if you count the risotto)—that's why South Minneapolis diners line up and cheerfully accept the no-reservations policy. Look for terrific dinner-for-two deals after 8 P.M. on Sundays and before 6 P.M. on weekdays, available seasonally. Across the street, at Broder's Cucina Italiana, you can pick up pasta to cook at home (and maybe a slice of pizza to munch along the way) and other imported goodies.

WEEKEND BRUNCH

Weekend brunch – best enjoyed at an hour that in many cities would be considered "breakfast" – is a beloved ritual in the Twin Cities. This is an early-rising town, even on the weekends. Great bets for hearty breakfasts built on local ingredients include downtown Minneapolis's **Hell's Kitchen** (80 S. 9th St., Minneapolis, 612/332-4700, www.hellskitcheninc.com, Mon.-Fri. 6:30 A.M.-2 P.M., Sat.-Sun. 8 A.M.-2 P.M.) and South Minneapolis's **The Zumbro** (2803 43rd St. S., Minneapolis, 612/870-7855, www.thezumbro.com, Tues.-Fri. 7 A.M.-2:30 P.M., Sat.-Sun. 7:30 A.M.-2:30 P.M., Mon. closed) and **French Meadow Bakery and Café** (2610 Lyndale Ave. S., Minneapolis, 612/870-7855, www.frenchmeadowcafe.com, Sun.-Thurs. 6:30 A.M.-9 P.M., Fri.-Sat. 6:30 A.M.-11 P.M.).

For a morning repast focused more on pastries than on eggs and bacon, head for the croissant-filled display case at **Bread and Chocolate** (867 Grand Ave., St. Paul, 651/228-1017, www.cafelatte.com, Mon.-Fri. 6:30 A.M.-6 P.M., Sat.-Sun. 7 A.M.-6 P.M.) or to one of **Turtle Bread**'s two tasty locations (3421 44th St. W., Minneapolis, 612/924-6013, daily 6:30 A.M.-8 P.M., and 4762 Chicago Ave. S., 612/823-7333, daily 6 A.M.-9 P.M.).

LATIN AMERICAN
MANNY'S TORTAS $

2700 Lake St. E., Minneapolis, 612/728-1778, www.mannystortas.com

HOURS: Mon.-Sat. 10 A.M.-10 P.M., Sun. 10 A.M.-4 P.M.

A *torta* is a complex thing. Layers of flavor pile up on a wide, thick baguette that barely seems to be able to contain it all. No matter what you order, there will be lettuce, tomato, avocado, peppers, mayo, and cheese. There may be beans and roasted vegetables. There may be several kinds of meat. You may think it will never come together into a single tasty whole, until it goes into the sandwich press and comes out born anew. The chorizo and egg sandwich will cure whatever ails you. Branches are in the Midtown Global Market and the Mercado Central (1515 Lake St. E., 612/728-5408).

MARIA'S ⓢ

1113 Franklin Ave. E., Minneapolis, 612/870-9842, www.mariascafe.com

HOURS: Mon.-Sat. 7 A.M.-3 P.M., Sun. 8 A.M.-3 P.M.

Norteamericanos have no monopoly on the best breakfasts. Maria Hoyos, a native of Colombia, serves up a mix of morning classics from North and South America. You've got your basic two eggs, toast, and bacon. But then there's *cachapas venezolanas* (Venezuelan corn pancakes), so tender they fall apart at the sight of a fork (sprinkled with Cotija cheese, they're the perfect combination of salty and sweet) and sautéed plantains and yucca (available on weekends). Breakfast is served all day and the lunch menu includes sandwiches and burgers.

TAQUERIA LOS OCAMPO ⓢ

809 Lake St. E., Minneapolis, 612/825-4978

HOURS: Daily 9 A.M.-8 P.M.

Spanish-language talk shows and *telenovelas* blare from the two television sets, and the happy crowds move noisily in and out, but you'll be too absorbed in your tasty, filling, and seriously inexpensive food to notice. A long and overly formal sign will warn you that this is not fast food and the tortillas, *gorditas*, *arepas* (a thick, chewy, corn-based holder for more toppings), and more are all made on site. But your order will likely arrive before you've finished reading it and noticing the woman behind the counter, slapping disks of masa into shape. There's a branch in the Midtown Global Market, just across Lake Street.

VICTOR'S 1959 CAFÉ ⓢ

3756 Grand Ave., Minneapolis, 612/827-8948, www.victors1959cafe.com

HOURS: Breakfast and lunch Sun.-Mon. 8 A.M.-2 P.M., Tues.-Sat. 7 A.M.-2:30 P.M.; dinner Tues.-Sat. 4:30-9 P.M.

A tiny shack painted very un-Minnesotan colors, Victor's has a subversive, makeshift feel to it. But it's actually a long-standing favorite, attracting people willing to wait in lines out the door for the corn pancakes and yucca and eggs in the morning, the authentic Cuban sandwich (ham, pork loin, pickles, and condiments pressed together in a soft, slightly sweet bun) at lunch, and the homey *ropa vieja* (shredded flank steak tossed with vegetables) at dinner.

MIDDLE EASTERN
SHIRAZ FIRE ROASTED CUISINE ⓢⓢ

6042 Nicollet Ave. S., Minneapolis, 612/861-5500, www.shirazmn.com

HOURS: Sun.-Thurs. 11 A.M.-10 P.M., Fri.-Sat. 11 A.M.-11 P.M.

You don't come to Minnesota to eat Persian food, but if you're craving the crispy bottom-of-the-rice-pan delight known as *tahdig*, or the pomegranate-infused chicken stew called *fesenjan*, you can find delicious versions of both right here. Housed in the shell of an old Mexican restaurant on a busy stretch of suburban street, Shiraz feels a little out of place, but you'll forget all that as you're enjoying lamb, beef, chicken, and mincemeat kebabs; rice infused with barberries, dill, or sour cherries; and the unbeatably refreshing *dugh*—a salty, cucumber-y, minty yogurt drink. Stick around for belly dancing on weekend nights.

SNACKS AND DESSERTS
CREMA ⓢ

3403 Lyndale Ave. S., Minneapolis, 612/824-3868

HOURS: Daily 8 A.M.-10:30 P.M.

For years Sonny Siron himself made Italian-style ice cream for fancy restaurants in the Twin Cities and as far afield as Chicago. Then, by popular demand, he opened Crema, a Tuscan-style jewel box with a hidden-garden patio, where neighbors could enjoy his tiny, intensely flavored scoops of cabernet chocolate chip, basil balsamic vinegar, green tea, cardamom black pepper, blackberry cassis, and an ever-changing list of other imaginative flavors. Sonny, a fondly remembered neighborhood fixture himself, has passed on, but his family continues to make the ice cream in five- and ten-gallon batches. You can't come to Crema without having ice cream, but while you're here, you might also have a bistro-style sandwich or a rich, dark brownie. Be aware that when the weather cools off, Crema may restrict its hours to weekend evenings.

PUMPHOUSE CREAMERY $

4754 Chicago Ave. S., Minneapolis, 612/825-2021, www.pumphouse-creamery.com

HOURS: Sun.-Fri. noon-10 P.M., Sat. 11:30 A.M.-10 P.M.

Milk and cream from local cows. Local berries. Handmade cookies. These are some of the main ingredients of Barb Zapzalka's ice cream. But for her more exotic flavors, like Guinness or *kulfi* (a cardamom- and rosewater-scented Indian dessert), she's willing to find sources farther afield. There are always 20 flavors to choose from, but there's just one table in the tiny parlor, so plan to take your ice cream with you on a stroll to nearby Minnehaha Creek. In the winter, Pumphouse closes a little earlier in the evening and closes on Mondays.

SEBASTIAN JOE'S $

1007 Franklin Ave. W., Minneapolis, 612/870-0065

HOURS: Daily 7 A.M.-11 P.M.

The signature flavor at Sebastian Joe's is Pavarotti, an addictive blend of caramel, banana, and chocolate. But the raspberry chocolate chip has partisans, as well. Other than that, you never know what you'll find in the ice cream case—cinnamon? green tea? malted vanilla? mango? Sebastian Joe's is a neighborhood family fixture and a favorite stop after soccer and T-ball games. But don't rule it out in the winter: In fact, as the temperature dips below freezing, the prices drop, as well! Also in the neighborhood of Linden Hills (4321 Upton Ave. S., 612/926-7916).

VEGETARIAN

BIRCHWOOD $

3311 25th St. E., Minneapolis, 612/722-4474, www.birchwoodcafe.com

HOURS: Mon.-Fri. 7 A.M.-10 P.M., Sat. 8 A.M.-10 P.M., Sun. 9 A.M.-8 P.M.

The Birchwood isn't strictly vegetarian, but

© BRUCE MANNING

Everyone loves Sebastian Joe's for its neighborhood atmosphere and creative flavors.

vegetarians, vegans, and their fish- and poultry-eating friends will all find common ground in this cheery neighborhood gem. The atmosphere is casual—you order at the counter and the place is teeming with kids—but pizzas, burgers, and light entrées are all a step above what you'd expect at a casual joint. Make it a pizza party on Saturday night, when two individual pizzas and a bottle of wine are $25. Live music on Monday nights.

SEWARD CAFÉ $

2129 Franklin Ave. E., Minneapolis, 612/332-1011, www.sewardcafempls.net

HOURS: Mon.-Fri. 7 A.M.-3 P.M., Sat.-Sun. 8 A.M.-4 P.M.

We're all in this together, this business of saving the earth, so tot up your own order on the pad provided and present it at the cash register (no credit cards, please). There isn't a scrap of meat in this rough-hewn throwback of a café, but there is an awful lot of tasty tofu, tempeh, and black beans. And eggs—organic and free-range—available all day long in big, filling scrambles and omelets. Even hungry carnivores can appreciate the hearty T(empeh)LT or tempeh gyro.

Nordeast and Dinkytown

Map 3

AFRICAN
TAM-TAM'S $

605 Cedar Ave. S., Minneapolis, 612/339-0854,
www.tamtamsrestaurant.com
HOURS: Sun.-Thurs. 11 A.M.-10 P.M., Fri.-Sat.
11 A.M.-midnight

African immigrants looking for a taste of home
and U of M students looking for a filling, inexpensive meal mingle at Tam-Tam's. The menu
is organized by region, with the *injera* (spongey
bread) of the Horn of Africa, palm butter-based
stews from Ghana, and peanut-based dishes
from Eastern and Central Africa. Large groups
and especially hungry diners can dig into the
Lion's Feast, a combination platter that includes
beef pies, chicken pies, stew, and ribs.

AMERICAN
ERTÉ $$

323 13th Ave. NE, Minneapolis, 612/623-4211,
www.ertedining.com
HOURS: Mon.-Thurs. 4:30-9 P.M., Fri.-Sat. 4-11 P.M.,
Sun. closed

A supper club doesn't have to be stuffy. Erté
takes luxurious, filling classics like filet mi-
gnon, shrimp cocktail, and Cobb salad and
serves them with a touch of humor on the side.
You'll find Northeast Minneapolis's more for-
tunate young professionals here, enjoying the
juxtaposition of the dark-wood-and-white-ta-
blecloths atmosphere and their own hip selves.
Vegetarians won't find much at all to satisfy
them—even most of the salads come packed
with animal protein. Hear live music Friday
and Saturday nights 7–10 P.M. in the Peacock
Lounge.

JAX $$$

1928 University Ave. NE, Minneapolis, 612/789-7297,
www.jaxcafe.com
HOURS: Mon.-Thurs. 11 A.M.-10 P.M., Fri.-Sat.
11 A.M.-11 P.M., Sun. 10 A.M.-9 P.M.

When Jax first opened in this largely Eastern
European neighborhood in 1933, "What
dining out was meant to be" was a formal

occasion, one you couldn't possibly replicate
at home. And that's what you still get at Jax—
dark wood, rich food (lots of steak and lobster),
and bygone pomp. But even the most formal
of dining institutions occasionally lets down its
hair: At Jax, you can net your own trout, while
they're in season, in a man-made brook in the
restaurant's charming back garden.

MODERN CAFÉ $$

337 13th Ave. NE, Minneapolis, 612/378-9882,
www.moderncafeminneapolis.com
HOURS: Tues.-Thurs. 11 A.M.-9 P.M., Fri. 11 A.M.-9:30 P.M.,
Sat. 8 A.M.-9:30 P.M., Sun. 8 A.M.-2 P.M.

Who orders pot roast at a restaurant? The
smart diners at the Modern Café, that's who.
Old-time, classic comfort food gets a modern
gussying-up at this small, care-worn neighborhood institution. New York strip might sit next
to quinoa; a pan-roasted chicken breast might
meet saffron mayo. The short menu—just a
half dozen or so entrées and as many appetizers—changes frequently, but that pot roast,
well, that's one of the few things you can count
on in life. Breakfast, served on weekends only,
is a popular affair. Bring the paper and pre-
pare to wait.

POP! A NEIGHBORHOOD
RESTAURANT $$

2859 Johnson St. NE, Minneapolis, 612/788-0455,
www.poprestaurant.com
HOURS: Mon.-Thurs. 11 A.M.-3:30 P.M. and 5-9 P.M.,
Fri.-Sat. 11 A.M.-3:30 P.M. and 5-10 P.M., Sun. closed

Why Pop!? Could be for the bright orange
walls. Could be because Snap! (for pizza and
ice cream) is two doors down. Could be because there are more than two dozen choices
on the soda menu (get it? soda pop?). In any
case, Pop! has captured the heart of the young,
family-oriented neighborhood. Come for the
walleye sandwich and be sure to get fries on
the side—skinny, crispy, and golden, they're
well worth it. Some dishes have a Latin flair—
a little *chimichurri* sauce on the steak, a little

chorizo in the polenta—but this is quintessentially fun American fare.

RED STAG SUPPER CLUB $$

509 1st Ave. NE, Minneapolis, 612/767-7766,
www.redstagsupperclub.com

HOURS: Mon.-Fri. 11 A.M.-2 A.M., Sat.-Sun. 9 A.M.-2 A.M.

(If you're tired of hearing about "green" this and "local" that, avert your attention for a moment.) Red Stag is the first LEED-certified restaurant in Minnesota—which means it was built using environmentally friendly building techniques—and buys as much of its meat and produce as possible from local farmers. But even if that does not interest you, you'll enjoy the food—updated renditions of supper club classics, from mac and cheese with truffle oil to liver and onions with green garlic gravy. The triple-cooked French fries are a sight to behold: about an inch on each side and as soft as batter inside. Friday is fish fry day, with an extensive menu of battered and fried in-season seafood, including tiny crispy smelt and whole trout.

RESTAURANT ALMA $$

528 University Ave. SE, Minneapolis, 612/379-3030,
www.restaurantalma.com

HOURS: Sun. 4-9 P.M., Mon.-Thurs. 11 A.M.-9 P.M.,
Fri.-Sat. 11 A.M.-10 P.M.

Alma's menu is short, meticulously chosen, and constantly changing to reflect the best each season has to offer, from spring nettle soup to wild halibut. While chef and owner Alex Roberts has twice been nominated for a James Beard Award and the *Washington Post, Gourmet,* and *Bon Appetit* have all taken note of Alma's strengths, it still has the feel of a cozy neighborhood bistro. The wide-ranging wine list includes few bargains but many hidden treasures.

THE SAMPLE ROOM $$

2124 Marshall St. NE, Minneapolis, 612/789-0333,
www.the-sample-room.com

HOURS: Mon.-Thurs. 11:30 A.M.-11 P.M., Fri.-Sat.
11:30 A.M.-1 P.M., Sun. 10 A.M.-11 P.M.

Your table fills up with little plates as if you're at a tapas joint or a sushi bar, but the fare is homey and full of Minnesota flavors—like the pork ribs, bratwurst, and breaded walleye fingers. The Sample Room allows you to fill up on appetizer-size portions of cheese, meat, veggie, and seafood dishes in a romantically dim and dark-wood dining room. You can also choose entrées not meant for sharing—hearty sandwiches, excellent burgers, and sausages worthy of Nordeast's East European heritage—but what's the fun in that?

SIGNATURE CAFÉ $$

130 Warwick St. SE, Minneapolis, 612/378-0237,
www.signaturecafe.net

HOURS: Lunch Tues.-Fri. 11 A.M.-1:30 P.M.; dinner
Sun.-Thurs. 4:30-9 P.M., Fri.-Sat. 4:30-10 P.M.

Imagine your best friend is a terrific cook with a sophisticated palate and she invited you over for dinner. That's what it feels like when Signature's chef and owner Nathalie Johnson is cooking for you. The restaurant itself is tucked in the middle of an otherwise totally residential neighborhood and the menu is a mix of American favorites with French bistro touches. Lunch on the porch with a cup of delicate bisque and a sandwich on crusty bread is a treat. A four-course tasting menu is available on Monday nights.

ASIAN
OBENTO-YA $$

1510 Como Ave. SE, Minneapolis, 612/331-1432,
www.obento-ya.com

HOURS: Mon.-Sat. 11:30 A.M.-2:30 P.M. and 5-9 P.M.,
Sun. closed

Obento-Ya describes itself as a "Japanese bistro"—and hits it spot on. While the menu is 100 percent authentic Japanese, the ambiance is that of a beloved, comfortable, welcoming neighborhood bistro. Familiar favorites (soba and udon noodles with tempura, unthreatening sushi rolls) sit on the menu alongside dishes that soon will be favorites, like tiny meat and vegetable skewers called *robata,* served à la carte, your choice of plain, tempura, or panko-covered.

BREAKFAST AND BRUNCH
AL'S BREAKFAST $

413 14th Ave. SE, Minneapolis, 612/331-9991

HOURS: Mon.-Sat. 6 A.M.-1 P.M., Sun. 9 A.M.-1 P.M.

Eleven stools—that's it, 11—are arranged along the single counter stretching from the front of the room to the back. In front of the counter are the grills, where the cook runs back and forth, conducting a symphony of short orders. And behind the stools stand all the people waiting to grab your seat as soon as you're gone. Al's is a University of Minnesota institution, known for its pancakes and its character.

EASTERN EUROPEAN
KRAMARCZUK'S $

215 Hennepin Ave. E., Minneapolis, 612/379-3018, www.kramarczuk.com

HOURS: Mon. 7 A.M.-4 P.M., Tues.-Sat. 7 A.M.-8 P.M., Sun. 11 A.M.-4 P.M.

Pick up sausages, cheese, and sweet pastries in the deli, or grab a tray and join the cafeteria line. Either way, you'd better be hungry. Kramarczuk's has served hearty Ukrainian specialties to the Eastern European residents of Nordeast for decades: potato- and cheese-filled *pelmeni* (dumplings nearly the size of a teacup), cabbage leaves stuffed with ground meat and swimming in tomato sauce, schnitzel, and hearty borscht (red and white).

GREEK
GARDENS OF SALONICA $$

19th 5th St. NE, Minneapolis, 612/378-0611, www.gardensofsalonica.com

HOURS: Tues.-Thurs. 11 A.M.-9 P.M., Fri.-Sat. 11 A.M.-10 P.M., Sun.-Mon. closed

This is the lighter, more Mediterranean side of Greek cuisine. The best things to eat are the small *meze*-like plates. Fill your table with them and share: hummus with pillowy Greek pita and olives, ultra-garlicky *skordalia* potato dip, pizzas built on pita bases, and the savory flaky pastries they call *boughatsa*. Of course, you can also build a traditional three-course meal and make a long, comfortable evening of it in the spare, serene dining room.

ITALIAN
LORING PASTA BAR $$

327 14th Ave. SE, Minneapolis, 612/378-4849, www.loringpastabar.com

HOURS: Mon.-Sat. 11:30 A.M.-1 A.M., Sun. 5:30 P.M.-1 A.M.

There's a trippy, through-the-rabbit-hole vibe to the Loring Pasta Bar, perhaps in tribute to this corner of Dinkytown and its not-so-distant past as a destination for student headshop-hunters. The prices keep out the truly penniless students, and sometimes the funky clientele seems like part of the baroque decor, along with the lush hanging plants. The best part of the menu is the longest section: plates of pasta (not overwhelmingly big) dressed with sausage, cream, tomato, peppers, and other classic Italian goodies. Stick around after dinner for live music most nights and the occasional salsa dance lesson.

PIZZA NEA $

306 Hennepin Ave. E., Minneapolis, 612/331-9298, www.pizzanea.com

HOURS: Mon.-Thurs. 11 A.M.-9:30 P.M., Fri.-Sat. 11 A.M.-10:30 P.M., Sun. noon-9 P.M.

True Neapolitan pizza is baked in a 900°F, wood-fired oven, just as it is here at Pizza Nea. The pies fall somewhere between individual and sharing size (depending on how hungry and how generous you are), and the crust is a bit thicker and chewier than the classic Neapolitan crust. It holds the toppings well, from the basic Margherita with basil to an inspired pie with two fried eggs and sharp parmesan cheese. Families are, of course, welcome, but this is a better choice for date night than pizza night after the soccer game.

LATIN AMERICAN
BRASA $$

600 Hennepin Ave. E., Minneapolis, 612/379-3030, www.brasa.us

HOURS: Mon.-Thurs. 11 A.M.-9 P.M., Fri. 11 A.M.-10 P.M., Sat. noon-10 P.M., Sun. closed

Brasa is the mostly Latin version of a meat-and-three: Pick your protein (spit-roasted chicken or pork), and your sides (fried yucca, creamed spinach, an ethereal muffin made with creamed corn). That's it, unless you'd like to turn that juicy chicken or pork into a sandwich or construct a meal entirely out of side dishes—which isn't a bad idea either. Or, get it to go and walk the mile to the Mississippi River for a picnic.

MIDDLE EASTERN
HOLY LAND $

2513 Central Ave. NE, Minneapolis, 612/781-2627, www.holylandbrand.com

HOURS: Sun.-Thurs. 9 A.M.-9 P.M., Fri.-Sat. 9 A.M.-10 P.M.

Don't worry, you're in the right place: Holy Land looks like a big, chaotic grocery store because it is one. But, just to the right as you walk in is the counter where you can order massive plates of gyros, kebabs, and falafel. And there in the center is the buffet. That's what you came here for. And I hope you came hungry. Ultra-fresh bread and hummus (the best in town), made on-site, flank a long line of chicken, beef, and lamb entrées—and sometimes even goat. You can also find Holy Land in the Midtown Global Market.

Downtown St. Paul and West Side   Map 4

AMERICAN
FOREPAUGH'S $$$

276 Exchange St. S., St. Paul, 651/224-5606, www.forepaughs.com

HOURS: Lunch Mon.-Fri. 11:30 A.M.-2 P.M.; dinner Mon.-Sat. 5:30-9:30 P.M., Sun. 5-8:30 P.M.; brunch Sun. 10:30 A.M.-1:30 P.M.

Forepaugh's is truly of another time. The setting is a three-story, 1870s mansion with a grand portico, antique tchotchkes, and several working fireplaces. The menu is the best of what was considered truly fine dining a couple of generations ago: beef Wellington, duckling pâté, escargot, baked Alaska. The service is formal and well trained. It even comes with a ghost story: Molly, an Irish maid in the household of Joseph Forepaugh, reputedly makes her presence known in the bar.

MICKEY'S DINER $

36 7th St. W., St. Paul, 651/222-5633

HOURS: Open daily 24 hours

In 1937, a prefab diner was shipped in from New Jersey and set up in downtown St. Paul. It hasn't closed since. Day and night the seats at the counter and the four booths are filled and the orders of pancakes, potatoes O'Brien (hash browns with the works), and tuna melts are flying off the griddle. In a world of slick, modern-retro diners, Mickey's is the real thing. And Hollywood has taken notice, giving Mickey's a role in the *Mighty Ducks, Jingle All the Way,* and *A Prairie Home Companion.*

ST. PAUL GRILL $$$

350 Market St., St. Paul, 651/224-7455, www.stpaulgrill.com

HOURS: Mon.-Fri. 11 A.M.-10 P.M., Sat. 11 A.M.-11 P.M., Sun. 10:30 A.M.-10 P.M.

This is old-school, make-a-grown-up-impression dining in the St. Paul Hotel. The dinner menu is almost entirely steaks, chops, and high-end seafood, with formal service in high-backed booths. (Did I say "almost?" Make that "entirely.") If you're not wearing your power suit, loosen your tie at the bar, where you can get an excellent burger. Breakfast, lunch, and Sunday brunch in the St. Paul Hotel, at the M Street Café (Mon.–Fri. 6:30 A.M.–2 P.M., Sat.–Sun. 7 A.M.–2 P.M.), are more casual and intimate—almost homey. For breakfast, have the Swedish pancakes with lingonberries or linger over the "sideboard," a buffet of fruit, pastries, and excellent house-smoked salmon. The lunch menu includes mid-priced sandwiches and salads.

WALLEYE AND WILD RICE

You undoubtedly have heard some snickering about Midwestern food – about hot dish and Jell-O salad, perhaps. And, as is often the case, there's some truth behind the jokes. Yes, as a rule, Minnesotans are a people grown hardy on hot dish (that's "casserole" to the rest of the country) and "salads" that are green only because they are made from green Jell-O (and fruit, and marshmallows, and served at the dinner, not for dessert).

But all that is home cooking. (Or, more accurately, church supper cooking.) When you are out at a restaurant and want to order something particularly Minnesotan, order the walleye. Walleye, the Minnesota state fish, is a mild, tasty freshwater species beloved by anglers and by eaters. It's often served breaded and fried, often in a sandwich. You'll find it on the menu in corner bars, in bowling alleys, and in white-tablecloth restaurants. At Hell's Kitchen in downtown Minneapolis, which may be the most unexpected and felicitous place of all, you'll find it crusted with parmesan, covered with bacon, and sandwiched between two slices of sourdough bread.

The irony here is that when you do order the Minnesota state fish in a Minnesota restaurant, what you're most likely eating is imported zander (also known as pike perch) from Canada or Europe. Because commercial fishing is strictly limited in Minnesota, it can't be caught in sufficient quantities to feed the local market. While this revelation caused a big stink locally a few years back, in the end most restaurant eaters realized that if they couldn't tell the difference it probably didn't make a very big difference. If you want to be sure that the walleye you're eating is truly walleye, you'll need a fishing line.

If you don't like fish but still want to choose a local flavor, order the wild rice. But, here as well we have some nomenclature issues. The Minnesota state grain, wild rice, is actually more closely related to oats than to rice. The Ojibwe, who call it *manoomin*, harvest the long, thin grains by knocking the stocks gently over canoes. It's a labor-intensive process and requires very specific growing conditions. More and more Native American-grown wild rice is available in specialty stores and direct from the tribes, but you have to seek it out. What you're more likely eating is not *manoomin* but a relative of it, grown commercially in a paddy (Minnesota law requires commercially grown wild rice to be labeled "paddy rice"). Hell's Kitchen serves authentic *manoomin* porridge for breakfast with nuts and blueberries.

W.A. FROST AND COMPANY 💲💲💲
374 Selby Ave., St. Paul, 651/224-5715, www.wafrost.com
HOURS: Lunch Mon.-Sat. 11:15 A.M.-1:30 P.M.; dinner Mon.-Thurs. 5-10 P.M., Fri.-Sat. 5-11 P.M., Sun. 5-10 P.M.; brunch Sun. 10:30 A.M.-2 P.M.

Three decades ago, W. A. Frost, in the 100-year-old building where a pharmacist of the same name once ran his store, was a pioneer in the revival of the Cathedral Hill neighborhood. Today, with its arched stained-glass windows, pressed-tin ceilings, and Oriental rugs, it's still a great place to take your mom or grandma out to dinner and enjoy the elegance of a bygone era. Frost's menu, however, is a little more up-to-date, focusing on local ingredients served in modern ways. If the beautiful patio and dining room are full, you can enjoy a full dinner in the bar. Sunday brunch at Frost is an institution.

ASIAN
MAI VILLAGE 💲
394 University Ave., St. Paul, 651/290-2585
HOURS: Mon.-Thurs. 11 A.M.-9 P.M., Fri.-Sat. 11 A.M.-10 P.M., Sun. noon-8 P.M.

The big draw at Mai Village is the spectacular setting: Cross the ornately carved bridge over the indoor koi pond to reach the dining room, where more wonders await, like walls full of Vietnamese art and elaborately inlaid tables. The menu and prices, however, are very much like what you'd find in the Twin Cities' best hole-in-the-wall Vietnamese places—*phô* soups, *bún* noodle salads, and stir-fries—with a few more festive additions, like whole grilled fish and *bo 7 mon*, or beef seven ways.

SAKURA RESTAURANT & BAR $$

350 St. Peter St., St. Paul, 651/224-0185,
www.sakurastpaul.com

HOURS: Lunch Mon.-Sat. 11:30 A.M.-2:30 P.M., Sun. noon-2:30 P.M.; dinner Mon.-Thurs. 5-10:30 P.M., Fri.-Sat. 5-11 P.M., Sun. 4-9:30 P.M.

Frequently named the best Japanese restaurant in the Twin Cities, Sakura has a little something for everyone, including inexpensive and filling *teishoku* dinners (like hearty, everyday combo plates), an elaborate sushi menu, and quick bento lunches. The dining room is bright and cheery—more the place for lively conversation than a romantic evening.

TANPOPO NOODLE SHOP $

308 Prince St., St. Paul, 651/209-6527,
www.tanpoporestaurant.com

HOURS: Lunch Tues.-Fri. 11 A.M.-2 P.M.; dinner

Mon.-Thurs. 5:30-9 P.M., Fri.-Sat. 5:30-10 P.M.; Sun. closed

This is Japanese comfort food. Heck, this is, or should be, comfort food the world over. Big bowls of rich broth, fat chewy noodles, enormous golden tempura shrimp. This isn't a full-menu Japanese restaurant, but a noodle shop that gets its limited menu exactly right. The serene atmosphere and spare decor are at least as comforting as the food. Finish your meal with the *mochi* (chewy, sweetened rice cake) or green tea ice cream.

FRENCH
MERITAGE $$$

410 St. Peter St., St. Paul, 651/222-5670,
www.meritage-stpaul.com

HOURS: Lunch Tues.-Fri. 11 A.M.-2 P.M., Sat.-Sun. 10 A.M.-2 P.M.; dinner Tues.-Thurs. and Sun. 5-9 P.M., Fri.-Sat. 5-11 P.M.

Mix a little joy, a little warm camaraderie with formal tableside service and serious culinary chops—and you have Meritage (rhymes with "heritage," a nod to the California Bordeaux-style wines of the same name). From the amusements—two-bite appetizers like the "tiny tuna tartar taco on a taro chip" (try to say

Looking out on St. Paul's Rice Park, Meritage serves a mix of haute French cuisine and bistro fare.

that without smiling)—to the proper starters (don't miss the baby beet salad) and the entrées (*steak frites,* roast chicken, sole Grenobloise), straight through to the marble-topped cheese cart, this is serious fine dining that doesn't take itself too seriously.

ITALIAN
PAZZALUNA $$$

360 St. Peter St., St. Paul, 651/223-7000, www.pazzaluna.com

HOURS: Mon.-Thurs. 5:30-10 P.M., Fri.-Sat. 5:30-11 P.M., Sun. 5:30-9 P.M.

Pazzaluna does not practice "hospitaliano." This is the real deal: real antipasti, like the *fritto misto* (delicate breaded calamari with onions and peppers); real *primi piatti,* all tangles of rich pasta; real *secondi piatti,* like mustard-crusted lamb, chicken with asparagus, and—because this is Minnesota—walleye baked in salt (the latter comes with quite the tableside show). This is one of the places where the beautiful people of St. Paul (and teenagers celebrating special occasions) come to see and be seen—the atmosphere is bright and cheery, rather than dim and romantic. On a budget? Order the excellent pizza. Really strapped? Order it at the bar.

LATIN AMERICAN
BOCA CHICA $

11 Cesar Chavez St., St. Paul, 651/222-8499, www.bocachicarestaurant.com

HOURS: Mon. 11 A.M.-9 P.M., Tues.-Thurs. 11 A.M.-10 P.M., Fri.-Sat. 11 A.M.-11 P.M., Sun. 10 A.M.-9 P.M.

The Frias family has been serving the well-established Mexican-American community of St. Paul's West Side since 1964. This is classic old-timey Mexican-American cuisine, the better-executed forerunner of every family taco night: flour and corn tacos, *chiles rellenos,* tamales, *flautas,* and tostados. Come hungry for the generous, filling lunchtime buffet, or hang out at the bar on weekend evenings while neighbors and visitors clutch buzzers waiting for a table. Yep, those tamales are good enough to pack the massive, bright yellow dining room with happy eaters.

© BRUCE MANNING

Pazzaluna offers high-end Italian dining.

EL BURRITO MERCADO $

175 Concord St., St. Paul, 651/227-2192, www.elburritomercado.com

HOURS: Daily 7 A.M.-9 P.M.

In the back of a grocery store, in the heart of St. Paul's Mexican-American community, you will find some of the biggest, best burritos this side of the border. To put together your lunch or dinner—or your filling single meal of the day—pick a *guisado* (a flavorful stew of pork, beef, or chicken) and then decide whether you want it in a taco, burrito, or gordita. It's all made fresh on-site, right down to the generous selection of salsas.

MIDDLE EASTERN
BABANI'S KURDISH RESTAURANT $$

544 St. Peter St., St. Paul, 651/602-9964

HOURS: Mon.-Thurs. 11 A.M.-9 P.M., Fri. 11 A.M.-10 P.M., Sat. 1-10 P.M., Sun. 3-9 P.M.

Babani's has long claimed to be the first Kurdish restaurant in the United States, a claim few are in any position to dispute.

In any case, that's a lonely place to be, educating diners about a little-known cuisine. Some dishes are recognizable: tabouli, stuffed grape leaves, the yogurt dip called *jaajic* here and *tzatziki* in Greece, the salty yogurt drink called a *lassi* in India and *dugh* in Iran. Others are entirely unique: *dowjic*, a lemony, yogurty chicken soup; grilled rice balls stuffed with ground meat; and the house specialty, Sheik Babani, an eggplant stuffed with tomato and meat sauce. It all comes with the warm welcome you might expect from a wandering people. The restaurant itself is small and comfortably worn about the edges.

STEAKHOUSES
MANCINI'S CHAR HOUSE $$$
521 W. 7th St., St. Paul, 651/224-7345,
www.mancinis.com
HOURS: Sun.-Thurs. 4:30-10 P.M., Fri.-Sat. 4:30-11 P.M.

If Frank Sinatra himself were to appear in Mancini's maroon and brass dining room, in your steak-stuffed state you might not even blink. Ol' Blue Eyes might even imagine himself to be in old-time Vegas. Mancini's

is the place in downtown St. Paul to celebrate anniversaries and big corporate deals with slabs of meat, lobster tails, and carb-heavy sides of potatoes and rolls. There's live music Wednesday–Saturday and a small dance floor.

STRIP CLUB $$$
378 Maria Ave., St. Paul, 651/793-6247,
www.domeats.com
HOURS: Lunch Tues.-Fri. 11 A.M.-2 P.M.; brunch Sat.-Sun. 9 A.M.-2 P.M.; dinner Tues.-Thurs. and Sun. 4-10 P.M., Fri. 4-11 P.M., Sat. 5-11 P.M.

The Strip Club serves up titillation of an entirely different sort: New York strip, filet, ribs—all of it local and grassfed. Pick your own sauce, from blue cheese to ginger and scallions. Unlike at traditional steakhouses, those who want something more than a slab of meat on their plate can also put together a satisfying dinner from the long and innovative list of small plates, including catfish fries and walleye fritters. In an out-of-the-way St. Paul residential neighborhood (one that is, shall we say, yet to be gentrified), the Strip Club is worth a trip.

Summit-University and Mac-Groveland   Map 5

AMERICAN
◖ CAFÉ LATTÉ $
850 Grand Ave., St. Paul, 651/224-5687,
www.cafelatte.com
HOURS: Sun.-Wed. 9 A.M.-10 P.M., Thurs. 9 A.M.-11 P.M., Fri.-Sat. 9 A.M.-midnight

Ladies who lunch love to lunch at Café Latté. Students, families, and young lovers also love it, along with anyone hungry for a relatively quick and relatively healthy bite. Choose pasta salads, tossed salads, soups, and sandwiches made to order as you slide your tray along the cafeteria side, or order wood-oven pizza specialties on the other side. Fair warning: Although service is quick, the line sometimes snakes out the door. Stop by on weekday afternoons for

a refreshing plate of sweets and savories in the style of an English afternoon tea.

CASPER & RUNYON'S NOOK $
492 Hamline Ave. S., St. Paul, 651/698-4347
HOURS: Sun.-Thurs. 11 A.M.-10 P.M., Fri.-Sat. 11 A.M.-11 P.M.

There is some dispute over the origin of the Jucy Lucy—an inside-out cheeseburger that, when made properly, sears the roof of your mouth in a delightful way—and there are even a few holdout partisans of other Jucy Lucys about town. But there is no disputing the fervent love St. Paulites hold for the Nook's burgers. The bar itself is tiny (and this is a bar, but it's unlikely that anyone has ever ordered a beer here without a burger), and during peak burger-eating hours you will have to wait. But you will know, when the hot cheese hits your mouth, that it has been worth it. And no, there's no i in Jucy. The bar is open until 2 A.M.

HEARTLAND ●●

1806 St. Clair Ave., St. Paul, 651/699-3536, www.heartlandrestaurant.com

HOURS: Tues.-Sat. 5:30-9:30 P.M., Mon. closed

Chef Lenny Russo has long been at the forefront of Minnesota's—and the Upper Midwest's—movement toward local, seasonal, chef-driven cuisine. He helped get the Guthrie Theater's Cue restaurant off the ground, but Heartland, with its intimate arts-and-crafts-inspired dining room, has always been his baby. Two prix-fixe menus are available each night, one—and this is not easy to find—entirely vegetarian. The à la carte menu may be brief, but it changes nightly and includes surprises like wild boar.

128 CAFÉ ●●

128 Cleveland Ave. N., St. Paul, 651/645-4128, www.128cafe.net

HOURS: Sun.-Thurs. 5-9 P.M., Fri.-Sat. 5-10 P.M.

The neighbors are fiercely loyal to this tiny basement restaurant—and perhaps a little possessive: If the secret gets out, competition for seats and parking spots might get even worse. But now that you know, come and order the baby back ribs in a sweet, tart glaze, and the roasted garlic appetizer. The kitchen is dedicated to buying the best local ingredients and, in a restaurant this small, they're able to walk the walk.

DESSERTS

GRAND OLE CREAMERY ●

750 Grand Ave., St. Paul, 651/293-1655, www.grandolecreamery.com

HOURS: Sun.-Thurs. 11:30 A.M.-11 P.M., Fri.-Sat. 11:30 A.M.-midnight

The smell of hot, fresh waffle cones is the smell of summer, and it flows out onto Grand Avenue, along with the overflow crowd of ice cream fiends. (The Grand Ole Creamery's waffle cones have a special extra touch: a malt

---

FROSTY TREATS IN FROSTY WEATHER

Don't expect the Twin Cities' beloved ice cream parlors to close up shop during the winter. The lines might be a little shorter – just a little – but the joints will still be hopping. In fact, Minneapolis's **Sebastian Joe's** offers ever-greater discounts as the mercury dips, and customers are always on hand to take advantage of them. Although there's no winter discount at the other ice cream shops in town, you don't want to miss the innovative flavors at **Izzy's** and **Pumphouse Creamery,** the Old World elegance at **Crema,** or the small-town atmosphere at **Grand Ole Creamery.**

---

ball in the bottom of each one. To stop drips, of course.) The flavors rotate daily, with 31 of a possible 200 on offer at any one time. Most are classics, with a few surprises like birthday cake and honey crunch. If you feel like jumping into the middle of a Twin Cities controversy, visit here and Minneapolis's Sebastian Joe's on the same day and declare your allegiance for one over the other. Winter hours may be shorter.

IZZY'S ICE CREAM CAFÉ ●

2034 Marshall Ave., St. Paul, 651/603-1458, www.izzysicecream.com

HOURS: Sun.-Thurs. 11 A.M.-10 P.M., Fri.-Sat. 11 A.M.-10:30 P.M.

Can't choose just one of Izzy's one-of-a-kind flavors, like key lime pie, Norwegian chai, or dark chocolate zin? Get two. Every scoop of ice cream comes with an "Izzy scoop"—a melon ball-sized bonus. Jeff Sommers, the man behind this beloved neighborhood ice cream shop, believes in high-quality ingredients and treading a little more lightly on the earth. (Izzy's is entirely solar-powered.) When the Food Network's Bobby Flay challenged him to an ice cream-making contest in 2006, Izzy's hot brown sugar flavor won handily.

ITALIAN
PUNCH PIZZA $$
704 Cleveland Ave. S., St. Paul, 651/696-1066, www.punchpizza.com

HOURS: Sun.-Thurs. 11 A.M.-9:30 P.M., Fri.-Sat. 11 A.M.-10 P.M., Mon. closed

Pizza—especially when it takes about four minutes to cook in an 800°F oven—is the ultimate fast food. But it doesn't feel like fast food when it's got gorgonzola and roasted red peppers on it and is served in a classy—but extremely family-friendly—dining room with a beer and wine license. This, the original Punch Pizza, has table service, unlike the equally great location in Minneapolis (3226 Lake St. W., 612/929-0006, daily 11 A.M.–10 P.M.), where the prices are a little lower. There is also a second Punch Pizza location in St. Paul's Grand Avenue shopping district (769 Grand Ave., 615/602-6068, daily 11 A.M.–10 P.M.).

JEWISH
CECIL'S DELICATESSEN $
651 Cleveland Ave. S., St. Paul, 651/698-6276, www.cecilsdeli.com

HOURS: Daily 9 A.M.-8 P.M.

Cecil's isn't kosher, but it is undeniably, authentically Jewish, from the mile-long menu exhorting you to "Eat, eat!" to the crisp latkes and sweet cheese blintzes. Get your sandwich "New York style"—just the meat, a heaping cup of it, and the bread—or with more Midwestern-style fixings. You know all those arguments about what really belongs in a Reuben? You can settle them here, where Cecil's serves several variations on the classic sandwich. Buy excellent pastrami and corned beef (kosher available) and house-baked loaves of pumpernickel and rye in the deli in front.

MEDITERRANEAN
BARBARY FIG $$
720 Grand Ave., St. Paul, 651/290-2085

HOURS: Lunch Mon.-Sat. 11 A.M.-2 P.M., dinner daily 5:30-9 P.M.

The Barbary Fig is everyone's secret favorite restaurant: They love it, they patronize it, but they are afraid to talk about it, lest the unwashed hordes discover it. The restaurant itself does a good job of flying under the radar, in a just-this-side-of-shabby two-story house on the increasingly flashy end of Grand Avenue. In the summer you can eat olives on the porch and pretend you are on some Mediterranean riviera. In the winter you can warm yourself with hearty *b'steeya* (braised chicken in phyllo) and lamb sausage in the welcoming wood-floored dining room.

NEPALI
EVEREST ON GRAND $$
1278 Grand Ave., St. Paul, 651/696-1666, www.hotmomo.com

HOURS: Mon.-Thurs. 11:30 A.M.-2:30 P.M. and 5-9 P.M., Fri.-Sat. 11:30 A.M.-10 P.M., Sun. 11:30 A.M.-9 P.M.

Nepali cuisine is a cross between northern Indian and Chinese, based on lots of ghee and very mild spices. *Momos,* Tibetan dumplings served either steamed or fried, are the highlight of the menu and reason enough to come. The curries, *pakoras* (batter-fried vegetables), and samosas will feel like milder versions of familiar Indian favorites. Keep in mind that this is hearty cuisine: The "lighter" side of the menu is a selection of fried rice dishes.

RUSSIAN
◖ MOSCOW ON THE HILL $$
371 Selby Ave., St. Paul, 651/291-1236, www.moscowonthehill.com

HOURS: Lunch Mon.-Fri. 11 A.M.-2 P.M.; dinner Mon.-Thurs. 5:30-10 P.M., Fri. 5:30-11 P.M., Sat. 4-11 P.M., Sun. 4-10 P.M.

Nobody does long, lavish celebrations better than the Russians. If you're looking for a quick bite before a show, go elsewhere. If you're looking for an experience that will last all evening long, there is nothing better than Moscow on the Hill. Russian meals are five courses long—soup, salad, *zakuski* (appetizers, served family style), main dish (often the least significant part of the meal), and dessert, with frequent stops for vodka in between. Musicians stroll the dining room, and as the evening wears on, it turns into one big party.

Como and St. Anthony Map 6

AFRICAN
FASIKA $

510 Snelling Ave. N., St. Paul, 651/646-4747,
www.fasika.com

HOURS: Daily 11 A.M.-midnight

The center of the Twin Cities' large and growing Ethiopian community is right here. On weekends, especially, the tables will be filled with large groups of family and friends, and if you are an Ethiopian cuisine newbie, you're likely to be the only one in the restaurant. Not to worry: The menu includes full descriptions in English, along with photos. Everything starts with *injera,* the spongy fermented bread that serves as both plate and eating utensil for the warmly spiced stews. You'll also find a real rarity: Ethiopian wine.

FINNISH
FINNISH BISTRO $

2264 Como Ave., St. Paul, 651/645-9181,
www.finnishbistro.com

HOURS: Mon.-Sat. 7 A.M.-8 P.M., Sun. 8 A.M.-8 P.M.

Finnish transplant Soile Anderson has brought some of the best of her homeland's cuisine to this friendly, elegant bistro in the leafy St. Anthony neighborhood, where the atmosphere, too, is pleasantly Scandinavian. Big salads; savory crêpes with vegetables, chicken, or salmon; and slices of "Finnish pie"—loaves layered with meat, cheese, veggies, wrapped in flaky pastry—all make this a popular lunch destination. If you're lucky—really, truly lucky—you'll find *karjalaiset piirakat,* rice-filled Finnish pastries topped with chopped egg and butter.

RUSSIAN
RUSSIAN TEA HOUSE $

1758 University Ave. W., St. Paul, 651/646-4144

HOURS: Tues.-Fri. 11 A.M.-3 P.M.

It doesn't look like much, and it certainly doesn't look like a restaurant, but inside this out-of-place two-story house on busy University Avenue, you'll find fat and filling *piroshki* (billed as "the Russian hamburger"), tangy borscht, tender cabbage rolls, and, on Fridays, homemade *pelmeni* (like potato ravioli). The Food Network's Alton Brown loved it all when he came through on his *River Run* tour in 2007. Ask the owner behind the counter about the day U2 played next door.

Greater Twin Cities Map 7

AMERICAN
CONVENTION GRILL $

3912 Sunnyside Rd., Edina, 952/920-6881

HOURS: Sun.-Thurs. 11 A.M.-10 P.M., Fri.-Sat. 11 A.M.-11 P.M.

The Convention Grill is a neighborhood classic: Get your hamburger flattened into a thin, lacy patty on the flat grill (a "California burger" comes with lettuce and tomato), order your malt to come with your meal, not as dessert, and be sure you plan to share your fries. A full order of the thin, greasy, golden beauties could satisfy a table of hungry diners. This isn't health food: The only thing green in the entire place is the throwback iceberg lettuce salad.

GOOD DAY CAFÉ $

5410 Wayzata Blvd., Golden Valley, 763/544-0242

HOURS: Daily 7 A.M.-3 P.M.

The very best of what American cuisine has offered the world is right here at the Good Day Café: hearty breakfasts and perfectly composed sandwiches. These are familiar classics with a few unexpected twists—guacamole on one of the many eggs Benedict variations, for example, and beignets on a Midwestern menu. The huge, sunny dining room still manages to fill up, but the perky waitstaff keep everything moving and everyone happy. Breakfast is served well into the lunch hour most days and until 3 P.M. on Sunday. This is a great choice for large groups.

BAKING CENTRAL: HOME OF BETTY CROCKER AND THE BUNDT CAKE

In the late 1800s, Minneapolis leaped to the top of the flour-milling world with the invention of a new milling technique. Rather than stone grindstones, Minnesota's Washburn-Crosby Mill started using metal and porcelain rollers and then blasting the wheat with air to remove the bits of shell and bran left behind. The pure white flour swept the world and Minneapolis produced more flour than any other city for several decades.

In 1921, Washburn-Crosby introduced the persona of Betty Crocker to help answer baking questions from customers. An artist created Betty's portrait and a secretary contributed her signature, which is still used today. Betty has had radio and TV shows and published cookbooks and even been voted the second-most famous woman in America (in 1945, after Eleanor Roosevelt). She's gotten a makeover seven times, most recently in 1996, but she's still the most recognizable face in baking.

Another baking icon that got its start here is the Bundt cake. In 1950, the Minneapolis chapter of the Hadassah Society, a Jewish women's aid organization, approached the Nordic Ware company, which is still based in the Minneapolis suburb of St. Louis Park, and asked for a lightweight, fluted, high-sided pan for baking ring-shaped coffee cakes. In 1966, a Bundt cake won the Pillsbury Bake-Off and the new pan quickly became the most-sold pan in the United States. Today, Nordic Ware has sold more than 50 million pans.

YUM! $

4000 Minnetonka Blvd., St. Louis Park, 952/922-4000, www.yumkitchen.com
HOURS: Daily 7 A.M.-8 P.M.

Grown-ups can be kids again and kids can learn to love grown-up foods, like chicken tortilla soup, tuna burgers, and Szechuan green beans. The menu is eclectic and the macaroni and cheese—curly cavatappi pasta in the kind of soupy, gooey, orangey sauce kids love—is worth driving miles for. Snag the first table you see (this place is popular) and order at the counter. The atmosphere is casual and child-friendly, but the food and the service are anything but low-brow.

ASIAN

◖ JUN BO $$

7717 Nicollet Ave., Richfield, 612/866-6888, www.jun-bo.com
HOURS: Mon.-Fri. 11 A.M.-11 P.M., Sat.-Sun. 10 A.M.-11 P.M.

Don't let first impressions fool you. Jun Bo is one seriously unattractive restaurant. It's right off the highway, a giant former fast food joint in a rippling suburban sea of fast food joints. If it looks like nobody has paid any attention to the landscaping or the paint job, it's probably because they've been too busy cooking—carts full of dim sum (available all day every day), Chinese hotpot, and authentic, real-deal Chinese food. The massive dining room seats 600 (perfect for the wedding parties it often hosts), but you won't even notice the echo as the dim sum cart rolls by again.

KING'S FINE KOREAN CUISINE $$

1051 Moore Lake Dr. E., Fridley, 763/571-7256, www.kingsrestaurant.com
HOURS: Tues.-Sun. 11:30 A.M.-9 P.M.

Classic Korean comfort food is *dolsot bibimbap*, a hot stone bowl filled with rice, pickled vegetables, stir-fried meat, and a raw egg, which cooks as you stir it all around. You can find that, fiery *bulgogi* (Korean barbecue), and more in this large, lavish dining room. If you're unfamiliar with Korean cuisine, throw yourself on the mercy of your helpful server, or order from the long sushi menu. After 9, King's becomes something entirely different: a karaoke-fueled nighttime hot spot for the local Korean community, with the fun raging into the wee hours.

FRENCH

PATRICK'S BAKERY AND CAFÉ $

2928 66th St. W., Edina, 612/861-7570,

www.patricksbakerycafe.com
HOURS: Sun.-Wed. 7 A.M.-9 P.M., Thurs.-Sat.
7 A.M.-10 P.M.

When Patrick Bernet opened his first bakery in a suburban strip mall in 2002, Twin Citians were gape-jawed: honest-to-*dieu* baguettes and *boules,* the best croissants you'd had since you backpacked through France at 18, shatteringly crisp meringues. Then he added warm quiches served with those perfectly dressed salads only the French can master and pastry puffs filled with wild mushroom sauce, and the jaws gaped even wider. Then he added things like a chicken ranch wrap and a Caesar salad to the lunch menu and, well, it's a good thing all those other wonderful things are still there (along with some tender little burgers on baguettes—those are good, too). Dinners include a limited menu of bistro specialties, like coq au vin and osso bucco. You can find the same great menu inside Bachmann's garden shop (6010 Lyndale Ave. S., 612/861-9277).

PATRICK'S BISTRO ⓈⓈⓈ

331 Broadway Ave. S., Wayzata, 952/345-6100,
www.patricksbakerycafe.com
HOURS: Mon.-Sun. 7 A.M.-10 P.M.

By day a bright and cheery bakery with the best croissants and apricot pastries around, by night a luxurious, intimate restaurant. Chef and owner Patrick Bernet shares his French heritage with classically prepared seafood and beef (the roasted scallops with lobster sauce are an excellent choice and you can't miss with *frites* with béarnaise sauce). Bernet is a pastry chef by training. What that means to you: absolutely save room for dessert. Kids eat free on Tuesdays and Thursdays.

SALUT BAR AMERICAIN ⓈⓈ

5034 France Ave. S., Edina, 952/929-3764,
www.salutbaramericain.com
HOURS: Mon.-Thurs. 11 A.M.-10 P.M., Fri.-Sat.
11 A.M.-11 P.M., Sun. 10 A.M.-5 P.M.

To get the joke at Salut, it helps to know a little bit about where it's located. The first-ring suburb of Edina (rhymes with whine-a) has a reputation for affluence and—we'll just come

out and say it—entitlement. So, clearly, what it needs is an upscale "French" restaurant with the cheery atmosphere of a fast-casual chain and "les cheesy puffs" and a "leetle beeg mac" on the menu. Fortunately, the folks in the kitchen aren't kidding around: They actually know their way around both a *croque monsieur* and an excellent array of steaks. There's another location in St. Paul (917 Grand Ave., 651/917-2345, Mon.-Thurs. 11 A.M.-10 P.M., Fri.-Sat. 11 A.M.-midnight, Sun. 10 A.M.-10 P.M.).

INDIAN
TASTE OF INDIA ⓈⓈ

5617 Wayzata Blvd., St. Louis Park, 952/541-4865,
www.tasteofindiaonline.com
HOURS: Daily 11 A.M.-2:30 P.M. and 5-10 P.M.

Whenever the local press asks readers to name the best Indian food in the Twin Cities, Taste of India nearly always tops the list. Minnesotans love this place because it doesn't dumb down or cool down the best of Indian cuisine. The lunchtime buffet is fresher and more varied than most Indian buffets. And the dinner menu is headlined by perfectly marinated tandoor dishes. It all tastes good in the cool, calm, dimly lit dining room.

RUSSIAN
ST. PETERSBURG ⓈⓈ

3610 France Ave. N., Robbinsdale, 763/587-1787,
www.myvodkabar.com
HOURS: Tues.-Thurs. 5-11 P.M., Fri.-St. 5 P.M.-1 A.M.,
Sun.-Mon. closed

You start with *zakuski*—appetizers like blini with caviar, *salad olivje,* pickles and black bread—and you move right on to heavy Russian entrées, but you had better be ready to get up and dance at any time, because the dance floor is right in the middle of the dining room and there's always a Russian pop band playing irresistibly low-brow music heavy on the bass and synth. A more authentically Russian experience couldn't be had in the real St. Petersburg, but here the guys in shiny double-breasted suits mean no harm. By the way, Russians don't do casual; come dressed to impress.

NIGHTLIFE

Minneapolis and St. Paul—especially St. Paul—are cities where people are nearly tribal in their loyalty to their own specific neighborhood bar. Each of these bars—and there are hundreds—is unique to its own fierce partisans, but all are rather similar to the untrained, nonnative eye. We've listed here the bars and clubs that attract patrons from a wider area. But an adventurous visitor could have fun seeking out the best of the neighborhood joints and never feel particularly out of place.

For a go-it-alone pedestrian bar crawl, start at Psycho Suzi's in Northeast Minneapolis and work your way south down Marshall or University Avenue until you can take it no more or—in a true feat of endurance—you hit downtown Minneapolis. You can do the same in downtown St. Paul by turning your back to the Xcel Energy Center and heading straight down West 7th Street. Either way, you'll get a true taste of everything Twin Citians love about their own favorite dive bars.

The nightclub scene in downtown Minneapolis—and thus the nightclub scene in the whole of the Twin Cities, because that is pretty much the sum of it—is a fluid thing. Just as soon as you think you've got the latest hot spots figured out, they all change hands, change names, and change decor. But the locations stay the same (outfitting a dance club being a rather expensive endeavor). So the safest thing to do is what

HIGHLIGHTS

LOOK FOR ◖ TO FIND RECOMMENDED NIGHTLIFE.

◖ **Best Place to Hear an Electric Hurdy-Gurdy:** Also the best place to hear any world music – the not-for-profit **Cedar Cultural Center** (page 76).

◖ **Best Place to Hear National Jazz Acts:** In downtown Minneapolis, the **Dakota Jazz Club and Restaurant** has the market cornered on great jazz and great dining (page 76).

◖ **Best Piece of Minneapolis's Musical Past, Present, and Future:** Prince got his start at **First Avenue and 7th St. Entry,** and you can still hear the musical greats of today and the stars of tomorrow (page 77).

◖ **Best Place for Lawn Bowling:** In truth, **Brit's Pub** has the only place for lawn bowling in town, but that doesn't diminish it in any way (page 79).

◖ **Best Place for the Hair of the Dog:** You won't be alone if you hit the **C.C. Club** when it opens at 8 A.M. (page 79).

◖ **Best Darn Bar in the Country:** Don't take our word for it. That's what *Esquire* magazine called **Nye's Polonaise Room.** Minneapolis heartily agrees (page 81).

◖ **Best Place to Rub Elbows with Power Brokers:** You never know what kind of important deals are going down at the **St. Paul Grill's** polished oak bar (page 82).

◖ **Best Hideaway:** The dim – and we mean dim – room at **Bev's Wine Bar** is perfect when you need a little break from the world (page 82).

◖ **Best Drag Show:** You don't have to be gay to appreciate a good drag show. And you don't have to be gay to have fun at the **Gay 90s.** But it helps (page 84).

© TRICIA CORNELL

the Dakota Jazz Club and Restaurant

NIGHTLIFE

the locals do: Put on your dancing clothes, head for the intersection of 1st Avenue and 5th Street in downtown Minneapolis, and see what looks happening.

Generally speaking, the Twin Cities are a very gay-friendly place. A nice benefit of that is that the gay bars and clubs are some of the most open, friendly—and downright rocking—hangouts in town, no matter what your persuasion.

Unless you're clubbing, this is a casual place. If you're a jeans-wearer in general, you will never feel uncomfortable in jeans. Last call in both Minneapolis and St. Paul is 2 A.M.

Live Music

ARTISTS' QUARTER

408 St. Peter St., St. Paul, 651/292-1359,
www.artistsquarter.com

HOURS: Mon.-Sat. 7 P.M.-1 A.M., Sun. opens half hour before show

Map 4

A jazz-lover's jazz club. No glitz, no glam, just serious music, from old-school to modern in this dim basement space beneath the Park Square Theater. The acoustics and atmosphere are so prized that nationally known musicians have recorded live here for the Artists' Quarter's own record label. Most shows are just $5 or $10, and you can't buy tickets in advance, but you can call for reservations for popular weekend shows. Participate in Monday open poetry slams—free if you get up to the mic yourself. You can order food from the Great Waters Brewery upstairs; just ask the bartender.

🌙 CEDAR CULTURAL CENTER

416 Cedar Ave. S., Minneapolis, 612/338-2674,
www.thecedar.org

Map 3

The warehouse-like gutted former movie theater packs in serious music lovers for more than 150 shows a year—indie rock, folk, roots, jazz, blues, world music, anything uncategorizable and out of the mainstream. One of the most anticipated events on the calendar each year is the late-September Nordic Roots Festival, when the quiet giants of the Scandinavian folk-rock movement bring their electric hurdy-gurdys to town and sell out shows. All ages at the Cedar means all ages: Kids and grandparents are welcome and likely to come.

🌙 DAKOTA JAZZ CLUB AND RESTAURANT

1010 Nicollet Mall, Minneapolis, 612/332-1010,
www.dakotacooks.com

HOURS: Lunch Mon.-Sat. 11:30 A.M.-1:30 P.M.; dinner Mon.-Thurs. 4:30-10 P.M., Fri.-Sat. 5:30-11 P.M., Sun. 5:30-9 P.M.

Map 1

The Dakota is Minnesota's premier jazz club, known as one of the best in the country. Local and national headliners perform every night in a lavish hall before a crowd with a bit of local glamour. The Dakota is a great place to eat, too, whether you munch smoked fish and fries with béarnaise sauce in the club or order a full, luxurious meal in the dining room. Look for early-evening and late-night happy hour deals. Shows generally start at 7, 8:30, and 11:30 P.M. and cost $5–60.

FAMOUS DAVE'S

3001 Hennepin Ave. S., Minneapolis, 612/822-9900,
www.famousdaves.com

HOURS: Mon.-Thurs. 11 A.M.-10 P.M.,
Fri.-Sat. 11 A.M.-11 P.M., Sun. 10 A.M.-10 P.M.

Map 2

Blues, jazz, and salsa acts take the stage at Famous Dave's, with a big dance floor and instructors on hand for salsa nights. Yep, this is part of a national barbecue chain, and you can certainly sit down to a plate of ribs and a sweet corn muffin while you're here, but what attracts people—crowds of young professionals—to this Famous Dave's location is the music. In fact, it's been named the Twin Cities' best blues bar more than once in recent years.

FINE LINE MUSIC CAFÉ

318 1st Ave. N., Minneapolis, 612/338-8100,
www.finelinemusic.com

Map 1

When the Pixies got back together in 2004, the Fine Line is where they launched their reunion tour. The dance floor isn't big (you can always escape to the balcony), but it has seen big names in music history since 1987, from Sheryl Crow to Bill Clinton. Look for shows nearly every night. For a taste of Minnesota's music scene right now, look for local music showcase nights (usually Tuesday, Wednesday, and Thursday). Shows are 21-plus unless otherwise noted and are general admission. Get there early if you want a table.

NIGHTLIFE

© TRICIA CORNELL

The Fine Line Music Café is a great place to catch live music performed by local musicians.

◖ FIRST AVENUE AND 7TH ST. ENTRY

701 1st Ave. N., Minneapolis, 612/332-1775, www.first-avenue.com
Map 1

First Avenue is a pilgrimage and a right of passage for young Minnesotans—and those not-so-young, who remember seeing U2 or Prince here for the first time (yep, that's First Avenue in *Purple Rain*). You can search out names of your favorite headlining acts on the curved outer walls of this former Greyhound station. Most nights see two or three shows, in the Main Room, VIP Room, and smaller Entry. Look for midweek, DJ-led dance nights, including Ritmo Caliente.

KITTY CAT KLUB

315 14th Ave. SE, Minneapolis, 612/331-9800, www.kittycatklub.net
HOURS: Mon.-Sat. 9 A.M.-1 A.M., Sun. noon-1 A.M.
Map 3

By day a hip, low-key coffee shop. By night a swank lounge that attracts a slightly older crowd than you might expect right here in Dinkytown, practically on the campus of the University of Minnesota. Most nights a rock band plays, but if not, there's a DJ (expect a small cover). The layout—lavishly furnished nook-like rooms—encourages conversation, socializing, and discreet people-watching.

TRIPLE ROCK SOCIAL CLUB

629 Cedar Ave. S., Minneapolis, 612/333-7399, www.triplerocksocialclub.com
HOURS: Mon.-Fri. 4 P.M.-2 A.M., Sat.-Sun. 10 A.M.-2 P.M.
Map 3

You've got your punks, you've got your preppy kids. You've got a lot traffic from the nearby University of Minnesota and Augsburg College. You've got a nearly solid schedule of music booked, much of it neo-punk, with a few DJ nights thrown in. And you've got free bacon Wednesdays. That's the Triple Rock Social Club. The concerts and the bar are side by side, but separated by sound-proof walls. All the better to enjoy your bar snacks (an even mix of carnivorous and vegan) in peace and to dance without getting a vegetarian hot wing in the face. Door time for most shows is 9 P.M.; for all-ages shows it's 5 or 6 P.M. Tickets are $5–15, sold at the door. No cover when there's a DJ.

VARSITY THEATER

1308 4th St. SE, Minneapolis, 612/604-0222, www.varsitytheater.org
Map 3

This converted vaudeville theater has been called the best place to hear a concert in the Twin Cities, thanks to 20-foot ceilings, a nearly infinitely reconfigurable space, and a top-notch sound system. In fact, depending on the show, you may have a choice of seating that includes café tables, club chairs, and queen-sized air mattresses. This isn't a music-every-night place, but it is where national touring indie acts, especially those just about to make it big, make their Twin Cities stops. Look for the art deco marquee and you'll know you're here.

Dance Clubs

ENVY

400 1st Ave. N., Minneapolis, 612/673-9694,
www.envympls.com
HOURS: Mon. and Wed.-Sat. 8 P.M.-2 A.M.,
Sun. and Tues. closed
Map 1

See and be seen at Envy, where Minneapolis's beautiful 20-somethings make a point of stopping on a Saturday night on the town. The impressive space, with modern build-outs imposed on the 19th-century interior, feels as much like a swank lounge as it does a dance club, with bars stretching the length of the walls and plush booths. Two rooms, divided by a frosted glass wall, mean two scenes: serious dancing in the front and, most nights, electronica in the back. Be prepared for a crowd—Envy is packed, especially on Saturdays—and remember, no T-shirts, sports attire, or hats.

THE LOUNGE

411 2nd Ave. N., Minneapolis, 612/333-8800,
www.theloungempls.com
HOURS: Thurs.-Sat. 9 P.M.-2 A.M., Sun. 10 P.M.-2 A.M.
Map 1

As other clubs come and go, The Lounge has endured since 1995, thanks to a loyal after-the-workday professional crowd and, at least in part, to some original programming. The Lounge will see your go-go dancers (they've got those) and raise you a magician and a fire dancer. Pick your scene among the several rooms, each like a smaller club in itself and each spinning different music, from top-40 to underground electronica. Keep the dress code

in mind—no white sneakers or white T-shirts, nothing saggy—and remember there may be a $5–8 cover.

MYTH

3090 Southlawn Dr., Maplewood, 651/779-6984,
www.mythnightclub.com
HOURS: Fri.-Sat. 9 P.M.-2 A.M.
Map 7

Myth is one of the few nightclubs that has broken free of the extraordinarily strong gravitational pull of downtown Minneapolis's Warehouse District. When it opened in the northern suburb of Maple Grove, the doubters said that true partygoers would never be caught dead in the 'burbs. But the lure of ample free parking, 36,000 square feet of dance floor, and big-name national DJs proved too strong. (Myth has even served as a concert venue for shows as unlikely as Elvis Costello.)

SPIN

10 5th St. S., Minneapolis, 612/333-5055,
www.spinmn.com
HOURS: Thurs.-Sat. 9 P.M.-2 A.M., Sun. 10 P.M.-2 A.M.
Map 1

When Twin Cities sports stars and media personalities are looking for a night on the town, they head to Spin, with three levels of dance floor inside the historic Lumber Exchange Building. Go-go dancers on the tables and out-of-town DJs with serious reputations give Spin an energy unlike anything else in Minneapolis. The dress code is simple: Come dressed to impress—really impress.

Bars

BRIT'S PUB
1110 Nicollet Mall, Minneapolis, 612/332-3908,
www.britspub.com
HOURS: Daily 11 A.M.-2 A.M.
Map 1

Footie and rugby on the telly, fish and chips, Scotch eggs, even the odd outdoor Shakespeare production. You might say Brit's has gone a smidge too far in its British pub theme—except that this is the real deal, with real English punters behind the scenes. The big attraction here is the second-floor rooftop deck, with 12 lanes of lawn bowling and numerous exhortations not to be "a tosser." Watch for open bowling nights when the leagues aren't playing and grab a lane for $5 per person per hour.

BULLDOG
401 Hennepin Ave. E., Minneapolis, 612/378-2855,
www.thebulldogmpls.com
HOURS: Daily 11 A.M.-2 A.M.
Map 3

The Bulldog is three great bars in three separate locations with the same great neighborhood feel and the same attraction for low-key young professionals. Both have flat-screen TVs, old-school shuffleboard tables, and other bar games. The Bulldog Northeast, on Hennepin, is the slightly more grown-up sibling, with a more grown-up and highly lauded bar menu (brisket on the nachos—yum). The Bulldog Uptown (2549 Lyndale Ave. S., 612/872-8893, daily 11 A.M.-2 A.M.) is a great place to have a beer and an authentic Chicago dog with a side of onion rings. The newest Bulldog in St. Paul has great food and pub games (237 6th St. E., 651/221-0750, daily 11 A.M.-2 A.M.).

C.C. CLUB
2600 Lyndale Ave. S., Minneapolis, 612/874-7226
HOURS: Mon.-Sat. 8 A.M.-2 A.M., Sun. 10 A.M.-2 A.M.
Map 2

Thousands, if not hundreds of thousands, of right-out-of-college Twin Cities youngsters

Brit's Pub, opposite Peavey Plaza, is favored by UK expats and downtown office workers.

have drunk through their aimless 20s right here in the C.C. Club. It's gritty. It's not particularly clean. It was smoky as hell until the smoking ban went into effect (and that smell never goes away). But it's home. All the tattoos might make you feel a little out of place as you open the door, but order a pitcher of beer, put some Hüsker Dü on the jukebox, and let some 20-something poor his drunken heart out to you. And if you need the hair of the dog the next morning, the C.C. Club opens up bright and early for a greasy breakfast.

CHATTERBOX
2229 35th St. E., Minneapolis, 612/728-9871,
www.chatterboxpub.net
HOURS: Sun.-Thurs. 11 A.M.-1 A.M., Fri.-Sat. 11 A.M.-2 A.M.
Map 2

If you're of a certain generation and your parents had a rec room, it probably looked an awful lot like the Chatterbox Pub: a scruffy Lazy-Boy, a beat-up couch, stacks of board games, and an Atari system hooked up to the TV. (But did you have 75 game cartridges? The Chatterbox does.) You probably didn't have a full menu of burgers, sandwiches, and beer, though. The St. Paul Chatterbox (800 Cleveland Ave. S., 651/699-1149), in a converted Perkins that still feels like a Perkins, is a family-friendly place on the English pub model.

HALF TIME REC

1013 Front Ave., St. Paul, 651/488-8245,
www.halftimerec.com
HOURS: Daily 10 A.M.–1 A.M.
Map 6

St. Paul is an old Irish town at heart, and Half Time Rec is St. Paul's favorite old Irish bar. Although the music half of the layout has stopped booking exclusively Irish bands, it's still the best place to hear Irish music in the cities. And you can play bocce (Hey, is that Irish?) on the two courts in the basement. If that doesn't sufficiently tire your arms out, try *hammerschlagen* (Again, Irish?): The point is to be the first to hammer a nail into a tree stump. What definitely is Irish is the warmth and energy of Half Time Rec's atmosphere and the way generations of serious drinkers come together for a good time.

HAPPY GNOME

498 Selby Ave., St. Paul, 651/287-2018,
www.thehappygnome.com
HOURS: Sun.–Thurs. 11:30 A.M.–1 A.M.,
Fri.–Sat. 11:30 A.M.–2 A.M.
Map 5

St. Paulites are so used to having a bar in this spot under some name or other that many have not noticed the subtle shift toward finer dining here at the Happy Gnome. Chef Matthew Hinman came to helm the kitchen from the lauded Minneapolis bistro Lucia's and now offers dinner in the Firehouse Room upstairs. The Happy Gnome offers 44 beers on tap and more than 180 bottles, along with a first-rate selection of scotch. This is a bar—a bar with great food (try the bison burger).

PERSON-POWERED PUB CRAWL

You could go on a typical pub crawl – the working-class neighborhoods of Nordeast are great for that – or you could bring the pub crawling – er, rolling – right along with you. You and up to 15 friends can rent the one and only **Pedal Pub** (952/703-9000, www.pedalpub.com, $150 per hour, two-hour minimum) and ride it from bar to bar or set up your own bar right on board. It's 100 percent BYOB and, yep, it's legal in Minnesota. Apparently, the mobile pub is based on a contraption known in Amsterdam as a *fietscafe*. Five people on each side pedal, while a company-provided driver steers. You can ride one of the Pedal Pub folks' 10 routes in Minneapolis and St. Paul – all pretty flat – or you can customize your own for an extra fee. If you've got a hankering to tailgate at a Twins or Vikings game and lack a tailgate itself, the Pedal Pub is a great option.

KIERAN'S IRISH PUB

330 2nd Ave. S., Minneapolis, 612-339-4499
HOURS: Mon.–Tues. 11 A.M.–11 P.M., Wed.–Thurs. 11 A.M.–1 A.M., Fri. 11 A.M.–2 A.M., Sat. 5 P.M.–2 A.M., Sun. closed (open some Sundays for special events and Vikings home games)
Map 1

Whether or not there's someone on stage playing an Irish jig (and, more often than not, there is), there's a big, friendly energy to Kieran's. Kieran Folliard, who himself came across the pond from Ireland, has created and sustained that energy in two other pubs—The Local on Nicollet Mall and The Liffey in downtown St. Paul. If music's not your thing, come for the pub quiz every third Wednesday. And with your pint, you can also fill up on shepherd's pie, corned beef and cabbage, and—in a nod to the locals—walleye and chips.

THE LOCAL

931 Nicollet Mall, Minneapolis, 612/904-1000,
www.the-local.com

HOURS: Mon.-Fri. 11 A.M.-2 A.M., Sat.-Sun. 10 A.M.-2 A.M.

`Map 1`

The Local is the best place in town to watch
international soccer, rugby, and hurling (it
might be the only place for hurling), with
screens showing Premiership and Champions
League games and plenty of enthusiastic fans.
It's also a great place to see young Minneapolis
office denizens in their natural environment
after work and to enjoy what is known as a
giant pint o' prawns. And, for the morning
after, a hearty brunch is served on Saturdays
and Sundays.

MONTE CARLO

219 3rd Ave. N., Minneapolis, 612/333-5900

HOURS: Mon.-Sat. 11 A.M.-1 A.M., Sun. 10 A.M.-midnight

`Map 1`

Once a bar for the Warehouse District working
class, now a swank bar and restaurant for the
Warehouse District young professional class—
and for a long line of downtown moneymakers.
The wall of bottles stacked to the ceiling behind the copper-topped bar is practically a Twin
Cities landmark in itself. The Monte Carlo is
also acknowledged by just about everyone in
the know to make the best martini in town. If
drinking makes you hungry, you'll find plenty
of filling eats, including a famed monte cristo
and a meatloaf sandwich with grilled onions.

◖ NYE'S POLONAISE ROOM

12 Hennepin Ave., Minneapolis, 612/379-2021,
www.nyespolonaise.com

HOURS: Daily 11 A.M.-2 A.M.

`Map 1`

Nye's Polonaise room is pure Minneapolis. It's
been here forever—well over 50 years, since
back in the day when all of Nordeast was a
working-class neighborhood with deep Eastern
European roots. Now the expensive condos
have crept over the river from downtown, but
Nye's is still here, with its formica tabletops,
glittery booths, Sweet Lou at the piano, and
the World's Most Dangerous Polka Band. You
can't feel out of place at Nye's, even if you don't
polka. In 2006, *Esquire* bestowed upon Nye's
the title of "Best Bar in America."

O'GARA'S BAR AND GRILL

164 Snelling Ave. N., St. Paul, 651/644-3333,
www.ogaras.com

HOURS: Sun.-Fri. 10 A.M.-1 A.M., Sat. 9 A.M.-1 A.M.

`Map 5`

O'Gara's has been serving beer to thirsty St.
Paulites since 1941. Since then it has added
the Shamrock Room, which hosts jazz and big
band music; the Garage, which attracts local
and national rock acts; and the Brew Pub,
where you can sample O'Gara's own housemade beer. The lunch and dinner menus are
lengthy and the atmosphere is warm. This
is the place to be if you're in St. Paul on St.
Patrick's Day.

PSYCHO SUZI'S MOTOR LOUNGE

2519 Marshall St. NE, Minneapolis, 612/788-9069,
www.psychosuzis.com

HOURS: Daily 11 A.M.-2 A.M.

`Map 3`

No temple to kitsch in the history of kitsch
worship has embraced the best of the low-
brow quite like Psycho Suzi's, with its year-
round patio with palm-frond umbrellas and
tiki-head drinking cups. The menu is like a
spoiled 10-year-old's dream: beer-battered
miniature hot dogs, tater tots, deviled eggs,
massive deep-fried cheese curds, and Suzi's famous pizza. The drink menu is like that spoiled
10-year-old's dream when he hits legal drinking age: The Suffering Bastard is described as
"Various blackberryish boozes, sour, spices,
and 151 mixed into a tasty delight."

STELLA'S FISH CAFÉ & PRESTIGE OYSTER BAR

1400 Lake St W., Minneapolis, 612/824-8862,
www.stellasfishcafe.com

HOURS: Sun.-Thurs. 11:30 A.M.-11 P.M., Fri.-Sat.
11:30 A.M.-2 A.M.

`Map 2`

Stella's Fish Café is actually a seafood restaurant—a rare enough thing in Minnesota—but

NIGHTLIFE

the hot young things lined up on Lake Street in skimpy blouses no matter the weather are not here for fish and chips (though the fish and chips are really pretty good). They're here because this is young Minneapolis's pickup joint of the moment. You can watch the scene unfold on the truly beautiful rooftop patio and avail yourself of fresh oysters at the same time.

ST. PAUL GRILL

350 Market St., St. Paul, 651/224-7455,
www.stpaulgrill.com
HOURS: Mon.-Thurs. 11 A.M.-11 P.M., Fri.-Sat. 11 A.M.-1 A.M., Sun. 10:30 A.M.-10 P.M.
Map 4

Feel like an old-time fat cat as you settle into the high-backed stools at the long, polished bar. Order a decades-old single malt, and strike up a conversation with the guy in the suit next to you. He might be a state senator. In truth, there are an awful lot of suits here, even though the jacket is not required. A classic shrimp cocktail or a bowl of lobster dip rounds out the whole living-large experience.

TURF CLUB

1601 University Ave., St. Paul, 651/647-0486,
www.turfclub.net
HOURS: Daily noon-2 A.M.
Map 5

Ask about great dive bars in St. Paul and you're going to hear about the Turf Club. And this is a town that knows its dive bars. In recent years this former 1940s music hall has left its country-music, line-dancing roots and become a rock-and-roll mecca. A young local band has made it—and is on its way to big things—when it plays the Turf Club. National acts swing through here, too, and you'll probably pay less to see them than you would anywhere else.

V.F.W. JAMES BALLENTINE POST NO. 246

2916 Lyndale Ave. S., Minneapolis, 612/823-6233
HOURS: Daily 11 A.M.-1 A.M.
Map 2

Yes, the V.F.W. In the young professional paradise that is Uptown, the V.F.W. is among the hottest hot spots. Cheap beer, strong drinks, bingo, karaoke (put your name in early; the schedule will fill up), and a veritable peaceable kingdom among patrons. Truckers, tourists, and Target marketing managers are all welcome here—as long as they don't try to snag two songs on the karaoke list. This is also the place to enjoy that quintessential Midwestern bar experience—the meat raffle. Buy your ticket, cross your fingers, and if you're lucky, take home some steaks, pork chops, or ground meat.

Wine Bars

BEAUJO'S

4950 France Ave. S., Edina, 952/922-8974,
www.beaujos.net
HOURS: Mon.-Thurs. 11 A.M.-11:30 P.M., Fri.-Sat. 11 A.M.-midnight, Sun. 3-10 P.M.
Map 7

Rather than dim and romantic, Beaujo's is bright and suburban and yet still manages to be chic—the perfect place to rest your shopping bags after a long day shopping at 50th and France. To watch the other shoppers, grab one of the high tables by the windows and settle in with a plate of olives or something more substantial, like salads, small plates, and sandwiches off the menu. A nice perk for light drinkers: Wines are available by the bottle, the glass, and the half glass.

BEV'S WINE BAR

250 3rd Ave. N., Minneapolis, 612/337-0102
HOURS: Tues.-Fri. 4:30 P.M.-1 A.M., Sat. 6:30 P.M.-1 A.M., Sun.-Mon. closed
Map 1

Don't be fooled by the dark windows: Bev's

is still open. Most nights the tea lights on the tables and the bar provide most of the light—and the ambiance works. The wine list isn't long, but it is carefully chosen and well priced. This is the perfect escape when a glass of peppery sangiovese and a plate of little cheeses in a quiet room is what you need.

RIVERVIEW

3747 42nd Ave. S., Minneapolis, 612/729-4200, www.theriverview.net
HOURS: Wed.-Thurs. 5-11 P.M., Fri.-Sat. 5 P.M.-midnight, Sun. 4-10 P.M., Mon.-Tues. closed
Map 2

A neighborhood wine bar is a great concept, and the Riverview is a reflection of the warmth and class of the Longfellow neighborhood around it. (It's a family-oriented neighborhood, so the Riverview Café, right next door, is equipped with one of the best play areas in the Twin Cities.) Pick a wine flight off the menu or tell your server what sorts of wines you like and have him or her put one together just for you. Beer lovers can have just as much fun, with more than 40 bottles from around the world to choose from.

TOAST

415 1st St. N., Minneapolis, 612/333-4305
HOURS: Tues.-Thurs. 5-11 P.M., Fri.-Sat. 5 P.M.-midnight, Sun. 5-11 A.M.
Map 1

With a well-known Twin Cities chef in the kitchen, Toast is a wine bar with something more to offer beyond the cheese and salami plates—excellent crostini, creative thin-crust pizzas, and hearty salads. It's a brighter and livelier space, rather than a dim and romantic one, and the beautiful crowd comes to mingle. Toast's wine list, studded inexpensive gems from Spain and Italy, has been lauded as "The Best in the Twin Cities" a nd Toast itself has taken the title of "Best Wine Bar."

Lounges

BAR LURCAT

1624 Harmon Pl., Minneapolis, 612/486-5500, www.cafelurcat.com
HOURS: Mon.-Thurs. 5-10 P.M., Fri.-Sat. 5 P.M.-1 A.M., Sun. 5-9 P.M.
Map 1

The thing to do at Bar Lurcat (opinions differ on the correct pronunciation) is to drape yourself over a vintage settee under a crystal chandelier and try to look as beautiful as the surroundings. Failing that, you can enjoy watching all the other artsy types trying to do the same thing. Order small plates from a kitchen run by one of the best food outfits in town (D'Amico and Sons) and choose from extensive wine list (more than 40 served by the glass).

BELLANOTTE

600 Hennepin Ave., Minneapolis, 612/339-7200, www.bellanottempls.com
HOURS: Mon.-Thurs. 11 A.M.-3 P.M. and 5-11 P.M., Fri. 11 A.M.-3 P.M. and 5 P.M.-midnight, Sat. 5 P.M.-midnight, Sun. 5-10 P.M.
Map 1

While Bellanotte is ostensibly an Italian restaurant—and a pricey one at that—the real action here is in the posh lounge area and on the dance floor, especially when the crowds flow out of the Target Center across the street after a Timberwolves game. That's when Bellanotte alone keeps the Twin Cities gossip columnist busy. The bold and the beautiful come dressed to the nines and ready to drop $15 on a martini.

CHAMBERS ROOFTOP LOUNGE

901 Hennepin Ave., Minneapolis, 612/767-6900, www.chambersminneapolis.com
HOURS: Thurs.-Sat. 9 P.M.-2 A.M.
Map 1

The full name of the rooftop lounge, as

© TRICIA CORNELL

The lounge in the Chambers hotel is full of contemporary art.

written in neon on the wall, is "Red, White, and [expletive] Blue." But that's not your first clue you're not in Kansas any more. The whole of the Chambers hotel, including both the rooftop and the lobby lounge (open Sun.–Wed. 2–11 P.M., Thurs. 2 P.M.–midnight, Fri.–Sat. 2 P.M.–1 A.M.) is so sleek, so polished that it seems to glow. The walls hold hundreds of thousands of dollars worth of modern art. Up on the roof there are striking views of Minneapolis.

Gay and Lesbian

◖ GAY 90S
408 Hennepin Ave., Minneapolis, 612/333-7755, www.gay90s.com
HOURS: Mon.-Sat. 8 A.M.-1 A.M., Sun. 10 A.M.-1 A.M.
Map 1

The party never stops at the Gay 90s, a sprawling complex with six bars and three dance floors. And even those not drawn by the "gay" part of the name know they'll find unstoppable dance music and a we're-all-friends-now atmosphere. Watch for karaoke nights, drag shows, and male strippers. Six nights a week some of the most professional, best-dressed, and best-coiffed drag queens in the Midwest strut their stuff in the La Femme lounge.

JETSET
115 1st St. N., Minneapolis, 612/339-3933, www.jetsetbar.com
HOURS: Tues.-Thurs. 5 P.M.-1 A.M., Fri. 5 P.M.-2 A.M., Sat. 6 P.M.-2 A.M., Sun. closed
Map 1

Small, sleek, and chic, Jetset is just a single spare room in the Warehouse District with low-slung, backless leather benches that encourage lounging and schmoozing. If you

A mixed crowd fills the Gay 90s dance club.

bravely push them aside, dancing is fine, too. Expect a small and self-selected crowd of sharp dressers, gay and straight, but don't expect the party to last much beyond midnight, when Jetset tends to clear out. Tuesday is neighborhood night, when Downtown's urban homesteaders make themselves at home and schmooze their neighbors.

19 BAR
19 15th St. W., Minneapolis, 612/871-5553
HOURS: Mon.-Fri. 3 P.M.-2 A.M., Sat.-Sun. 1 P.M.-2 A.M.
Map 1
The 19 Bar dates to a time in the Twin Cities when the marginalized gay community was centered right here in the Loring Park neighborhood near downtown. (In fact, some say it's

the oldest gay bar in the cities.) As doors have opened and closets closed down for good, 19 has survived and remains a welcome and welcoming haven in what can otherwise be a wild scene. This is just a bar, very much like any other small-town bar, with a crowd of regular young professionals.

THE SALOON
830 Hennepin Ave., Minneapolis, 612/332-0835, www.saloonmn.com
HOURS: Daily 9 A.M.-2 A.M.
Map 1
Did old western saloons have dance floors like this one? Highly unlikely. The focus here is on dancing, not drinking, and several evenings a week there are go-go boys to keep the crowd going. The back patio is secluded enough for things to get a little rowdy. Spend afternoons enjoying more sedate pursuits, like parlor games, trivia, and bingo. The Saloon is the old-school cornerstone of the Twin Cities' longstanding gay community.

TOWN HOUSE
1415 University Ave. W., St. Paul, 651/646-7087, www.townhousebar.com
HOURS: Mon.-Fri. 3 P.M.-1 A.M., Sat.-Sun. noon-1 A.M.
Map 5
The operative word here is fun. Gay men and lesbians come to the clean, comfortable Town House, near the U of M campus, for a casual night of dancing. Sundays and Thursdays the Pumps and Pearls Drag Revue performs. On other nights you'll find raucous karaoke or live entertainment. Wednesday is the Original Cheapie Night, with a $5 cover and $1 beers. For an even more mellow time, head to the piano bar in the back.

NIGHTLIFE

© TRICIA CORNELL

ARTS AND LEISURE

Far from the 80-hour work weeks and hour-long commutes of the coasts, Twin Citians often find themselves with some time on their hands—but they are rarely at a loss for what to do with it. From the arts to parks, residents know they're blessed with true gems and work hard to take advantage of them. It may be an "idle hands do the devil's work" philosophy handed down subconsciously from the cities' largely German and Scandinavian ancestry. It may be the appreciation for nature that comes from being a generation or two off the farm. It may just be there's so darned much to do here. But, for whatever reason, this is a population that rarely sits still.

Both cities—but Minneapolis in particular—are known for having some of the best park systems in the country, with more per capita parkland than nearly anywhere else. The parks, as well, are more than mown lawns and children's playgrounds. Well-maintained sports fields, public wading pools, tennis courts, boating facilities, and park buildings—as well as classes and programming that do much to maintain the quality of life even for segments of the population that can't afford much on their own—are the norm. We expect a lot from our park systems. And, by and large, we get it.

Indoor pursuits are overwhelmingly popular, as well. On any given weekend night during the theater season—and even in the summer—somebody with an urge to see a play will have more than 40 shows to choose from. The metro area, in fact, is second only to New York City in per capita attendance at theater and arts events. Which means you'll find high

© BRUCE MANNING

HIGHLIGHTS

LOOK FOR (TO FIND RECOMMENDED ARTS AND ACTIVITIES.

(**Most Accessible – and Stunning – Architectural Landmark:** Downtown St. Paul's **Landmark Center** is free and open to the public every day of the week. Visitors can marvel at 20-foot ceilings and hand-carved mahogany and (for small admission fees) visit several museums (page 93).

(**Best Introduction to Minneapolis History:** Minneapolis built its early economy and reputation on flour, and the **Mill City Museum,** in a rehabbed flour mill, makes that important history come alive for children and adults (page 94).

(**Best Arts Deal in Town:** The **Minneapolis Institute of Arts** is a free, first-rate art museum with a world-class Asian collection (page 94).

(**Most Unexpected Museum Find:** Nobody comes to Minnesota expecting to find one of the finest collections of 20th-century Russian art – yet. **The Museum of Russian Art,** founded in 2005, will soon change that (page 95).

(**Top Theater Choice for Any Age:** You don't have to be a kid or have one in tow to enjoy the award-winning, visually stunning, and smartly scripted shows at the **Children's Theatre Company** (page 99).

(**Must-See Theater, Even Without a Ticket:** Seeing a show at the **Guthrie Theater** is almost guaranteed to be a great experience. But the modern building itself is open almost all day, every day and worth a visit to walk on the "endless bridge" cantilevered over the Mississippi (page 99).

(**Best Way to Enjoy the Cold:** Don't hide from the cold; revel in it at the **Winter Carnival.** Although the ice castle isn't built

every year, there's always plenty of snowy, icy fun (page 106).

(**Best 10 Days of the Year in Minnesota:** Visitors have been known to plan their trips to Minnesota around the **Minnesota State Fair** – a strategy we highly endorse (page 110).

(**Best Outdoor Activity:** Rent or borrow a bike and hit the **Grand Rounds National Scenic Byway.** The only urban National Scenic Byway showcases the best of life in the Twin Cities (page 120).

(**Best Guided Tour:** Rather than trudge along on your own two feet, on the **Magical History Tours** you get to ride a Segway along the Mississippi River (page 127).

© TRICIA CORNELL

The ice castle is the highlight of the St. Paul Winter Carnival, although it isn't built every year.

ARTS AND LEISURE

quality, full houses, and enthusiastic audiences as well as just plain variety. Don't expect safe old chestnuts to dominate the playbills, either. Several theaters, including Minneapolis's Jungle Theater and St. Paul's History Theater, are well known for presenting original scripts, and the venerable Guthrie Theater regularly premieres works by internationally known playwrights, including Arthur Miller's penultimate play, *Resurrection Blues,* in 2002.

A final testament to the cities' appreciation for the arts: A building boom in 2003–2005 brought five new arts-related buildings to Minneapolis, all designed by renowned international architects. The explosion brought national and international attention to the city, but, more importantly, here at home it brought sold-out opening galas and crowds that continue to this day. It awakened an attitude that said, "Of course, it all happened here. What took the rest of you so long to notice?"

The Arts

Come as you are—that's the attitude at Twin Cities art galleries, theaters, and concert halls. Whether you packed a suit, a designer dress, or jeans and a fleece, you will be welcomed and you're likely to look around and see someone dressed just like you are. (The same attitude, by the way, goes at even the poshest restaurants in town. The only place where someone is likely to give you guff about your attire is at a nightclub.)

And, while you're at it, bring the kids! Whether you see it as a pro or a con, you should know that, for the most part, arts institutions from museums to galleries to theaters are very accommodating of children, and you are likely to encounter plenty of families enjoying the arts together. (And, if I may say so myself, Minnesota children tend to know how to behave themselves in those situations.)

Another welcoming aspect: the price. Theater tickets, except for the big Broadway productions that blow through town, never top $50 (and most hover around $20–30). Museum admission—again, except for high-profile touring exhibits—is almost universally under $10, and some of the most worthwhile museums are free. And if you've got your heart set on seeing a show but don't have tickets in hand, rush seats, especially at the Guthrie, are almost always available.

MUSEUMS
ALEXANDER RAMSEY HOUSE
265 Exchange St. S., St. Paul, 651/296-8760, www.mnhs.org
HOURS: Fri.-Sat. 10 A.M.-3 P.M.
COST: $8 adults, $6 seniors, $5 children, children 5 and under free
Map 4

Alexander Ramsey's elegant three-story home in St. Paul has been called one of the best preserved Victorian houses in the country. Ramsey served as an appointed territorial governor of Minnesota and later as the state of Minnesota's second elected governor, and held a host of other public offices. Costumed guides dressed as his wife Anna and servants now lead tours through the home and offer insight into the upstairs/downstairs lives of the period. Guided tours leave on the hour. An additional tour is added June–August Tuesday, Wednesday, and Thursday at 1 P.M.

AMERICAN SWEDISH INSTITUTE
2600 Park Ave., Minneapolis, 612/871-4907, www.americanswedishinst.org
HOURS: Tues. and Thurs.-Sat. noon-4 P.M., Wed. noon-8 P.M., Sun. 1-5 P.M.
COST: $6 adults, $5 seniors, $4 children, children 5 and under free
Map 2

In the late 1800s, waves of Swedish immigrants began making their homes in

TWIN CITIES WITH KIDS

Minneapolis and St. Paul are, in general, very kid-friendly. Unless you've chosen one of the poshest restaurants in town, it's not hard to find booster seats, kids' menus, and crayons. Arts venues, too, welcome kids, although you should note that some, including the **Guthrie,** have a minimum age for most of their shows.

The must-see list for families visiting the Twin Cities is long: the **Minnesota Children's Museum,** the **Science Museum of Minnesota,** the **Minnesota History Center,** the **Mill City Museum, Historic Fort Snelling,** and the **Minnesota Zoo** and **Como Zoo** are all good bets.

Keep an eye out for monthly special deals: Admission to the Minnesota Children's Museum is free on the third Sunday of the month. The **Walker Art Center** hosts an all-out family-oriented bash on the first Saturday of the month, free of charge. The joint is hopping as families work on two crafts projects, rock out at the dance party in the auditorium, and watch offbeat films and live performances. (Note to those traveling without children: This is not a good day to try

to enjoy the exhibits.) And admission to the **Minneapolis Institute of Arts** is always free, but the museum hosts Target Family Day one Sunday a month, with art projects, performers, and special tours for families. Finally, on select winter Saturdays, the **Jungle Theater** collaborates with the **Wild Rumpus** bookstore to put on live readings of favorite children's books. For a schedule of all children's theater shows and all family-oriented activities in the Twin Cities, go to the calendar section at www.mnparent.com.

If you're traveling with toddlers, you need somewhere for them to get their wiggles out. You'll find great playgrounds in downtown Minneapolis's **Loring Park,** on the shores of **Lake Calhoun** and **Lake Harriet** in South Minneapolis, and in St. Paul's **Como Park.** Inclement weather? Run the kids ragged in the empty hallways of the **Mall of America** in the hours after the doors open at 7 A.M. and before the stores open at 10 A.M.

Got older kids who have to move, move, move all the time? Take them to **3rd Lair** skate park, rent them a board and a helmet, and say, "See you in three hours."

Minnesota, where the terrain, with its lakes, rivers, and gentle rolling fields and forests, reminded them of home. Among them was Swan Turnblad, who rose from typesetter to newspaper publisher and built the massive 33-room mansion (rumored at the time to cost $1 million to build) on Park Avenue. The building, with its turrets and stately portico, was completed in 1903, and in 1929, Turnblad revealed why he had built such a grand house for his small family: He had intended all along to create a museum of Swedish-American culture. Today several rooms display examples of early-20th-century furnishings, while others host traveling exhibits. The third floor is dedicated to the history of Swedish culture in the Twin Cities.

THE BAKKEN

3537 Zenith Ave. S., Minneapolis, 612/926-3738, www.thebakken.org

HOURS: Tues.-Wed. and Fri.-Sat. 10 A.M.-5 P.M., Thurs. 10 A.M.-8 P.M., Sun.-Mon. closed

COST: $7 adults, $5 students and seniors, children 5 and under free

`Map 2`

At The Bakken, visitors can experience electricity in just about every form, starting in the front hall, where cranking a machine from the 1920s delivers a powerful jolt of electricity. Farther along in the museum's warren of small rooms and hallways, a theremin (one of the first electronic musical instruments) hums and whistles as visitors pass their hands through it, electric fish spark in dark aquariums, and the monster in Mary Shelley's Frankenstein

ARTS AND LEISURE

lies on his inventor's table. Visitors can even play Mindball—a game you win by moving a ball with your mind. In 1957, Earl Bakken invented the first wearable pacemaker. His company, Medtronic, went on to become one of Minnesota's most important companies and a major player in medical electronics. Medtronic's collection of devices and documents was opened to the public in its current location in 1976.

BELL MUSEUM OF NATURAL HISTORY

10 Church St. SE, Minneapolis, 612/624-7083, www.bellmuseum.org

HOURS: Tues.-Fri. 9 A.M.-5 P.M., Sat. 10 A.M.-5 P.M., Sun. noon-5 P.M.

COST: $5 adults, $3 students and seniors

Map 3

Dioramas are part art and part science and, for the first half of the 20th century, played a huge role in the way the general public viewed the natural world. The Bell Museum uses its well-regarded collection of dioramas for two purposes: to present the animals themselves and to illuminate the history of dioramas. Under the auspices of the University of Minnesota, the museum is an excellent introduction to the birds and animals of the Upper Midwest and includes some specimens from other parts of the world. It also hosts a number of science-related films and lectures as well as excellent children's programs throughout the year. In the Touch and See Room, children can touch dinosaur fossils, pet live turtles and snakes, and even sit on a whale vertebrae.

FREDERICK R. WEISMAN ART MUSEUM

333 E. River Road, Minneapolis, 612/625-9494, www.weisman.umn.edu

HOURS: Tues.-Wed. and Fri. 10 A.M.-5 P.M., Thurs. 10 A.M.-8 P.M., Sat.-Sun. 11 A.M.-5 P.M., Mon. closed

COST: Free

Map 3

The silver curves and planes of architect Frank Gehry's Weisman Art Museum float high above the Mississippi River. The Weisman—Gehry's first and so far only museum design in the United States—looks familiar to those who know his design for the Guggenheim Museum in Bilbao, Spain. But, in fact, the 1993 Weisman predates the Guggenheim and was where Gehry first started working in this distinctive style. The interior galleries—ingeniously simple and functional—are both a contrast and a complement to the wild exterior, as well as a beautiful backdrop for art. The museum's permanent collection includes an impressive number of works of American modernism, including Charles Biederman, Roy Lichtenstein, and Georgia O'Keeffe, as well as an unrivaled collection of traditional Korean furniture. The Weisman has a major expansion (also designed by Gehry) in the works.

GIBBS MUSEUM OF PIONEER AND DAKOTAH LIFE

2097 Larpenteur Ave. W., St. Paul, 651/646-8629, www.rchs.com

HOURS: May-Oct. Tues.-Sun. noon-4 P.M., closed Nov.-Apr.

COST: $7 adults, $6 seniors, $4 children

Map 6

Young newlyweds Jane and Heman Gibbs moved to this spot in 1849 and built a dugout sod hut. They later built a one-room cabin and then expanded it to an elegant Victorian farmhouse. Their Dakota neighbors—childhood friends of Jane—would often pass through the farm while traveling between their summer and winter homes. Because of this long and rich history, the small Gibbs homestead offers a varied look at the lives of both the early pioneers and their Native American neighbors. Visitors are free to walk through the buildings—including the farmhouse, sod house, school, bark lodge, and tepees—without guides, but costumed interpreters are on hand to answer questions and tell stories.

GOLDSTEIN MUSEUM

364 McNeal Hall, 1985 Buford Ave., St. Paul, 612/624-7434, http://goldstein.che.umn.edu

HOURS: Mon.-Wed. and Fri. 10 A.M.-4 P.M., Thurs. 10 A.M.-8 P.M., Sat.-Sun. 1:30-4:30 P.M.

COST: Free

© BRUCE MANNING

The Gibbs Museum of Pioneer and Dakotah Life recreates life in the 19th century.

Map 6

A Christian LaCroix dress, an Eames chair, a high-concept magazine, a Turkish woven towel—all examples of design and the way it interacts with our everyday life. This intersection of art and life was the passion of two sisters, Harriet and Vetta Goldstein, who taught at the University of Minnesota and built the foundation of what is now the Goldstein Museum. The permanent collection is not on display but can be viewed by appointment (call 612/625-2737). The museum's temporary exhibitions run the gamut from housing to fashion to surface design and may focus on a single item—the chair—or a single designer—Russel Wright—or look boldly and broadly into the future. A smaller gallery with temporary exhibitions is also open in the lobby of **Rapson Hall,** on the East Bank of the Minneapolis campus (89 Church St., Minneapolis, daily 8 A.M.–6 P.M.).

HENNEPIN HISTORY MUSEUM
2303 3rd Ave. S., Minneapolis, 612/870-1329

HOURS: Tues. 10 A.M.-2 P.M., Wed. 1-5 P.M., Thurs. 1-8 P.M., Fri.-Sun. 1-5 P.M., Mon. closed
COST: $5 adults, $1 seniors and children under 18
Map 2

Sadly often overlooked, the Hennepin History Museum takes advantage of its under-the-radar status to put on some zany exhibits: A memorable recent one traced the history of burlesque in early-20th-century Minneapolis, and another focused on everyone's favorite accessories—shoes and purses. The permanent exhibit in this 1919 mansion mixes whimsy with some somber truth. The Century of the Child displays children's toys, books, clothes, and other artifacts from throughout the 20th century, but it also looks hard at darker subjects, like child labor and child trafficking. The museum's library and collections—with photographs, maps, government documents, and ephemera—are open to researchers and the curious public Tues. 10 A.M.–2 P.M. and Wed.–Sat. 1–5 P.M. (closed Sun. and Mon.). The museum is not wheelchair-accessible.

ARTS AND LEISURE

JAMES J. HILL HOUSE

240 Summit Ave., St. Paul, 651/297-2555,
www.mnhs.org
HOURS: Tours Wed.-Sat. 10 A.M.-3:30 P.M., Sun.
1-3:30 P.M.; art gallery open Mon.-Tues. 10 A.M.-4 P.M.
COST: $8 adults, $6 seniors and students, $5 children,
children 5 and under free
Map 4

Railroad baron James J. Hill personifies
Minnesota's Gilded Age, when cities like
Minneapolis and St. Paul were exploding in
population and wealth and grand stone homes
lined St. Paul's Summit Avenue. His private
home, now owned by the Minnesota Historical
Society, is a shining example of the excesses of
that time. Completed in 1891, the house cost
nearly $1 million to build—all 36,000 square
feet of it, on five floors, with more than 40
rooms and intricate carving on nearly every
wooden surface. It was also something of a
technological marvel for its time, with modern conveniences like a security system and a
telecom. Visitors need to take a 75-minute tour
to see most of the house (tours leave on the

half hour), but three rooms in the art gallery,
with changing exhibitions, are open without
a tour.

THE LANDING

2187 Hwy. 101 E., Shakopee 763/694-7784,
www.threeriversparkdistrict.org
HOURS: Mid-May-Thanksgiving Mon.-Fri. 10 A.M.-4 P.M.,
Sat. 10 A.M.-5 P.M., Sun. noon-5 P.M.; December
weekends Sat. 10 A.M.-4 P.M., Sun. 11 A.M.-4 P.M.
COST: Weekends in summer and December $8.50
adults, $7 seniors and children 3-11, children 3 and
under free; other times $5 with a guided tour,
$3 without a guided tour
Map 7

In the tiny village of Eagle Creek, tucked in a
bend in the Minnesota River, it is still 1890.
A blacksmith shapes nails and door hinges,
women in long dresses cook at wood stoves,
and the village schoolteacher rings an enormous bell to call students to the one-room
schoolhouse. Two draft horses bring a trolley
full of guests to a small settlement of original
1840s cabins or all the way to Eagle Creek's

The Landing recreates a settlement in 19th-century Minnesota.

town square, surrounded by houses, a church, and a general store. On weekends in the summer and in December, most of the buildings are open and staffed by costumed interpreters. On summer weekdays and throughout the week in the early fall, guided and self tours are available, but without the interpreters to bring it to life. December weekends bring a merry recreation of 19th-century Christmas traditions. A mile-long hiking trail hugs the river.

◖ LANDMARK CENTER

75 5th St. W., St. Paul, 651/292-3233,
www.landmarkcenter.org
HOURS: Mon.-Wed. and Fri. 8 A.M.-5 P.M.,
Thurs. 8 A.M.-8 P.M., Sat. 10 A.M.-5 P.M., Sun. noon-5 P.M.
COST: Free
Map 4

The pink granite Landmark Center in downtown St. Paul's Rice Park is very much a local landmark. The 1902 Romanesque structure is also something of a one-stop shop for unique niche museums. The permanent exhibition Uncle Sam Worked Here tells the Landmark's own story—built as a post office, it has also served as the federal courthouse where John Dillinger and his girlfriend Billie Frechette and the St. Paul gangsters Machine Gun Kelly and Baby Face Nelson were tried. The Landmark Center Archive Gallery shows artifacts from 150 years of local postal history, and the Ramsey County Historical Society rotates exhibits, as well. (Those exhibits are all open during normal building hours.)

The Gallery of Wood Art (651/484-9094, www.woodturners.org, Tues.–Fri. 11 A.M.–4 P.M.) features exhibitions of some of the nation's finest examples of woodturning. **The Schubert Club** (651/292-3267, www.schubert.org, Mon.–Fri. 11 A.M.–3 P.M., Sun. 1–5 P.M., Sat. closed) displays musical instruments in the basement gallery space and manuscripts on the second floor. **TRACES Center for History and Culture** (651/292-8700, www.traces.org, Sat. 10 A.M.–4 P.M., Sun. noon–4 P.M., $5 adults, $4 seniors and veterans, $3 children) gives a glimpse into how Midwesterners experienced World War II.

FAVORITE LITERARY SONS

In Rice Park, in the heart of St. Paul, are modest and playful monuments to two of St. Paul's favorite literary sons – men who were, in truth, a little ambiguous about the city of St. Paul itself.

F. Scott Fitzgerald was born in St. Paul in 1896. He spent much of his childhood on the East Coast but attended St. Paul Academy for three years. After three years at Princeton, a couple in the army, and a couple at an ad agency in New York, Fitzgerald returned to his parents' house in St. Paul to revise his first novel and, having sold it, to convince Zelda that he would be able to support her. He spent the remainder of his too-brief adult years on the East and West Coasts. Fitzgerald is honored with a life-size statue by artist Michael Price. He stands casually, coat over arm, as if, as Garrison Keillor said, "you could walk up and talk to" him.

Charles Schulz was born in St. Paul a generation later, in 1922. His first comic strip, *Li'l Folks,* was published in the *Pioneer Press.* He moved to California permanently in his 30s, after he had hit it big, and made it known that much of the darkness in the early strips came from his bitter memories of his childhood in St. Paul. Despite that, St. Paul has maintained a deep fondness for Schulz. A public art project that ran from 2000 to 2004 featured individually decorated *Peanuts* characters you're likely to see around town. In Rice Park, a bronze Marcie reads on a bench with Woodstock, Schroeder plays the piano while Lucy listens, Peppermint Patty kicks a football, Sally and Linus lean on a wall, and Charlie Brown sits under a tree with Snoopy.

The Landmark Center's interior is worth a quick stop and look even if you don't have time to tour the museums. A number of concerts and special events are held in the building's five-story central atrium, as well.

(MILL CITY MUSEUM

704 2nd St. S., Minneapolis, 612/341-7555,
www.millcitymuseum.org
HOURS: Tues.-Sat. 10 A.M.-5 P.M., Thurs. till 9 P.M.,
Sun. noon-5 P.M.
COST: $10 adults, $8 seniors and college students,
$5 children ages 6-17, free ages 5 and under
Map 1

Minneapolis's reputation as the Mill City was cemented in the 1880s, with the development of a revolutionary process for milling flour that maximized quality and output, and it held its place until the flour market shifted to Buffalo and Chicago in the 1930s. The Washburn A. Mill continued to produce flour until 1965, then sat empty on the waterfront until it was mostly destroyed by fire in 1991. The Minnesota Historical Society saw the beauty and potential in the ruins of the structure, transforming it into the Mill City Museum in 2003 but keeping much of the burned-out shell. The museum itself is small, but the two multimedia presentations are must-sees on your visit: the Flour Tower Tour and *Minneapolis in 19 Minutes Flat,* a humorous look at local history by beloved Minneapolis writer and comedian Kevin Kling.

(MINNEAPOLIS INSTITUTE OF ARTS

2400 3rd Ave. S., Minneapolis, 888/642-2787,
www.artsmia.org
HOURS: Tues.-Wed. and Fri.-Sat. 10 A.M.-5 P.M.,
Thurs. 10 A.M.-9 P.M., Sun. 11 A.M.-5 P.M., Mon. closed
COST: Free
Map 2

A neoclassical surprise in a gentrifying neighborhood, the MIA welcomes half a million people every year. The museum was founded in 1883 and moved into its present home in 1915. Two additions—a 1974 minimalist wing and a 2006 Michael Graves–designed wing—contrast with the main facade. While the main collection covers nearly every period and area of the globe, the MIA is particularly well known for its Asian collection.

Families can take a break in the Family Center, where they can read a book, play a game, have a snack, and emerge ready for more art. One Sunday a month, the museum hosts special kid-oriented events. Grown-ups get the run of the museum on third Thursday evenings, with music and drinks (6–9 P.M.). A fee is charged for some special exhibitions.

Perhaps the most unusual item in the MIA's collection is the **Purcell-Cutts House,** about

The Mill City Museum (center) was built in an old flour mill.

© TRICIA CORNELL

a mile away on Lake of the Isles. Tours of the elegant Prairie School home are offered the second weekend of every month (2328 Lake Pl., 612/870-3131, $5 adults, $4 students and seniors).

MINNESOTA CHILDREN'S MUSEUM

10 7th St. W., St. Paul, 651/225-6000, www.mcm.org

HOURS: Sun.-Thurs. 9 A.M.-5 P.M., Fri. 9 A.M.-8 P.M., Sat. 9 A.M.-5 P.M.

COST: $7.95

Map 4

Kids need room to move and to explore the world on their own terms—and that is exactly what the popular Minnesota Children's Museum gives them. The fun spreads over three floors, with a good mix of standing and traveling exhibits. The tiniest visitors can hang out in the Habitot, a soft environment where kids under four can climb, slide, and play with puppets. Braver kids can don ant costumes and tunnel through the ant hill, make a thunderstorm, blow giant bubbles, and help run a Korean restaurant. Everything is built with kids in mind, such as the kid-level handrail on the stairs. At midmorning and midafternoon, an announcement invites everyone to gather on the mezzanine for story time or Big Fun—when the parachutes, carpet skates, stilts, and other big-motor toys come out. The museum is closed Mondays Labor Day through Memorial Day.

◖ THE MUSEUM OF RUSSIAN ART

5500 Stevens Ave. S., Minneapolis, 612/821-9045, www.tmora.org

HOURS: Mon.-Wed. and Fri. 10 A.M.-5 P.M., Thurs. 10 A.M.-8 P.M., Sat. 10 A.M.-4 P.M., Sun. closed

Map 2

What is one of the finest collections of Russian art doing in a renovated church in a mostly residential neighborhood of South Minneapolis? It all comes down to one man—Minnesota businessman and passionate art collector Ray Johnson, who was among the first Westerners to start poking around in attics, country homes, and artists' cluttered apartments as the Soviet Union began opening up under *glasnost* in the late 1980s. He found paintings—officially sanctioned and not—that reflected a side of Russian art most Western eyes would not recognize even today. Beyond Wassily Kandinsky and early Modernist propaganda posters, Soviet realism embraced and encouraged art that was meant to speak even to uneducated peasants. Villages, fields, forests, and other beloved icons of Russian culture are rendered realistically and sympathetically. The gallery space itself, while small, has excellent lighting and an inviting mezzanine.

PAVEK MUSEUM OF BROADCASTING

3515 Raleigh Ave., St. Louis Park, 952/926-8198, www.pavekmuseum.org

HOURS: Tues.-Fri. 10 A.M.-6 P.M., Sat. 9 A.M.-5 P.M., Sun.-Mon. closed

COST: $6 adults, $5 students and seniors

Map 7

As the story goes, Joe Pavek was an instructor at the Dunwoody College of Technology who couldn't bear to see his students tear up beautiful old radios. So he took one home. With the help of other radio enthusiasts, including the inventor of the implantable pacemaker, Earl Bakken, that one radio has now grown into a collection of broadcasting and recording equipment that fills more than 12,000 square feet. Visitors can create their own radio broadcasts in a 1960s studio, try their hand at operating a ham radio, and watch and listen to vintage television and radio programs.

SCIENCE MUSEUM OF MINNESOTA

120 Kellogg Blvd. W., St. Paul, 651/221-9444, www.smm.org

HOURS: Sun.-Wed. 9:30 A.M.-5 P.M., Thurs.-Sat. 9:30 A.M.-9 P.M.

COST: Museum admission $11 adults, $8.50 seniors and children; additional cost for Omnitheater

Map 4

Try your hand at piloting a river barge, see real human tissue through a microscope, handle dinosaur fossils, explore the science behind magnetism, and walk through a traditional Hmong house. These exhibits attract more than a million visitors a year (on weekends it can feel

ARTS AND LEISURE

like they're all in line, waiting to buy tickets). A favorite exhibit includes the artifacts from Minneapolis's beloved Museum of Questionable Medical Devices, a small private museum that donated its collections when it closed. See a phrenology machine, which divines a person's personality from the bumps on his or her head, and all manner of vibrating and electricity-conducting "medical cures." The museum is open extended hours during the summer, the winter holidays, and school vacation periods. It is closed Mondays during the fall.

The lobby is also home to the **Mississippi River Visitor Center** (651/293-0200, www .mississippirivervisitorcenter.org), where you can learn about the river, buy maps and souvenirs, and talk to National Park Service rangers about outdoor activities in the area. Check their website for the most current hours of operation.

TWIN CITIES MODEL RAILROAD MUSEUM

1021 Bandana Sq., St. Paul, 651/647-9628, www.tcmrm.org
HOURS: Tues. 11 A.M.-3 P.M. and 6-8 P.M., Wed.-Thurs. 11 A.M.-3 P.M., Fri. 11 A.M.-7 P.M., Sat. 10 A.M.-5 P.M., Sun. noon-5 P.M., Mon. closed
COST: $4, children 5 and under free
Map 6

Although the museum is small, it is situated in a wonderful and expansive old rail foundry building, listed on the National Register of Historic Places. The O-scale layout will delight train buffs, history buffs, and kids. Volunteer train enthusiasts run up to six trains at a time on the scale two-mile track. The train table is expansive, and easily viewed by kids as young as three years old. Trains from many eras, along with a few street cars, run through a scaled historic Minneapolis riverfront, the Grand Northern rail terminal, a fictitious rural town, and along the bluffs of the Mississippi (including a painstakingly detailed steamboat). The museum sells a full range of model train equipment, historic photos, and train paraphernalia—and is quite happy to let the littlest ones run wild on the toy train tables in front.

GALLERIES
FRANKLIN ART WORKS

1021 Franklin Ave. E., Minneapolis, 612/872-7494, www.franklinartworks.org
HOURS: Wed.-Sat. noon-5 P.M., Sun.-Tues. closed
Map 2

This old movie theater in Minneapolis's economically depressed Phillips neighborhood has been reborn as a culturally and artistically important place for the community. First a reputable silent movie house, then an adult movie theater, then an underground performance venue, the 120-seat theater, with many of its original features, now hosts dancers, speakers, and performance artists. The spacious main gallery stages more than a dozen one-person exhibitions a year, all drawing on some of the most cutting-edge contemporary artists from around the country.

HOUSE OF BALLS

212 3rd Ave. N., Minneapolis, 612/332-3992, www.houseofballs.com
HOURS: Daily noon-4 P.M. and 9 P.M.-midnight
Map 1

Sculptor and House of Balls proprietor Allen Christian makes art out of everything he can get his hands on, from old typewriter parts to doll heads to alabaster. Ring the doorbell, and if Christian is home, he'll invite you in to see and touch and be a part of his art-filled space. If he's not, read the question on the blackboard by the door and leave your answer on the tape recorder. If you're in downtown Minneapolis's Warehouse District anyway for a night on the town, even the outside of the gallery is worth a look.

INTERMEDIA ARTS

2822 Lyndale Ave. S., Minneapolis, 612/871-4444, www.intermediaarts.org
HOURS: Mon.-Fri. noon-7 P.M., Sat. noon-5 P.M., Sun. closed
Map 2

Inside this old auto-repair garage is the heart of a decades-old arts community uniquely tied to its own neighborhood. Each spring Intermedia Arts hosts the *Minneapolis 55408* exhibit, open to any artist living in this diverse section of town. Many, but not all, of the exhibits in the two intimate galleries have local ties. You're likely to find photography, painting, or mixed-media installations giving voice to underrepresented communities, from immigrants to teenage girls. The 125-seat theater hosts film screenings and performance art, also on the cutting edge, and Intermedia Arts is a well-known supporter of artistic endeavors throughout the city, including some of those wildly decorated "artcars" you might see around town.

MINNESOTA CENTER FOR BOOK ARTS

1011 Washington Ave. S., Minneapolis, 612/215-2520, www.mnbookarts.org

HOURS: Mon.-Sat. 10 A.M.-5 P.M., Tues. until 9 P.M., Sun. noon-4 P.M.

COST: Free

Map 1

Books are art. Books can be transformed into art. And the skills we use to construct books, like papermaking and binding, can be used in other arts. The Minnesota Center for Book Arts, which shares space with The Loft Literary Center, the independent press Milkweed Editions, a coffee shop, and the visual arts-oriented **Rosalux Gallery** (612/747-3942, www.rosaluxgallery.com, Wed.–Thurs. noon–8 P.M., Fri.–Sat. noon–5 P.M., Sun.–Tues. closed) is dedicated to all of these things. There are studios where you might find someone making paper or setting type and exhibition spaces where national and international book artists display their work. The center is the largest of its kind in the country.

NORTHERN CLAY CENTER

2424 Franklin Ave. E., Minneapolis, 612/339-8007, www.northernclaycenter.org

HOURS: Tues.-Wed. and Fri.-Sat. 10 A.M.-6 P.M., Thurs. 10 A.M.-7 P.M., Sun. noon-4 P.M., Mon. closed

Map 2

The Northern Clay Center celebrates pottery in every form, from functional to fantastical. The two-room gallery—cool and inviting in blond wood tones—hosts about a dozen exhibitions every year, drawing on works from local, national, and international artists. Programming also includes a number of popular classes and special events. The center's shop is a great place to find works of art as gifts and souvenirs, especially if you happen to come during the American Pottery Festival in the fall or in time for the special sale around the winter holidays.

ROGUE BUDDHA GALLERY

357 13th Ave. NE, Minneapolis, 612/331-3889, www.roguebuddha.com

HOURS: Wed.-Thurs. noon-4 P.M., Fri.-Sat. 3-8 P.M.

Map 3

This storefront gallery in Nordeast Minneapolis regularly makes local and national lists of the best places to see and buy art. In fact, owner and artist Nicholas Harper was recently named to CNN's list of artists to watch. As a rule, the artists displayed push the edges of visual arts, with raw images and unusual techniques. Harper himself takes traditional portraiture and distorts it, adding a disturbing emotionality. The gallery space is pure Nordeast: tin ceilings, rough floors, and an ersatz feel.

SOAP FACTORY

518 2nd St. SE, Minneapolis, 612/623-9176, www.soapfactory.org

HOURS: Thurs.-Fri. 2-8 P.M., Sat.-Sun. noon-5 P.M.

Map 1

Judging from the venue alone, the Soap Factory might not seem likely to last. The cavernous 40,000-square-foot space in the old National Purity Soap Company is almost exactly the way the soap makers left it long ago. And there is no heating system. At all. And yet the gallery celebrated its 20th anniversary in 2008 and has watched the former warehouses around it transform into coveted real estate, while garnering nationwide attention as a leader in contemporary art. To get around the heating the Soap Factory programs furiously between April and November and shuts down for the winter. Exhibitions often combine media and artists thematically, exploring questions of identity and perception, rather than showcasing a particular artist.

SOO VISUAL ARTS STUDIOS

2640 Lyndale Ave. S., Minneapolis, 612/871-2263, www.soovac.org

HOURS: Wed. noon-6 P.M., Thurs. noon-8 P.M., Fri. noon-6 P.M., Sat.-Sun. noon-4 P.M.

Map 2

The distinctive murals on the facade of the Soo Visual Arts Center signal that this is a bold contemporary art space. It's also a particularly accessible one. The shows are curated with a particular sense of whimsy—based, for example, around a single play on words—and may feature artists entrenched in the local art scene or take a chance on the relatively new. The gallery's shop, Soo Too, is an excellent place to find affordable paintings, prints, jewelry, and other pieces by emerging local artists.

TEXTILE CENTER

3000 University Ave. SE, Minneapolis, 612/436-0464, www.textilecentermn.org

HOURS: Mon.-Thurs. 10 A.M.-7 P.M., Fri.-Sat. 10 A.M.-5 P.M.

Map 3

Originally a Ford dealership, the Textile Center has big, beautiful front windows and a wide-open gallery space for works by textile artists of all stripes—knitters, quilters, weavers, and those that defy description. There's also a small library with a collection of books and periodicals on all fabric arts (open to everyone; members can check books out). The Textile Center is also a great place to connect with its member organizations, such as the Weavers Guild of Minnesota and the Minnesota Quilters.

THEATER
BEDLAM THEATRE

1501 6th St. S., Minneapolis, 612/341-1038, www.bedlamtheatre.org

Map 3

Bedlam's shows have been called fun, avant garde, daring, gutsy, risky, radical, and, in

some corners, obscene. It's not a place for those looking for refined, classical entertainment. Any given season—a fluid, yearlong affair—is likely to include all types of performance, from plays to dance to puppetry to music and, most often, a mix of all of the above. In 2007, the theater moved into new digs with a main stage and a lounge, for an even greater mix of performances, and a restaurant and bar, quickly becoming the hip new theater hangout.

BRAVE NEW WORKSHOP

2605 Hennepin Ave. S., Minneapolis, 612/332-6620, www.bravenewworkshop.org

Map 2

The Brave New Workshop lays claim to the title of longest-running satirical theater company in the United States, with roots that go back to 1958. The company has been performing at its present location since 1965 (with a brief hiatus in St. Paul). Nationally known performers got their start here, including Al Franken, who took the political and social satire he learned on to *Saturday Night Live* and the political arena. Some of the show titles tell you this is a no-holds-barred place—*The Lion, the Witch, and the War Hero; or Is McCain Able?, Bushwacked II: One Nation Under Stress,* and *Martha Stewart's Prison Jamboree.* In addition to the main shows, the BNW troupe does improv Tuesday at 7:30 P.M. ($1), Friday at 10 P.M. ($8), and Sunday at 8 P.M. ($1).

BRYANT-LAKE BOWL

810 Lake St. W., Minneapolis, 612/825-8949, www.bryantlakebowl.com

Map 2

It's a restaurant! It's a bowling alley! It's a cabaret-style theater! Bryant-Lake Bowl is most definitely all three, as well as a South Minneapolis institution—and you never know what you'll find in the theater. It might be a family-friendly production on a weekend morning. It might be bawdy improv late in the evening. It might be sociopolitical commentary presented by Dykes in Drag. It might be a roundtable discussion on environmental science. It might be hard to hear over the din of bowling balls and restaurant chatter. It might be so mesmerizing that even the bowlers and the diners stop to listen in.

CENTENNIAL SHOWBOAT

Harriet Island, St. Paul, 612/625-4001,
http://showboat.umn.edu

Map 4

A classic paddleboat with a Victorian jewel box theater is the perfect setting for classic vaudeville-style theater, full of melodrama, physical comedy, and witty musical numbers appropriate for the whole family. (Actually, the paddleboat itself isn't all that old: It was built in 2000 after a fire destroyed the 19th-century original.) Since 1958 (Minnesota's centennial year), the Showboat Players, all University of Minnesota students, have staged one play a summer on the water. Alums include many who are still favorites on Twin Cities and national stages. Dinner is served at 6:30 on Fridays and Saturdays, with advance reservations.

◖ CHILDREN'S THEATRE COMPANY

2400 3rd Ave. S., Minneapolis, 612/874-0400,
www.childrenstheatre.org

Map 2

In 2003 the Children's Theatre Company won a Regional Theatre Tony Award—the first children's theater company to do so—and that was even before its lush new wing opened to the public and attracted even larger audiences and greater loyalty among Twin Cities fans. No matter what your age, this is a great place to see theater (and there's no shame in buying a ticket for yourself without a kid in tow). The main proscenium stage holds lavish, sophisticated sets for the big musical productions, and the innovative, welcoming Cargill Stage is the perfect place to introduce the youngest kids to theater. In fact the Children's Theatre is a leader in this area: Shows for preschoolers are geared expertly toward tiny attention spans, and actors always introduce themselves and then, like Pied Pipers, lead the kids personally into the theater.

© BRUCE MANNING

The Guthrie Theater fits in comfortably among the old industrial buildings in downtown Minneapolis's milling district.

◖ GUTHRIE THEATER

818 2nd St. S., Minneapolis, 612/377-2224,
www.guthrietheater.org

Map 1

When Sir Tyrone Guthrie decided the country needed a resident repertory theater, Minneapolis won him over. The Guthrie opened in 1963 with *Hamlet* and has stayed true to its founder's artistic vision ever since. The company's bread and butter is classics—from Shakespeare to Noel Coward—but the Guthrie is also known for world premieres from leading contemporary playwrights.

In 2006, the Guthrie moved into the industrial-looking building overlooking the Mississippi River. Three stages allow for a wide range of programming, from experimental works by new playwrights in the Dowling lab to classics on the asymmetrical thrust stage and contemporary American works on the proscenium stage.

You don't need tickets to a show to enjoy the Guthrie. Come for lunch or dinner at Cue or the Level Five restaurant, or walk out the "endless bridge" over the river. Take a self-guided

ARTS AND LEISURE

audio tour narrated by Guthrie artistic director Joe Dowling ($5 a person) or schedule a guided architectural tour in advance (call 612/225-6172). Backstage tours are also available Friday, Saturday, Sunday, and Monday mornings and after some weekend matinees ($10 adult, $6 student or senior).

IN THE HEART OF THE BEAST PUPPET AND MASK THEATRE
1500 Lake St. E., Minneapolis, 612/721-2535, www.hobt.org
Map 2

Towering larger-than-life-size puppets, marionettes, hand puppets, and multi-actor dragons interact with live actors on fantastical, folk art–inspired sets. In the Heart of the Beast takes social issues—like water conservation, immigration, even the Holocaust and the Korean DMZ—and makes them understandable for the whole family. It also stages fun folk tales from around the world and an annual Nativity play. Housed in a 1930s art deco theater, In the Heart of the Beast has been around since 1973 and is also the force behind the annual May Day parade on the first Sunday of May, when massive puppets made and carried by community members wind down to Powderhorn Park.

JUNGLE THEATER
2951 Lyndale Ave. S., Minneapolis, 612/822-7063, www.jungletheater.org
Map 2

The Jungle is a snug and intimate theater with just 150 seats and a reputation, since its very first season in 1991, for excellent contemporary plays. A season at the Jungle—which runs January through December, rather than September through June—might include plays by David Mamet or Craig Wright (who wrote for the television series *Six Feet Under* and whom the Jungle nurtured), or an adaptation of Dylan Thomas. Whether comedy or drama, you can expect a tight and emotionally charged production with a finely tuned, if not showy, set. And you are allowed to bring your wine or coffee or cookie from the lobby concession stand into the theater—a friendly touch.

MINNESOTA HISTORY THEATRE
30 10th St. E., St. Paul, 651/292-4323, www.historytheatre.com
Map 4

The Minnesota History Theatre's bland name doesn't do it justice. Far from a high school field trip destination, the theater has built a nationwide reputation for supporting new work and staging world premieres. As the theater itself describes it, these are "real plays about real people": from the infamous Duluth lynchings to the founding of Minneapolis's Guthrie Theater to *Wellstone!*, about the late progressive senator from Minnesota. A single season might explore several decades or even centuries of Minnesota's past, from the points of view of all of the state's myriad ethnic groups. A mix of newcomers and longtime stalwarts in the Twin Cities theater scene take on the roles, always admirably.

MIXED BLOOD THEATRE
1501 4th St. S., Minneapolis, 612/338-0937, www.mixedblood.com
Map 3

Founded in 1976 by 22-year-old Jack Reuler, Mixed Blood showcases works by and for groups that are often left out of traditional theater—immigrants, people of color, people with disabilities, the elderly, and more. The converted fire station in the Cedar-Riverside neighborhood—itself an ever-shifting portrait of the area's newest immigrant groups—is on the small side and a bit rickety, but the atmosphere is always one of shared discovery and pure joy in the theater. You may feel like everybody but you knows somebody, but grab a glass of wine in the lobby, strike up a conversation, and that will soon change.

OLD LOG THEATRE
5185 Meadville St., Greenwood, 952/474-5951, www.oldlog.com
Map 7

Seeing a show at the Old Log is a little like going to a classy summer camp. Near Lake Minnetonka, the grounds do in fact include an old log cabin. The season, which runs year-round, includes new comedies and musicals that appeal across generations, and the annual holiday show is especially popular. Arrive with plenty of time to enjoy the fireplace in the lobby and some time on the broad porch. If you plan to dine at the theater, make reservations when you buy your ticket and choose your entrée ahead of time. Your choices will include classics worthy of the Old Log's ambience, like prime rib, walleye, and roast crown of pork.

OPEN EYE FIGURE THEATRE

506 24th St. E., Minneapolis, 612/874-6338,
www.openeyetheatre.org
`Map 2`

The intimate Open Eye Theatre seats barely 100 people in a single room that doubles as the lobby, but what goes on on the tiny stage seeks to reach beyond the confined space. Performers combine storytelling with music and puppetry, and some of the Twin Cities' most innovative playwrights and actors, including beloved NPR commentator Kevin Kling, have made Open Eye their local theater home. While the neighborhood is a little dodgy, the well-tended garden in back is a quiet haven.

PARK SQUARE THEATER

20 7th Pl. W., St. Paul, 651/291-7005,
www.parksquaretheatre.org
`Map 4`

When it was founded in 1974, the Park Square Theatre set out to bring the classics to St. Paul. But after a couple of decades of Shakespeare and Wilde, the theater decided to go bolder—and more professional at the same time—with more new and contemporary plays each season. The Park Square is still more staid and traditional than other theaters you might find in the Twin Cities, and the venue itself feels a little anonymous, but the draw here is the extraordinary level of talent on stage. The majority of the cast in any show is likely to be made up of Actor's Equity members, many on a break from the Guthrie or bigger shows on the coasts.

© BRUCE MANNING

The Park Square Theater in downtown St. Paul stages contemporary plays.

PENUMBRA THEATRE

270 Kent St. N., St. Paul, 651/224-3180,
www.penumbratheatre.org
`Map 5`

Penumbra Theatre, founded in 1976, is proud to be one of just three African American theaters in the United States to offer a full season of plays. The theater, founded by Twin Cities theater-scene stalwart Lou Bellamy, who remains at its head today, helped launch the career of Pulitzer Prize–winning playwright August Wilson. By 2013, Penumbra plans to stage all 10 plays in Wilson's *Century Cycle*—a decade-by-decade look at the 20th-century African American experience. Each December, the popular *Black Nativity* show combines gospel music, storytelling, and dance.

STAGES THEATER

1111 Mainstreet, Hopkins, 952/979-1111,
www.stagestheatre.org
`Map 7`

Children's literature comes to life in Hopkins, staged by kids and for kids. While some of the plays are obvious choices for the stage—like *Seussical* and *The Wizard of Oz*—others are delightful surprises, like children's classics *Goodnight Moon* and *The Paper Bag Princess*. Young audiences relate well to the actors on stage, all ages 10–21, and many will be inspired to join the Stages theater classes.

STEPPINGSTONE THEATRE

55 Victoria St. N., St. Paul, 651/225-9265,
www.steppingstonetheatre.org

Map 5

When SteppingStone moved into its own beautiful performance space in a converted neoclassical church in 2007, the Twin Cities gained yet another superb place to introduce young audiences to theater. The theater seats 430—twice the capacity of SteppingStone's old space in the Landmark Center, which regularly sold out—and offers an awe-inspiring first theater experience. The kids on stage may be young (actors are 8–18 years old), but their training, professionalism, and talent show in plays with themes from around the world. During the holiday season, watch for *The Best Christmas Pageant Ever*.

CONCERT VENUES
FITZGERALD THEATER

10 Exchange St. E., St. Paul, 651/290-1200,
www.fitzgeraldtheater.org

Map 4

The Fitz, as it is affectionately known, is the home of the quintessentially Minnesotan radio show *A Prairie Home Companion*. Unless they're on the road—as they often are—Garrison Keillor and the gang perform "The News from Lake Wobegon," "Guy Noir, Private Eye," "The Lives of the Cowboys," and other beloved skits and songs live, right here, on Saturday evenings. Keillor hobnobs with the audience a bit before the familiar music rises up ("Oh, hear that old piano, from down the avenue . . ."), and loyal fans can't get enough of watching him schlump around the stage in his trademark red sneakers. On other nights, the historic theater, built in 1910 and owned by Minnesota

© BRUCE MANNING

The Fitzgerald Theater is the long-time home of the radio show *A Prairie Home Companion*.

Public Radio, hosts musical and comedy acts, speakers, and authors in the popular "Talking Volumes" book discussion series.

HENNEPIN THEATRE DISTRICT

Hennepin Ave., Minneapolis, 612/673-0404,
www.hennepintheatredistrict.org

Map 1

The Hennepin Theatre District comprises four theaters. **Hennepin Stages** (824 Hennepin Ave.) is the place to see modern comedies—often bawdy. **The Orpheum** (910 Hennepin Ave.) hosts Broadway shows and big names in music, while the **Pantages** (710 Hennepin Ave.) is a popular concert and comedy venue and the **State Theatre** (805 Hennepin Ave.) does a little bit of everything. The four share a central box office at the State Theatre and an online booking system.

The Orpheum, Pantages, and State all share a rich history. In the 1910s and '20s, Hennepin Avenue was the place to see vaudeville in lavish theaters. At the end of the 1920s, vaudeville's popularity had declined and the

© TRICIA CORNELL

The Orpheum sits at the heart of the Hennepin Theatre District.

theaters embraced movies. By the 1970s, Hennepin Avenue was no longer a safe destination. The buildings sat empty for many years before being refurbished and revived by the Hennepin Theatre Trust. Call 612/373-5696 to arrange a tour of any of the buildings ($5 per person).

NORTHROP AUDITORIUM

84 Church St. SE, Minneapolis, 612/624-2345, www1.umn.edu/umato

`Map 3`

When Northrop Auditorium was built in 1929 on the campus of the University of Minnesota, promoters called it "the Carnegie Hall of the Midwest." Today the building's soaring classical pillars are an iconic image. From the very early seasons, when Rachmaninoff, Stravinsky, and other luminaries made this their Midwest tour stop, the Northrop has attracted the top names in classical music, jazz, dance, and literature. The 4,800-seat auditorium looks much as it did more than eight decades ago, and the Northrop Organ has been recognized for the high quality of its preservation. The massive organ, Æolian-Skinner's Opus 892, has nearly

ALL THE LAUGHS ARE ABOVE AVERAGE

By the time *A Prairie Home Companion* debuted, in a format similar to today's, in 1974, Garrison Keillor had been dabbling for a few years in radio, hosting a morning program on Minnesota Public Radio. Public-supported radio was a new and innovative concept at the time, but young Keillor looked to an older tradition, the Grand Ole Opry, as a model for his live variety show. Since then, *A Prairie Home Companion* has become permanently intertwined with the identity of its creator and, for many, with Minnesota.

On Saturday evenings, 5–7 P.M. central time, nearly four million people listen to Keillor, Guy's All-Star Shoe Band, actors Tom Keith, Fred Newman, Sue Scott, and Tim Russell, and his many guest stars. Many wait eagerly for the stories that always begin "It's been a quiet week in Lake Wobegon, my hometown," others for Guy Noir and the Ketchup Advisory Board. Crowds pack the bandstand for the annual show at the Minnesota State Fair each year, and tickets for the live broadcasts sell out fast. Another popular event, usually held in early October, is the street dance and meatloaf supper, held outside the theater after the broadcast.

The show was off the air for a few years, from 1987 to 1993, while Keillor lived abroad and then in New York. Its home is now the Fitzgerald Theater in St. Paul, though Keillor takes the whole show on the road for many weeks a year. Tickets for the Saturday night live broadcasts and for the Friday preview shows are available from the **Fitzgerald Theater** (651/2901221, http://fitzgeraldtheater.publicradio.org).

ARTS AND LEISURE

7,000 pipes, ranging from the size of a pencil to 32 feet tall. Members of the university community look forward to the free summer concerts on the lawn, held weekdays in June and July, and featuring a wide range of music.

ORCHESTRA HALL

1111 Nicollet Mall, Minneapolis, 612/371-5656,
www.minnesotaorchestra.org

Map 1

With the Minnesota Orchestra, you are as likely to hear Copland and Bernstein as Mahler and Shostakovich. The 100-plus-year-old orchestra has a history of commissioning original pieces and nurturing new American composers. You're also likely to hear some Sibelius or other Nordic-influenced work, thanks to music director Osmo Vänskä, who hails from Finland and has found a very receptive audience for the sounds of his homeland here in the Twin Cities. Sommerfest in July and August brings a particularly audience-friendly schedule.

The building itself, with its trademark blue pipes, is a landmark, anchoring the south end of Nicollet Mall. In front of Orchestra Hall, Peavey Plaza is part massive fountain, part village square. It fills with music at lunch time and in the early evening nearly all summer long.

ORDWAY CENTER FOR THE PERFORMING ARTS

345 Washington St., St. Paul, 651/224-4222,
www.ordway.org

Map 4

On any given day on the Ordway stage, you're likely to find a nationally known modern dance troupe, the beloved local ensemble VocalEssence, a big Broadway show, or the musicians of one of the three major musical organizations that make their home here—the Minnesota Opera, the St. Paul Chamber Orchestra, or the Schubert Club. In fact, the massive glass-fronted building facing St. Paul's lovely Rice Park hosts more than 500 varied performances a year in the 1,900-seat Main Hall and the 300-seat McKnight Theater. Although the building, funded by local arts-lover Sally Ordway Irvine, opened in 1985, the plush two-story lobby with its thick carpet and dazzling chandeliers has a certain forgotten elegance.

THE O'SHAUGHNESSY

2004 Randolph Ave., St. Paul, 651/690-6700,
http://oshaughnessy.stkate.edu

Map 5

The College of St. Catherine's impressive theater—fully overhauled in 2003—attracts big-name national acts in its Women of Substance Series (this is a respected women's college after all). Over the past decade or so, Allison Kraus, Sweet Honey and the Rock, Maya Angelou, Madeleine Albright, and many, many more have played and addressed packed houses. The venue itself is conducive to a great show: Steeply raked, comfortable seats bring audience members even closer to the performers on stage.

TARGET CENTER

600 1st Ave. N., Minneapolis, 612/673-1600,
www.targetcenter.com

Map 1

Home to the **Minnesota Timberwolves** basketball team and the WNBA team the **Minnesota Lynx,** the Target Center is a major landmark in downtown Minneapolis. When it opened in 1990, it was the first entirely non-smoking arena in the country. Along with St. Paul's **Xcel Energy Center,** this is where you can expect to see major national and international tours when they come to town, including pop stars of all stripes, family shows, wrestling, and even the Cirque du Soleil. The arena seats about 20,000 for basketball games and 13,000–19,000 for concerts. Also in the building, which is connected to the skyway system, is a **Lifetime Fitness** gym and the **NBA City Restaurant.** Call 612/673-1600 to find out if a parents room—where chaperones of event ticket holders can wait during shows—will be available.

XCEL ENERGY CENTER

199 Kellogg Blvd. W., St. Paul, 651/265-4800,
www.xcelenergycenter.com

Map 4

Home of the **Minnesota Wild** hockey team, the Xcel Energy Center opened in St. Paul in 2000 to give Minneapolis's Target Center a run for its money. And it has, selling out nearly every hockey game, snagging major international acts of all stripes, and attracting the 2008 Republican National Convention as well as 2008 Democratic presidential contender Barack Obama's first speech as the presumptive nominee. The arena seats around 20,000 and offers two large restaurants—**Headwaters Bar and Grill** and **Iron Range Grill,** both named for geographical features of hockey-crazy northern Minnesota—and dozens of concession stands. During some events, a family room is available, where chaperones of ticketholders can hang out for free. Call in advance to find out if this is the case.

INDEPENDENT CINEMA
HEIGHTS THEATER
3951 Central Ave. NE, Minneapolis, 763/788-9079, www.heightstheater.com
Map 3

The atmosphere is 100 percent classic—from the heavy velvet drapes to the chandeliers, orchestra pit, and Wurlitzer organ—but the shows are a mix of high-quality first-run Hollywood movies, foreign films, and unforgettable classics. You might even get to hear the organ on Friday and Saturday nights, sometimes before a show, sometimes accompanying a silent film. But don't expect the usual half-hour lead-up to the main attraction: The Heights shows no advertisements and just a few previews. This is the Twin Cities' oldest continually operated movie theater, in business since 1926.

OAK STREET CINEMA
309 Oak St. SE, Minneapolis, 612/331-3134, www.mnfilmarts.org
Map 3

When University of Minnesota students and other series film buffs want to see Akira Kirosawa retrospectives, the latest political skewer piece, or whatever's hot in France and Italy, they're likely to look for it at the Oak Street Cinema. This is also the hub for the annual **Minneapolis-St. Paul International Film Fest,** held in the spring in venues throughout town. The building, near the University campus, is a bit rundown, inside and out, but perhaps that's most fitting for the gritty film noir that's its stock in trade. While financial troubles have forced Minnesota Film Arts to cut back on the schedule, this is still a Minneapolis institution.

RIVERVIEW THEATER
3800 42nd Ave. S., Minneapolis, 612/729-7369, www.riverviewtheater.com
Map 2

The lobby of the Riverview today looks much as it did when it was built in 1948, with mirrored and tiled walls, midcentury sofas and lamps, marble tabletops, and a copper fountain. The screening room is updated, but only for comfort, with modern stadium seating in front of the classic stage. This is one of the last places in the Twin Cities to see second-run Hollywood films for just $3. The theater is also a popular venue for film festivals and special showings.

UPTOWN THEATRE
2906 Hennepin Ave., Minneapolis, 612/825-6006, www.landmarktheatres.com
Map 2

The Uptown Theatre's 50-foot-tall marquee is a landmark on Hennepin Avenue. The large single-screen theater—the largest screen in the Twin Cities—shows indie films, often of the lefty documentary sort, as well as fun Saturday midnight showings of cult classics. After a week or two at the Uptown, movies often move on to the screens at the larger sister theaters **Lagoon Theatre** (1320 Lagoon Ave., 612/825-6006) and **Edina Cinema** (3911 50th St. W., 651/649-4416). The Lagoon and Edina, with four and five screens of their own, also show foreign, independent, and small studio films.

ARTS AND LEISURE

Festivals and Events

Map 2

High festival season starts in June, and the events—big and small—fill summer weekends with art, music, and revelry until it all wraps up in the "Great Minnesota Get-Together," the Minnesota State Fair, on Labor Day. It's no surprise that the fall festival schedule is thin in Minnesota: We're all bushed. The energy level picks up again in the winter, however, with skiing, skating, and that odd and energetic ritual—more than a century old—known as the Winter Carnival.

WINTER

FOOD AND WINE EXPERIENCE

Minneapolis Convention Center, 1301 2nd Ave. S., Minneapolis, 612/371-5800, www.foodwineshow.com

For one long weekend in February, when nearly everyone is sick of winter's outdoor pursuits, but nobody is yet ready to start dreaming of outdoor grilling and beachwear, the **Minneapolis Convention Center** (1301 2nd Ave. S., Minneapolis, 612/335-6025, www .minneapolisconventioncenter.com) becomes foodie central. Everyone connected with food in the Twin Cities—from restaurateurs to wine suppliers to critics to serious eaters—finds their way to the Food and Wine Experience. While eating, drinking, and socializing are the order of the day, seminars and learning lunches are also popular. Tickets to these and to the main event all sell out fast.

MACY'S HOLIDAY SHOW

700 Nicollet Mall, 8th floor, Minneapolis, www.macys.com/events

HOURS: Mid-November-Christmas Mon.-Fri. 8 A.M.-8 P.M., Sat. 9 A.M.-9 P.M., Sun. noon-6 P.M.

COST: Free

Department store holiday window displays are popular in many cities, but the Macy's on Nicollet Mall takes the concept one step further: The 8th-floor auditorium is transformed into an elaborate animatronic storybook during the winter holiday season. Visitors walk along an elaborately decorated path, surrounded by glitter and magic, as the story unfolds around them in individual displays. Past shows have been based on *The Nutcracker, Mary Poppins,* and *Pinocchio.* During peak hours—weekends and evenings—lines can snake for hours. Avoid them by visiting during the work day if you can.

MACY'S HOLIDAZZLE

Nicollet Mall between 12th St. and 4th St., Minneapolis, www.macysholidazzle.com

HOURS: Thanksgiving-Christmas Thurs.-Sun. 6:30 P.M.

Four nights a week, throughout the winter holiday season, families line Nicollet Mall to get a glimpse of Santa Claus. The big man himself is preceded by marching bands, brightly lit floats, and hundreds of costumed marchers, wearing tens of thousands of light bulbs. The whole parade takes about half an hour. To get the best view, stake out a spot on one of the skyways overlooking the mall to get the best view—and get there early.

ROCK THE CRADLE

Minneapolis Institute of Arts, 2400 3rd Ave. S., Minneapolis, 888/642-2787, www.mpr.org

One Sunday in January, a rocking party takes over the **Minneapolis Institute of Arts** and the adjacent **Children's Theatre.** But, in this case, the raucous guests are toddling tots and their families, dancing at the kids' disco, going on air with DJs from Minnesota Public Radio's hip music station The Current, and exploring their musical future at the "instrument petting zoo." The fun, sponsored by MPR, stretches from morning nap time to dinner, and—given South Minneapolis's family-heavy demographics—it's wall-to-wall kids the whole time.

◖ WINTER CARNIVAL

Rice Park, St. Paul, 651/223-4700, www.winter-carnival.com

Map 4

A fateful insult in the late 1800s launched a beloved festival that now draws about 350,000 visitors a year. That's when a New

York newspaper reporter called St. Paul—then the fastest-growing city in America—"another Siberia, unfit for human habitation in the winter." St. Paulites took up the challenge and, since 1886, have spent much of the month of January thoroughly enjoying the winter weather. While the Ice Palace is the biggest draw, it isn't built every year, for economic and weather reasons. The entire city of St. Paul bustles with ice skating, ice carving contests, and a 5K run and half marathon (yes, outside). Warm up in the Hotdish Tent with Minnesotans' favorite comfort food: hot dish (that's casserole to the rest of the country). Most of the action centers around Rice Park and the Landmark Center, but events are also held at other locations.

SPRING
ART-A-WHIRL
Nordeast Minneapolis, 612/788-1679, www.nemaa.org
If ever an art event could be said to fill a neighborhood, this is it. Art-A-Whirl, held the third weekend in May, takes over Northeast Minneapolis, where much of the city's art scene fled after condo developers discovered downtown's Warehouse District. Each year, 500 artists—sculptors, painters, photographers, glass artists, and even musicians—open their studios and galleries to the public. Other local businesses get in on the fun, and area bars book local bands through much of the weekend. To get your bearings, start at the welcome booth at 13th and Marshall or on Quincy Street NE. Trolleys run periodically around the main sites.

CINCO DE MAYO
Cesar Chavez St., St. Paul, 651/222-6347, www.districtdelsol.com
The roots of the Latino population on St. Paul's West Side go back well over 100 years, and a strong community is still centered on the area around Cesar Chavez Street. That is undoubtedly the place to be during the first weekend in May, when over 100,000 people show up to celebrate Cinco de Mayo, the historic celebration of the 1962 Battle of Puebla, when the Mexican army defeated the invading

French. Music, art, sports, and children's activities fill Cesar Chavez between Wabasha and Anita Streets on Friday evening and all day Saturday during this decidedly family-oriented event. And food—of course there's food and plenty of it—from a salsa tasting contest to street vendors.

EDINA ART FAIR
50th St. and France Blvd., Edina, 952/922-1524, www.edinaartfair.com
For some in South Minneapolis, the Edina Art Fair, generally held the first weekend of June, signals that, yes, summer really is coming and it is time to start shoehorning in all the outdoor activities, bratwurst, and kettle corn that the brief, intense warm weather demands. More than 400 artists bring their paintings, pottery, quilts, and more to the juried sale, squeezed onto the intersection of 50th Street and France Avenue in this decidedly upscale shopping district. Live music, cooking demonstrations, fashion shows, and food vendors help visitors make a real day of it, although

Cinco de Mayo festival

© MEETMINNEAPOLIS.COM

ARTS AND LEISURE

there isn't much to keep antsy kids satisfied. This is a good time to watch for real deals at the 50th and France boutiques, many of which hold sidewalk sales.

FESTIVAL OF NATIONS

Rivercentre, 175 Kellogg Blvd. W., St. Paul, 651/647-0191, www.festivalofnations.com

The Latvian children's dance troupe takes the stage after the Japanese drums and sometime before the Karen dancers. Somebody wanders by with a Finnish rice pie in one hand and a Somali *sambuza* in the other. This is St. Paul's Rivercentre for four days in early May. And, while the festival has changed and grown a great deal as Minnesota has grown and its ethnic makeup has changed, this happy fusion has been going on in some form since the first Festival of Nations in 1932, sponsored by the International Institute of Minnesota. More than 90 ethnic groups are represented, with food booths, dance and musical performances, and craft demonstrations. Come hungry and ready to see something you've never seen before, no matter where you're from.

MINNEAPOLIS-ST. PAUL INTERNATIONAL FILM FESTIVAL

Theaters around Minneapolis, 612/331-3134, www.mspfilmfest.org

When an 80-something curmudgeonly film buff puts together an international film festival for over two decades—not quite singlehandedly, but certainly infusing his own unique spirit—you get a great depth of film choices and a whole lot of quirk. M-SPIFF, as it's known, has been curated by local fixture Al Milgrom for nearly as long as it's been around. This late-April festival, which some years includes as many 150 films from 50 countries, has a good mix of international Oscar nominees and long shots from obscure Baltic countries. (Actually, given Minnesota's history and the artistic proclivities of the audience, there's always a good selection from Scandinavia and the Baltics.)

The **Childish Film Festival,** which runs concurrently, is a refreshingly unexpected selection of films, many suited for children as young as preschoolers, showing a quieter, funnier, more independent sort of childhood.

SUMMER
AQUATENNIAL

Venues throughout the Twin Cities, 612/376-7669, www.aquatennial.org

Teams clad in swimsuits, shorts, or elaborate costumes launch boats into **Lake Calhoun** in South Minneapolis. First to make it across wins, of course, but points are also given for creativity. Sounds unremarkable and a little dull. Except that these boats are all made—100 percent—out of paper milk cartons. (How does this work? Easy: Wash 'em out, seal 'em tight, and do some math. Each carton supports about four pounds.) The milk carton boat race is but one reason to look forward to Aquatennial, a festival spread out over the third full week of July and across the city. The Torchlight Parade through downtown Minneapolis, the crowning of the Aquatennial royalty, the water ski shows on the Mississippi, the fireworks, the

The sandcastle-building competition on the beach at Lake Calhoun is a much-awaited part of the annual Aquatennial celebration.

block party, and the triathlon are other good reasons, as is the general sense that summer has truly hit its peak.

BASILICA BLOCK PARTY
Basilica of St. Mary, 88 17th St. N., Minneapolis, 612/317-3511, www.basilicablockparty.com

Party at the Catholic Church? You bet. This is one of the biggest parties of the summer. Every July, about 25,000 people pack into the area around the Basilica of St. Mary for two days of music. The good-natured crowds and party atmosphere—as well as the traffic and the music itself—spill over into the rest of downtown and even beyond. In the past, headliners have include Ziggy Marley and the Jayhawks. You'll want to buy your tickets early; they tend to sell out.

DRAGON FESTIVAL
Phalen Lake Park, St. Paul, www.dragonfestival.org

St. Paul's Phalen Lake Park is a beautiful backdrop for this annual pan-Asian celebration, which began in 1996 and now attracts more than 10,000 visitors. The highlight of the two-day festival is the dragon boat races. Two dozen 20-person teams—many of which have never paddled a dragon boat before—race the long, skinny boats across the lake. Each boat is 40 feet long and just 4 feet wide and glides swiftly across the water, as dragon boats have done for two and a half millennia. The entire festival, held in mid-July, is free and includes Japanese *taiko* drumming, dragon dancing, martial arts, and plenty of children's activities.

FRINGE FESTIVAL
Throughout Minneapolis, 612/872-1212, www.fringefestival.org
COST: Fringe button $3, plus individual tickets for each show: $12 adults, $10 seniors, $5 children

Minnesota's Fringe Festival is among the largest of its kind in the nation. More than 150 productions in 14 locations go up during the 11-day festival held in late July and early August. Up to 50,000 tickets have been sold. You'll find comedy, drama, and the truly uncategorizable, but keep in mind that this is

potluck: Productions are chosen by lottery rather than jury, so to say you'll find some gems and some duds is wild understatement. Die-hard Fringe fans hit dozens of shows, so don't be surprised if everybody waiting in line seems to know each other already. In recent years, a limited number of shows for kids and teens have been added.

GRAND OLD DAY
Grand Ave., St. Paul, 651/699-0029, www.grandave.com/grandoldday

How much fun can one neighborhood pack into one day? On Grand Avenue, on a Saturday in early June, they can pack in more than you ever thought possible: more than three dozen outdoor concerts on nine stages (some free, some for a nominal ticket price), four footraces, an art fair, a parade, and, oh, yeah, a quarter of a million people—all in the space of 20 city blocks. The beer flows freely on some blocks, while others are given over to petting zoos and bouncy castles. Devotees of the Grand Old Day plan far in advance to cope with the exhaustion that inevitably follows. Grand Avenue is known as St. Paul's favorite shopping district, and with the purchase of a $5 "grandee" button, you get discounts for most of the summer at retailers all up and down Grand Avenue.

JUNETEENTH
Theodore Wirth Park, Minneapolis, 612/238-3722, www.juneteenthminnesota.org

The day kicks off with a free community breakfast, followed by a parade with drum corps and community leaders, and then turns into something resembling the biggest family reunion you've ever seen. Theodore Wirth Park is filled with music, games, dancing, reminiscences, and the telling of shared histories as 60,000 people gather for the day. Juneteenth—June 19th—marks the day in 1865 federal troops rode into Texas to enforce the emancipation of slaves, nearly three years after the Emancipation Proclamation. While it is primarily an African American celebration, all are welcome.

MINNESOTA ORCHESTRA SOMMERFEST

1111 Nicollet Mall, Minneapolis, 612/371-5656,
www.minnesotaorchestra.org

This festival features three weeks of music, from opera to jazz to pop and kids' performers, some of it in the Orchestra Hall, much of it is on Peavey Plaza out front. And for one long night in July, music continues for a full 24 hours in the **Macy's Day of Music** celebration. Every genre is represented as the music starts outside on the plaza and then moves inside for the wee hours and then outside again as soon as the sun comes up, culminating in a children's concert, often with a big name in the world of kiddie pop. All of the outdoor shows are free, but many of the concerts in Orchestra Hall require tickets.

◖ MINNESOTA STATE FAIR

State Fairgrounds, 1265 Snelling Ave. N., St. Paul, 651/288-4400, www.mnstatefair.org
HOURS: 6 A.M.–10 P.M.
COST: $11 adults, $9 seniors, $8 kids 5-12, children under 5 free
Map 6

If you are anywhere near St. Paul during the 12 days leading up to Labor Day, the Minnesota State Fair is not to be missed. The 320-acre fairgrounds becomes the third-largest city in Minnesota, with around 200,000 visitors each day. What began as an agricultural fair in 1855 has evolved to include more than 100 musical acts, a massive midway, butter carving, daily marching band parades (at 2 P.M.), and nightly fireworks (around 10 P.M.). Fuel up with a gut-bedeviling array of foods, including more than 60 served on a stick.

With all that going on and only 9,000 parking spaces at the fair itself, driving and parking in the northwest corner of St. Paul is pretty tight. You're better off using one of the dozens of park-and-ride lots around the Twin Cities (many are free, and buses operate 8 A.M.–10 P.M. daily). Call 651/603-6808 after August 1 for park-and-ride information.

In Minnesota, you know summer is over when you have eaten your last deep-fried cheese curd.

The Minnesota State Fair is the highlight of summer in Minnesota.

TASTE OF MINNESOTA

Harriet Island, St. Paul, 651/772-9980,
www.tasteofmn.org

Minnesota—or, at least, Minnesota as sampled at Taste of Minnesota—may be tasty, but it is certainly not healthful: beer-battered fries with cheese, pork chops on a stick, crab cakes on a bun, and—if you have room for dessert—mini donuts. The justification must be that it takes a lot of energy to muscle your way through the crowds and get the best seats for the free concerts and nightly fireworks held over the July 4th weekend. (Or, perhaps everyone digging into a corn dog participated in that morning's 5K?) Every year an astonishing array of popular artists from all genres and eras finds its way onto the Taste of Minnesota schedule, prompting the whole state to remark, "So *that's* what happened to REO Speedwagon."

TWIN CITIES HOT SUMMER JAZZ FESTIVAL

Throughout Minneapolis and St. Paul,
www.hotsummerjazz.com

Outside of jazz circles, the Hot Summer Jazz Festival doesn't get a whole lot of attention—it competes with milk carton boat races, after all—but a total of 75,000 people find their way to the concerts. For 10 days in July, more than two dozen nationally known jazz acts come to the Twin Cities to play shows in eight locations in front of very appreciative audiences. The bulk of the action is at the **Dakota Jazz Club and Restaurant** in Minneapolis and **Artists' Quarter** in St. Paul, but free outdoor concerts are offered on **Peavey Plaza** in Minneapolis and in **Mears Park** in St. Paul, as well as at other locations around the cities.

TWIN CITIES PRIDE

Loring Park, Minneapolis, 612/305-6900,
www.tcpride.org

Every June, the Twin Cities Pride festival kicks off with a picnic in Como Park in St. Paul and culminates in a concert, day-long festival, and parade in Minneapolis. In the 10 days in between, look for a full schedule of concerts, readings, and get-togethers throughout the cities.

Most of the activity is centered around Loring Park, where the Twin Cities' first GLBT march took place in 1972. Revelers fill downtown bars and nightclubs during the final weekend, so you're likely to get swept up in the celebration even if it's not what you came here for.

UPTOWN, POWDERHORN, AND LORING PARK ART FAIRS

Art lovers in the Twin Cities once faced a problem: art-fair fatigue. The **Uptown Art Fair** (Lake St. and Hennepin Ave., 612/823-4581, www.uptownminneapolis.com/art-fair)—by far the biggest of the summer—had its considerable charms. And they wanted to enjoy the edgier **Loring Park Art Fair** (Loring Park, 612/203-9911, www.loringparkartfestival.com) and the small, community-oriented **Powderhorn Art Fair** (Powderhorn Park, 612/722-4817, www.powderhornartfair.org). But three art-fair weekends in one summer was enough to put them off the experience of wandering from one pottery-filled booth to the next. The solution? Combine forces. Now all three art fairs are held the second weekend in July, although they remain separate events with separate identities. Metro Transit provides free bus service for all three art fairs. And art lovers can sate themselves on paintings, photographs, sculptures, and more, while cherry picking the best of the musical offerings (probably Uptown) and food (definitely Loring Park).

FALL

MEDTRONIC TWIN CITIES MARATHON

Downtown Minneapolis to downtown St. Paul,
763/287-3888, www.mtcmarathon.org

The Twin Cities Marathon has been called "the most beautiful urban marathon in America"—albeit by the organizers, who have a considerable stake in the matter. But there's undoubtedly something to the claim. The course starts at the Metrodome in downtown Minneapolis and then winds its way around four lakes in South Minneapolis before heading back north along the Mississippi to St. Paul, where it ends at the State Capitol. The flat and shady course attracts top runners from all over the world and is an Olympic qualifying race. Every year the race is booked to its full capacity of 10,500 runners, and a quarter million spectators cheer them on. Family events and 1-mile, 10-mile, and 5K races are also held. Out-of-towners shouldn't worry about the weather: Minnesota is beautiful in October, with highs in the mid-60s. Perfect for running. Or watching.

MINNESOTA RENAISSANCE FESTIVAL

12364 Chestnut Blvd., Shakopee, 800/966-8215, www.renaissancefest.com

HOURS: Late Aug.-Sept. Sat.-Sun. 9 A.M.-7 P.M.

COST: $19.95 adults, $10.95 children

For a half dozen weekends a year, a medieval village emerges in the southern suburb of Shakopee. Minstrels and maidens wander the streets. Jugglers, clowns, and fire-eaters perform. Potters, jewelers, and tailors hawk their wares. Giant turkey legs and funnel cake are consumed. In fact, a lot of turkey legs are consumed: This is the largest renaissance festival in the United States and it attracts about 275,000 people every year. And, as medieval villages go, this is a pretty big one, with 275 craft booths, 120 food sellers, and about 700 costumed entertainers wandering around, most of them remarkably faithful to the festival's demands for period dress and staying in character. Watch for themed weekends each year, celebrating Irish, Scottish, and Italian heritage, and more. The festival is also open on Labor Day itself.

Sports and Recreation

Despite their urban centers and urbane attitudes, both cities make it easy to get outdoors, hit the water, find solitude in the woods, breathe clean air, and get pleasantly sweaty—without ever leaving the city itself. And outdoor pursuits barely slow down in the winter. Locals switch out their Rollerblades for cross-country skis and their canoes for ice fishing houses when the weather gets a little colder, but they certainly don't hide indoors.

PARKS

COMO PARK

Horton Ave. and Lexington Pkwy. N., St. Paul, www.stpaul.gov

HOURS: Daily dawn-11 P.M.

Map 6

Como Park is the center of outdoor life in St. Paul, a beloved haven of nearly 400 varied and well-kept acres. More than 2.5 million people come every year to play tennis, soccer, baseball, football, golf, or mini golf; to swim in the outdoor pool or fish on Como Lake; or just explore the grounds, with sculptures, ponds, a waterfall, and a labyrinth. The **Historic**

Streetcar Station (1224 Lexington Pkwy. N., Sun. noon–4 P.M.) includes a small exhibit on the history of streetcars in the Twin Cities. Park visitors can bring picnics, use public grills, or grab a sandwich at the **Como Lakeside Pavilion café** (1360 Lexington Pkwy. N., 651/488-4920). This is also where you can rent canoes and paddleboats for a ride on Como Lake and hear concerts several nights a week during the summer.

GOLD MEDAL PARK

2nd St. S. and 11th Ave. S., Minneapolis

HOURS: Daily 6 A.M.-10 P.M.

Map 1

A spiral pathway ascends a 32-foot grass-covered mound in the center of Gold Medal Park, which takes its name from a brand of flour once milled right here in the former mills district. From there, you get terrific views of the bridges across the Mississippi River, St. Anthony Falls, and downtown Minneapolis. The eight-acre park, created in 2007, is a popular lunch spot for office workers in the area and a welcome spot of green in downtown.

FRISBEE GOLF

Frisbee of all sorts, from ultimate to disc golf, is well established in the Twin Cities. In fact, there are more than two dozen disc golf courses in the greater metro area. The best known course, which is among the most highly rated in the Twin Cities, is in **Kaposia Park** (1028 Wilde Ave., South St. Paul, www.southstpaul.org), a beautiful park in its own right. 'Bee enthusiasts like the well-marked holes, which start in an open field and then wind through the woods. In the west metro area, **Bryant Lake Park's course** (6800 Rowland Rd., Eden Prairie, 763/559-9000, www.threeriversparkdistrict.org) is also highly regarded. Maintained by the Three Rivers Park District, it is groomed to a degree that will surprise DIY disc golfers, with wood chip "greens" around the baskets. A day pass costs $3, available online or by calling the park. Discs are available for rent, as well.

© PAT LAUREL/ST. PAUL CVA

Harriet Island Regional Park

HARRIET ISLAND REGIONAL PARK

Harriet Island, Minneapolis, www.stpaul.gov
HOURS: Daily dawn-11 P.M.
Map 4

While the channel of the Mississippi River separating Harriet Island from the bank filled in long ago, the park retains the name. A stage and a wide, open lawn host a number of massive public events (including Taste of Minnesota), but even when there's nothing in particular going on, this is a popular place to stroll along the riverbank and boardwalk, looking up at the skyline of downtown St. Paul. The **Clarence W. Wigington Pavilion,** the beautiful limestone building combining art deco and classic elements at the center of the park, was designed by the nation's first African American municipal architect. Wigington (1883–1967) was a senior designer for the city of St. Paul for 34 years, and 60 of his buildings are extant today. Harriet Island is also the place to board **Padelford Cruises** and the **Centennial Showboat.**

HIDDEN FALLS PARK AND CROSBY FARM PARK

1415 Mississippi River Blvd. S., St. Paul, 651/632-5111,
www.stpaul.gov
HOURS: Daily dawn-9 P.M.
Map 5

These two wooded havens line the deep bend on the St. Paul side of the Mississippi for several miles and nearly connect where Highway 5 crosses the Mississippi. Nearly undeveloped except for miles of paved paths and shady picnic pavilions, both offer quiet, up-close-and-personal access to the Mississippi and its wildlife that's hard to find even in these two cities that hug the river so tightly. There is, in fact, a man-made waterfall in Hidden Falls Park, as well as a convenient boat launch area for canoes.

LORING PARK

15th St. W. and Willow St. S., Minneapolis,
www.minneapolisparks.org
HOURS: Daily 6 A.M.-10 P.M.
Map 1

A decade or so ago, Loring Park was the place suburban parents warned their kids

ARTS AND LEISURE

against when they came into Minneapolis to see a show. Today it's a great place to recommend to visitors for a stroll around the lake, a game of shuffleboard or horseshoes, or a moment to relax in the gardens. (This is also where you'll find downtown's only off-leash dog park.) Loring Park, created in 1883 and named after one of the architects of Minneapolis's public park movement, is among the city's oldest parks. Today it is connected by a footbridge to the Walker Art Center and Sculpture Garden and by the Loring Greenway to Nicollet Mall. On Monday nights in the summer, come for a concert and an outdoor movie at dusk.

LYNDALE PARK

4124 Roseway Rd., Minneapolis, 612/230-6400,
www.minneapolisparks.org
HOURS: Daily 6 A.M.-10 P.M.
Map 2

Lyndale Park slopes gently down to the parkway circling Lake Harriet and contains several delightful gardens in its 60 acres. A favorite is the **Lyndale Park Rose Garden,** designed in 1907 by Theodore Wirth, an early and influential Minneapolis parks superintendent. Rose lovers can see 100 varieties of plants laid out in neat rows (sadly encircled by chain-link fencing). The best time to see the roses in bloom is mid-June through early September. The **Peace Garden** was created through the efforts of dedicated neighbors and combines some elements of a traditional Japanese garden and of a formal rock garden. Two large stones in the garden were brought in from the cities of Nagasaki and Hiroshima, Japan. **Stevie Ray's Improv Company** has been performing in the park on summer Sundays (shows at 5 and 7 P.M., free) for nearly two decades.

MILL RUINS PARK

West River Pkwy. and Portland Ave., Minneapolis,
www.minneapolisparks.org
HOURS: Daily 6 A.M.-10 P.M.
Map 1

At the base of the Stone Arch Bridge, on the

© BRUCE MANNING

The Heffelfinger Fountain is the highlight of the Lyndale Park Rose Garden.

banks of the Mississippi River, you can see several layers of Minneapolis history exposed. Archaeologists have been digging here since the 1980s, when several road construction projects were underway. When they found railway footings and extensive traces of the water power and milling systems, they decided to preserve them for the public to explore. Today, interpretive signs lead from the wooden-plank section of West River Parkway down to the river and around catwalks that bring you close to the remains of the old mills.

MINNEHAHA FALLS

4825 Minnehaha Ave. S., Minneapolis, 612/230-6400,
www.minneapolisparks.org
HOURS: Daily 6 A.M.-10 P.M.
Map 2

The 53-foot waterfall that inspired Henry Wadsworth Longfellow to write *The Song of Hiawatha* is the main attraction at this popular park, but there is so much else to do. Wander the gardens in the upper park or take

Mill Ruins Park, on the bank of the Mississippi, showcases the exposed remains of an old flour mill.

a slightly more strenuous hike through the wild lower park.

Rent a bike, including four- and six-person surreys (Wheel Fun Rentals, 612/729-2660, www.wheelfunrentals.com, Memorial Day–Labor Day daily 10 A.M.–sunset; May, Sept., and Oct. weekends only). Visit the historic **Princess Depot,** a small transport museum (4801 Minnehaha Ave. S., 612/230-6400, Sun. 2–6 P.M., free), or the **John H. Stevens House** (Memorial Day–Labor Day, Sun. noon–4 P.M.), the first wood-frame house built west of the Mississippi, or the replica of **Longfellow's home** (4800 Minnehaha Ave. S., 612/230-6520, Memorial Day–Labor Day Mon.–Fri. 10 A.M.–2 P.M.), where you can learn about the history of Minneapolis's park system. There's also a disc golf course, a wading pool, and fish tacos at **Sea Salt.**

THEODORE WIRTH PARK

1339 Theodore Wirth Pkwy., Minneapolis, 612/230-6400, www.minneapolisparks.org

HOURS: Daily 6 A.M.–10 P.M.

Map 2

Named for the father of the Minneapolis Park System, Theodore Wirth Park is the jewel in a very beautiful crown. By far the city's largest park at 759 acres, the park is nearly as large as New York City's Central Park (843 acres). In addition to two golf courses, park visitors will find a small sandy beach for swimming on Wirth Lake and a quiet pier for boating and fishing on Birch Pond. During the winter the popular winter sports area (1301 Theodore Wirth Pkwy., Minneapolis, 763/522-4584, Mon.–Fri. 5–9 P.M., Sat. 10 A.M.–9 P.M., Sun. 10 A.M.–6 P.M.) offers inexpensive snowboarding, cross-country skiing, and snowtubing, as well as classes and equipment rental.

But the real wonders of the park are things you'll find almost nowhere else: the five-acre **Quaking Bog,** shaded by tall tamarack trees, and the 15-acre **Eloise Butler Wildflower Garden,** home to 500 plant species and 140 bird species.

ARTS AND LEISURE

WATER POWER PARK

Hennepin Island, 206 Main St. SE, Minneapolis,
800/895-4999, www.waterpowerpark.com
HOURS: March-Nov. 8 A.M.-30 min. after sunset
Map 1

This is as close as you can possibly get to St. Anthony Falls: Standing on the viewing platform, you can feel sometimes feel the spray from one of the best natural sources of water power in the nation. One of the country's first hydroelectric plants was built here on Hennepin Island more than 120 years ago, and to this day Xcel Energy operates a plant on the island that powers downtown Minneapolis. Water Power Park, with walking paths and interpretive signs, is owned by Xcel Energy and open to the public as a provision of their license to operate here. You can enjoy a stroll and a picnic in the park on your own, but for a tour of the plant, call 800/895-4999.

SPECTATOR SPORTS

The most sports-obsessed Twin Citians will often claim—usually when supporting public financing for stadiums or ballparks—that without their professional sports franchises, Minneapolis and St. Paul would be nothing more than a cold Omaha. (U.S. Senator Hubert H. Humphrey actually coined the phrase in 1976 when arguing for funding for the Metrodome, soon to be abandoned by the baseball Twins and still—for now—home to the football Vikings.) There's no need to insult the wonders of Omaha, whatever they may be, and there's no need to discount the deep and diverse charms of the Twin Cities at the expense of four mostly hapless big league franchises and a host of smaller and collegiate squads.

The Minnesota Twins last won the World Series in 1991 (and first won it in 1987, more than 25 years after they came into existence), and no Minnesota professional team has taken home its sport's biggest title since. The Minnesota Vikings have a well-deserved reputation for futility, being the first team to play and lose in the Super Bowl four times. The Minnesota Timberwolves are rightfully most closely associated with Kevin Garnett, who,

after years of yeoman-like service, left for the Boston Celtics and promptly earned a championship ring. The Minnesota Wild, a recent addition to the NHL, feature a roster made up almost exclusively of Canucks sneaking south. The Wild have had two recent strong playoff runs and can boast of having sold out every home game in franchise history, but Lord Stanley's cup has yet to make St. Paul its home.

There are a few notable exceptions to this recent history of spirited failure. The University of Minnesota's men's and women's hockey teams continue a proud tradition on the ice that has made Eveleth, Minnesota, the "Capital of American Hockey" and the home of the U.S. Hockey Hall of Fame; they have each won two titles since 2002. (If you include the University of Minnesota Duluth, the women have won six.) The feather in Minnesota's hockey helmet is the now-deceased, much-loved Herb Brooks, considered by many to the best hockey coach of all time and the man running the show for 1980's Miracle on Ice.

Baseball
MINNESOTA TWINS

Hubert H. Humphrey Metrodome, 900 5th St. S.,
Minneapolis, 612/375-1366, http://twins.mlb.com
Map 1

The Minnesota Twins will move to new Target Stadium, on the west side of downtown Minneapolis, with a beautiful downtown view and connections to bus and rail transit, in time for Opening Day in 2010. Their previous home, the Hubert H. Humphrey Metrodome on the east side of downtown Minneapolis, will serve them through that day and remain the home of the Minnesota Vikings. The highs of a pair of World Series wins in 1987 and 1991, spearheaded by local heroes Kirby Puckett, Kent Hrbek, Frank Viola, and Jack Morris, have not been reached recently, although the team is consistently competitive. An afternoon in the outfield will set you back $7–12, with better seats topping out around $55, but it is a fine way to spend a summer day, even more so once the new open-air stadium opens.

ST. PAUL SAINTS
Midway Field, 1771 Energy Park Dr., St. Paul,
651/644-6659, www.saintsbaseball.com
`Map 6`

The second-level league success of the
Minneapolis Millers (who disbanded in 1960
but featured, at times, Ted Williams, Willie
Mays, and Carl Yastrzemski) is still going
strong with the St. Paul Saints. The Saints
play at Midway Field, a small, old-style open-
air park about halfway between downtown
Minneapolis and downtown St. Paul. Owned
by Mike Veeck, the son of legendary Major
League Baseball showman Bill Veeck, the
Saints play decent ball in the North Division
and provide a tremendous amount of entertainment—from the usual (beer, sunny days) to the
unusual (a mascot pig delivering game balls
while spectators getting haircuts in the stands
cheer), all the while embodying Veeck's mantra
that "Fun is Good." Tickets ($5–12) are fairly
hard to come by and should be bought as early
as possible.

Football
GOLDEN GOPHERS FOOTBALL TEAM
TCF Bank Stadium, 2009 University Ave. SE,
800/846-7437 or 612/624-8080,
http://stadium.gophersports.com
`Map 3`

The University of Minnesota Golden
Gophers are about to be rewarded with a
new on-campus horseshoe stadium, TCF
Bank Stadium, opening September 12, 2009.
The Gophers will leave the Tupperware-like
feel of the Metrodome to march across the
river and play nestled among labs and dorms
right in the heart of Dinkytown. It is hoped
that the new venue will produce a change
of direction for a program that hasn't won
a conference championship since 1967. The
days of Bronko Nagurski are long gone, but
fierce rivalries for Floyd of Rosedale (the
pig statue trophy awarded to the winner
of the Minnesota-Iowa game) and for Paul
Bunyan's Axe (awarded to the winner of the
Minnesota-Wisconsin game) continue. The
Battle of the Little Brown Jug (Minnesota-

Michigan) has only gone for the Gophers
three times since 1978. The hilarious tro-
phies bespeak a fun, if collegiately drunken,
afternoon.

MINNESOTA VIKINGS
Hubert H. Humphrey Metrodome, 900 5th St. S,
Minneapolis, 651/989-5151, www.vikings.com
`Map 1`

The Minnesota Vikings play in the Metrodome
in Minneapolis but are perpetually angling
for a new stadium. Home games are incredibly loud affairs, starting from Ragnar the
Viking's motorcycle (or snowmobile) entrance
and continuing on as the hordes in Helga Hats
(purple hats, white horns, yellow braids) hol-
ler for gridiron greatness. Greatness has been
in short supply of late, but high hopes start
up every September. The famed Purple People
Eater defenses, anchored in the 1970s by current Minnesota Supreme Court Justice Alan
Page, are gone, as are trips to the Superbowl.
Minnesotans remain committed fans of
the team and archenemies of neighboring
Wisconsin's Green Bay Packers, and regularly
spend up to $135 for tickets (the cheap seats
can sometimes be had for $15), with another
$20 thrown in for parking—and that's before
anyone decides to eat anything or buy a souvenir Helga Hat.

Hockey
GOLDEN GOPHERS HOCKEY TEAMS
Mariucci Arena, 1901 4th St. SE, Minneapolis,
612/625-8365, www.gophersports.com
`Map 3`

Mariucci Arena at the University of Minnesota,
the only hockey facility to make *Sports
Illustrated*'s list of top campus sporting venues,
is home to top-shelf men's collegiate hockey.
Just across the street, the women's team plays
in Ridder Arena, the first facility nationwide
exclusively dedicated to women's hockey. The
Golden Gophers are perpetual contenders, the
men having brought home back-to-back tro-
phies from the Frozen Four in 2002 and 2003
and the women doing the same in 2004 and
2005. Both teams feature, nearly exclusively,

U.S. POND HOCKEY CHAMPIONSHIPS

There's a difference between the hard-checking, high-stakes hockey of the NFL and hockey as nature intended it: outside, on any frozen body of water, with kids skating their hearts out in the freezing cold before the winter sun disappears.

That is the hockey celebrated at the U.S. Pond Hockey Championships (www.uspondhockey.com). Conceived by a couple of grown-up kids who had skated their hearts out on Minnesota's frozen lakes and ponds, the first tournament, in 2006, attracted 120 teams from across the country. It was an instant success: *Sports Illustrated*, ESPN, and even Jeopardy! have all taken notice.

The three-day tournament has grown to more than 200 games and moved from its original location on Lake Calhoun to Lake Nokomis in South Minneapolis, where volunteers groom as many as 25 rinks.

talent from the state of Minnesota, which instills an even greater sense of pride in the already rabid college hockey fan. The women's tickets are more affordable (topping out at $10 compared with $35), but the games are no less entertaining. Getting to a men's game requires more planning and a higher tolerance for alcohol-fueled spectators.

MINNESOTA WILD
Xcel Energy Center, 199 Kellogg Blvd. W., St. Paul, 651/265-4800, www.xcelenergycenter.org
Map 4

Minnesota's first NHL team was the beloved Minnesota Northstars, who hightailed it for Dallas (and became the Stars) in 1993. In 2000, the Minnesota Wild brought professional hockey back to Minnesota, showcasing the record-holding Slovenian right wing Marián Gáborík since their inaugural season. With an eight-year sell-out streak at the state-of-the-art Xcel Energy Center, it is no

surprise that tickets ($25–100) are hard to come by.

The X is also home to the boys' and girls' state high school hockey tournaments. There is hardly a better way to get a true Minnesota sports experience than to spend an evening watching teams from around the Twin Cities and from greater Minnesota duke it out for statewide supremacy for three days in March. Check out www.mhshl.org for current information.

Basketball
GOLDEN GOPHERS BASKETBALL TEAMS
Williams Arena, 1925 University Ave. SE, Minneapolis, 612/625-3007, www.gophersports.com
Map 3

The University of Minnesota Golden Gophers, men and women, provide an opportunity for the sports enthusiast to don maroon and gold and enjoy Big Ten basketball and the occasional run in March Madness (the women reached the Final Four in 2004). The teams play in Williams Arena (a.k.a. "the Barn"), located on the East Bank of the university. Students sitting in "the Barnyard" can cheer on the state's highest paid employee, men's coach Tubby Smith, whose first-year earnings of $1.75 million bought a return to the upper half of conference standings but not to the big dance. The women's team misses Minnesota product Lindsay Whalen, and Minnesotans still talk about the Connecticut Sun star reverentially, but this is nevertheless an entertaining evening.

MINNESOTA LYNX
Target Center, 600 1st Ave. N., Minneapolis, 612/673-1600, www.wnba.com/lynx
Map 1

During the NBA off-season, there are still plenty of chances to watch basketball at the Target Center. The Minnesota Lynx, the WNBA franchise attached to the Minnesota Timberwolves, play 34 games (17 at home) during the regular season, which runs May through August. The Lynx have been mediocre for years, with one playoff victory to their credit since inception in 1999. On the plus side, however, guard and gold-medal Olympian Seimone Augustus is one of the most exciting players in the league, and the team's games are affordable, fun, and a welcome option for mothers and fathers to show their kids that professional athletes aren't all men. Tickets ($10–60) are easy to come by: The crowd averages 7,000 a game, about one-third of the Target Center's capacity.

MINNESOTA TIMBERWOLVES

Target Center, 600 1st Ave. N., Minneapolis, 612/673-1600, www.nba.com/timberwolves

`Map 1`

Professional basketball returned to Minnesota in 1987—the Minneapolis Lakers having long ago become the oddly named Los Angeles Lakers. The Minnesota Timberwolves call Minneapolis's Target Center home, and from the rafters hangs a single division title (2004). From 1995 to 2007 the Timberwolves were synonymous with Kevin Garnett, one of the most gifted and loyal players to play the game. Although the team made the playoffs from 1997 to 2004, it peaked in 2004, losing in the conference finals. Garnett took home the league MVP, stuck it out for a few additional seasons, then headed to the Boston Celtics. When the Timberwolves play the Celtics, the Target Center sells out (not a regular occurrence these days) and Garnett is greeted with great warmth. The current squad, among the youngest in the NBA, is not without its charms but is many years off from becoming a force in the league.

Soccer
MINNESOTA LIGHTNING

Elizabeth Lyle Robbie Stadium, 1745 Cleveland Ave. N., St. Paul, 651/917-8326, www.mnlightning.com

`Map 6`

Minnesota's professional women's soccer team, the Minnesota Lightning, plays in the Midwest Division of the United Soccer League's W-League. The league was founded in 1995, and the Lightning joined in 2006. While the

team advanced to the semifinals in its first year and made the finals in the second, it didn't qualify the third time around, putting it right in the middle of the league. The women play at Elizabeth Lyle Robbie Stadium on the St. Paul campus of the University of Minnesota. The stadium, which holds about 1,000 spectators, is one of the nation's finest women's soccer facilities. It is named for the first woman owner of a professional sports franchise in the United States. In the mid-1970s, Robbie owned the Miami Toros, which relocated and became the Minnesota Strikers in the mid-1980s, before disbanding in 1988. The women's season runs May through July.

MINNESOTA THUNDER

National Sports Center, 1700 105th Ave. NE, Blaine, 763/785-5600, www.mnthunder.com

`Map 7`

The Lightning's male counterpart, the Minnesota Thunder, plays in the United Soccer League's First Division, one step down the hierarchy from Major League Soccer. In 2008, the team moved back to the polished, modern National Sports Center in the northwestern suburb of Blaine after five seasons at the grittier James Griffin Stadium in St. Paul. The move to the urban core was an attempt to reach more soccer-loving populations that didn't quite pan out. The men's season runs April through September, and about 3,000 people turn out for games in a stadium with a capacity of 8,500. Since the team's creation in 1990, it has won a single championship, in 1999, and reached the final a handful of times. The 2005–2008 seasons have been particularly dispiriting, with the Thunder placing toward the bottom of the division every year.

BICYCLING

The Twin Cities have a well-deserved reputation for a vibrant cycling culture and a strong infrastructure for two-wheeled transportation. St. Paul maintains 101 miles of paved off-street trails, 24 miles of dirt trails, and 30 miles of dedicated bike lanes. Minneapolis has 40 miles of dedicated bike lanes on city streets and 82

ARTS AND LEISURE

© BRUCE MANNING

Cyclists take advantage of the fall weather at Minnehaha Park.

miles of off-street bike trails, with plans to add 45 miles in 2009–2010.

According to the U.S. Census Bureau, Minneapolis has the second-highest percentage of bike commuters—2.4 percent—right behind Portland, Oregon (3.5 percent) and ahead of Seattle (2.2 percent). The Minneapolis Department of Public Works estimates that city bike lanes and trails see about 10,000 cyclists a day—and, yes, while some park their bikes for the winter, many more bike year-round. One thing that makes all this biking possible is that all Metro Transit buses have two bike racks in front, available for use for no extra charge. On the light rail, cyclists can walk their bikes onto the trains and stand with them or hang them in designated areas.

Downloadable maps of bike paths are available for Minneapolis (www.ci.minneapolis .mn.us) and St. Paul (www.ci.stpaul.mn.us). The Metropolitan Council has region-wide maps at www.metrotransit.org.

Trails
GATEWAY TRAIL
Trail runs from State Capitol to Pine Point Regional Park, www.gatewaytrailmn.org
Map 4

St. Paul's beloved rail-to-trail venture is the Gateway Trail, which connects the city to Pine Point Regional Park, just north of Stillwater. The 18-mile ride starts one mile north of the State Capitol building and passes through the northeastern suburbs of Maplewood, North St. Paul, and Oakdale. Eventually supporters hope to expand it all the way to the river town of Taylors Falls. A horse path runs parallel to a 10-mile section of the trail, which follows the old Soo rail line. A nice stopping point for those who don't want to make the whole 36-mile round-trip is at **Lake Phalen Regional Park,** which has a nice trail network of its own. Although the narrow paved trail can get crowded, riding through the woods feels like an instant escape from the city.

GRAND ROUNDS NATIONAL SCENIC BYWAY
Start at Minnehaha Park,
www.minneapolisparks.org/grandrounds
Map 2

One of the most beautiful and accessible rides—and a good way to see Minneapolis's leafy green residential neighborhoods—is the Grand Rounds National Scenic Byway, a 50-mile ring of interconnected bike trails. It loops around the outer edges of the city, taking in Theodore Wirth Park, the Chain of Lakes in Southwest Minneapolis, about 10 miles of riverfront on the Mississippi, downtown Minneapolis, and the parkways of north Minneapolis. The Grand Rounds, the only urban trail system designated as a National Scenic Byway, was part of the original vision for the Minneapolis Park System. That route has always had a three-mile "hole" in it, north of I-94 and east of the Mississippi River. In 2008, the Minneapolis Park Board approved plans to acquire the rights-of-way to complete the circle, though it may be years before the funding and road improvements necessary are in place.

LUCE LINE TRAIL

10th Ave. N. and Vicksburg Ln., Plymouth, www.luceline.com
Map 7

For a more ambitious ride, set out on the 63-mile Luce Line Trail, which heads northwest to the small town of Cosmos. The trail originally started in the Minneapolis suburb of Plymouth, but work is underway to extend the trail southward to Theodore Wirth Park in Minneapolis, adding another eight miles to its length. The former railroad line is paved with crushed limestone for most of the way, with a dirt surface in the last few miles. The trail is very flat, owing to its past as a railroad bed and, of course, to Minnesota's very bicycle-friendly terrain. A parallel path for horses runs alongside.

MIDTOWN GREENWAY

Trail runs from Chowen Ave. to West River Pkwy., South Minneapolis, www.midtowngreenway.org
Map 2

The Midtown Greenway, beloved by commuters, families, and recreational cyclists alike, crosses South Minneapolis from the lakes to the Mississippi River, along a rail corridor (running alongside active rail lines in one stretch). Planners hope that the greenway will eventually cross the river, connecting cyclists to St. Paul. The easy, almost entirely flat 5.7-mile ride runs parallel to

WINTER CYCLING

Yes, it's cold. And, yes, Minnesota sees a great deal of snow. But not all locals lock their bikes up for the winter. A growing community of winter bikers are out to convince their fellow cyclists to join them. If you hit the roads in the winter, there are a few things you need to keep in mind. With snowbanks piled high on both sides, city streets get considerably narrower. Stick to dedicated bike lanes or, better yet, to off-street trails. Always use a blinking light and reflectors. The sun sets early, and even winter daylight can be deceptive. Use a fat-tired bike, ride slowly, and give motorists a wide berth: They've got plenty to concentrate on when the roads are slick. And, of course, dress in layers and cover up exposed skin.

busy Lake Street, with plenty of opportunities to stop for a bite or a drink. One particularly recommended stop is at the **Midtown Global Market.** There are about two dozen access points along the trail, many right at street level, and the path crosses the light rail line, making it a fun, car-free way to get into downtown Minneapolis. The western end of the greenway hooks up to the South Loop of the **Southwest Regional LRT Trail,** if you want to extend your ride.

SOUTHWEST REGIONAL LRT TRAIL

Trailheads on 8th Ave. N. in Hopkins and off Lake St. W. in Minneapolis, www.threeriversparkdistrict.org
Map 7

Heading west from Minneapolis, the two loops of the Southwest Regional LRT Trail are maintained by the Three Rivers Park District. The 10-foot-wide crushed limestone trails total over 30 miles. The North Loop begins in the near suburb of Hopkins, just north of Mainstreet, and ends in the tiny town of Victoria, 15 miles away, with great views of Lake Minnetonka along the way. The South Loop hooks right up to the end of

ARTS AND LEISURE

Minneapolis's Midtown Greenway and ends 15.5 miles away in Chanhassen, passing along Minnehaha Creek and the Minnesota River Valley. Both loops pass through several parks with picnic and restroom facilities. If all goes according to plan, the trails will share part of the corridor with a commuter light rail line from Minneapolis through Hopkins and Minnetonka to Eden Prairie, currently slated to open in 2015.

Events
MINNEAPOLIS BIKE TOUR
612/230-6400, www.minneapolisbiketour.com

Two annual events—the Minneapolis Bike Tour and the St. Paul Classic—bring together avid bikers and newbies each year, and both take advantage of Minnesota's temperate, picture-perfect September weather (though registration tends to close much earlier in the summer, so you need to plan ahead). Both are noncompetitive—downright supportive, as a matter of fact—and offer the unique chance to ride on city streets free from traffic. The Minneapolis Bike Tour is organized by the Minneapolis Park Board. The 14-mile short route circles Southwest Minneapolis's Chain of Lakes. The 37-mile route largely follows the Ground Rounds Scenic Byway. There are refreshment stops along the way and a big "Aftour" party at the end of the route.

ST. PAUL CLASSIC
952/882-3180, www.bikeclassic.org

Riders in the St. Paul Classic can choose a 15-mile course, a 30-mile course, or a 45-mile course that combines the two. All three start at St. Thomas University. The short course (and hence the longest course, as well) follows the Mississippi River and then climbs up a hill so steep into downtown St. Paul that most riders choose to walk it (no shame there!). The 30-mile course also follows the river, then climbs up to **Indian Mounds Park** and heads north to Lake Phalen and **Como Lake,** in some of St. Paul's most beautiful neighborhoods. You'll know this is not a competitive race when you see cyclists happily parking their bikes at the numerous rest stops to enjoy coffee and pastries and listen to music. A portion of the fees supports the Neighborhood Energy Commission, which promotes energy-efficient living.

Bike Shops and Rentals
CALHOUN RENTAL
1622 Lake St., Minneapolis, 612/827-8231, www.calhounrental.com
HOURS: Daily 9 A.M.-7 P.M.
Map 2

If you're riding the Grand Rounds, Calhoun Rental, just a block from Lake Calhoun, is a great place to start—you can rent your bike and be right on your way. They've got reasonable rates on all kinds of bikes, including tandems and recumbents, and even in-line skates and child trailers, but rentals require a major credit card and photo ID. Look for the unassuming sign on the side of what looks like a residential house.

FREEWHEEL MIDTOWN BIKE CENTER
2834 10th Ave. S., Minneapolis, 612/238-4447, www.freewheelbike.com
HOURS: Mon.-Fri. 6:30 A.M.-8 P.M., Sat. 9 A.M.-6 P.M., Sun. 9 A.M.-5 P.M.
Map 2

Right on the Midtown Greenway, which is a convenient place to start for just about any Twin Cities ride, Freewheel Bike Shop will set you up with a rental for $45 a day ($99 for high-end bikes), with some hourly rates available. But this is so much more than a rental shop. In addition to a full line of bikes and accessories available for sale, Freewheel does repairs, provides public shop space for a small fee if you want to do your own repairs, holds classes, rents bike lockers, and offers public showers for commuters. There's also a small café, all built directly into the hill right at the greenway level. The bike center is a joint effort of the City of Minneapolis and Allina Health Systems, the major tenant of the office space in the nearby Midtown Global Market.

GATEWAY CYCLE
6028 N. Hwy 36, Oakdale, 651/777-0188,
www.gatewaycycle.com
HOURS: Mon.-Fri. 10 A.M.-8 P.M., Sat. 9 A.M.-5 P.M.,
Sun. noon-4 P.M.
Map 7

If you're headed east, Gateway Cycle, right across from the entrance to the Gateway Trail, is the place to go. It rents mountain bikes, road bikes, hybrids, tandems, recumbents, and trailers starting at $20 a day (prices go up on the weekends). Weekly and monthly rentals are also available, at even lower daily rates. Valid driver's license, credit card, and a signed waiver are required with all rentals. Gateway also sells a range of bikes and does repairs and tune-ups.

Resources
TWIN CITIES BICYCLING CLUB
www.biketcbc.org

The Twin Cities Bicycling Club is the metro area's largest cycling club, with more than 1,000 members. The club organizes more than 1,800 rides a year, of all difficulty levels. Rides are free for members, and nonmembers pay just $2. A schedule is available on the website, and most rides do not require advance registration. Just show up about 20 minutes before the scheduled start time. The club also publishes the *Minnesota Bike Atlas,* now in its 7th edition. It's available to order on the website for $21.25 and comes with a CD with maps and cue sheets.

GOLF
The Minneapolis Park Board (www.minneapolisparks.org) maintains seven public golf courses and the City of St. Paul (www.stpaul.gov) maintains four—which adds up to a lot of inexpensive golfing right in city limits. The golf season in Minnesota runs a lot longer than you might expect: Avid golfers are out on the greens as soon as it's dry in the spring and have been known to putt in the snow well into November or December.

BAKER NATIONAL GOLF COURSE
2935 Parkview Dr., Medina, 952/473-0800,
www.bakernational.com
HOURS: Daily 6:30 A.M.-sunset
Map 7

Twenty miles outside of the cities proper, the award-winning Baker National Golf Course has been recognized by *Golf Digest* as a terrific deal. The Three Rivers Park District, which maintains the course in the heart of the Baker Park Preserve, keeps greens fees under $30. The bluegrass course totals nearly 7,000 yards, with a par of 72 on the 18-hole course and 30 on the 9-hole course. Practice areas, a driving range, a pro shop, snack cart, cart rental, and lessons are also available.

LES BOLSTAD UNIVERSITY OF MINNESOTA GOLF CLUB
2275 Larpenteur Ave. W., St. Paul, 612/627-4000,
www.uofmgolf.com
Map 6

On the St. Paul campus of the University of Minnesota this bit of University of Minnesota sports history could be described as the people's golf course. Thanks to the convenient location, low greens fees (just $25, with discounts for off hours), and complete lack of pretension, the fairways can get pretty crowded. Opened in 1929 and home to the U of M's championship men's and women's golf teams, the course features tight fairways and rolling, shaded terrain over more than 6,000 yards. The 18-hole course has a par of 71.

RUSH CREEK GOLF CLUB
7801 Troy Ln. N., Maple Grove, 763/494-0400,
www.rushcreek.com
Map 7

In the northeastern suburb of Maple Grove, Rush Creek is the posh and pricey option (greens fees top out over $100). The clubhouse looks like the archetypal suburban golf chateau, with its gabled roofs rising above a sea of gently rolling green. Inside, the decorating style harks back to golf's Scottish origins. Even the restaurant, the Highlander, reaches for a little bit of Scottish cachet (although the menu is all-American). This 18-hole championship course with more than 7,000 yards of golf and a par of 72 has hosted three LPGA Tour events and has frequently been voted best public golf course in the Twin Cities.

WATER ACTIVITIES
Boating on the Chain of Lakes
LAKE CALHOUN SAILING SCHOOL

3000 Calhoun Pkwy. E., 612/822-8328,
www.lakecalhoun.org

`Map 2`

The Lake Calhoun Sailing School, one of the largest schools of its kind in the Midwest, is based just south of the park building on the north end of Lake Calhoun. The school offers classes for all experience levels and nearly all ages—from four-year-olds to adults. (It's quite a sight to watch the little square boats with their stubby little sails round the buoys on lesson day.) Classes are organized in intensive two- to six-week sessions, meeting several times a week for a full or half day, at the end of which rank beginners can rig, launch, and handle a boat. The sailing school is a part of the Calhoun Yacht Club, which organizes races throughout the summer.

LAKE HARRIET YACHT CLUB
Lake Harriet, Minneapolis, 612/920-9420,
www.lhycsailing.com

`Map 2`

The Lake Harriet Yacht Club, based in the small sailing pavilion on the north side of the lake, organizes regattas and offers specialized clinics for new racers, women, and people who want more safety instruction. Also based in the sailing pavilion, the **Minneapolis Park Board** (www.minneapolisparks.org) offers multi-session classes for children and adults in the summer. Schedules are available at the website. The **Twin Cities Sailing Club** offers members access to a fleet of boats and informal instruction on Tuesday and Saturday mornings throughout the summer. While membership in the club is limited, those mornings are definitely the time to be hanging around the sailing pavilion if you're interested in getting to know the Twin Cities boating scene or picking up some tips.

Sailboats skim across Lake Harriet and Lake Calhoun in the Chain of Lakes all summer long.

WHEEL FUN RENTALS

3000 Calhoun Pkwy. E., Minneapolis, 612/823-5765,
www.wheelfunrentals.com

HOURS: Memorial Day–Labor Day daily 10 A.M.–sunset;
May and Sept.–Oct. Sat.–Sun. 11 A.M.–7 P.M.

COST: $11-21 per hour

Map 2

Lake Calhoun, the largest of the four lakes in the Chain of Lakes at 3.2 miles around, is connected by a picturesque channel to Lake of the Isles, which is connected to Cedar Lake. You could spend an hour or a half a day paddling and exploring Lake of the Isles, Lake Calhoun, and Lake Harriet in a kayak, double kayak, paddleboat, or canoe from the Wheel Fun Rentals franchise on Lake Calhoun. Keep in mind that, while Lake of the Isles does, indeed, have two islands, they are both protected and you are not allowed to land there. A separate Wheel Fun franchise (612/823-0077, early June–Labor Day daily 10 A.M.–8 P.M.) is located on the north side of Lake Harriet, which is not connected by water to the other three lakes. The same equipment is available to rent.

Canoeing and Kayaking on the Mississippi

KETTER CANOEING

7878 Mississippi Ln., Brooklyn Park, 763/560-3840,
www.kettercanoeing.com

HOURS: Mon.–Sat. 10 A.M.–5 P.M., Sun. closed

COST: $40/day

Map 7

The Mississippi River in the Twin Cities area is not for novice paddlers. You'll meet Class I rapids, boulders, a swift current, larger boat traffic throwing heavy wakes, and, of course, a series of locks and dams. If you've got some boating skills under your belt, you can rent canoes and kayaks from Ketter Canoeing for $40 a day. The rental facility (also a sales center for canoes and kayaks) backs right up on the river itself and you can launch right there, about eight miles north of Minneapolis. Kenn Ketter also offers a number of guided canoe tours throughout the summer for $50 a person. Always call in advance, as Ketter is a one-man show. For more information on the conditions on the

FISHING

Fishing is legal and convenient in nearly all of Minneapolis and St. Paul's urban lakes. Throwing a line in from a boat, a pier, or even a street overpass is very common. The most common species are bluegills, crappies, muskellunges, walleye, and carp, many stocked by the Minnesota Department of Natural Resources. All anglers over the age of 16 need a license, which can be purchased over the phone at 888/665-4236 or online at www4.wildlife-license.com/mn, for $9.50 for 24 hours, $23 for 72 hours, and $26.50 for a week.

The Minnesota Health Department (www.health.state.mn.us) tests fish from 1,000 lakes in Minnesota, including most of those in the metro area, and publishes a lake-by-lake and species-by-species list of guidelines on which to eat and which to throw back. Many species fall on the "limit consumption to once per week" list; the most common contaminants are mercury and perfluorocarbons. The full list is available on the website.

river, contact the **Minnesota Department of Natural Resources** (651/296-6157, www.dnr.state.mn.us).

River Cruises

PADELFORD CRUISES

100 Yacht Club Rd. W., St. Paul, 651/227-1100,
www.riverrides.com

HOURS: June–Aug. Tues.–Sun. departures at noon and 2 P.M.

COST: $15 adults, $13.50 seniors, $7.50 children

Map 4

Three large boats depart from Harriet Island in downtown St. Paul almost daily throughout the summer. Ride inside the cabin or on the open upper deck as the boat slips down the river under the St. Paul High Bridge, past the caves where St. Paul began, and beneath Fort Snelling. Tour guides share historical and geographical tidbits the whole way. The high bluffs of the river in this area are a beautiful

© TRICIA CORNELL

A tour boat passes under the Stone Arch Bridge in downtown Minneapolis.

sight no matter what the season, but especially during September and October, when Padelford runs longer fall color cruises. Watch for other special cruises on the schedule, including Sunday brunch cruises, Mother's Day and Father's Day excursions, and more. On particularly busy days, the *Betsey Northrup*, a converted barge, is hooked up behind the riverboat *Anson Northrup*, and the two together carry more than 700 passengers.

PARADISE CHARTER CRUISES

Boom Island Park, Minneapolis, 952/474-8058, www.twincitiescruises.com

HOURS: Mother's Day–October Sun. brunch cruise 11 A.M., other tours daily at noon, 2 P.M., 6 P.M., and 6:30 P.M., depending on the season

COST: $16.95–59.95

Map 1

The *Minneapolis Queen* (a retro paddleboat) and the *Paradise Lady* (a sleek modern ship) ply the Mississippi riverfront near downtown Minneapolis. The comfortable ships, which hold up to 125 and 145 passengers respectively, are a terrific way to get a unique view of the city—from inside the comfortable cabin or out on the open deck. The cruise route passes through the locks at the St. Anthony Falls dam—a fun experience in itself. Evening

cruises include cocktails or dinner. Reservations are recommended for all tours and are required for dinner and brunch cruises.

GYMS AND HEALTH CLUBS
THE FIRM

245 Aldrich Ave. N., Minneapolis, 612/377-3003, www.thefirmmpls.com

HOURS: Mon.-Wed. 5:30 A.M.-10 P.M., Thurs. 5:30 A.M.-8 P.M., Fri. 7 A.M.-7 P.M., Sat. 8 A.M.-6 P.M., Sun. closed

COST: Day pass $20

Map 1

Back in 1985, when everybody was wearing headbands and doing the grapevine to get fit, three aerobics-loving friends founded The Firm. Now it's one of the top clubs in the cities for people who are serious about fitness, whether it's spinning, weights, boxing, yoga, pilates, or—most likely—a combination. A $20 day pass buys entry to the equipment and classes. To keep you company in the highly charged atmosphere, you'll have young downtown professionals who work out at least as hard as they work.

LIFETIME FITNESS IN TARGET CENTER

600 1st Ave. N., Minneapolis, 612/486-3600, www.lifetimefitness.com

HOURS: Mon.-Thurs. 5 A.M.-10 P.M., Fri. 5 A.M.-8 P.M., Sat.-Sun. 6:30 A.M.-8 P.M.

Map 1

What could be more motivating than working out in the Target Center, where pro basketball players themselves sweat? This state-of-the-art facility, geared toward serious fitness enthusiasts, offers a full-size track and a lap pool; saunas and a whirlpool; basketball, racquetball, and squash courts (the latter aren't easy to find in the Twin Cities); and free towels and lockers. To pile on even more convenience, it's connected to the skyway system and opens at the crack of dawn— perfect for business travelers. Lifetime Fitness offers a seven-day trial pass, downloadable from the website.

YWCAS OF MINNEAPOLIS AND ST. PAUL

1130 Nicollet Mall, Minneapolis, 612/332-0501, www.ywca-minneapolis.org; 375 Selby Ave., St. Paul, 651/222-3741, www.ywcaofstpaul.org

HOURS: in Minneapolis Mon.-Fri. 5:30 A.M.-9 P.M., Sat. 7:30 A.M.-5 P.M., Sun. 9 A.M.-4 P.M., closed Sun. in the summer; in St. Paul Mon.-Thurs. 5:30 A.M.-10 P.M., Fri. 5:30 A.M.-9 P.M., Sat. 7 A.M.-7 P.M., Sun. 7 A.M.-9 P.M.

Map 1

Unlike the YMCAs in the Twin Cities, which are part of a unified system, the YWCAs of Minneapolis and St. Paul are separate entities, but they have much in common in terms of their philosophies and services. The Minneapolis YWCA operates three locations (the downtown one is listed here), while the St. Paul YWCA maintains a single facility in the Cathedral Hill neighborhood just west of downtown. Both offer cardiovascular equipment, weights, a pool, and a large gym, but neither has a running track or racquetball courts. (The Minneapolis YWCA has an indoor track at its Midtown location. Call for information.) The St. Paul YWCA offers a guest pass for $12. To use the Minneapolis YWCA, ask about reciprocity if you are a member of a YWCA elsewhere.

GUIDED AND WALKING TOURS

MAGICAL HISTORY TOURS

125 Main St. SE, Minneapolis, 952/888-9200, www.humanonastick.com

HOURS: Apr.-Oct. daily 10 A.M. and 3 P.M.

COST: $69.95

Map 1

This three-hour tour follows a seven-mile loop from St. Anthony Main to the Stone Arch Bridge, past the Guthrie Theater and Mill City Museum and up to Boom Island and Nicollet Island. All the while, knowledgeable guides introduce you to the highlights of Minneapolis history. Plus, you get to say you rode a Segway. All tours start with training and helmets are provided. Riders must be 13–80 years old and less than 280 pounds. (The human-on-a-stick joke, by the way, refers to Minneapolis's beloved State Fair, where all manner of edibles are served impaled.)

METROCONNECTIONS

Tours leave from the Mall of America, 612/333-8687, www.metroconnectionstours.com/public

COST: $28-42, depending on length

Map 7

A bus tour is a good way to cram a lot of sightseeing into a very short time. MetroConnections' three-hour Twin Cities Highlights Tour certainly hits the highest of the highlights, albeit from the windows of a bus—from Minneapolis's skyline to St. Anthony Falls to St. Paul's Summit Avenue and the State Capitol. Knowledgeable guides fill nearly the entire trip with patter. Riders get out to stretch their legs and get a breath of fresh air at Minnehaha Falls. Minneapolis and Mississippi River Tours, offered on summer Thursdays, take visitors through Minneapolis's beautiful residential neighborhood of Kenwood and then down the Mississippi River Road. After the tour, riders have time to explore the farmers market on Nicollet Mall. Tours leave several times a day. Holiday lights tours, offered weekends in December, fill up fast.

ARTS AND LEISURE

© TRICIA CORNELL

Segways used on the Magical History Tours park outside the Guthrie Theater.

MILL CITY MUSEUM TOURS

704 2nd St. S., Minneapolis, 612/341-7555,
www.millcitymuseum.org
HOURS: June–Sept. most Thursdays, Saturdays,
and Sundays
COST: $12 adults, $10 seniors and college students,
$8 children 5–17
Map 1

Capable and enthusiastic guides from the Minnesota Historical Society lead tours of downtown's riverfront district. The Minneapolis Riverfront Walking Tour begins and ends at the Mill City Museum and takes you across the Stone Arch Bridge, focusing on the city's milling history.

The Historic Main Street Walking Tours begins and ends at Pracna Restaurant (117 Main St. SE). Visitors will get to explore just beyond the riverfront in what was once the city of St. Anthony, including Our Lady of Lourdes Church and the Ard Godfrey House, the oldest existing wood-frame house in Minneapolis, dating from 1849. Museum admission is included in the price of both tours.

ST. ANTHONY FALLS HERITAGE TRAIL

Main St. SE, Minneapolis
Map 1

Plenty of history is crammed into this two-mile loop, which crosses the river at the Stone Arch and Hennepin Avenue Bridges and follows its banks along West River Parkway and Main Street. Be sure to leave ample time in your stroll to read about the geology and history of the area on the many interpretive signs. On the western end of the Hennepin Avenue bridge, be sure to stop under the bridge in First Bridge Park and see some of the archaeological remains of the first bridge ever to cross the Mississippi.

ST. PAUL GANGSTER TOURS

215 Wabasha St. S., 651/292-1220,
www.wabashastreetcaves.com
HOURS: Sat. noon
COST: $22
Map 4

Your guide, "Dapper Dan Hogan," leads the two-hour bus tour in character as the proprietor of a real 1920s joint called the Green Lantern. Prohibition was authored by teetotalers in St. Paul's Landmark Center, and its eventual passage left a brutal mark on the city: an extensive kickback and protection racket involving the St. Paul police, shootouts with John Dillinger, and a whorehouse rumored to be connected to the State Capitol by a secret but well-traversed tunnel. The tour, by air-conditioned coach, includes a number of parks and facades around St. Paul (where, often as not, villainy of some sort once happened) and also covers a general history of the city through the mid-20th century. Reservations are required. The company also offers a more detailed tour of historic Summit Avenue and a Minneapolis Gangster tour, as well as specialty seasonal tours. For a quicker peek into St. Paul's underbelly, take a 45-minute cave tour, no bus involved (Thurs. 5 P.M., Sat.–Sun. 11 A.M., $5).

ARTS AND LEISURE

WINTER SPORTS
Cross-Country Skiing

With die-hard skier and Minneapolis mayor R. T. Rybak in the lead, the metro area is one of the most enthusiastic cross-country ski towns in the country. The North Star Ski Touring Club (www.north-stars.org) is the largest ski touring club in the United States outside of Alaska, with 800 members. And Minneapolis hosts the City of Lakes Loppet, a beautiful race that attracts skiers from around the region.

If you've got your own skis with you, there are about four dozen trails right in the cities or the near suburbs, groomed and maintained by the city and state park systems. Three of the best, listed here, also rent skis. All skiers over the age of 16 on public trails (including within city, state, and regional parks) must purchase

a ski pass: $5 for the day, $15 for the season, or $40 for three seasons, available online at www4.wildlifelicense.com/mn or by phone at 888/665-4236. Have your driver's license and credit card handy.

COMO SKI CENTER
1431 Lexington Pkwy. N., St. Paul, 651/488-9673
HOURS: Mid-Dec.-mid-Feb. Tues.-Wed. 3-9 P.M., Sat. 9 A.M.-6 P.M., Sun. 11 A.M.-6 P.M.; Mon., Thurs., and Fri. closed
Map 6

The Como Ski Center in Como Park takes over the open, rolling terrain of the golf course as soon as the snow flies, with 3.5 miles of groomed classical and freestyle trails and a one-mile loop for beginners. The beginner's loop stays lighted until 11 P.M. Equipment rental is

CURLING

Curling is widely known as "chess on ice" – well, insofar as it's widely known as anything anywhere, and that's largely in Scotland, Canada, and Minnesota. In fact, Minnesotans regularly pack the U.S. Olympic curling team. The game looks a little odd to outsiders, but it is strangely addicting: One team member slides a large, smooth stone with a handle down the lane toward a series of concentric circles, aiming to get it as close to the center as possible. Two sweepers hurry ahead of the stone, brushing the ice hard with their brooms, to reduce friction and speed the stone on its way. The fourth team member, the skip, stands down by the target (the "house"), giving direction. Rounds of play are scored like bocce: The team with the stone closest to the center gets to count toward its score all the stones that are closer than the opponents' first stone.

St. Paul boasts the largest and one of the oldest curling clubs in the country, the **St. Paul Curling Club** (470 Selby Ave., St Paul, 651/224-7408, www.stpaulcurlingclub.org). This storied club, founded in 1888, however, is not the right place to turn if you are a novice curler or even if you're a long-time pro looking to get some ice time. The membership rolls

are so packed that there's no public ice time available and even longtime members vie for good slots. Missing your curling night is just not done in Minnesota.

Thank goodness, then, that two new curling clubs have opened since 2006 to pick up some of the slack. The **Dakota Curling Club** (251 Civic Center Pkwy., Burnsville, 952/895-4651, www.dakotacurlingclub.org) rents ice at the Burnsville Ice Arena. Most of its ice time is also filled by the league schedule, but the club does offer occasional curling classes and open ice times. You are also welcome to come during regular league play (generally Saturdays and Sundays) and watch the pros. If there's an open lane, someone is very likely to be willing to show you the ropes. (Curlers are like that.) Remember that curling is played in teams of four, so you'll want to bring along some friends, along with some soft-soled, clean shoes. The club has some equipment (brooms and sliders, which fit over your shoes) to lend.

The third club in the area, the **Edina Curling Club** (7300 Bush Lake Rd., Edina, www.edina-curlingclub.org) does not have open curling times or lessons.

ARTS AND LEISURE

available at the chalet for very reasonable fees (cross-country skis, poles, and boots for $12 for two hours). Group and private instruction is available for all levels, but preregistration is required. Call 651/266-6400 during business hours for trail conditions.

HYLAND LAKE PARK PRESERVE

10145 Bush Lake Rd., Bloomington, 763/694-7687, www.threeriversparkdistrict.org

HOURS: Daily in season 5 A.M.–10 P.M.

Map 7

South of Minneapolis, the Hyland Lake Park Preserve has six trails totaling seven miles, winding through beautiful wooded terrain. Skis and poles are available to rent at the visitors center. Non-lighted trails close at sunset. Two trails—Lake and Star—are lighted 5 A.M.–sunrise and sunset–10 A.M. daily. The Three Rivers Park District, which maintains the park, also operates seven other ski areas, with a total of 70 miles of groomed trails that see as many as 78,000 skiers annually. Minnesota Ski Passes are not required in the Three Rivers Park District system, but skiers must buy a ski pass from the park itself for $4 a day. If skiing isn't your thing, or if you want to try something new, the park also has two dedicated snowshoe trails. Snowshoes are available to rent at the Richardson Nature Center (763/694-7676), within the park.

THEODORE WIRTH PARK

1339 Theodore Wirth Pkwy., 763/522-4584, www.theodorewirth.org

HOURS: Mon.–Fri. 5-9 P.M., Sat. 10 A.M.–9 P.M., Sun. 10 A.M.–6 P.M.

Map 2

The seven-plus miles of groomed cross-country ski trails in Theodore Wirth Park snake throughout the whole park—winding through the golf course, the gardens, across the lake, even through the Quaking Bog. They even connect directly to trails on and around Cedar Lake and Lake of the Isles. Expert and practice loops near the ski chalet are lit and have snowmaking abilities. Rentals are downright cheap at $10 for everything you need. And you can drop in on a Saturday or Sunday lesson (10 A.M., noon, 2 P.M., and 4 P.M.) if you're lucky. Preregistration is recommended because classes with fewer than four students will be canceled. The 1.5-hour lessons cost just $15, not including rental fees. The views of downtown Minneapolis as you emerge from the woods make this a beautiful way to see the city. A map of the trails is available for download at www.minneapolisparks.org; search for "Theodore Wirth ski."

Downhill Skiing and Snowboarding

Sitting as it does on the edge of the prairie, the Twin Cities metro area could hardly be expected to offer world-class downhill skiing. In fact, at least one East Coast transplant has been heard to laugh involuntarily upon glimpsing the *top* of a favorite ski slope from a moving car on the highway. But that is uncharitable and even these Nordic ski–loving flatlanders have some skilled die-hard downhill skiers among them.

COMO PARK

1431 Lexington Pkwy. N., St. Paul, 651/488-9673

HOURS: Mid-Dec.–mid-Feb. Tues.–Wed. 3-9 P.M., Sat. 9 A.M.–6 P.M., Sun. 11 A.M.–6 P.M., Mon., Thurs., and Fri. closed

Map 6

Como Park in St. Paul offers a very gentle downhill ski slope with a not-entirely-necessary tow rope back to the top in an easy-going, family atmosphere. There are no show-offs swooshing down the slopes at Como, but there are plenty of kids learning to snowplow. The area also has the added benefit of very inexpensive equipment rental (just $9 for children and $12 for adults). Snowboards are allowed on the hill as well (snowboard equipment rental is $16). A rope tow day pass is $9 for kids and $11 for adults. Private downhill ski and snowboard lessons are available for $25 (call ahead to schedule). Six-week group lessons at all levels are also available; preregistration is required.

HYLAND SKI AND SNOWBOARD CENTER
8800 Chalet Rd., Bloomington, 763/694-7800,
www.hylandski.com
HOURS: Mon.-Thurs. 10 A.M.-9 P.M., Fri. 10 A.M.-10 P.M.,
Sat. 9 A.M.-10 P.M., Sun. 9 A.M.-9 P.M.
COST: $29 adults, $26 children, $14.50 seniors
Map 7

Hyland Ski and Snowboard Center offers more challenge, more glitz, and—frankly—more verticality. Here three chairlifts and three rope tows carry skiers and snowboards to the tops of some genuinely challenging slopes spread out over 35 acres, the whole of which is groomed and equipped for snowmaking. Skiers are treated to glimpses of the Minneapolis skyline peeking out over the pines. Alpine ski equipment rental is $20; snowboarding equipment is $28. Private and group lessons are offered, with preregistration.

Hyland Lake Park is also home to three alpine ski jumps run by the **Minneapolis Ski Club** (612/709-6429, www.minneapolisski-club.com). You must be a member to jump, but memberships cost just $25 and can be purchased on the spot from a coach. Call for exact directions or to arrange a time. The small jumps, where beginners must start, are open Tues. and Thurs. 7–9 P.M. and Sat. 10 A.M.–noon. Equipment rental is $20, but you should bring your own helmet.

THEODORE WIRTH PARK
1301 Theodore Wirth Pkwy., 763/522-4584,
www.theodorewirth.org
HOURS: Mon.-Fri. 5-9 P.M., Sat. 10 A.M.-9 P.M.,
Sun. 10 A.M.-6 P.M.
Map 2

Theodore Wirth Park jumped on the snowboarding bandwagon a few years and has been a big hit. The terrain changes every few weeks and includes a 24-foot-long staircase and a wall. Day passes cost $10, equipment rental is $15, and lessons—offered Saturday and Sunday at 10 A.M., noon, 2 P.M., and 4 P.M.—are a very reasonable $15. Families and those less athletically inclined can rent a snowtube ($12 adults, $8 children) and slide down the hill without all

that exertion. There's even a tow rope to take you to the top.

Ice Skating
In hockey-mad Minnesota, skating is a way of life. The Minneapolis Park Board maintains 30 outdoor ice rinks in city parks and St. Paul maintains 20. The temperature generally has to stay below 25°F for a week before it's possible to flood them and create a nice hard surface. Generally speaking, these are no-amenities spots: just a rink with some sideboards and overhead lights and a warming house if you're lucky. Many Minneapolis rinks also have a limited number of used skates available to borrow for free, usually in the park building near the rink. (For a list, go to www.minneapolisparks.org and search for "outdoor rinks.") Some rinks are divided into designated areas for hockey and for figure skating. Be courteous—and safe—and stay out of the hockey players' way. Slower skaters stay to the outside of the rink. If you see teams of people out on the ice chasing a ball with sticks that look like giant Q-Tips, that's broomball. Similar to hockey but played without pads, it's a quintessentially Minnesotan thing and a good way to get some really nice bruises to take home as a souvenir.

THE DEPOT
225 3rd Ave. S., Minneapolis, 612/339-2253,
www.thedepotminneapolis.com/icerink
HOURS: Nov.-March, hours vary widely, check website for schedule
COST: $8 adult, $6 seniors and children
Map 1

In a converted railyard that is now home to a Marriott and a water park, The Depot is a nice mix of indoors and outdoors and a surprisingly lovely spot on this busy stretch of Washington Avenue. Rather than shivering under the stars on one of Minneapolis's lakes, you can skate in comfort under the arches of the old train depot. The rink is heated and attached to heated underground parking. You'll find lockers, refreshments, and skate rental. Look online or call ahead. Hours vary widely week to week. Skate rental is $7 and child's metal trainer is $2.

LAKE OF THE ISLES
26th St. and Lake of the Isles Pkwy. E., ice hotline 612/313-7708
HOURS: Daily 6 A.M.-10 P.M.
COST: Free
Map 2

One of the most beautiful spots to skate in the Twin Cities is on Lake of the Isles. Minneapolis Parks maintains two separate rinks for figure skating and for hockey right out on the lake, along with a warming house. As you whoosh around the rink you can enjoy the open sky, the quiet pace of traffic around the parkway, and the twinkling lights from the stately homes that ring the lake. Before you venture out, however, call the hotline to learn about the condition of the ice.

LANDMARK CENTER RINK
Rice Park, 651/291-5608,
www.capitalcitypartnership.com/events/winterskate
HOURS: Mon.-Thurs. 11 A.M.-5 P.M., Fri. 11 A.M.-10 P.M., Sat.-Sun. 10 A.M.-10 P.M.
Map 4

In downtown St. Paul, the Landmark Center Rink combines the beauty of outdoor skating with the convenience of (cheap! $2!) skate rental. There's truly a festival atmosphere, as locals and visitors enjoy skating among St. Paul's most beautiful buildings and drinking hot chocolate around a roaring fire. Skate rentals are limited and the rink does fill up, so be prepared to wait your turn.

PARADE ICE GARDEN
600 Kenwood Pkwy., 612/370-4846,
www.minneapolisparks.org
Map 1

If you prefer to skate indoors, or if you long for the ice in the middle of June, head for the Parade Ice Garden, which is open year-round. The hours for public skating vary widely, as hockey practices and skating lessons get juggled among the three rinks. During the warmer months, one rink is converted to a gym

for indoor soccer and lacrosse. Public skate admission is $3 and skate rental is $2.

WATER PARKS
THE DEPOT
225 3rd Ave. S., Minneapolis, 612/339-2253,
www.thedepotminneapolis.com/waterpark
HOURS: Fri. noon-10 P.M., Sat., 9 A.M.-10 P.M., Sun. 9 A.M.-3 P.M.
COST: $20
Map 1

From the late 1800s to the 1970s, freight trains from all over the country pulled into the train depot in downtown Minneapolis. Now the trains parked inside The Depot are painted bright colors and spout water from all sides as children slide out of them into splash pools. This indoor water park has four pools and is a nice, manageable size for families with small kids, without the hectic atmosphere of the bigger water parks. One of the pools is just one foot deep, so even the tiniest kids can join in the fun. Older kids can play water basketball, climb ropes, and ride a floating log. When they need to dry off a little, kids can enjoy good, old-fashioned arcade games and air hockey. Guests at the Renaissance Marriott (attached to the park) can ask for water park packages that include up to four tickets, with additional tickets available for purchase for $10. The number of passes for non-hotel guests is limited, so call ahead. Some additional days are added during the heat of summer.

GRAND RIOS
6900 Lakeland Ave. N., Minneapolis, 763/566-8855,
www.grandrios.com
HOURS: Fri. 4-9 P.M., Sat. 10 A.M.-9 P.M., Sun. 10 A.M.-5 P.M.
COST: $18.95
Map 7

From a four-story slide to a slow-moving "lazy river" (like a slide in slow motion), Grand Rios is flashy and splashy (and kind of loud). The decor is faux-tropical, with plastic palm trees in among the geysers. Families with very tiny tots will appreciate the zero-depth entry pool, while older kids can enjoy the 500-gallon splash bucket and the arcade. Deals are available on 4 P.M.–4 P.M. admission, giving you access to the park two days in a row. Those not swimming can pay a $9.95 "dry" admission fee. Hours vary widely as the seasons change. Packages are available for Ramada guests. If you're not staying at the hotel, call about ticket availability, especially on Saturday mornings when hotel guests tend to fill the park.

WATER PARK OF AMERICA
1700 American Blvd. E., Bloomington, 952/854-8700, www.waterparkofamerica.com
HOURS: Fri.-Sat. 10 A.M.-9 P.M., Sun. 10 A.M.-5 P.M.
COST: $17-26
Map 7

One of the 10 largest indoor water parks in the United States, the Water Park of America promises an over-the-top splash-filled experience—and it delivers. Water slides wind down the outside of the 10-story building, weaving in and out of the building itself. A "lazy river" flows around the perimeter. Surfers and boogie boarders catch a wave on the surf simulator. And water, kids, and happy families fill the 70,000-square-foot area. The Radisson by Mall of America is connected to the park and offers hotel/park packages. Hours and admission price vary by season, with additional days in the summer. Saturday mornings tend to fill up fast.

OTHER RECREATION
CANTERBURY PARK
1100 Canterbury Rd., Shakopee, 952/445-7223, www.canterburypark.com
HOURS: 24 hours
COST: Live racing: $5 adults, $3 seniors, children under 17 free; otherwise free
Map 7

From May to Labor Day, you can watch the ponies run at Canterbury Park in suburban comfort. Lacking much grit or history, the track will never be confused with Churchill Downs, but it still attracts both the dyed-in-the-wool racing fan and the purely curious looking for a relaxing afternoon. In between races you can grab a bite to eat at one of the four restaurants or play a round of Texas Hold'em in the 34-table poker room. The track has hosted the Claiming Crown—known as the "blue-collar Breeders' Cup"—for most of the race series' short history. Even when the horses aren't running, Canterbury Park's doors are open 24 hours for betting on simulcast horse racing and poker. Keep in mind that the legal gambling age, for the track and the tables, is 18.

ROLLER DOME
Metrodome, 5th St. and 11th Ave., 612/825-3663, www.roller-dome.com
HOURS: Vary widely depending on events; call or check online
COST: $6.50 adults, $5.50 students, $4.50 seniors and children, $5 skate rental
Map 1

What is an empty sports stadium good for? Think of all that smooth empty concrete—the answer could only be Rollerblading, which was born right here in Minnesota in 1984. When the Dome isn't otherwise in use November–April, up to 1,000 skaters at a time come spin around the upper and lower levels, enjoying music, exercise (2.5 laps make a mile), and a respite from the weather. To make this as easy as possible, there's free attached parking, free lessons, free coat check, and free protective gear.

3RD LAIR SKATE PARK
850 Florida Ave. S., Golden Valley, 763/797-5283, www.3rdlair.com
HOURS: Sun.-Thurs. noon-9 P.M., Fri. noon-midnight, Sat. 8 A.M.-9 P.M.
COST: $11-13
Map 7

Teenagers dominate the 25,000-square-foot indoor-outdoor facility, full of pipes, walls, banks, rails, and pyramids, but people of all ages are welcome. The owners and staff are all skaters themselves who seem to have a special affinity for kids. New riders and kids 12 and under are encouraged to come to the park Saturday mornings before noon when it's less busy and there are instructors on hand (classes cost $35 and walk-ins are welcome). All equipment is available to rent for very reasonable prices. You pay admission per three-hour session. First-time users must buy a $5 pass and bring photo ID or have a parent sign for them. Hours vary with the school year. Parents can stay and watch for free, hang out in the parents' lounge, or leave their kids in the capable hands of the "lifeguards." There's a second facility in Burnsville (3260 County Rd. 42 W., 952/224-3316).

VERTICAL ENDEAVORS

845 Phalen Blvd., St. Paul, 651/776-1430,
www.verticalendeavors.com
HOURS: May-Oct. Mon.-Fri. noon-10 P.M., Sat.
11 A.M.-6 P.M., Sun. 11 A.M.-6 P.M., Nov.-April Mon.-Fri.
noon-10 P.M., Sat. 10 A.M.-10 P.M., Sun. 10 A.M.-6 P.M.
COST: Day pass $13 weekdays, $15 weekends
Map 4

Hard-core climbers love Vertical Endeavors. The state-of-the-art facility has climbing walls of all degrees of difficulty and bouldering caves with up to 60 degrees of overhang. The facility is fastidiously maintained and friendly and filled with climbing enthusiasts. If you're a novice climber, you're welcome as well, but you'll want to sign up in advance for one of the beginning classes. A day pass gives you access to the entire facility, including exercise equipment and showers. You can even leave, rest up, and come back for even more climbing. Equipment rental is $10.

SHOPS

It's hard to talk about shopping in the Twin Cities without mentioning the Mall of America. It's true; many locals have a love/hate relationship with The Mall: It sure is convenient to have all those national chains in one climate-controlled place. And all that parking! Right at the intersection of two major highways! Right next to IKEA! You'll find locals who sniff at the Mall of America, but you'll be hard-pressed to find one who doesn't visit on occasion.

But, while the Twin Cities have their fair share of big-box shopping (this is the home of our much-beloved Target Corporation, after all) and a ring of suburban malls known colloquially as "the Dales" (Southdale, Rosedale, Ridgedale), the "shop locally" ethos is alive and well here. Local fashionistas would rather boast about a one-of-a-kind piece by a young, up-and-coming designer than a recognizable label.

Serious shoppers head to the mile-long stretch of Grand Avenue in St. Paul, park at one end, and make a day of visiting one small boutique after another, many just a few rooms on the ground floor of a converted bungalow. Serious shoppers with bigger budgets have the same routine at 50th and France in Edina, the closest thing Minnesota has to Rodeo Drive.

There are a couple of other good reasons to keep your credit card close at hand in the Twin Cities: There's no sales tax on clothing here, shaving a few bucks off the expense, and this place is crawling with bookstores—new bookstores, used bookstores, specialty bookstores catering to small and happy slices of the reading population, and some of the best children's

© TRICIA CORNELL

HIGHLIGHTS

LOOK FOR 【 TO FIND RECOMMENDED SHOPS.

【 **Best Place to Read to the Kids:** The worn armchairs at **Wild Rumpus** in the Linden Hills neighborhood of Minneapolis are so inviting you won't be able to resist spending a few minutes, or even longer, test-running a kids' book (page 141).

【 **Best Place to Find Vintage Glam:** If you can carry off a mink stole or a full 1950s skirt, you'll find plenty of new additions to your wardrobe at **Via's Vintage** (page 144).

【 **Best Place to Be a Kid Again:** Remember the joys of imaginative play at **Wonderment,** where nearly everything is made from wood or wool (page 146).

【 **Best Place to Find Thoughtful Gifts for Everyone on Your List:** Even if you don't know what you're looking for, you're likely to find it at **The Bibelot's** four shops, from women's clothing and accessories to kitchen necessities to smart baby toys (page 146).

【 **Best Place to Find Absolutely Anything for the Kitchen:** Serious cooks can find anything they can dream up at **Cooks of Crocus Hill**'s two locations, on Grand Avenue in St. Paul and 50th and France in Edina (page 146).

【 **Best Place to Get an Authentically Minnesotan Souvenir:** Minnesota's Scandinavian roots are represented at **Ingebretsen's** in hand-knit sweaters, painted Swedish dala horses, and intricate rosemaling (page 149).

【 **Best Place to Shop Responsibly:** Everything at **Twin Cities Green** is made from recycled or sustainable materials. And it's all modern and beautiful, as well (page 150).

【 **Best Place for Expert Wine Advice:** The wine purveyors at **France 44** know their stuff. Tell them what you like and they'll put together a custom case to take home (page 151).

【 **Best Place to Spend a Summer Saturday Morning:** Join the crowd at the **Mill City Farmers Market** in downtown Minneapolis. While you munch on pastries, check out handmade jewelry and clothes made from reclaimed fabrics (page 152).

© BRUCE MANNING

Bibelot means a decorative ornament or trinket.

bookstores in the country. In fact, Minneapolis has sat at the top of the Most Literate Cities in the United States list for the past couple of years, and St. Paul is always in the top 10.

SHOPPING DISTRICTS
Downtown Minneapolis

A bronze Mary Tyler Moore flings her tam in the air in front of Macy's (which die-hard Minnesotans may still refer to as Dayton's), and downtown office workers hurry down Nicollet Mall, squeezing in a little shopping on their lunch hour. Visitors will find familiar chains, from the Gap and Banana Republic to Nieman Marcus and Off 5th. Inside Gaviidae Common—a surprisingly flashy upscale shopping center at 6th Street and Nicollet Mall—you'll find more interesting local boutiques, like the lifestyle boutique Finnstyle. Bad weather never keeps shoppers away from downtown (everything is connected by the skyways), but weekend activities might: The pace is slow on Saturdays and barely alive on Sundays. Come on a summer Thursday and pick up fruits, vegetables, flowers, tamales, and more from the vendors at the weekly farmers market, set up all along the mall.

50th and France

The shady crossroads of 50th and France, a roughly four-block shopping district on the border between South Minneapolis and the tony suburb of Edina, is the sort of place where you'll find toned, fashionable women swinging shopping bags as they saunter from one boutique to another and then sit down, exhausted, to a light and expensive lunch. National chains like Anthropologie and Chico's sit alongside local shops like Bumbershute, Hot Mama (cutting-edge clothes for the expecting and no longer expecting), and the salon of local designer darling Monique Lhuillier. Those who know their way around a kitchen as well as a charity luncheon might spend hours in Cooks of Crocus Hill and then pop across the street to the Premier Cheese Market for a well-chosen treat.

Grand Avenue

Grand Avenue stretches from the Mississippi River to downtown St. Paul, with pockets of retail and restaurants scattered along its length, but most of the action is at the intersection of Grand and Victoria Avenues. Here tasteful new construction mingles with converted stucco homes. Although the occasional chain pops up (J. Crew has been here for years), mostly you'll find well-established, creative, local shops, like the delicious Cooks of Crocus Hill, the irresistible Red Balloon Bookshop for kids, and the absolutely inimitable Golden Fig for handmade gourmet goods. Wear good walking shoes and head west to Grand and Lexington Avenues for even more unique boutiques.

Hopkins Mainstreet

Mainstreet in the family-oriented, first-ring suburb of Hopkins is the sort of thing newer suburbs try, unsuccessfully, to recreate with out-of-the-box storefronts and chains. But Hopkins is the real deal: a shady three- or four-block stretch of quaint buildings, some dating to the late 1800s. Antiques are the big draw here, with 10 antiques stores within an easy stroll and sometimes right next to each other. Some dealers specialize in jewelry or trains, while others, like the Hopkins Antique Mall, represent multiple dealers. If you want to do more than shop, you can download and print a historic walking tour map at www .thinkhopkins.com, or consider combining your shopping trip with a show at the Hopkins Center for the Arts and definitely stop for Blue Moon Ice Cream at Pine Cone Cottage. Just a few minutes from downtown Minneapolis, Hopkins feels like a whole different world.

Linden Hills

The neighborhood of Linden Hills has been called a small town in the middle of the city— the kind of place where everybody really might know your name, whether it's at the Dunn Bros. coffee shop or Sebastian Joe's ice cream parlor. The shopping district is packed onto a single intersection—where Upton Avenue meets 43rd Street—but the variety could keep diehard shoppers busy all day. Browse tchotchkes and clothes at Bibelot, discover the marvel of modern childhood at Creative Kidstuff and Wonderment, and spend as much time as you like chasing the cats and chickens and reading books at Wild Rumpus. On weekdays you'll have plenty of parents pushing strollers to keep you company, and on weekends the whole neighborhood turns out.

Uptown

While chain stores have moved in on the one-time center of Twin Cities counterculture at the corner of Lake Street and Hennepin Avenue, the whole of the Uptown neighborhood is still a lively retail area with an independent bent. The two main north–south axes are Hennepin and Lyndale Avenues, with Lake Street connecting them east–west. Minneapolis's post-college crowd comes to Uptown to browse books at Magers and Quinn, fashions at Local Motion, and hipster housewares at Twin Cities Green.

Antiques

ART AND ARCHITECTURE

3338 University Ave. SE, Minneapolis, 612/904-1776
HOURS: Mon.-Sat. 10 A.M.-5 P.M., Sun. noon-5 P.M.
Map 3

Poking around the dim, crowded corners of Art and Architecture is like finding an enchanted attic, where the best architectural remnants of another time have come to rest, from the very large—church pews, stained-glass windows, and solid wood doors—to the rather small—printing press blocks, doorknobs, boxes of brass hinges. Nearly every decade and major design era is represented, and everything is sorted almost compulsively, so you don't have to go digging in the bathroom fixtures for that perfect chandelier.

HOPKINS ANTIQUE MALL

1008 Mainstreet, Hopkins, 952/931-9748,
www.hopkinsantiquemall.com
HOURS: Mon.-Sat. 11 A.M.-6 P.M., Sun. 11 A.M.-5 P.M.
Map 7

One-stop shopping for antiques aficionados—more than 60 dealers show their wares, from furniture to jewelry, Tiffany lamps to collectible lunch boxes, kitchenware to books. Just when you think you've seen it all, there's another level to explore. Many dealers are eager to buy as well. Be sure to stroll up and down Mainstreet,

where there are nearly a dozen other antiques dealers, though none as big as this.

Mainstreet in Hopkins, a small town within minutes of downtown Minneapolis, is a popular destination for antiques shoppers and families.

Arts and Crafts

CRAFTY PLANET

2833 Johnson St. NE, Minneapolis, 612/788-1180, www.craftyplanet.com

HOURS: Mon.-Sat. 10 A.M.-7 P.M., Sun. 11 A.M.-5 P.M.

Map 3

If the words "Amy Butler," "Malabrigo," and "Addi Turbo," make you sit right up and hunt for your wallet, you can't miss Crafty Planet. (Those, by the way, are—respectively—smart, modern sewing patterns; yummy, hand-dyed yarn; and the Cadillac of knitting needles.) Proprietors Trish and Matt are crafters themselves and happy to chat about your project and show you around the walls and walls of fabric, yarn, and notions. You'll feel particularly at home here if you've got a slightly subversive bent—maybe there were skulls in your first knitting project. Extra bonus: inexpensive choices like Lion Brand Yarn among the pricier stuff.

NEEDLEWORK UNLIMITED

4420 Drew Ave. S., Minneapolis, 612/925-2454, www.needleworkunlimited.com

HOURS: Mon.-Wed. and Fri. 10 A.M.-6 P.M., Thurs. 10 A.M.-8 P.M., Sat. 10 A.M.-5 P.M., Sun. noon-4 P.M.

Map 2

If you can name a brand of yarn, the experienced knitters at Needlework Unlimited can find it for you here—or offer a good reason why they don't carry it. You'll find the walls stacked to the ceiling with Rowan, Koigu, Berroco, and Debbie Bliss. Bring your pattern and you'll get expert advice on substituting yarns and sizing. Bring your unfinished project in for advice on how to get over the rough spots. Check their schedule for workshops and signings. This is where the big shots in the knitting world stop when they come through town. Needlepointers will also find a range of designer canvases and fibers.

TREADLE YARD GOODS

1338 Grand Ave., St. Paul, 651/698-9690

HOURS: Mon.-Thurs. 10 A.M.-8 P.M., Fri. 10 A.M.-6 P.M., Sun. 1-5 P.M.

Map 5

You might walk right by Treadle's plain-Jane storefront without even noticing. But inside it's a different story. Are those the latest Japanese import fabrics (very big in the crafting world) on that modest stand? Are those full fabric lines from hot designers Amy Butler and Joel Dewberry? Why, yes, they are. And there in the corner may be the best collection of oilcloth you've seen. Treadle feels as much like a welcoming community as a shop, with home garment makers (that's the focus here, rather than quilting or other crafts) stopping by to chat about projects and even help out a newcomer.

THE YARNERY

840 Grand Ave., St. Paul, 651/222-5793, www.yarnery.com

HOURS: Mon.-Thurs. 10 A.M.-8 P.M., Fri.-Sat. 10 A.M.-6 P.M., Sun. noon-5 P.M.

Map 5

Before knitting was hip—before there was the Yarn Harlot or a Stitch and Bitch Nation—there was The Yarnery, a cozy bungalow stuffed to the rafters with yarn. You will invariably find a table of women (and maybe men) knitting—very likely winter clothes for a local organization or squares for a blanket raffle. This is a community-minded place, with a particular penchant for supporting local designers. Clinics are free and classes are inexpensive. If you crave the company of other knitters, stop by for Friday Knit Nights, 6:30–8:30 P.M. on the first and third Fridays of the month.

Books and Music

BOOKS

BIG BRAIN COMICS

1027 Washington Ave. S., Minneapolis, 612/338-4390,
www.bigbraincomics.com

HOURS: Mon.-Sat. noon-8 P.M., Sun. noon-5 P.M.

Map 1

Leave your preconceptions about comic book shops at the door: Big Brain is far from the dim, dank, disorganized den you might imagine. It's small, but it's expertly organized, with an eye to helping you find exactly what you're looking for. ("New this week?" Got it right here.) But the clerks fit the standard comic book mold in one important aspect: They are way into their work. Big Brain stocks both new and back-issue comics, from small presses as well as big publishers. There's a wide selection of graphic novels, trade paperbacks, and figurines as well.

BIRCHBARK BOOKS

2115 21st St. W., Minneapolis, 612/374-4023,
www.birchbarkbooks.com

HOURS: Mon.-Fri. 9 A.M.-6 P.M., Sat. 10 A.M.-5 P.M.,
Sun. noon-5 P.M.

Map 2

Novelist Louise Erdrich has created a haven for book lovers in just 800 square feet of space on a quiet, tree-lined, mostly residential street. While there is a special focus on Native American books (including a few published by BirchBark), the other quirks of the staff's interest show through as well, including a fine selection of books on language. The store also features the work of Native American artisans, including baskets, silver, and dolls.

COMMON GOOD BOOKS

165 Western Ave. N., St. Paul, 651/225-8989,
www.commongoodbooks.com

HOURS: Mon.-Sat. 10 A.M.-10 P.M., Sun. 10 A.M.-10 P.M.

Map 4

"Common Good Books, G. Keillor"—there's a Minnesota story right there. A humble sign, a humble name, affixed to the name of one of our most famous native sons. The bookstore is the pet project of Garrison Keillor, host of the public radio program *A Prairie Home Companion* and an excellent place to pick up a book by a local writer, hear a speaker, or buy some "quality trash"—that's how the shelf is labeled—to read upstairs in Nina's Coffee Cafe (165 Western Ave. N., 651/292-9816, daily 6:30 A.M.–10 P.M.).

FRIENDS OF THE MINNEAPOLIS PUBLIC LIBRARY BOOKSTORE

300 Nicollet Mall, Minneapolis, 612/630-6170,
www.friendsofmpl.org

HOURS: Tues., Wed., and Fri. 10 A.M.-5 P.M., Thurs.
10 A.M.-7 P.M., Sat. 10 A.M.-4:30 P.M., Sun.-Mon. closed

Map 1

Sure, you can find deeply discounted library books at plenty of libraries, but here at the Minneapolis Public Library's Central Library, you get a few things you can't find anywhere else, not least of which is an excuse to visit the stunning building. The bookstore goes way beyond books, stocking fun book- and library-related kitsch, including librarian action figures, totes, T-shirts, and baby onesies.

MAGERS AND QUINN

3038 Hennepin Ave. S., Minneapolis, 612/822-4611,
www.magersandquinn.com

HOURS: Sun.-Thurs. 10 A.M.-10 P.M., Fri.-Sat.
10 A.M.-11 P.M.

Map 2

It might say something about the people of Minneapolis that Magers and Quinn is a popular date destination. Or it might say something about Magers and Quinn. Books of all kinds—new and used, rare collectibles and discounted bestsellers, children's books and foreign philosophers—fill three floors, floor to ceiling. High ceilings, antique prints, glass-fronted display cases, and a general feeling of reverence make this, one of the Midwest's largest bookstores, feel as much like a museum as a shop.

MICAWBER'S BOOKS

2238 Carter Ave., St. Paul, 651/646-5506,
www.micawbers.com
HOURS: Mon.-Fri. 10 A.M.-8 P.M., Sat. 10 A.M.-6 P.M.,
Sun. 11 A.M.-5 P.M.
Map 6

To anyone who has ever passed through Micawber's quaint half-timbered door more than once, it is more a book club than a bookstore. The passionate owners and staff are not only ready to share their recommendations but to really listen to what their customers are saying about what they love to read. Come with an open mind about what you're looking for: Bestselling books aren't automatically disqualified, but being on the bestseller list is not enough to guarantee a spot on the rigorously edited shelves at Micawber's.

THE RED BALLOON BOOKSHOP

891 Grand Ave., St. Paul, 651/224-8320,
www.redballoonbookshop.com
HOURS: Mon.-Fri. 10 A.M.-8 P.M., Sat. 9 A.M.-5 P.M.,
Sun. noon-5 P.M.
Map 5

For book-loving families, the Red Balloon is a regular pilgrimage. While the shop specializes in children's books, there's a small selection of titles just for adults, with a preference for new voices, indie bookseller's faves, and local nonfiction. There's plenty of room on the carpeted floor to give your purchases a test run, and a knowledgeable staff who will gladly introduce you to the latest releases. Watch the website for signings and events, and join in a story time if you're there on Tuesday (10:15 A.M. for babies, 11 A.M. for toddlers) or Wednesday (10:30 A.M. for preschoolers).

UNCLE EDGAR'S MYSTERY BOOKSTORE & UNCLE HUGO'S SCIENCE FICTION BOOKSTORE

2864 Chicago Ave. S., Minneapolis, Uncle Hugo's
612/824-6347, Uncle Edgar's 612/824-9984,
www.unclehugo.com
HOURS: Mon.-Fri. 10 A.M.-8 P.M., Sat. 10 A.M.-6 P.M.,
Sun. noon-5 P.M.
Map 2

Genre fiction fans will know they're in the right place when they nearly trip over the large cardboard box labeled "Nick Carter, box 3"—and it's stacked on top of boxes 4 and 5 of the popular detective series. Uncle Hugo's, founded in 1974, claims to be the oldest science fiction bookstore in America; Uncle Edgar, Hugo's Siamese twin, joined him six years later. Both are straight out of geeky bookstore central casting: musty, silent, with walls packed vertigo-inducingly tight with bright paperback spines, and boxes of new and used books knee-deep on the floor.

◖ WILD RUMPUS

2720 43rd St. W., Minneapolis, 612/920-5005,
www.wildrumpusbooks.com
HOURS: Mon. 10 A.M.-5 P.M., Tues.-Fri. 10 A.M.-8 P.M.,
Sat. 10 A.M.-5 P.M., Sun. noon-5 P.M.
Map 2

Yes, that is a chicken wandering around. And a cat. The Wild Rumpus's menagerie includes birds, rodents, and the occasional lizard and arachnid. This makes the kids feel right at

© BRUCE MANNING

Wild Rumpus invites families to browse, read, and chase the resident chickens.

SHOPS

home, even if it makes a few adults nervous. Go ahead, sit in one of the worn, comfy armchairs and read, because the proprietors of Wild Rumpus, one of the best kids' bookstores in town, if not the country, know you will eventually buy something, so well chosen is their selection. From classic board books to popular tween series and even carefully selected adult titles for mature young adult readers, the staffers know books.

MUSIC
ELECTRIC FETUS

2000 4th Ave. S., Minneapolis, 612/870-9300,
www.electricfetus.com
HOURS: Mon.-Fri. 9 A.M.-9 P.M., Sat. 9 A.M.-8 P.M.,
Sun. 11 A.M.-6 P.M.
Map 2

Four decades of Minneapolis music history have accreted on the creaky racks at the Electric Fetus (or maybe that's the accumulated grime from more than 40 years of burning incense). In this time of niche marketing and specialization, the Fetus has survived by making musicheads of all stripes deliriously happy. Spend hours browsing rock, jazz, metal, hip-hop, and every permutation thereof. Then sidle over to the used, vinyl, and local sections. New locations have opened in Duluth and St. Cloud, but this, in its unlikely spot on a frontage road off I-35W, is the original.

HYMIE'S VINTAGE RECORDS

3318 Lake St. E., Minneapolis, 612/729-8890
HOURS: Mon.-Sat. 11 A.M.-7 P.M., Sun. 1-6 P.M.
Map 2

Hymie's is like a museum tracing the evolution of popular sound from 45s to 78s to eight-tracks to cassette tapes to CDs, even relevant books and videos. While Hymie himself—a stalwart in the vinyl collecting world—is gone, his successors are knowledgeable and passionate about music. Building a collection? Start here. Already have a collection and need accessories like sleeves? Here as well.

Clothing and Accessories

BIRCH

2309 50th St. W., Minneapolis, 612/436-0776,
www.birchclothing.com
HOURS: Mon.-Wed. and Fri.-Sat. 10 A.M.-6 P.M.,
Thurs. 10 A.M.-8 P.M., Sun. 1-5 P.M.
Map 2

If ever there was a clothing store perfectly suited to its neighborhood, it would be Birch here in liberal-leaning South Minneapolis. The muted palettes, nubby weaves, and drapey shapes fit the neighborhood's casual, family-oriented lifestyle, and the insistence on sustainably harvested fibers, fair wages for workers, and toxin-free dyes fits its values. The small, friendly boutique focuses on women's clothes and bags (including Relan, made from old billboards) but also carries a few items for men and babies.

COVERED

402 14th Ave. SE, Minneapolis, 612/378-4776,
www.shopcovered.com
HOURS: Mon.-Sat. 11 A.M.-9 A.M., Sun. noon-6 P.M.
Map 3

The young women behind Covered claim to be able to fit any body, within certain parameters: You've got to have a waist between 24 and 32 inches and you have to be willing to drop some serious dough on a fabulous pair of jeans. Covered stocks Joe's Jeans, Citizens of Humanity, True Religion, and about 10 other brands of premium denim, along with hip casual tops and dresses. The original store in the Dinkytown neighborhood near the university is for women only, but men and women can both find the perfect denim at the Uptown location (1202 Lagoon Ave., 612/825-1610, Mon.–Sat. 11 A.M.–9 P.M., Sun. noon–6 P.M.).

HOT MAMA

3940 50th St. W., Edina, 952/746-8255,
www.shopmama.com

HOURS: Mon. 10 A.M.-6 P.M., Tues.-Fri. 10 A.M.-7 P.M.,
Sat. 10 A.M.-6 P.M., Sun. noon-5 P.M.

Map 7

The folks at Hot Mama are dedicated to making expecting and no-longer-expecting mothers feel at least as hot as they did pre-baby. And they are enthusiastic about it: Don't be surprised to find your arms draped with $150 pairs of jeans and $35 tanks as you walk in the door. For all the high prices and chic atmosphere, this is a kid-friendly space: Park the kids at the train table and they'll most likely have plenty of company. This is the original, but there's a sister store on Grand Avenue in St. Paul (867 Grand Ave., 651/209-0222, Mon.–Fri. 10 A.M.–7 P.M., Sat. 10 A.M.–6 P.M., Sun. noon–5 P.M.).

LOCAL MOTION

2813 Hennepin Ave., Minneapolis,
612/871-8436

HOURS: Mon.-Thurs. 11 A.M.-7 P.M., Fri. 11 A.M.-8 P.M.,
Sat. 10 A.M.-6 P.M., Sun. noon-6 P.M.

Map 2

The look at Local Motion is grown-up, feminine, and a little boho, heavy on dresses, skirts, and feminine blouses in the colors and cuts of the moment. While the boutique started as a showcase for local designers—and you'll still find many here—the owners now keep a close eye on fashion in New York and L.A., bringing the best of what they find to the Twin Cities. Come in serious shopping mode: The racks are packed, the aisles small, and the prices make these clothes indulgences.

LULA'S VINTAGE WEAR

1587 Selby Ave., St. Paul, 651/644-4110

HOURS: Mon. noon-6 P.M., Tues.-Thurs. noon-7 P.M.,
Fri. noon-6 P.M., Sat. 11 A.M.-6 P.M., Sun. noon-5 P.M.

Map 5

Feminine dresses (many of them handmade by skilled seamstresses) from the 1950s through the '80s fill two walls, and costume jewelry from all eras fills the display case. Men get more rack space here than they do in most vintage stores—a solid collection of sports coats, weekend button-downs, and ties. Be prepared to enjoy the hunt—most racks aren't arranged by size—and don't be afraid to ask the incredibly friendly staff for help.

PICKY GIRL

1326 Grand Ave., St. Paul, 651/698-4107,
www.pickygirlmn.com

HOURS: Mon.-Sat. 11 A.M.-8 P.M., Sun. noon-5 P.M.

Map 5

The picky girl for whom this shop is intended is indeed very picky. She is also young, slender, and fashionable, and has plenty of disposable income. This small shop is, as they say in the fashion business, meticulously edited. Rather than racks and racks of options, each piece—many handmade and all by small designers—is chosen to wow. The spare space feels almost like your girlfriend's closet: no artwork needed, the clothes are the stars here.

QUINCE

850 Grand Ave., St. Paul, 651/225-9900,
www.quincegifts.com

HOURS: Mon.-Tues. 11 A.M.-6 P.M., Wed.-Sat. 11 A.M.-9 P.M., Sun. 11 A.M.-6 P.M.

Map 5

Bold, bright, fun fashion for big girls and little girls (in fact, the pasties and ruffled undies are on the opposite side of the display of baby onesies with sassy sayings and ballerina skirts). College kids and those who can still carry off a college look will find pieces that stand out, including accessories and trinkets. And who doesn't know a little girl who needs purple cowboy boots? Mixed in with the clothes are artsy gifts of the sort no one actually knows they want until you give it to them, like sock monkeys and joke books.

◖ VIA'S VINTAGE

2408 Hennepin Ave. S., Minneapolis, 612/374-3649,
www.viasvintage.com

HOURS: Mon.-Sat. 11 A.M.-7 P.M., Sun. noon-5 P.M.

Map 2

© TRICIA CORNELL

Via's Vintage has a 1950s vibe.

If your wardrobe comfortably accommo-
dates ruffled Edwardian blouses, 1950s fur
stoles, and mod shift dresses, you can out-
fit yourself very, very nicely at Via's—and
have fun doing it, too. For a store featuring
items that are 30 to 100 years old, Via's is
bright, clean, and free of that musty used-
clothes feeling. There's a smaller collection
of men's clothes and a rack of kids' stuff, as
well as vintage pieces reworked into one-of-
a-kind couture artifacts. Keep in mind that
vintage sizing isn't kind to larger women:
The biggest sizes you're likely to find here
fit 30- and 32-inch waists.

Kids' Stores

BABY GRAND

1137 Grand Ave., St. Paul, 651/224-4414,
www.babyongrand.com

HOURS: Mon.-Fri. 10 A.M.-8 P.M., Sat. 10 A.M.-5 P.M.,
Sun. noon-5 P.M.

Map 5

You don't have to go to a big box store to
stock up for a baby or to pick out a shower
gift. This converted single-family home on
St. Paul's hottest shopping street is like the
Mary Poppins bag of baby stores: It holds
far more than it ever looks like it could from
the outside. From cribs and gliders to onesies and burp cloths, from high-end brands
like Stokke and Inglesina to more everyday
stuff like Chicco, it's all packed tightly in
here. And they know their stuff: Bring a list
or show up completely clueless and an experienced salesperson will walk you through every
daunting choice. Baby Grand's second store
opened in the western suburb of Hopkins in
2008 (1010 Mainstreet, 952/912-1010, Tues.-
Fri. 11 A.M.-8 P.M., Sat. 10 A.M.-6 P.M., Sun.
noon-5 P.M., Mon. closed).

CREATIVE KIDSTUFF

4313 Upton Ave. S., Minneapolis, 612/927-0653,
www.creativekidstuff.com

HOURS: Mon.-Fri. 10 A.M.-8 P.M., Sat. 10 A.M.-6 P.M.,
Sun. noon-5 P.M.

Map 2

At Creative Kidstuff, they seem to know what
the next hot toys will be before anybody else
does. We're not talking about movie tie-ins or
action figures (you won't find those here), but
creative, hands-on toys for babies right on up
through the early teens. The stores also stock
plenty of relative classics, like Playmobil, Brio,
Ryan's Room, Groovy Girls, and Corolle
dolls. Most of the friendly sales staff are parents themselves and eager to share their exper-
tise. There are five other locations in the Twin
Cities, including in St. Paul (1074 Grand Ave.,
651/222-2472, Mon.-Fri. 9:30 A.M.-8 P.M.,
Sat. 9:30 A.M.-6 P.M., Sun. noon-5 P.M.) and
in the Galleria mall in the western suburb of
Edina (3555 69th St., 952/926-4512, Mon.-
Fri. 10 A.M.-9 P.M., Sat. 10 A.M.-8 P.M., Sun.
11 A.M.-5 P.M.).

KIDDYWAMPUS

4400 Excelsior Blvd., St. Louis Park, 952/926-7871,
www.kiddywampus.com

HOURS: Mon.-Sat. 10 A.M.-6 P.M.

Map 7

You've never seen a toy store like this. Spare, open, and modern, Kiddywampus lets the toys—and the kids—take center stage. You probably haven't seen most of these toys before, either. Owner Amy Saldanha hunts down the kind of high-design, high-concept building blocks, art sets, children's furniture, and more that a modern parent might not mind seeing scattered all over the living room. (Kids can test drive many of the toys, to be sure that fun hasn't been sacrificed to design.) Antsy kids can hang out in the Kiddyplay area (Mon.-Sat. 10 A.M.-4:30 P.M., $5/hour) or make art in the open studio (Mon. and Fri. 10 A.M.-4:30 P.M., Tues.-Thurs. 12:30-4:30 P.M., $8).

PEAPODS

251 Snelling Ave. S., St. Paul, 651/695-5559,
www.peapods.com

HOURS: Mon.-Sat. 10 A.M.-6 P.M., closed Sun. except during the Christmas season

Map 5

What started as a home business selling slings and cloth diapers is now an award-winning natural toy and baby care mini-emporium, with everything from Butt Balm to the best princess hats around. What you won't find is anything plastic or a single "two AA batteries required" sign. Everything in the store is made from wood or natural fibers—the sorts of things husband and wife Millie Adelsheim and Dan Marshall were looking for when they first started their family more than 12 years ago. The family is still behind the cash register and still a great source for information on natural parenting in the Twin Cities.

© BRUCE MANNING

Creative Kidstuff, in South Minneapolis, is widely recognized as one of the best toy stores around.

SIJI KIDS
1326B Grand Ave., St. Paul, 651/699-5290,
www.sijikids.com
HOURS: Mon.-Sat. 10 A.M.-7 P.M., Sun. noon-5 P.M.
Map 5

Style-minded parents of boys have it rough:
If you don't want footballs all over your kids'
clothes you have to dress them like little bankers. SIJI Kids solves that problem with comfortable, fashionable, upscale play clothes
for little boys from Tea Collection, Esprit,
American Apparel, and others. Little girls
don't get left out either (do they ever?), with
fashion-forward dresses and separates. The
best selection is for toddlers and preschoolers,
but sizes do run up to 8, and there's a rack of
sweet cotton duds for babies. If you've got the
kids along with you, they can chill in the large
playroom in back.

◖ WONDERMENT
4306 Upton Ave. S., Minneapolis, 612/929-2707,
www.wondermentshop.com
HOURS: Mon.-Fri. 10 A.M.-6 P.M., Thurs. untill 8 P.M.,
Sat. 10 A.M.-5 P.M., Sun. noon-4 P.M.
Map 2

There's barely a scrap of plastic in the whole
of this Waldorf-inspired wonderland. Instead
you'll find wooden play sets, soft cotton dolls,
HABA games from Germany, and plenty of
dress-up and art supplies. Everything here
is designed to inspire kids to do something,
rather than observe passively—even the store
itself. The wooden tree in the back corner
is full of young explorers climbing and hid-
ing while their parents shop. Three friends
founded Wonderment in the Linden Hills
neighborhood of Minneapolis in 2005 to share
some of what their children had experienced
together in the local Waldorf school, then expanded to St. Paul in 2008 (949 Grand Ave.,
651/291-5099). Watch for workshops in needle
felting, paper marbling, basic woodworking,
and more.

Gifts and Home

◖ THE BIBELOT
1082 Grand Ave., St. Paul, 651/222-0321,
www.bibelotshops.com
HOURS: Mon.-Fri. 9:30 A.M.-8 P.M., Sat. 9:30 A.M.-7 P.M.,
Sun. 11 A.M.-5 P.M.
Map 5

You need a spatula, a cute tote bag, something
for a friend's new baby, and maybe an inter-
view suit. And you can find it all in one place at
the Bibelot. More likely, however, you'll spend
your time browsing the shelves (arranged more
by theme than anything else; e.g., here's where
you'll find all the gifts that say, "You go, girl!)
and walking out with something completely
unexpected. So beloved is this local shop that it
has expanded to four locations, all of which will
have lines out the door on big sale days, especially when the clothes go on sale (the selection
runs to the mature and eccentric, like Eileen
Fisher). Sister shops are located in St. Paul's
St. Anthony neighborhood (2276 Como Ave.,
651/646-5651, Mon.–Fri. 9:30 A.M.–8 P.M.,
Sat. 9:30 A.M.–7 P.M., Sun. 11 A.M.–5 P.M.)
and two neighborhoods in Minneapolis
(4315 Upton Ave., 612/925-3175, Mon.–
Fri. 9:30 A.M.–8 P.M., Sat. 9:30 A.M.–7 P.M.,
Sun. 11 A.M.–5 P.M.; 300 Hennepin Ave. E.,
612/379-9300, Mon.–Fri. 9:30 A.M.–8 P.M.,
Sat. 9:30 A.M.–6 P.M., Sun. noon–5 P.M.).

◖ COOKS OF CROCUS HILL
877 Grand Ave., St. Paul, 651/228-1333,
www.cooksofcrocushill.com
HOURS: Mon.-Fri. 10 A.M.-9 P.M., Sat. 10 A.M.-7 P.M.,
Sun. noon-5 P.M.
Map 5

Both expert and aspiring home cooks will find
what they're looking for at Cooks of Crocus
Hill, from Le Creuset and All-Clad cookware
to shelves of cookbooks and a small collection

The Bibelot sells tempting trinkets and elegant clothing.

of pantry wares. The staff all know their way around a kitchen themselves and are more than happy to answer questions. If you're looking to improve your cooking chops yourself, see if there's room in an upcoming cooking class, held in professional kitchens at both locations. Also at 50th and France in Edina (3921 50th St. W., 952/285-1903, Mon.–Fri. 10 A.M.–9 P.M., Sat. 10 A.M.–6 P.M., Sun. noon–5 P.M.).

DANISH BOHEMIA
1144 Grand Ave., St. Paul, 651/222-8383,
www.danishbohemia.com
HOURS: Tues.-Fri. noon-6 P.M., Sat. 10 A.M.-5 P.M.,
Sun.-Mon. closed
Map 5

Beyond the stark metal and polished wood of Scandinavian design, there's another aesthetic in the cold northern countries. Think of a country house where everything is worn and well-cared-for and loved. That's the Denmark you'll find here, in this shop that still bears the original layout of the family home it once was.

There's a small collection of women's clothes and accessories, housewares—lots of inviting felted pillows—and a nursery area in muted colors and elegant lines.

FINNSTYLE
651 Nicollet Mall (2nd flr.), Minneapolis, 612/333-2127,
www.finnstyle.com
HOURS: Mon.-Fri. 10 A.M.-7 P.M., Sat. 10 A.M.-6 P.M.,
Sun. closed
Map 1

Fans of Finnish design are often single-minded in their passion. They love Marimekko's bold, modern fabric designs (which are getting lots of attention lately), Iitala's elegant and functional glassware, jewelry by Aarikka and Kalevala, and anything with children's writer Tove Jansson's Moomintrolls on it. These things aren't very easy to find, or they weren't until Finnstyle opened in downtown Minneapolis's Gaviidae Common and gathered them all into one place. Grab a Fazer milk chocolate by the cash register.

SOUVENIR HUNTING AT THE LARGEST MALL IN AMERICA

There's no need to be intimidated by the **Mall of America** (60 E. Broadway, Bloomington, 952/883-8800, www.mallofamerica.com, Mon.-Sat. 10 A.M.-9:30 P.M., Sun. 11 A.M.-7 P.M.). In a lot of ways, it's just like your local mall. Well, okay, four or five local malls put together, with an amusement park in the middle and a shark tank underneath. But, aside from its sheer size, the shopping experience – from the chain stores to the food court – will be very familiar to anyone who's spent time in any mall in the country. There's a good reason, however, for visitors to make a side trip to the mall, beyond just being able to say they've seen it: It's a great place to pick up Minnesota-themed souvenirs and gifts for family and friends.

A note about store addresses: The letter in front indicates the side of the mall the store is on – E for east, and so on – and the first of the three digits indicates the floor, so E350 is on the east end of the third floor.

A handful of specialty stores, tucked in among the Gap and Long John Silver's, make the mall a one-stop shopping destination for mugs, T-shirts, and key chains, as well as more specialized gifts. **Lake Wobegon USA** (E350, 952/854-3795, www.prettygood-goods.org) has everything a dedicated fan of Garrison Keillor's *A Prairie Home Companion* could want, from a Guy Noir cap to a Professional Organization of English Majors shirt. Outdoors enthusiasts will enjoy **Minnesota Bound** (W372, 952/854-9100, www.love-frommn.com), based on a locally beloved television show. The faux-rustic store is packed with gadgets and kitschy decor for the home and cabin.

The mall itself sells souvenirs at the **Mall of America Gift Store** (N128, 952/854-8257, www.mallofamericagifts.com), and three separate stores sell the typical sort of destination gear you might find in a college bookstore or airport shop: **Destination Minnesota** (E132, 952/883-9024), **Love from Minnesota** (W380, 952/854-7319, www.lovefrommn.com), and **Minnesot-ah!** (E157, 952/854-5882, www.lovefrommn.com).

© MEETMINNEAPOLIS.COM

THE GRAND HAND

619 Grand Ave., St. Paul, 651/312-1122,
www.thegrandhand.com

HOURS: Tues.-Sat. 11 A.M.-5 P.M., Thurs. untill 7 P.M.,
Sun. noon-5 P.M., Mon. closed

`Map 5`

This is where craft meets art meets great shopping. Pottery, jewelry, silk scarves, wrought iron, glasswork, and more—all made by hand and much, but not all, by artists from the Upper Midwest. The atmosphere is somewhere between a gallery and boutique: Come to look—especially in the River Gallery, attached to the shop, where there are regular exhibitions of fine art—but you may find it irresistible to buy.

█ INGEBRETSEN'S

1601 Lake St. E., Minneapolis, 612/729-9333,
www.ingebretsens.com

HOURS: Mon.-Fri. 9 A.M.-5:50 P.M., Sat. 9 A.M.-5 P.M.,
Sun. closed

`Map 2`

When a craving hits for Finnish licorice, Swedish *lefse* (a bland flatbread), or the universally Scandinavian lingonberry jam, folks in Minneapolis—whether descended from Scandinavian stock or not—head to Ingebretsen's. Half the store is given over to foodstuffs and the other half to exquisite and authentic handicrafts, including sweaters, rosemaling (Norwegian folk painting), and Swedish dala horses. Knitters will find a treasure trove of high-end natural fibers in the annex next door. Keep in mind that Ingebretsen's hews to the old ways in more ways than one: No credit cards are accepted.

PAPER SOURCE

3048 Hennepin Ave. S., Minneapolis, 612/377-0700,
www.paper-source.com

HOURS: Mon.-Sat. 10 A.M.-7 P.M., Sun. 11 A.M.-6 P.M.

`Map 2`

Good stationery and thoughtful wrapping paper are some of the subtle niceties that make life just a little bit better. You'll find terrific selections of them both in the only Minnesota outpost of this small but growing national chain. Racks of flat sheets of lush papers from India, Japan, and Italy line two of the walls and a third is taken up entirely by stationery sets. Displays devoted to rubber stamps and photo albums round things out, along with many off-beat baby shower gifts.

PATINA

1009 Franklin Ave. W., Minneapolis, 612/872-0880,
www.patinastores.com

HOURS: Mon.-Sat. 9:30 A.M.-9 P.M., Sun. 11 A.M.-6 P.M.

`Map 2`

A little kitsch, a little humor, a little modern design, a little inspiration. Mix it all up and that's what you'll find in Patina. There isn't a single object in a Patina store that anyone actually needs, but it takes just a few minutes to find something you never knew you wanted—or wanted very badly to give to a friend. A tape dispenser shaped like a frog, a cake server that looks like a high heel, a trout stapler. But not all is fun and games: You'll also find seriously

Patina shops are filled with trinkets you never knew you needed.

beautiful bags, jewelry, and modern kitchen goods. Patina has four other locations, including two in St. Paul (2057 Ford Pkwy., 651/695-9955, and 1581 Selby Ave., 651/644-5444) and two more in Minneapolis (2305 18th Ave. NE, 612/788-8933, and 5001 Bryant Ave. S., 612/821-9315), all open the same hours.

◀ TWIN CITIES GREEN

2405 Hennepin Ave. S., Minneapolis, 612/374-4581, www.twincitiesgreen.com

HOURS: Tues.-Sat. 11 A.M.-7 P.M., Sun. noon-5 P.M., Mon. closed

Map 2

When eco-minded artists and artisans get their hands on the detritus of modern life, you never know what they might come up with: a playhouse made out of mailing tubes, baby slippers out of ramen packets, furniture from old bowling alleys. And when they do, it is very likely to end up at Twin Cities Green, a perky store dedicated to the second part of the "reduce, reuse, recycle" mantra. And what little they sell that's not made from reclaimed materials is made with an eye toward sustainability and lower toxicity levels. While you're here, have a seat in the Do It Green! Resource Center in the back and browse resources related to green building and living.

Bath, Beauty, and Spa

GARDEN OF EDEN

867 Grand Ave., St. Paul, 651/293-1300, www.gardenofedenstores.com

HOURS: Mon.-Fri. 10 A.M.-8 P.M., Sat. 9:30 A.M.-8 P.M., Sun. 11 A.M.-5 P.M.

Map 5

Garden of Eden's own line of natural beauty products, which has been available since 1972, is totally customizable. Pick your product (shower gel, lotion, and more) and pick your scents, and have them mixed up right there. The store, in a small mall at the corner of Victoria and Grand, also offers a huge line of essential oils and products from Thymes and Caldrea (both Minnesota companies), Kiehl's, and Burt's Bees.

INTELLIGENT NUTRIENTS

983 Hennepin Ave. E., Minneapolis, 612/617-2000, www.intelligentnutrients.com

HOURS: Tues.-Sat. 11 A.M.-7 P.M., Sun.-Mon. closed

Map 3

When the founder of the internationally known Aveda line of styling products needed a new challenge, he decided to turn himself to the care of the entire body, inside and out. Horst Rechelbacher, Austrian transplant and longtime Twin Citian, created the Intelligent Nutrients line of aromatherapy oils, dietary supplements, hair care, chocolate bars, and teas—all organic. While those products are distributed in salons throughout the country, here at the national headquarters you will find a lush retail showroom, extraordinarily enthusiastic staff, and a small café serving healthful sandwiches, soups, and salads for lunch.

Wine and Gourmet Goodies

CHOCOLAT CELESTE

2506 University Ave. W., Minneapolis, 651/644-3823
HOURS: Tues.-Fri. 10 A.M.-6 P.M., Sat. 9:30 A.M.-5 P.M.,
Sun. closed
Map 6

It's a modern fairy tale: Successful business-woman chucks her high-powered career to find fulfillment in her passion—chocolate. That's what drove Mary Leonard to create Chocolat Celeste in 2002. Since then, chocolate lovers, the media, and the Food Network's Rachael Ray have all taken notice. In addition to the truffles and bonbons made on-site, Chocolat Celeste sells hard-to-find imported chocolates from France, Switzerland, and Venezuela. Heavenly chocolate doesn't come cheap: A four-piece box of bonbons is about $15.

█ FRANCE 44

4351 France Ave. S., Minneapolis, 612/925-3252,
www.france44.com
HOURS: Tues.-Sat. 11 A.M.-7 P.M., Sun.-Mon. closed
Map 2

Three generations of the Anderson family have sold wine at the corner of France Avenue and 44th Street on the border between South Minneapolis and the suburb of Edina, and you're likely to find an Anderson there during your visit. But what started out as a mom-and-pop store has grown into something far more ambitious: a full-service high-end wine shop with a decent selection of beer and liquor, a cheese shop, and a deli with sit-down service. While the focus at France 44 is on higher end wines, a bold customer can ask for a bottle under $15 and find a staffer eager for the challenge—and it is a challenge here.

THE GOLDEN FIG

790 Grand Ave., St. Paul, 651/602-0144,
www.goldenfig.com
HOURS: Mon.-Wed. and Sat. 10 A.M.-6 P.M.,
Thurs.-Fri. 10 A.M.-7 P.M., Sun. 10 A.M.-4 P.M.
Map 5

Jars of homemade jams, pickles, and chutneys. Cruets of flavored vinegars. Infused sugars, spice mixes, compound butters. Homemade caramels and marshmallows. All of it made in small batches, by hand, mostly right here in Minnesota. The Golden Fig is like a food lover's dream pantry. There is no way to walk into this small, friendly shop and not put together a fabulous gourmet snack. This is a great place to find local favorites, B. T. McElrath chocolates. Friday, by the way, is cupcake day, with flavors like limoncello and roasted peach on offer.

LEGACY CHOCOLATES

2042 Marshall Ave., St. Paul, 651/646-0644,
www.legacychocolates.com
HOURS: Mon.-Sat. 11 A.M.-7 P.M., Sun. noon-5 P.M.
Map 5

Serious chocolate lovers know there's one number that counts—the percentage of cocoa used in the mix. That's why all the truffles in this small, family-owned shop are labeled, from 41 percent all the way up to 99—yes, that's 99 percent cocoa, formidably dark chocolate. The truffles are all made without preservatives and may not travel well, but if you're looking for gifts, you can pick up Legacy's hot cocoa mix, their beloved Potion No. 9 chocolate sauce, and a sipping chocolate known as the Mayan Experience.

PREMIER CHEESE MARKET

5013 France Ave. S., Minneapolis, 612/436-5590,
www.premiercheesemarket.com
HOURS: Tues.-Sat. 9 A.M.-7 P.M., Sun. 11 A.M.-3 P.M.,
Mon. closed
Map 7

Cheese isn't the ideal souvenir, but it is a great way to experience one of the passions of the Upper Midwest—dairy products. Premier Cheese Market showcases award-winning local cheeses, like Big Woods Blue from Shepherd's Way Farm and Black River Blue from Wisconsin, right alongside the imported *delice de Bougogne* (a double cream brie) and the ultimate stinky cheese, *epoisses*. The staff are happy to show off their knowledge and even offer a taste. If you come around lunchtime, grab a sandwich or some bread, olives, and—of course—cheese, and have a picnic.

SURDYK'S

303 Hennepin Ave. E., Minneapolis, 612/379-3232, www.surdyks.com
HOURS: Mon.-Thurs. 9 A.M.-9 P.M., Fri.-Sat. 9 A.M.-10 P.M.
Map 3

What Surdyk's lacks in ambience it makes up

for in so, so many other ways: history (theirs was reputedly the first liquor license issued in Minneapolis after Prohibition), selection (name a country, they've probably got a bottle from there), and price. (Under $12? No problem. Under $10? Still no problem.) Even better is that you can pick up your fabulous $9 bottle of wine, then head next door to Surdyk's unmissable gourmet shop and blow all your savings on imported cheeses and chocolates.

Farmers Markets

LYNDALE MARKET

312 East Lyndale Ave. N., Minneapolis, 612/333-1718, www.mplsfarmersmarket.com
HOURS: Mid-Apr.-mid-Nov. daily 6 A.M.-1 P.M.
Map 1

Serious shoppers come to the Lyndale Market, one of the biggest produce markets in the Midwest. On weekend mornings, you may need to throw some elbows or block with a bag of bok choy to make it down the crowded aisles, but the bargains and the quality of the produce make it worth it. Vendors sell bratwurst and other treats, and artisans sell jewelry and other handicrafts at the Farmers Market Annex (the three covered sheds to the south). Competition for parking spots under the I-94 overpass is fierce, but the market is just a short walk from Loring Park.

◖ MILL CITY FARMERS MARKET

704 2nd St. S., Minneapolis, 612/341-7580, www.millcityfarmersmarket.org
HOURS: Mid-May-mid-Oct. Sat. 8 A.M.-1 P.M.
Map 1

More than just a place to buy some local, organic beets, the Mill City Farmers Market is an all-in-one Saturday morning experience. Start with a cup of coffee and a fruit tart, watch demonstrations and cooking competitions by local chefs, pet the chickens and tip the musicians, then swing through again for vegetables, meat, cheese, and bread to take home. By this time you're probably hungry again, so get a kebab or bratwurst

to eat on the steps overlooking the river. All this (and more!) is crammed into the old train yard connected to the Mill City Museum, next to the Guthrie Theater on the riverfront.

NICOLLET MALL MARKET

Nicollet Mall, between 5th St. and 12th St., Minneapolis, 612/333-1718, www.mplsfarmersmarket.com
HOURS: May-Nov. Thurs. 6 A.M.-6 P.M.
Map 1

One of the best ways to enjoy downtown Minneapolis is to join the river of people moving up and down Nicollet Mall at lunchtime on Thursdays, picking up string beans at one stall, flowers at the next, and bread or tamales one block down. Although much of the produce is grown locally, vendors are allowed to bring fruits and vegetables from outside the area. That means you can grab a peach and a roll from the St. Agnes bakery stall and enjoy it in the sunshine on Peavey Plaza (Nicollet Mall and 12th Street).

ST. PAUL FARMERS' MARKET

290 5th St. E., St. Paul, 651/227-8101, www.stpaulfarmersmarket.com
HOURS: late Apr.-mid-Nov. Sat. 6 A.M.-1 P.M., Sun. 8 A.M.-1 P.M.
Map 4

In a town where people have their pick of farmers markets and often have very strong opinions about them, the St. Paul Farmers' Market in the Lowertown neighborhood is widely regarded to be the best. It's just big enough to bustle a bit and offer a fantastic selection of vegetables and treats, without the overwhelming oppression of large crowds. All products must be locally grown and sold directly from the producer to the consumer. Most days there is live music 9 A.M.–noon.

Shopping Centers

ALBERTVILLE PREMIUM OUTLETS
6415 Labeaux Ave. NE, Albertville, 763/497-1911, www.premiumoutlets.com
HOURS: Mon.-Sat. 10 A.M.-9 P.M., Sun. 10 A.M.-7 P.M.
`Map 7`

With more than 100 stores, Albertville is worth the 45-minute drive from the Twin Cities. You'll find the usual suspects, from Ann Taylor and the Gap to Van Heusen and Tommy Hilfiger, and some rarer treats in the outlet world—Le Creuset cast iron cookware and Hanna Andersson clothing from Sweden. Aside from a small Dunn Bros. coffee shop, it's hard to find much in the way of a decent lunch near the outlets, so plan accordingly or be prepared for fast food. Watch for live music on summer weekend afternoons.

THE GALLERIA
3510 70th St. W., Edina, 952/925-4321
HOURS: Mon.-Fri. 10 A.M.-9 P.M., Sat. 10 A.M.-8 P.M., Sun. 11 A.M.-5 P.M.
`Map 7`

The Galleria, in the tony western suburb of Edina, is where you go in the Twin Cities if you want to have breakfast at Tiffany's. The other upscale stores arrayed along the mall's long central corridor (an oddly gloomy one, strangely enough) include the perfumery L'Occitane, Coach, the French children's clothier Oililly, and gardening great Smith and Hawken, to name just a few. When the ladies who shop and lunch get tired of the former, they have a healthy sandwich at the Good Earth Restaurant and Bakery (952/925-1001, Mon.–Sat. 7 A.M.–10 P.M., Sun. 7 A.M.–9 P.M.) or a big old steak at Kozy's Steaks and Seafood (952/224-5866, Sun.–Thurs. 11 A.M.–10 P.M., Fri.–Sat. 11 A.M.–11 P.M.).

THE SHOPPES AT ARBOR LAKES
I-94 and I-694 at Hemlock Ln., Maple Grove, 763/424-0504, www.shoppesatarborlakes.com
HOURS: Mon.-Sat. 10 A.M.-9 P.M., Sun. 11 A.M.-6 P.M.
`Map 7`

The sheer size of the Arbor Lakes shopping center is the draw, along with the piazzas and fountains that add a pleasant touch of fantasy to your suburban shopping experience. There are more than 75 stores and restaurants in this complex and well over two dozen in the nearby Fountains shopping area. You'll find nearly every major national chain and some local gems like Hot Mama. During the summer you might run into an outdoor music performance.

HOTELS

A building boom in the summer of 2008, just before the Republican National Convention came to St. Paul, added six major new hotels—five of them in downtown Minneapolis—and as many as 2,000 rooms to the Twin Cities area. That's good news for travelers looking for a little luxury, as each swank new hotel tried to top the last in style and amenities. It's also good news for travelers' budgets, as the new rooms eased up a hotel market with very high occupancy rates and made it a little more of a buyer's market.

There are still a few holes in the Twin Cities accommodation market. While prices in general will pleasantly surprise guests used to paying for hotels on the coasts, there aren't a lot of truly low-budget options—just a single small hostel. There also isn't a big bed-and-

breakfast culture in town, beyond a handful of lovely options in residential neighborhoods. For bed-and-breakfast options, the town of Stillwater, about 30 miles east of St. Paul (see the *Excursions* chapter) is the place to go.

CHOOSING A HOTEL

Most hotels in the Twin Cities are clustered in two areas. In downtown Minneapolis, you'll find high-end chains, many of which do a very fine job of masquerading as stand-alone hotels with an individual flair to suit the area. While, in general, downtown is your most expensive accommodation choice, there are also one or two surprising bargains. Keep in mind that, because downtown hotels cater to business travelers, prices tend to go down, rather than up, on the weekends, sometimes remarkably

© HYATT PRESS PHOTO LIBRARY

HIGHLIGHTS

LOOK FOR (TO FIND RECOMMENDED HOTELS.

(**Best Hotel for Art Lovers:** Downtown Minneapolis's **Chambers Minneapolis** prides itself on its multimillion-dollar art collection and even opens a small gallery space to the public (page 156).

(**Best Downtown Value:** In an expense-account world, the **Hotel Minneapolis** offers value and oodles of style for guests paying their own way and watching their budget (page 157).

(**Most Romance within View of the Downtown Skyscrapers:** It's easy to forget that the **Nicollet Island Inn,** on an island in the Mississippi, is within an easy walk of the central business district (page 158).

(**Best Way to Relive the Gilded Age:** The **W Minneapolis-The Foshay** is where 21st-century swank meets 1920s verve (page 158).

(**Best Place to See the Mississippi:** The best place to see the river is right on it, in the floating **Covington Inn Bed and Breakfast** (page 160).

(**Best Place to Impress Your Guests:** One of the oldest hotels in Minnesota, the **St. Paul Hotel** is the classic embodiment of all that a high-end hotel should be (page 160).

(**Best Hotel for Families:** The **Marriott Residence Inn, Edinborough** in Minneapolis's southern suburb of Edina comes with the best amenity of all: a three-story indoor play structure (page 163).

The St. Paul Hotel is among the oldest and most elegant in Minnesota.

so. Because it's so easily navigable on foot and is the hub for much of the area's public transportation, including light rail to and from the airport and Mall of America, downtown is a good choice if you're arriving without your own transportation.

In the southern suburbs, clustered around the Mall of America and the Minneapolis-St. Paul airport, you'll find just about every chain hotel you can name—upwards of 30, as a matter of fact. Nearly all of these offer shuttle service to and from the mall—convenient not only if shopping is your primary reason for visiting the Twin Cities, but also because the light rail trains depart from the mall to downtown Minneapolis. You won't,

however, find very much charm in the generic concrete jungle.

Downtown St. Paul offers a couple of reasonably priced chain options, as well as two that are truly unique and tempting—the grand St. Paul Hotel and the floating Covington Inn.

The Dinkytown neighborhood around the University of Minnesota, more or less directly between Minneapolis and St. Paul, also offers a couple of less-expensive chain hotel options catering to university guests (meaning that graduation, homecoming, and move-in weekends tend to be booked full), along with the homey inns mentioned here.

When you look to accommodations outside of Minneapolis and St. Paul proper, be sure to pay attention to which "side" of things you'll be staying on: The metro area sprawls, and while the town of Afton, for example, is very convenient for visitors to St. Paul and the east metro, it is quite a trek for those with business in Minneapolis or the west metro. The reverse is true of the cities of Chanhassen and Chaska.

Price ranges given here are for double occupancy in the high season (summer).

PRICE KEY

$ less than $150 per night

$$ $150-250 per night

$$$ more than $250 per night

Downtown Minneapolis   Map 1

ALOFT $
900 Washington Ave. S., Minneapolis, 612/455-8400, www.alofthotels.com

Is the typical chain hotel a little too stuffy for you? Aloft, part of the Starwood chain, wants you to feel right at home. Or, rather, to feel like you're right in your much cooler friend's loft-like home. Nine-foot ceilings, platform beds, huge walk-in showers, and funky furnishings (love the faux cowhide on the walls) feel very downtown and very of-the-moment, as do the Euro-inspired lobby lounge and bar. You also can't beat Aloft's location. A block from the river and right across from the Guthrie Theater, it's the first hotel to open in downtown's Mill District.

CHAMBERS MINNEAPOLIS $$$
901 Hennepin Ave. S., Minneapolis, 612/767-6900, www.chambersminneapolis.com

By the time you get to your room, you will have passed about $30 million worth of contemporary art displayed in the lobby. Valuable oil canvases hang in the guest rooms, and if that's not enough art, you can tune to the art channel on your plasma TV and watch video art. In fact, you don't even need to be checked in to soak up some of the art: The Burnet Art Gallery on the ground floor hosts several shows a year and is free and open to the public. The contemporary rooms themselves show a careful attention to aesthetics, with clean comfortable furnishings, two plasma TVs, and an iPod deck in every room. The

Rock Star Suite, which has been a temporary home to Sarah Jessica Parker, Francis Ford Coppola, and baseball star Alex Rodriguez, boasts a massive balcony with unique views of downtown.

THE DEPOT $$
225 3rd Ave. S, Minneapolis, 612/375-1700, www.thedepotminneapolis.com

The Depot is actually two hotels in one, both by Marriott—The Depot Minneapolis, a Renaissance Hotel, and, for extended stays, Residence Inn at The Depot. Both offer Marriott-level services in a fantastic location—just a block or so off the river on one side and a short walk to the skyway system on the other. Rates go way, way down on the weekends, when The Depot transforms from a business hotel to a comfortable family retreat (look for affordable packages including water park passes).

GRAND HOTEL MINNEAPOLIS $$$
615 2nd Ave. S., Minneapolis, 612/339-3655, www.grandhotelminneapolis.com

From the red-coated doorman to the ornate furnishings to the Godiva chocolate on your pillow at night, the Grand Hotel harks back to a time of great luxury and service. In fact, AAA has given it the highest rating of any Minneapolis hotel. Guests will appreciate the full range of business services and the direct connection to the skyway system, as well as complimentary access to the Lifetime Fitness

Center, with a full-size pool and indoor running track.

GRAVES 601 $$

601 1st Ave. N., Minneapolis, 612/677-1100,
www.graves601hotel.com

Sleek, sophisticated, and modern, Graves 601 offers a little bit of glamour during your stay in Minneapolis. Some of the extra touches are for comfort—rain showers and robes and slippers—while some are more practical—complimentary high-speed Internet access and shoeshines. The Graves is connected to the skyway system and convenient to the Target Center, the Hennepin Theatre District, and central business district. Ask for an upper-level room with a view of the skyline.

HILTON MINNEAPOLIS $$

1001 Marquette Ave., Minneapolis, 612/376-1000,
www.hilton.com

The Hilton makes a show-stopping first impression—all marble and mirrored columns, with chandeliers and bronze statues in the lobby. The lobby's always a lively place, too, with frequent events in the ballrooms upstairs and a large, popular bar. The 800-plus guest rooms aren't quite so lavishly appointed but, with carved oak furniture and up-to-date fabrics, go beyond the typical hotel room. The top two floors of the 25-story hotel are the executive level, with complimentary breakfast and hors d'oeuvres. The Hilton Minneapolis is consistently recognized by event organizers as one of the top hotels in the Pinnacle Awards. Even its pool area is far more pleasant than at most hotels.

HOTEL IVY $$$

201 11th St. S., Minneapolis, 612/746-4600,
www.thehotelivy.com

Comfortable, unfussy luxury is the Hotel Ivy's signature, from the cream-and-ivy color scheme to the elegant limestone bathrooms and the 400-thread-count sheets. (A nice touch: All guest rooms feature both a tub and a separate shower.) Part of the Starwood chain, it opened in summer 2008 and offers an accommodation option just off the skyway system and convenient to Orchestra Hall and the Minneapolis Convention Center. Porter & Frye, the Ivy's restaurant, has received good reviews. And the Ivy Spa Club, right on the premises, offers top-of-the-line fitness facilities and spa services.

◖ HOTEL MINNEAPOLIS $

215 4th St. S., Minneapolis, 612/340-2000,
www.thehotelminneapolis.com

When the Hotel Minneapolis opened in the summer of 2008, it hit some magical sweet spot, combining up-to-the-minute style and unbelievable value for a downtown hotel (rooms start at $129). While it is part of the Doubletree chain, the furnishings and design are entirely unique and rooted in local history. Originally built as a bank in 1906, the building still has original vaults in the lobby and in Restaurant Max, where they serve as conversation pieces, art, and—in the restaurant—a wine

The Hotel Minneapolis is a great bargain.

cellar. In the lobby, the bank's commanding marble columns are now surrounded by long couches and television sets that would feel at home in a modern loft. The rooms are spacious and equipped with modern toys like flat-screen TVs and iPod docking stations.

THE MARQUETTE HOTEL $ $

710 Marquette Ave., 612/333-4545,
www.marquettehotel.com

In 2008, *Budget Travel* named the Marquette to its list of best values in travel—in fact, it came in at number 28 worldwide. Located in the IDS Center, Minneapolis's tallest building, the Marquette has been around long enough to have mastered the art of customer service and earned that reputation. Rooms are extra large and comfortably appointed for business travelers, with particularly broad and comfortable desks. The decor is spare and grown-up, and many rooms look out on the elegant obelisk that was the city's tallest until the IDS surpassed it:

The Marquette Hotel's balcony in its in-house restaurant, Basil's, is featured in the opening credits of *The Mary Tyler Moore Show*.

the Foshay tower. The hotel restaurant, Basil's, is home to the indoor balcony featured in the credits of *The Mary Tyler Moore Show*.

NICOLLET ISLAND INN $ $

95 Merriam St. S., 612/331-1800,
www.nicolletislandinn.com

Would you like the river side, the park side, the city side, or the bridge side? The Nicollet Island Inn sits smack in the middle of the island from which it takes its name, so all of its 24 rooms offer distinctive views. The furnishings are distinctive as well, from the modern comfort of Sleep Number beds to the Victorian chairs and damask wallpaper. There's no pool or workout room—but who needs it when some of the most inviting walking paths in the city are right out the front door? While the inn is starting to attract more business travelers as downtown's central business district creeps closer to the river, the clientele are primarily here on pleasure, often celebrating weddings and anniversaries. (That also means that, unlike at other downtown hotels, prices go up rather than down on the weekends.)

SALOON HOTEL $

828 Hennepin Ave. S., 612/228-0459,
www.saloonmn.com

Gay-owned and gay-friendly, the Saloon (look for the "Hotel Amsterdam sign" and go upstairs) compares itself to the no-frills, inexpensive pensions in Europe. And that's about right. You won't find a better price (rooms start at $65), and everything is comfortably frayed, from the living-room-like lounge with its collegiate couches to the rooms themselves. The bar and dance club of the same name is right downstairs, so things might get a little rowdy. Longer-term rentals are available.

W MINNEAPOLIS- THE FOSHAY $ $ $

821 Marquette Ave., Minneapolis, 612/215-3700,
www.starwoodhotels.com

Wilbur Foshay's tribute to the Roaring '20s barely saw the glories of that high-flying

© TRICIA CORNELL

The gay-friendly Saloon Hotel is downtown Minneapolis's only truly low-budget option.

decade: It was completed just weeks before the stock market crashed in 1929. Nearly 80 years later, the building's rebirth as one of Minneapolis's poshest hotels is at least as showy as Foshay's original dream, if not more so. The original ceiling was restored at enormous cost, but the opulent furnishings and forward-thinking lighting are entirely 21st century. Wilbur's own office, notoriously extravagant, is now a bar called Prohibition, and his boardroom is available to rent for private events. Two other restaurants—the high-end Manny's Steakhouse and the more proletarian Key's Cafe, share the building. Guest rooms show a meticulous attention to detail—there are 230 of them, in more than 50 different designs. But it doesn't come cheap: Doubles range $400–4,000 a night.

South Minneapolis   Map 2

HISTORIC KING INN AND MINNEAPOLIS HOSTEL $

2400 Stevens Ave. S., Minneapolis, 612/874-0407, www.historickinginn.com, www.minneapolishostel.com

This 1909 mansion in a gentrifying section of South Minneapolis leads a double life. The Historic King Inn features seven private rooms, including a "bridal suite"—a converted dining room with a fireplace and early-20th-century antiques. The Minneapolis Hostel has 30 beds in five dormitory-style rooms segregated by sex. Together they're housed in this gracious and comfortable brick house, and all are decorated in a homey style, right down to the country-style floral bedspreads. All guests share the spacious and inviting sitting room and the fully equipped kitchen. Hostel guests need to show out-of-town ID and can inquire about longer-term housing during the off-season.

Nordeast and Dinkytown   Map 3

LEBLANC HOUSE
BED AND BREAKFAST $$

302 University Ave. NE, Minneapolis, 612/379-2570,
www.leblanchouse.com

Buffered from the traffic and bustle of downtown by the Mississippi River, the LeBlanc House sits in a remarkably quiet residential neighborhood and yet is still convenient for business travelers and tourists who want to take in downtown by foot. From the shady front porch to the tidy parlor, to the three guest rooms (each with its own private bathroom), the LeBlanc House feels like a step back in time, to the Victorian period in which it was built. Perhaps the biggest bonus: authentic Swedish pancakes—thin like crepes—with lingonberry jam for breakfast on weekend mornings.

WALES HOUSE $

1115 5th St. SE, Minneapolis, 612/331-3931,
www.waleshouse.com

The Carver family makes guests at Wales House feel like family. On the edge of the University of Minnesota's East Bank, the inn is located on a very quiet residential street, giving guests, many of whom are visiting the university from overseas, a taste of authentic neighborhood life. The 10 guest rooms—spare, homey, and comfortable—are a remarkable deal, just $60 for a room with a shared bath, $70 for a private bath (rates go down for weekly and monthly rentals). Guests gather for an organic continental breakfast each morning and have the use of the well-stocked kitchen and three common areas.

Downtown St. Paul and West Side   Map 4

◖ COVINGTON INN BED
AND BREAKFAST $$

100 Harriet Island Rd., St. Paul, 651/292-1411,
www.covingtoninn.com

This is the closest you'll ever get to the Mississippi without getting in and swimming. The Covington is a 1946 tugboat permanently moored at Harriet Island, right in downtown St. Paul. The four suites—remarkably spacious for having been carved out of the tight decks of a small ship—mix nautical touches with more typical bed-and-breakfast decor. In fact, you won't have to give up any of the comforts of home while staying on the boat, from private bathrooms and air conditioning to a working fireplace—the only thing missing is a television, which your hosts chose to leave out on purpose. Spring for the two-floor Pilot House Suite and you can see the lights of downtown.

◖ ST. PAUL HOTEL $$$

350 Market St., St. Paul, 651/292-9292,
www.saintpaulhotel.com

Old-school elegance is the rule at the St. Paul Hotel. The current building was built in 1910, but a hotel has operated on this spot in the heart of downtown St. Paul almost continuously since 1856. From the sweeping curved drive to the uniformed doormen in the grand lobby to the four-poster beds in the rooms, it almost feels like you're stepping back into that gilded age yourself. The St. Paul Hotel regularly wins top honors from respected national agencies, including AAA's Four-Diamond Award 24 years in a row, and is the only Minnesota hotel on *Condé Nast Traveler's* Gold List. Guests should be sure to pack their gym shoes: The fitness center, open 24 hours, is on the roof of the hotel and commands stunning views of St. Paul.

Como and St. Anthony
Map 6

BEST WESTERN BANDANA SQUARE $
1010 Bandana Sq., St. Paul, 651/647-1637,
www.bestwesternminnesota.com

It's not posh, but the setting is unique and the location, almost exactly halfway between downtown Minneapolis and downtown St. Paul, is very convenient for anyone with transportation. The people who will most appreciate this particular Best Western, however, are families with children. The hotel is located in an old rail depot that is also home to the Twin Cities Model Railroad Museum. Even if you don't have the time to visit the museum, the old train tracks and the small exhibit in the lobby will amuse the little ones.

Greater Twin Cities
Map 7

AFTON HOUSE INN $$
3291 St. Croix Tr. S., Afton, 651/436-8883,
www.aftonhouseinn.com

When you need a getaway in the midst of your getaway, the Afton House Inn is a good choice. Located 20 miles east of St. Paul, it's convenient to everything in the eastern metro area, and yet the quiet river town of Afton can be a destination in itself. With two dozen individually decorated rooms of all sizes (some start as low as $80), the inn has the charm of a bed-and-breakfast with the convenience of a small hotel. Ask about special treats like a Jacuzzi in the room (in some cases right next to the bed) and a private balcony overlooking the St. Croix River. The Afton House Inn also offers riverboat cruises and is well known in the Twin Cities for the high quality of its restaurant.

BIRD HOUSE INN $$
371 Water St., Excelsior, 952/474-0196,
www.birdhouseinn.com

Make yourself at home, borrow the kind innkeepers' bikes, check out their extensive DVD collection—that's the ethos here at Bird House Inn, about 20 miles from downtown Minneapolis. The Victorian house with the wide wraparound porch and second-story deck sits three blocks from the parks and public docks on the shores of Lake Minnetonka. The living and dining rooms are prim and formal, but the seven guest rooms are more relaxed (the Garden Room, in particular, is unique with its themed murals). Prices are much lower October through May, with discounts on weekdays and for multinight stays.

CHANHASSEN INN $
531 79th St. W., Chanhassen, 952/934-7373,
www.chaninn.com

When you need just the basics, at a very basic price, the Chanhassen Inn is ideal. Family-run, with 71 rooms, the inn is more comfortable, friendly, and clean than the chains in this price range (rooms start around $75). You won't find fancy furnishings, but you will find a couple of important touches, like free wireless Internet access and a small exercise room. The inn is about 20 miles west of Minneapolis.

CROWNE PLAZA BLOOMINGTON $$
5401 Green Valley Dr., Bloomington, 952/831-8000,
www.cpmsp.com

The Crowne Plaza is one of a host of chain hotels convenient to the Mall of America and the Minneapolis-St. Paul airport, but there are a few things that set it apart. One is its Olympic-size indoor swimming pool, pleasantly surrounded by lounge chairs in a space that—unlike at many hotel pools—actually invites lounging. It's also just one block away from the Hyland Lake Park Preserve,

CAMPING

You have to get pretty far outside of the central cities to pitch a tent or park an RV, but it's still possible to combine a trip to the Twin Cities with some good old-fashioned camping.

The **Three Rivers Park District** (www .threeriversparkdistrict.org) maintains three campgrounds within easy driving distance of Minneapolis. Call 763/559-6700 to make reservations at any of the campgrounds. A $7.50 fee per reservation will be charged. Campgrounds are open May–October. The campground in **Baker Park Reserve** (763/694-7662, $17-25 per night) is 20 miles west of Minneapolis and has 210 sites, about half with electricity. The 54 sites at **Lake Auburn Campground** (952/443-2911, $11) near Victoria, about 25 miles west of Minneapolis, are more rustic, with no electric or water hookups and no showers. The sites at **Red Pine Family Camping Area** (763/694-7777, $11) near Prior Lake, about 26 miles south of Minneapolis, are hike-in only, with no amenities beyond pit latrines.

Two **Minnesota State Parks** campgrounds are within easy driving distance of the metro area. Make reservations for campsites up to one year in advance at 866/857-2757 or www.stayatmnparks.com. The reservation fee is $8.50. Campsite fees are $12-20 per night.

In the far east metro area, **Afton State Park** (6959 Peller Ave., South Hastings, 651/436-5391, www.dnr.state.mn.us) is about 20 miles southeast of St. Paul and open year-round. There are 24 tenting sites located about one mile from parking lot, with wood and water available there. Flush toilets are located in the camp office, with vault toilets near the camping area. **Minnesota Valley State Park** (19825 Park Blvd., Jordan, 952/492-6400, www.dnr.state.mn.us) is about 40 miles southwest of Minneapolis, with 25 drive-in sites (good for car camping or RVs up to 50 feet long), eight hike-in sites, and three sites that can accommodate horses. The campground is open mid-May through Labor Day.

The nationwide chain of RV parks KOA has two campgrounds (or is that "kampgrounds?") in the metro area. **Minneapolis Northwest KOA** (10410, Brockton Ln. N., Maple Grove, 763/420-2255, www.koa.com) is 20 miles north of Minneapolis. **Minneapolis Southwest KOA** (3315 166th St. S. W., Jordan, 952/492-6440, www.koa.org) is about 35 miles south of Minneapolis. Both are open May–October and have RV and tent sites and cabins available, as well as a swimming pool and a mini-golf course on-site.

an oasis in here in concrete-covered suburbia. While at other suburban hotels, you might not even be able to walk around the block, here you can walk, jog, or even ski in the 1,000-acre preserve.

GRAND LODGE $

1700 American Blvd. E., Bloomington, 952/854-8700, www.waterparkofamerica.com

It's all about location at the Grand Lodge: This Radisson Hotel is inside the country's largest water park (or is it the other way around?) and right across the highway from the Mall of America. Some rooms even overlook the water slides and splash pools (the others look

out on the suburban knot of highways here, south of Minneapolis). All of the rooms are well equipped for traveling families, with refrigerators and microwaves. Plenty of deals combining accommodations with water park passes are available.

GRAND RIOS $$

6900 Lakeland Ave. N., Brooklyn Park, 763/566-8855, www.grandrios.com

Guests are likely to find this Ramada Inn crawling with little kids: It's within one of the Twin Cities' favorite indoor water parks. The water theme carries into the rooms, where the art and furniture all have a beach-vacation feel. Packages including water park passes are available, as are pool-side suites. Families will appreciate the extra-large rooms and fold-out furniture. Just north of Minneapolis, the hotel is conveniently located even for those not interested in getting wet.

◖ MARRIOTT RESIDENCE INN, EDINBOROUGH ❸

3400 Edinborough Way, Edina, 952/893-9300, www.marriott.com

All Residence Inn hotels offer affordable suites with kitchenettes. This one, however, also comes with an indoor park. Edinborough, maintained by the city of Edina, is a one-acre indoor park with flowers, trees, a small waterfall, and a concert stage, along with an indoor pool, gym, and a three-story children's climbing structure called Adventure Peak. It's all attached to the hotel—along with a child-care center and senior citizens' residence—and guests get free entry. The park itself can be deafeningly loud, but the hotel is completely insulated from the noise.

EXCURSIONS FROM MINNEAPOLIS AND ST. PAUL

Residents of the Twin Cities—as blessed as they are with ready access to lakes and trails—have a time-honored tradition of getting the heck out of town whenever they possibly can. They go "up north" or "to the cabin"—vague answers to the question "What did you do this weekend?" that are as evocative to a native Minnesotan as a full description of the destination and the route. They tend to do this, en masse, on summer Fridays, when the highways headed out of town (especially going north and east) clog up in the early afternoon.

Even if you don't have a family cabin in Minnesota, you can enjoy a little bit of the "up north" lifestyle with a weekend in Duluth, on the shore of Lake Superior. Or you can spend a day in one of Minnesota's most charming small towns—shopping for antiques in Stillwater, hiking up the bluffs of Red Wing, or soaking up the college-town atmosphere in Northfield. When you head out of the cities, the transformation is dramatic. You can leave behind the skyscrapers and mild congestion of either downtown in a matter of minutes and find yourself in a compact grid of single-family homes. You can put the straight urban streets behind you and find the curvy lanes of suburbia in another easy quarter of an hour, and then a few moments later you're driving through farmland. Stick to the two-lane rural highways and you'll come upon two-intersection towns in a steady rhythm, the sort with a church, a coffee shop, and a hardware store.

Minnesota's flat prairie is a stunning sight for natives of the hillier, woodsier, more crowded coasts, who may never have seen the

© TRICIA CORNELL

HIGHLIGHTS

LOOK FOR (TO FIND RECOMMENDED SIGHTS, ACTIVITIES, DINING, AND LODGING.

(**Best Antique Shopping in Minnesota:** With a half dozen large antiques stores and antiquarian booksellers within easy walking distance, Stillwater's **Historic Main Street** takes the prize, hands down (page 169).

(**Most Jaw-Dropping View of the Mississippi River:** Near Red Wing, the great river broadens into the stunning Lake Pepin, easily viewed from a 20-mile stretch of the **Great River Road** (page 174).

(**Best Birding, Even for Non-Birders:** Eagles and other raptors congregate around Lake Pepin's warm waters on the Mississippi River and are easily spotted from the **National Eagle Center** (page 175).

(**Best Place to Enjoy the Student Lifestyle:** In the quiet college town of Northfield, students from both Carleton and St. Olaf Colleges have long enjoyed the pleasure

of hiking and running in **Carleton College's** 800-acre Cowling Arboretum (page 178).

(**Best Treat for Shipping Buffs:** With a copy of the *Duluth Shipping News* in hand, you can be sure to time your stop in **Maritime Duluth** at the aerial lift bridge in **Canal Park** to see it lift straight up and allow a massive freighter to pass through to the docks (page 182).

(**Most Iconic Minnesota Sight:** The **Split Rock Lighthouse** looks impressive on a postcard or Minnesota Historical Society brochure, but that's nothing compared to marveling at the building in person and staring straight down the bluff at Lake Superior 600 feet below (page 184).

(**Best Way to Go Back in Time:** The railroad helped transform Duluth from a swamp to a major shipping port. Now you can enjoy pleasure rides along the North Shore of Lake Superior or the wooded St. Louis River, leaving from the **Union Depot** (page 184).

Split Rock Lighthouse

© MINNESOTA HISTORICAL SOCIETY

EXCURSIONS

EXCURSIONS

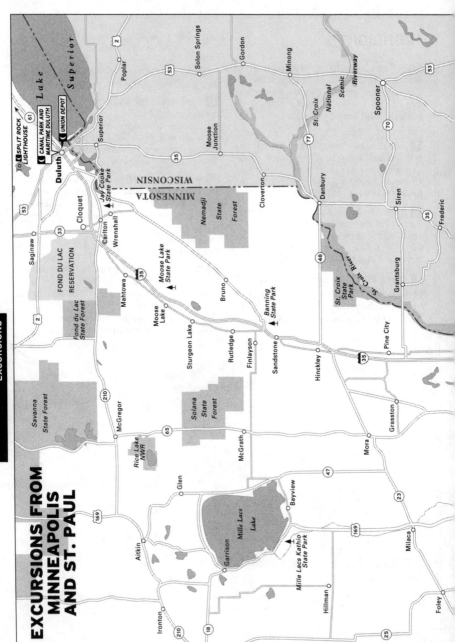

EXCURSIONS FROM MINNEAPOLIS AND ST. PAUL

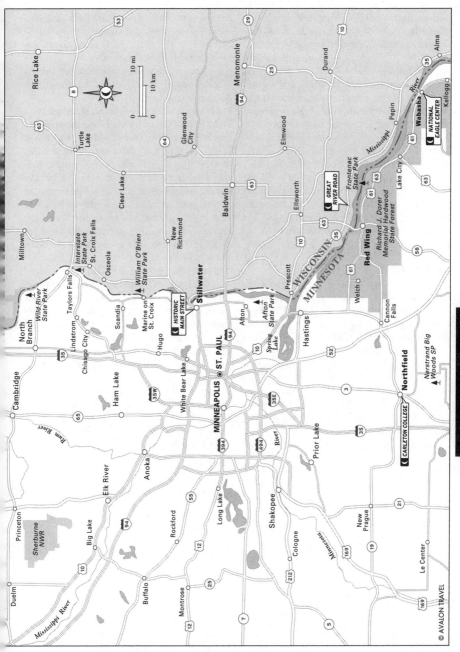

EXCURSIONS

horizon over land. Watching lightning strike where the land meets the sky, miles away, during early summer thunderstorms is simply unforgettable (if a little ill-advised, unless you're familiar with the local weather patterns). As you head south and east toward Red Wing and the bluff country, the prairie starts to roll and then spike into majestic hills whose downward slant drops you right at the Mississippi River. North of the Twin Cities, the ancient mountains of the Iron Range touch down lightly at Duluth, a city built between the foothills and Gitchigami—the "great water"—as the Ojibwe call Lake Superior. And all along the way, there are lakes—well more than the advertised "10,000"—and the Minnesota landscape that calls Twin Citians inexorably to head "up north" and "to the cabin."

PLANNING YOUR TIME

If you have an extra day or two in the Twin Cities, it's easy enough to head for the small towns and farmland that surround them—easy, that is, if you have your own transportation. Stillwater, just 20 miles from St. Paul, is close enough to be considered a commuting suburb, but it has enough history and personality of its own to make it worth exploring. This is our top pick if you've got limited time. It's a very comfortable day trip, but the huge selection of bed and breakfasts and the great dining options could easily tempt you to stay longer.

Two of Minnesota's most charming small towns, Red Wing and Northfield, are also within short driving distance, to the southeast and south of the cities, respectively. An ambitious sightseer could combine the two trips into one day but would lose out on the whole point of a relaxing, laid-back southern Minnesota jaunt.

Duluth is both a popular weekend getaway and a good place to kick off a more outdoorsy expedition on the North Shore. While you could certainly get a taste of the city in a day of wandering Canal Park, the 300-mile round-trip drive (straight north on I-35) might take the joy out of it. A better idea would be to plan at least one overnight, preferably in a homey bed-and-breakfast, and make sure you have enough time to drive up the stunning shore of Lake Superior, at least as far as the Split Rock lighthouse.

Summer brings out the boating crowd and the T-shirt–buying hordes, but Duluth's famous "air-conditioning" (the lake keeps the center of town as much as 10–20°F cooler than the surrounding area) can make braving the crowds worth it. The North Shore, like much of Minnesota, truly shines in September and October. (Fall foliage typically peaks in early October.)

Any expedition outside the Twin Cities will require a car, with a couple of possible exceptions: An Amtrak train makes one trip a day each way to Red Wing, and Greyhound services Duluth.

Stillwater

Stillwater is where Twin Citians go to relax. Just half an hour from St. Paul, the small town on the St. Croix River is close enough to be a commuting suburb but is distinct enough in its history to be an easy escape from the daily grind. From May to October, tourists fill the historic downtown on the riverfront, an easy all-in-one stop for shopping, boating, fine dining, and drinking beer on a long summer evening on a deck overlooking the river. In the off-season—Minnesota's beautiful autumn and fleeting spring, even the cold winters—the crowds are smaller, but all of Stillwater's delights are still open and available. Stillwater can easily be enjoyed in a day—or even just a long evening.

SIGHTS
◖ Historic Main Street

A trip to Stillwater can start and end quite satisfactorily on historic Main Street, which stretches along the riverfront. Storefronts dating to the mid-19th century crowd the sidewalk, now occupied by bookstores, candy shops, and tchotchke boutiques as well as antiques stores, antiques stores, and more antiques stores. Start at the south end, where Nelson Street crosses Main Street, and stroll north about half a mile to the train station. How long it takes you will depend on how avid a shopper you are. At either end of your trip, long, steep flights of steps (the steps at the south end are known as the **Stillwater Steps**) will take you to the top of the bluff for spectacular views of the St. Croix and the still green and undeveloped Wisconsin side of the river.

Joseph Wolf Brewery

At the south end of Main Street, at the base of the Stillwater Steps, a unique piece of Stillwater history is open for tours. In the late 19th century, the Joseph Wolf Brewery dug caves into the limestone cliffs to house its operations. At its high point, the brewery shipped 25,000 barrels of beer a year. Prohibition put the brewery out of business and the caves lay vacant for half a century. Today the **Luna Rossa** Italian restaurant (402 Main St. S., Stillwater, 651/430-0560) occupies the facility and offers half-hour cave tours Thursday–Sunday noon–5 P.M., on the hour. Tour times may be more limited during the off-season. Tickets are $5 and may be purchased at Luna Rossa's European-style gelato and espresso bar (where a gelato on the outdoor patio makes an excellent treat after the tour).

Stillwater Aerial Lift Bridge

The Stillwater aerial lift bridge, built in 1931, is one of only two of its type left in Minnesota (the other is in Duluth). The central part of the bridge lifts straight up, rather than tilting, to let boats pass through. Although the bridge is of tremendous sentimental value to locals and visitors alike, its days may be numbered. Its single lanes in each direction are simply insufficient to handle the traffic through

Stairways lead up the bluffs for great views of the St. Croix River and the Stillwater aerial lift bridge.

EXCURSIONS

© TRICIA CORNELL

downtown Stillwater, and it is known to have serious structural issues.

Warden's House Museum

At the north end of Main Street, the Washington County Historical Society displays another piece of Stillwater's history in the Warden's House Museum (602 Main St. N., Stillwater, 651/439-5956, May–Oct. Thurs.–Sun. 1–5 P.M., $5 adults, $1 children 6–17). From the time it was completed in 1853 until 1914, the building housed 13 wardens who presided over the Minnesota Territorial—and then State—Penitentiary in Stillwater. Most of its 14 rooms are decorated in late-19th-century period style. Others house exhibits on the lumbering industry and some famous residents of the prison, including Jesse James's partners in crime, Jim, Bob, and Cole Younger.

RESTAURANTS

Even natives of the Twin Cities—who are now spoiled for choice when it comes to fine dining—have been known to drive to Stillwater for a memorable meal. One particular destination is **◖ Savories European Bistro** (108 Main St. N., Stillwater, 651/430-0702, www.savories-bistro.com, breakfast Sat.–Sun. 8 A.M.–1 P.M., lunch Tues.–Fri. 10:30 A.M.–3 P.M. and Sat.–Sun. 11:30 A.M.–3 P.M., dinner Tues.–Sun. 5–9 P.M., Mon. closed). The menu changes every month or so but always features pizzas and pastas with a touch of luxury—whether it's lobster or housemade sausage. You may also find a Moroccan-inspired lamb burger or the classic bistro *steak frites*. Entrées run $12–20. Lunch features creative sandwiches on housemade bread. The dining room itself is cosy, bright, and homey, stuffed with bric-a-brac.

An equally luxurious meal can be had at **The Dock Café** (425 Nelson St. E., Stillwater, 651/430-3770, www.dockcafe.com, Mon.–Thurs. 11 A.M.–9 P.M., Fri.–Sat. 11 A.M.–10 P.M., Sun. 11 A.M.–8 P.M.), with the added bonus of a broad shaded patio right on the river. Although none of the fish itself comes from the St. Croix River, the location calls for

a menu heavy on the seafood, from the local favorite walleye to scallops, shrimp, tuna, and salmon. Non–fish lovers can enjoy chicken, steaks, and burgers, but vegetarians will have a tough time filling up. Expect to pay $15–30 for an entrée. Even if the weather isn't right for dining alfresco, the large plate glass windows in the dining room make every meal feel like outdoor dining.

For a different sort of treat, stop into **Aprille's Showers Tea Room** (120 Main St. N., Stillwater, 651/430-2004, www.aprilleshowers.com, Mon.–Sat. 10 A.M.–4 P.M., Sun. noon–4 P.M.). The main dining room and balcony are filled with frilly, flowery knick-knacks straight from Grandma's house (many for sale). High tea, with both sweets and savories, is $19.95. A lighter snack is $13.95. Teas, sandwiches, and salads are also available à la carte. Watch for frequent American Girl teas, where girls and their dolls are welcome, and for Christmas teas around the holidays.

There's no reason you can't fuel your stroll through Stillwater with a more down-market, but entirely enjoyable, meal at **Chicago Dogs** (402 Main St. N., Stillwater, 651/323-7150, www.chicagodogsmn.com, April–Nov. daily 11 A.M.–9 P.M.). Order from the window at this little nook in the Isaac Staples Sawmill building and grab one of the handful of seats. You can get an honest-to-goodness Vienna all-beef dog in a poppy seed bun with all the Chicago-approved toppings, or pick your own toppings. Chicago Dogs also serves Italian beef sandwiches, gyros, and veggie pitas.

RECREATION

While you can have a terrific time in Stillwater without ever getting on the water, the St. Croix River is an obvious attraction. The **St. Croix Riverboat and Packet Co.** (525 Main St. S., Stillwater, 651/430-1234, www.stillwaterriverboats.com) offers two or three cruises a day, most with a meal included for $12–30 depending on the time and menu. Six boats, with capacities of 50 to 675, make the tours north up the picturesque St. Croix, passing under the lift bridge.

© TRICIA CORNELL

Tour boats take passengers up and down the St. Croix River in Stillwater.

You can also ride smaller—much smaller—boats on the river, namely the two-passenger gondolas of **Gondola Romantica** (Nelson St. on the riverfront, Stillwater, 651/439-1783, www.gondolaromantica.com). Rides on the Venetian-style boats poled by burly men in striped sailor's shirts start at $95 for 45 minutes. Packages combining a ride with a meal at the **Dock Café** are also available.

If you want to be in control of your own craft, rent a kayak from **P.J. Asch Otterfitters** (413 Nelson St. E., Stillwater, 651/430-2286, www.pjaschotterfitters .com, Mon.–Fri. 10 A.M.–9 P.M., Sat. 10 A.M.–6 P.M., Sun. noon–5 P.M.) for $35 a day or $50 for two days. P.J. Asch, located in an old grain elevator, also offers kayak classes, Nordic ski rental, and an indoor climbing wall with more than 6,000 square feet of surface. Climbers should come in pairs or be prepared to pay someone to belay them. Beginner's lessons cost $30 and a climbing day pass is $6 plus equipment rental ($14 for a package including shoes, harness, helmet, chalk bag, and belay plate).

SHOPS

Shopping is a pastime and a passion for many visitors to Stillwater, many drawn specifically by the well more than half a dozen antiques shops and antiquarian booksellers downtown. You'll encounter rare finds but none too many deals. One of the largest antiques shops is **Staples Mill Antiques** (410 Main St. N., Stillwater, 651/430-1816, daily 10 A.M.–6 P.M.), located in the old mill building at the north end of Main Street. As many as 30 dealers sell in the store's three levels, on more than 10,000 square feet of sales floor. You'll find pieces large and small, including furniture, depression glass, jewelry, and old magazines.

Midtown Antiques (301 Main St. S., Stillwater, 651/430-0808, www.midtownan-tiques.com, Mon.–Thurs. 10 A.M.–5 P.M., Fri.–Sat. 10 A.M.–7 P.M., Sun. 11 A.M.–6 P.M.; open Mon.–Thurs. until 5 P.M., Thurs. until 8 P.M. during summer) is even larger, with 100 dealers in an overwhelming 30,000 square feet. With so much on offer, you could stumble across virtually anything on one of the three floors. Appropriate to the setting, many dealers specialize in Victorian pieces, others in Modern or Middle Eastern. A particularly nice selection of old advertisements is available.

Books are another Stillwater passion. At one time there were 35 booksellers in this small town, though some have fallen on hard times. In 1994 Stillwater was "officially" named the first North American "Booktown" by the equally book-obsessed city of Hay-on-Wye in Wales. **Loome Theological Booksellers** (320 4th St. N., Stillwater, 651/430-1092, www.loomebooks.com, Mon.–Sat. 9 A.M.–5 P.M., Sun. closed) has more than a quarter million volumes on religion, housed, appropriately and beautifully, in the Old Swedish Covenant Church. Right on the main drag, **St. Croix Antiquarian Booksellers** (232 Main St. S., Stillwater, 651/430-0732, Tues.–Sun. 11 A.M.–5 P.M.) is everything a used bookstore should be but so often is not: It's brightly lit and spacious enough to house its 40,000 volumes without stacking them willy-nilly on the floor. There's plenty of room to browse in dignity—at tables and chairs. The store has recently added new and used globes and maps to its inventory, including a huge searchable collection of 19th-century house plans. Watch for signs advertising occasional theater performances at the store.

Valley Bookseller (217 Main St. N., Stillwater, 651/430-3385, www.valleybookseller.com, Sat.–Wed. 10 A.M.–7 P.M., Thurs.–Fri. 10 A.M.–8 P.M.) is an independent bookseller with a serious independent streak, right down to the birds living in a beautiful glass house in the middle of the store. While most of the selection is new books, a few good bargains on used are mixed in. Free Wi-Fi is available for use.

HOTELS

Stillwater is known for its historic inns and bed-and-breakfast options. The **Stillwater Bed and Breakfast Association** (www.stillwaterbb.com) represents seven of them, all within easy walking distance of Main Street and the waterfront. High-season weekend rates are given here. Prices drop considerably in the winter and on weekdays. Some inns have a two-night minimum on the weekends.

Among the best known is the 🄲 **Elephant Walk Inn** (801 Pine St. W., Stillwater, 651/430-0359, www.elephantwalkbb.com, $169–299 d). Proprietors Rita and Jon Graybill have filled the Victorian mansion with mementos from their diplomatic tours in Europe and Asia, and each of the four rooms reflects the flavor of one of their favorite countries. The house and owners are both filled to bursting with charm, right down to the complimentary bottle of wine and four-course breakfast that comes with each night's stay.

Particularly convenient to downtown, the **Rivertown Inn** (306 Olive St. W., Stillwater, 651/430-0359, www.rivertowninn.com, $200–325 d) has nine rooms each decorated in the style of a favorite author, from Agatha Christie to Oscar Wilde to Lewis Carroll. The mansion, with its broad, comfortable porch, and the carriage house are surrounded by fantastical gardens with fountains and a gazebo. The large professional kitchen offers cooking classes about once a month. Plan ahead if you want to include one in your trip: These sell out fast.

High above the southern end of downtown, the **Ann Bean Mansion** (319 Pine St. W., Stillwater, 651/430-0355, www.annbeanmansion.com, $179–199 d) represents a lumberman's wife's determination to show up her neighbors with a grand house. The five rooms are all comfortably, though not sumptuously, furnished. The fourth-floor tower room is as cozy as a treehouse and has one of the best views in Stillwater. The mansion does have a resident cat, but guests may ask that it be kept in the innkeeper's residence.

PRACTICALITIES
Tourist Office

The Greater Stillwater Chamber of Commerce maintains a well-stocked visitors center right in the middle of town (106 Main St. S., Stillwater, 651/439-4001, www.ilovestillwater.com). During the summer you can stop by to ask questions or pick up brochures (Mon.–Fri. 9 A.M.–6 P.M., Sat. 10 A.M.–6 P.M., Sun. 11 A.M.–5 P.M.). Hours during the off-season are slightly shorter (Mon.–Fri. 9 A.M.–5 P.M., Sat. 10 A.M.–2 P.M., Sun. closed). The office also has a host of information about the rest of the St. Croix Valley.

Media

Stillwater's daily newspaper is the **Stillwater Gazette,** part of the Sun community newspaper chain. The **Stillwater Courier** comes out weekly on Thursdays. Both focus very closely on local news. The Twin Cities dailies, as well as the several Twin Cities free monthly and weekly magazines, are widely available all over town. **Valley Bookseller** stocks English-language international papers.

Getting There

One Metro Transit bus—the 294—travels between downtown St. Paul and downtown Stillwater (Water St. and Myrtle St. in the parking lot on the riverfront). It's a commuter bus, so it runs 6–9 A.M. and 4–6:30 P.M., about every half hour. The ride takes about an hour. Pay your fare ($2.75) in cash as you board. No change is given.

For convenience's sake, you'll most likely want to drive. Highway 36 east from Minneapolis or St. Paul (it runs across the northern half of the metro area) will drop you directly on Main Street.

Getting Around

Once you're in Stillwater, navigating on foot is very easy, as everything is within a block or two of the main half-mile stretch of Main Street.

Red Wing and the Mississippi Bluffs

The city of Red Wing began on the site of a Dakota farming village. White missionaries and settlers began arriving in 1837, but the city saw a huge boom in population in the 1860s and '70s, when this became a key—and even for a time the *most* important—shipping point in the world for wheat. When the wheat trade shifted elsewhere, Red Wing became an important manufacturing city—most notably (and this is where you've heard the name before, in case you've been wondering) for shoes and pottery.

Red Wing work boots and Red Wing pottery are still a big draw for tourists, who come for good prices and to see the famous products at their source. The city itself is compact and can be enjoyed in a single full day, including a trip to the **Red Wing Stoneware Factory.** But if you want to enjoy the other wonders of the bluffland, including the glistening **Lake Pepin** and charming small river towns like **Wabasha,** add in an overnight.

Pleasure boats speed up and down the wide Mississippi River, south of Red Wing.

SIGHTS
Red Wing's Historic Downtown

Red Wing's historic downtown district is a well-preserved and welcoming area of a half dozen blocks, just steps from the Mississippi River. While tourists will find plenty to do, this is a modern, working business district, where barbers, hardware stores, and appliance stores sit in among the gift shops. A perfect example of the mix of old and new is the **Sheldon Theatre** (443 W. 3rd St., Red Wing, 651/388-8700, www.sheldontheatre.org). A landmark since 1905, the playhouse, with its ornate interior restored to its original splendor, now shows a thoroughly modern mix of comedies, children's shows, concerts, and lectures.

Just four miles north of downtown, you can get a taste of Red Wing's manufacturing past and present. The **Red Wing Stoneware Factory** (4909 Moundview Dr., Red Wing, 651/388-4610, www.redwingstoneware.com) offers 20-minute tours weekdays at 10:30 A.M., 1 P.M., and 3:30 P.M. Watch potters and painters at work on the distinctive, heavy gray and blue crocks, butter churns, bowls, and more. (Note that Red Wing Pottery, with a factory store also located off Highway 61, is a separate company.)

The river bluffs that make this area unique are another draw in Red Wing. The easiest way to get a panoramic view of the city is to take the short but winding drive to the top of Sorin's bluff in **Memorial Park** (entrance at 542 E. 7th St., Red Wing). You'll also find hiking trails and disc golf. For a more rewarding but much harder-won view, head to **Barn Bluff** (steps at 500 E. 5th St., Red Wing). The steps to the top of the 350-foot limestone cliff may leave you huffing and puffing, but you'll have a nearly 360-degree view of Red Wing.

◖ Great River Road

Minnesota's Great River Road follows the Mississippi River from the headwaters in Itasca State Park to the Iowa border. In bluff country, the Great River Road curves along **Lake Pepin,** one of Minnesota's most popular destinations, for most of the lake's 22-mile length.

Red Wing, once a busy port, is now a popular tourist destination.

© TRICIA CORNELL

EXCURSIONS

Lake Pepin is the name given to the widest part of the Mississippi River from Red Wing to Reads Landing. It was formed by sediment carried down by the much narrower and steeper Chippewa River and dumped at the confluence of the two rivers, blocking the flow of the water upstream in the Mississippi. Spectacular views can be had from the road, especially on sunny summer days, when the wide smooth water glistens on one side and 450-foot bluffs soar on the other. There are several opportunities to pull off the highway at observation points and rest stops.

◖ National Eagle Center

The stretch of the Mississippi River below Lake Pepin doesn't freeze over in the winter, thanks to the warm water pouring down from the lake and the turbulence that forms at the confluence with the Chippewa River. This attracts, among other hungry species, bald eagles, who feed in the ice-free water. While hundreds of eagles live here year-round, peak eagle-viewing time comes when the cold weather hits, mid-November to mid-March. As many as 700 eagles have been counted in the area on a single day, according to the National Eagle Center (20 Pembroke Ave., Wabasha, 651/565-4989, www.nationaleagle-center.org, daily 10 A.M.–5 P.M., $6 adults, $5 seniors, $4 children). The Eagle Center, a modern building among century-old storefronts in the tiny historic town of Wabasha, sits directly on the river, with a small observation deck and spotting scopes aimed at the highway stretching over the river into Wisconsin. That's where eagles and other birds like to congregate. The center itself is home to four bald eagles who were all injured in the wild and now live in the exhibit hall, where visitors can get up close and personal without glass or fencing in the way. After visiting the eagles, it's worth sparing some time to wander down Wabasha's Main Street to **Beach Park** and the marina, passing the **tourist information office** (137 W. Main St., Wabasha, 651/565-4158) along the way.

LARK Toys

Farther south down Highway 62 (about 35 miles from Red Wing), the focus shifts from natural wonders to the wonder of childhood. LARK Toys (171 LARK Lane, Kellogg, 507/767-3387, www.larktoys.com, Mon.–Fri. 9 A.M.–5 P.M., Sat.–Sun. 10 A.M.–5 P.M.) grew up in this off-the-beaten-path location thanks to one family's passion for wooden toys. LARK stands for Lost Arts Revival by Kreofsky. Now the 20,000-square-foot store sells original LARK designs (including rockers, doll houses, and puzzles) as well as carefully selected toys, art supplies, science kits, and books in seven showrooms. While the 85-mile trip from the Twin Cities may seem like an awful lot for a toy store, even a truly great one, LARK is much more than a toy store: An 18-hole mini-golf course (May–Oct., $5 adults, $4 children) stays open until 9 P.M. on warm summer Fridays and Saturdays, and, almost worth the trip in itself, a fantastical carousel with carved moose, beavers, flamingos, and ostriches operates right in the middle of the café. Like any good children's fantasy, the café serves hamburgers, hot dogs, onion rings, ice cream, and fudge. In January and February, LARK Toys takes a little break, staying open only on Fridays, Saturdays, and Sundays.

RESTAURANTS

Even the most upscale restaurants in Red Wing have a casual, resort-town air to them in the summer. The swankest hotel in town, the **St. James Hotel** (406 Main St., Red Wing, 651/388-2846, www.st-james-hotel.com) has two restaurants and a pub where it's definitely no-jackets-required. **The Veranda** (Mon.–Sat. 6:30 A.M.–8 P.M., Sun. 7:30 A.M.–8 P.M.) serves breakfast (try the Sturdiwheat pancakes with maple-vanilla sauce), lunch, and a light dinner (hearty batter-fried walleye or a lighter sandwich) on the patio or inside, both with a great view of Levee Park and the Mississippi. Downstairs, **Port** (daily 5–9 P.M.) serves steak and seafood in a former bank vault.

A more casual—and thoroughly modern— meal is available at **Lily's Coffee House** (419 W. 3rd St., Red Wing, 651/388-8797, www.lily-scoffeehouse.com, Mon.–Fri. 7 A.M.–5:30 P.M., Sat. 7 A.M.–4:30 P.M., Sun. closed). Generous, classic sandwiches and updated wraps can be had for under $7. Sit in the comfortable dining room or on the flower-bedecked patio in the alley. Very hearty sandwiches can also be had at the **Subhouse** (210 Bush St., Red Wing, 651/388-0111, Mon.–Tues. 10 A.M.–7 P.M., Wed.–Fri. 10 A.M.–8 P.M., Sat. 10 A.M.–5 P.M., Sun. 11 A.M.–4 P.M.).

Liberty's Restaurant and Lounge (303 W. 3rd St., Red Wing, 651/388-8877, www.lib-ertysonline.com, Sun.–Thurs. 8 A.M.–11 P.M., Fri.–Sat. 8 A.M.–midnight) has white tablecloths and a long menu that mixes a bit of the upscale (steak and lobster) with a bit of the downscale (breakfast all day). Family-owned for more than 30 years, Liberty's keeps everybody happy, with Friday fish fry buffets and free shuttle service to and from area marinas and hotels.

RECREATION

One of the most popular ways to experience the natural beauty of southeastern Minnesota is on the **Cannon Valley Trail** (trail office: 825 Cannon River Ave., Cannon Falls, 507/263-0508, www.cannonvalleytrail.com). Nearly 100,000 cyclists, hikers, skaters, and skiers traverse the trail every year between the cities of Cannon Falls and Red Wing. The 20-mile paved trail follows the Chicago Great Western rail right of way along the Cannon River. Anybody on wheels—whether bike, skates, skateboard, or scooter—needs a wheel pass, available for $3 from the trail office and a variety of local businesses, including the **St. James Hotel** and the **Red Wing Visitors Center.** You can buy your pass and rent your bike at **Cannon Falls Canoe, Kayak and Bike Rental** (615 5th St. N., Cannon Falls, 507/263-4657, Mon.–Fri. 10 A.M.–sunset, Sat.–Sun. 9 A.M.–sunset). A full-day rental is $20 and a half day is $15.

If you want to get in or on the water, **Lake City,** more or less halfway down the Minnesota side of the lake, is the place to be. **Hok-Si-La Municipal Park and Campground** (2500 N. Hwy. 61, Lake City, 651/345-3855, www .ci-lake-city.mn.us) is a convenient swimming spot, with a shady park and a broad sandy beach, as well as 41 tent camping sites. There's also a big public beach at the **Lake City Marina** in the center of town. To rent speedboats, pontoons, and sailboats, head to **Hansen's Harbor** (35853 Hwy. 61 Blvd., Lake City, 651/345-3022). If you happened to bring your own boat, there's convenient public water access at **Roschen Park,** just south of the Lake City Marina.

Popular with skiers and snowboarders from around the region, **Welch Village Resort** (26685 County 7 Blvd., Welch, 651/258-4567, www.welchvillage.com) covers 120 acres of skiable terrain, with two dozen trails and eight lifts. The average annual snowfall in this area is 45 inches, but Welch Village is prepared to supplement that with plenty of snowmaking equipment, to make sure the season lasts from November to March. A day pass costs $45 and hours vary throughout the season.

Some may say there is no better recreation than drinking a $3 beer on a lingering summer evening at a small-town baseball game. The whole town turns out to cheer and the sun sets over the cornfield. That's exactly what you can find at a **Miesville Mudhens** game, 15 miles northwest of Red Wing, along Highway 61 and just a 30-minute drive from the Twin Cities. The Mudhens play at Jack Ruhr Field (Hwy. 61, center of Miesville, www.miesvil-lemudhens.com) and took the state amateur championship in 2007. Their regular season is in the Classic Cannon Valley League against teams like the Dundas Dukes, the Red Wing Aces, and the Northfield Knights.

For recreation of an altogether different sort, the Mdewakanton Sioux of Prairie Island, a band of Dakota, own and operate **Treasure Island Resort and Casino** (5734 Sturgeon Lake Rd., Welch, 800/222-7077, www.treasureisland.com). The complex includes half a dozen restaurants, slots and gaming tables, a bowling alley, 18-hole golf course overlooking Lake Pepin, a massive hotel, marina, and RV park.

SHOPS

A dedicated shopper in Red Wing can easily fill half a day or more exploring the shops downtown—even more if that person is a dedicated antiques shopper. **Memory Maker Antiques** (415 Main St., Red Wing, 651/385-5914, daily 10 A.M.–5 P.M.) has two floors of antique furnishings, kitchenware, jewelry, and more.

The **Red Wing Shoe Company** (314 Main St., Red Wing, www.redwingshoe.com, Mon.–Fri. 9 A.M.–8 P.M., Sat. 9 A.M.–6 P.M., Sun. 11 A.M.–5 P.M.) occupies most of the Riverfront Centre block. The company, which has been making work boots since 1905 (the first pair sold for $1.75), keeps its corporate offices here, along with an extensive display on its history and a store selling all its brands (watch for terrific semiannual sales).

"Uffda" is what a Minnesotan says when confronted with disappointment, consternation, or mild pain. It's a quiet, characteristically stoic two syllables, usually said under one's breath. At the **Uffda Shop** (202 Bush St., Red Wing, 651/388-8436, Mon.–Fri. 9 A.M.–8 P.M., Sat. 9 A.M.–6 P.M., Sun. noon–5 P.M., shortened hours Jan.–Apr.) you can experience a little more of the Scandinavian national character—and a lot of the aesthetic. The Norwegian, Swedish, Finnish, and Icelandic wares are typically spare and elegant, and the extensive Christmas selection is a nice change from other schlocky and sentimental holiday stuff.

An excellent souvenir to bring back from Red Wing is a piece of the gray, salt-glazed pottery the city is known for. **Red Wing Pottery and Shops** (1920 W. Main St., Red Wing, 651/388-3562, www.redwingpottery.com, Mon.–Sat. 9 A.M.–6 P.M., Sun. 9 A.M.–5 P.M.) offers discounted stoneware and Fiestaware and other kitchen items in a row of shops. Watch potters at work in the back of the store, seven days a week. Next door is the 1883 Minnesota Stoneware/Red Wing Potteries factory. That long brick building, with the remains of the original kilns outside, is now **Pottery Place** (2000 W. Main St., Red Wing, 651/388-1428, www.rwpotteryplace.com, Mon.–Sat. 10 A.M.–6 P.M., Sun. 11 A.M.–5 P.M.), a mall with antiques and specialty shops. It is also home of the **Red Wing Pottery Museum,** a largish room displaying pottery examples from throughout Red Wing's manufacturing history.

HOTELS

The **$\mathbb{C}$ St. James Hotel** (406 Main St., Red Wing, 651/388-2846, www.st-james-hotel.com, $159 s, $209 d) has been a landmark in Red Wing since 1875. Today the hotel is like a one-stop getaway for weary Twin Citians, especially those who take advantage of the weekend meals-included packages. The Victorian ambiance of the lobby extends to the 60-plus guest rooms, all individually decorated with period furniture and quilts. On the mezzanine level, take a quick break to see the artifacts in the American Ski Jumping Hall of Fame, or look for monthly book signings with Minnesota authors at Clara's Coffee in the main lobby.

A few miles outside of downtown Red Wing, you'll find the more intimate **Round Barn Farm** (28650 Wildwood Ln., Red Wing, 651/385-9250, www.roundbarnfarm.com, $159–249 d), which calls itself a B&B&B—or bed & breakfast & bread, after the sourdough bread the proprietors bake in the wood-fired stone oven. Five double rooms with feather beds, massage tubs, and fireplaces make this a welcoming retreat, and with extensive hiking trails on the farm itself, you may never feel the need to explore much further.

For something a little different on longer trips, rent a houseboat from **Great River Houseboats** (1009 E. Main St., Wabasha, 651/565-3376, www.greatriverhouseboats.com). The family-owned company rents boats sleeping 2–4 people for a minimum of two nights ($600 for two nights), or 10 people for the long weekend ($1,100–$1,600) or the week ($1,700–$2,400). The boats are fully equipped and—provided you're ready to pilot a 48-foot boat—can move up and down the river within a 70-mile range.

PRACTICALITIES
Tourist Office
The Red Wing **Tourist Information Office** (420 Levee St., Red Wing, 651/385-5934, www .redwing.org, Mon.–Fri. 8 A.M.–5 P.M., Sat.–Sun. closed) is inside the historic train station, built in 1904 and modeled, like many buildings of the time, after the neoclassical revival style made popular by the 1893 Colombian Exposition. Even outside of regular hours, when the information office is staffed, the main lobby of the train station is stocked with brochures and information and has some historic photos on display.

Media
Red Wing's daily newspaper is the *Republican Eagle* (www.republican-eagle .com), owned by Forum Communications, a media company based in Fargo, North Dakota, that owns about three dozen newspapers in Minnesota, Wisconsin, and the Dakotas. The Twin Cities major dailies, the *Minneapolis Star Tribune* and *St. Paul Pioneer Press,* are also widely available.

Getting There
Train travel is rarely a convenient option in Minnesota, but the Twin Cities' only passenger train is, in fact, timed for a nice day trip to Red Wing. The Empire Builder, Amtrak's most popular long-distance train, carries half a million passengers a year between Chicago and Seattle, passing through both Red Wing and St. Paul. One train a day passes in each direction, leaving St. Paul at 7:50 A.M. and arriving in Red Wing about 9 A.M., then departing Red Wing at 8:50 P.M. and arriving in St. Paul about 10:30 P.M. The train, however, is notoriously unpredictable and is often delayed for hours in the Rocky Mountains.

If you want to explore the area outside of the downtown historic district, you'll want your own transportation. From the Twin Cities, many roads lead to Red Wing, each more picturesque than the last. Taking Highway 55 south to Highway 52 to Highway 61 will take you through small towns and rolling farmland. For a few more glimpses of the river, take I-94 to Highway 61, then cross into Wisconsin at Prescott and take Highway 55 south, crossing back into Minnesota at Red Wing.

Getting Around
Red Wing's historic downtown district is easily navigated on foot, from the train station on the riverfront park to the small shops in the area. But if you want to appreciate the rest of Lake Pepin or tour the Red Wing Stoneware Factory, you'll need your own transportation. Bus service in Red Wing is very limited.

Northfield

When the city of Northfield tried to replace its long-time slogan, "Cows, colleges, and contentment," the good citizens led a quiet rebellion, and the phrase simply refused to go away, eventually returning to a place of honor on a sign on the main road into town. Apparently this happy, agricultural city of 17,000, 20 percent of whom are students, wants the world to know it just that way.

History buffs are more likely to know Northfield as the end of the road for the James-Younger gang, which tried to rob the First National Bank in 1876 and was thwarted by an angry mob of citizens. Visitors can absorb Northfield's college-town charms in a morning or an afternoon, stretching it out to a full day by adding a trek through Carleton College's 800-acre arboretum.

SIGHTS
◖ Carleton College
Two colleges, Carleton and St. Olaf, together help shape much of life in town, from attracting professors and staff members as residents to supporting arts and cultural life. Both colleges were founded by Protestant

Northfield's Bridge Square is a popular gathering place.

organizations—Carleton by Congregationalists in 1866 and St. Olaf by Lutherans in 1874—but only St. Olaf has retained the religious tie. Both schools rank highly among small liberal arts schools and were coeducational from the very first class. In local lore, a great rivalry rages, but in truth, the rivalry comes down to an annual football game—a sport neither school is known to play all that well—and a few ribald chants in an otherwise peaceful coexistence, with neither side paying the other much attention. Carleton (1 N. College St., Northfield, 507/222-4000, www.carleton.edu) sits immediately adjacent to downtown Northfield, along the river. Most of the school's historic buildings are arranged around a quadrangle known as the Bald Spot, where students play Frisbee in all sorts of weather and skate and play broomball in the winter. On the west side of the Bald Spot is Willis Hall, the campus's oldest building. Like the iconic "Old Main" at many schools, Willis was once a classroom building, dormitory, chapel, and cafeteria all in one. Today it houses several social science departments.

To the north and east of the Bald Spot is the historic **Goodsell Observatory,** built in 1887 and given to the school by the railroad magnate James J. Hill. For many years it sent daily time signals to railroads around the country. Goodsell has two domes, the larger with a 16-inch refractor—one of the largest in the world when it was installed in 1890—and the smaller an 8-inch refractor. The telescopes are open to the public on the first Friday of every month, starting at dusk, for about two hours.

The gem of the Carleton campus is the **Cowling Arboretum,** 880 acres of natural beauty originally dubbed "Cowling's Folly" by those who disagreed with then-President Donald Cowling's investment. But, like so many so-called "follies" in history, the Arb, as it is known, has been vindicated and is now central to campus life. The Upper Arb, the area closest to the main campus, includes playing fields and is crisscrossed by paved and unpaved paths for running and biking. The much larger portion, the Lower Arb, is less developed and a lovely place for more solitary hiking and running (but no biking is allowed). The easiest place to access the Lower Arb is behind West Gymnasium (321 Division St. N., Northfield). Cross Division Street and walk north a few hundred yards to access the Upper Arb. (Note that the Lower Arb, so named because it lies low in the Cannon River valley, actually lies to the north of the Upper Arb.)

Defeat of Jesse James

Northfield's claim to fame is the 1876 bank robbery that proved the downfall of the James-Younger Gang. Five men held up the First National Bank of Northfield with guns and Bowie knives, thwarted by a brave cashier and quick-acting local citizenry. The bank itself has moved up the street, and the **Northfield Historical Society** (408 Division St., Northfield, 507/645-9268, www.northfieldhistory.org, Tues.–Sat. 10 A.M.–4 P.M., Sun. 1–4 P.M.) has restored the original location to its 1870s appearance. Visitors can see the cashier's booth and safe, as well as some of the weapons used in the raid. Rumor has it a skeleton of one of the Younger brothers was once on display in the museum but has now been moved into storage.

St. Olaf College

St. Olaf (1520 St. Olaf Ave., Northfield, 507/786-2222, www.stolaf.edu) sits on a hill overlooking Northfield's compact downtown. Strolling through the shady campus, one can enjoy the beautifully unified architecture, much of it in the Norman Gothic style. Rølvaag Memorial Library (1510 St. Olaf Ave.) is a good example of this. Built in 1942, it is named for Ole Edvart Roølvaag, an Olaf alum and author of the 1927 bestselling immigrant epic *Giants in the Earth.* Next door, Holland Hall, completed 20 years earlier, is like a brotherly bookend to the library, and the pair make a familiar Northfield sight.

St. Olaf is well known for its musical programs, including the annual St. Olaf Christmas Festival concert, broadcast nationally. About one-third of the school's roughly 3,000 students are involved in music somehow, many of

them in the 17 instrumental ensembles and 10 vocal groups. The college also rates some pop-culture references, in times because its name sounds humorous to non-Midwesterners. In his radio program *A Prairie Home Companion,* Garrison Keillor will sometimes throw in a story or two about St. Olaf, and Jay Gatsby, in F. Scott Fitzgerald's *The Great Gatsby,* attended the school.

RESTAURANTS

For years Northfield residents had to drive to the Twin Cities for any cuisine other than American. But now Twin Citians have been known to drive to Northfield for **Chapati** (214 Division St. S., Northfield, 507/645-2462, www.chapati.us, Sun.–Thurs. 11:30 A.M.–2 P.M. and 5–9 P.M., Fri.–Sat. 11:30 A.M.–2 P.M. and 5–10 P.M., Mon. closed). Located inside the Archer House building, along with a host of small shops, the Archer House hotel, and a couple of other restaurants, Chapati offers fresh, authentic Indian cuisine, including excellent tandoori dishes and *biryani* (similar to rice pilaf). The daily lunch buffet includes as many as eight curries, plus rice and side dishes. Expect to pay $8–17 for an entrée.

In a college town like Northfield, academic types need a place to gather over a pint or a meal. **The Contented Cow** (302 Division St., Northfield, 507/663-1351, www.contentedcow.com, Sun.–Thurs. 3 P.M.–midnight, Fri.–Sat. 3 P.M.–1 A.M.) offers just that, informally and formally, with its Politics and a Pint gab fests on Sunday nights, starting at 6 P.M. The pub also hosts live music on Sundays and Tuesdays, as well as frequent poetry readings, and it makes good use of its riverside deck, with outdoor barbecues when the weather permits. The menu is lighter in the summer (salads and sandwiches) and heavier in the winter, with the addition of dishes like shepherd's pie and pork stew, and there are 13 beers on tap (also changing seasonally) to wash it down.

Another pub with a great riverside view is **Froggy Bottoms** (302 Water St. S., Northfield, 507/664-0260, www.froggybottoms.com,

Mon.–Sat. 11 A.M.–11 P.M.). Owned by a St. Olaf graduate who, no doubt, had noted the long-famous dearth of bars in this college town, Froggy Bottoms has a cozy, stone-walled main dining room and a small, flower-filled patio right on the river. The menu includes filling sandwiches, pizzas, and pasta dishes ($8–12) and a long list of goofily named cocktails (Sex on the Cannon, anyone?). Karaoke on Thursdays and Saturdays starts at 9 P.M.

HOTELS

Rooms in and around Northfield fill up fast—as in four years in advance—for St. Olaf and Carleton graduation and homecoming weekends. During the Defeat of Jesse James Days festival (the weekend after Labor Day) and the St. Olaf Christmas Festival, rooms are also hard to come by. During those special events many hotels may have higher rates and minimum stays.

Right on the Cannon River in the center of town is the charmingly old-fashioned **Archer House** (212 Division St., Northfield, 507/645-5661, www.archerhouse.com, $75–160 d). The Archer House was built as a hotel in 1877 and has been welcoming visitors to town ever since (even through a couple of decades of relative disrepute and decrepitude during the 1960s and '70s). Rooms are on the small side and individually decorated in a sweet country style. Many have old-timey details like sleigh beds, four-posters, and clawfoot tubs. Be sure to specify whether you want a full or a queen bed and ask for a river view. Rates are higher on weekends and during special events.

For longer stays, or for more convenience during a single overnight, the **Froggy Bottoms Suites** (309 Water St. S., Northfield, 507/650-0039, www.froggybottoms.com), next door to the pub of the same name, are a unique option. The one- and two-bedroom suites sleep four or six people and come with fully equipped kitchens and on-site laundry facilities. The price is the same no matter how many in your party: $100–150 for a weekday overnight, more on weekends and during special events, $600–900 weekly, and $1,800–2,700 monthly. The suites are casually decorated, like spare, comfortable student apartments, with a goofy frog theme throughout. Several have decks directly overlooking the river.

PRACTICALITIES
Tourist Office
The **Northfield Convention and Visitors Bureau** (205 3rd St. W., Northfield, 507/645-5604, www.visitingnorthfield.com, Mon.–Fri. 8 A.M.–5 P.M.) doesn't see all that many drop-in visitors, but staff will happily answer questions and supply you with materials.

Media
Northfield's newspaper is the **Northfield News** (www.northfieldnews.com), published Wednesdays and Saturdays. It covers the local politics, sports, and school news very well. For national news, the Twin Cities papers and *New York Times* are widely available. Carleton's student-run radio station, **KRLX** (www.krlx.org), broadcasts on 88.1 FM, with a music-focused schedule that changes with every school term.

Getting There
No buses or trains serve Northfield, which is about 45 minutes to an hour's drive south of the Twin Cities. Take I-35 to exit 69. State Highway 19 will take you straight past the Malt-O-Meal factory to the center of town.

Getting Around
Once you're in Northfield, the main drag, Division Street, is easy to navigate on foot and immediately adjacent to Carleton College. If you want to head the couple of miles up the hill to St. Olaf, you'll want to be able to get there on your own power. Northfield's single taxi is notoriously difficult to summon.

Duluth and the North Shore

Duluth was once the definition of a boom town: After financier Jay Cooke convinced the Lake Superior and Mississippi Railroad to open a line to Duluth in 1869, the population ballooned from practically zero to 3,500 in a matter of months. By the early 20th century, the rail, timber, mining, and shipping industries were exploding, the port of Duluth handled more freight than any other port in the United States, and Duluth was home to more millionaires per capita than anywhere else in the world.

Some shadows of those boom times are still visible in the steep neighborhoods of Duluth, where today tourism easily surpasses shipping as the city's major industry. Grand mansions are now inns and the railroads offer nostalgic pleasure rides. But one thing remains: Here at the westernmost edge of the Great Lakes, where the St. Louis River opens out into Lake Superior, Gitchigami ("great water" as the Ojibwe call the lake) shapes everything, from the food to the weather to the economy.

SIGHTS
◖ Canal Park and Maritime Duluth

A great way to get acquainted with Duluth is to walk along the three-mile **Lakewalk** from the **Bayfront Park Pavilion** through Canal Park and then north beyond the **Fitger's Brewery Complex.** You'll pass Duluth's iconic **aerial lift bridge,** which connects Canal Park with a narrow peninsula known as Park Point. The central portion of the bridge rises straight up (rather than at an angle) to let boats pass underneath. The bridge can make it all the way to the top in about three minutes and lifts about 40 times a day during peak shipping season. You can pick up a copy of the *Duluth Shipping News* (www .duluthshippingnews.com) to find out when ships are expected to pass through or listen for the long-short-long-short series of horn blows that signals a request to raise the bridge. The bridge is an especially beautiful sight at night, when it is fully illuminated.

© BRUCE MANNING

The aerial lift bridge in Duluth is one of only two of its kind in Minnesota.

THE DULUTH LYNCHINGS

In June of 1920, four black men were falsely accused of rape. Three were lynched by a mob of nearly 3,000 and the fourth was convicted in a mockery of a court trial. At the time, the lynchings earned headlines in newspapers across the country. But memories receded to the point where most Minnesotans were unaware of the crime. Court records were burned and the Duluth Historical Society discouraged research into the event. In 1992, the play *The Last Minstrel Show* premiered at Penumbra Theater and helped resurrect the tragedy. Since then, the play has been reprised, the Minnesota Historical Society Press published Michael Fedo's *The Lynchings in Duluth* and Warren Read's *The Lyncher in Me,* and Duluth has erected a memorial to Elias Clayton, Elmer Jackson, and Isaac McGhie, the three men who were murdered.

At the base of the bridge, the surprisingly diminutive tugboat *Essayons,* which takes its name from the Army Corps of Engineers motto "Let us try," stands outside the **Lake Superior Maritime Visitor Center** (south end of Canal Park Dr., Duluth, 217/727-2479, www.lsmma .com, daily 10 A.M.–9 P.M., free). Inside, you can get a good look at the tug's engine and learn more about the 1908 boat's history. Like any good ship, the visitors center crams more than you would think possible into a small space: exhibits on shipwrecks in Lake Superior, the history of shipping on the lake, and early passenger travel conditions, as well as a working radar and marine radio. You can even try your hand at steering a large ship. Serious shipping buffs can call the **Boatwatcher's Hotline** at 218/722-6489 for news on which ships are expected to dock or leave port that day. This information is also listed on the *Duluth Shipping News,* a one-sheet distributed free at the visitor centers around town daily during the summer and occasionally during the spring and fall.

The center's staff is small, and it may close earlier between Labor Day and Memorial Day.

You can get even closer to Lake Superior's maritime past and present aboard two ships docked just off Canal Park. One ticket gets you access to both the **U.S. Coast Guard Vessel *Sundew*** and the **SS *William A. Irvin*** (350 Harbor Dr., Duluth, 218/722-7876, www .decc.org, May daily 10 A.M.–4 P.M., Memorial Day–Labor Day daily 9 A.M.–6 P.M., Sept.–early Oct. daily 10 A.M.–4 P.M., adults $9, kids under 10 free.). The *William A. Irvin,* built in 1937, carried both serious cargo and serious dignitaries, which means the one-hour tour will give you a look at a 2,000-horsepower engine and the lavishly furnished staterooms. In October the ghosts of Halloweens past come aboard for Haunted Ship Tours. The *Sundew* was decommissioned in 2004 after 60 years tending buoys and cutting ice on Lake Superior.

Glensheen

In the early 1900s, Chester and Clara Congdon raised seven children in Glensheen mansion (3300 London Rd., Duluth, 218/726-8910, www.glensheen.org, mid-May–late Oct. daily 9 A.M.–5:30 P.M., late Oct.–mid-May Sat.–Sun. 9:30 A.M.–3:30 P.M.; grounds only $5; standard tour $13 adults, $7 children; expanded tour $24 adults, $13 children), and much of the elaborate decor is still in place for the public to view. But that is not necessarily what draws Minnesotans to the house and grounds. In 1977, one of Chester and Clara's children, Elisabeth Congdon, was murdered, along with her nurse, Velma Pietila, by Elisabeth's son-in-law, in one of Minnesota's most notorious crimes.

Great Lakes Aquarium

The Great Lakes Aquarium (353 Harbor Dr., Duluth, 218/740-3474, www.glaquarium.org, daily 10 A.M.–6 P.M., $14.50 adults, $11.50 seniors, $8.50 children) is 120,000 gallons of freshwater, focusing on fish found in the Great Lakes. Some 70 species of freshwater fish, birds, amphibians, and reptiles are spread out over

© BRUCE MANNING

The Great Lakes Aquarium in Duluth is the largest freshwater aquarium in the country.

two floors, along a self-guided tour. The aquarium is fairly well curated and includes some historical perspective on lake life. Lake fish, by and large, lack the color and flash of the more commonly exhibited tropical species, but that in no way diminishes the appealing oddity of the paddlefish, the sturgeon, and the catfish on display in carefully chosen habitats, the most impressive of which recreates the base of a waterfall. There are plenty of interactive exhibits, a touch pool, a wave maker, and an expansive model of the Great Lakes where you can pilot a plastic boat from Duluth to the Atlantic Ocean and gain a working understanding of the lock and dam systems along the way.

◖ Split Rock Lighthouse

While it lies nearly 30 miles north of Duluth, along the scenic North Shore Drive, the Split Rock Lighthouse (3713 Split Rock Lighthouse Rd., Two Harbors, 218/226-6372, www.mnhs .org, May 15–Oct. 15 daily 10 A.M.–6 P.M., $8 adults, $6 seniors and students, $5 children 5–17) is an iconic Minnesota sight and worth the drive for anyone who has time. It stands a full 600 feet above the surface of Lake Superior, built here after a 1905 storm damaged

29 ships. The Minnesota Historical Society has restored the lighthouse to its 1920s appearance and leads tours that focus on the lonely life of a lighthouse keeper. It is no longer operational, but the beacon shines across the water once a year, on November 10, to commemorate the wreck of the *Edmund Fitzgerald*. Call ahead for winter hours.

◖ Union Depot

Built in 1892, the Union Depot was serving seven different rail lines and 5,000 passengers daily by 1910 and served as an important hub for the transport of logs and iron ore for decades. In 1971, the building was placed on the National Register of Historic Places and "The Depot" (www.duluthdepot.org) now houses the Duluth Playhouse, the Duluth Art Institute, the Duluth Children's Museum, the St. Louis County Historical Society, and the Lake Superior Railroad Museum. It also serves as the launch point for the North Shore Scenic Railroad, which offers a seasonal schedule of 90-minute trips starting in Canal Park and running along the craggy shoreline of Lake Superior and into the Northwoods.

The **Duluth Children's Museum** (506

Michigan St. W., Duluth, 218/733-7543, www.duluthchildrensmuseum.org, Memorial Day–Labor Day daily 9:30 A.M.–6 P.M., Labor Day–Memorial Day Tues.–Sat. 10 A.M.–5 P.M., Sun. 1–5 P.M., Mon. closed, $10 adults, $5.50 children 3–13) aims to spark imaginative play more than it tries to educate, and it succeeds. The centerpiece is a large room with a thoroughly medieval theme, complete with costumes, stables, a blacksmith's shop, knights' armor, a royal feast, a keep, and a dragon. Upstairs is a campsite milieu, featuring a rowboat, a tent, and the chance to play in a pretend Northwoods. Worthwhile even in the summer, the museum is at its best on colder days.

The same admission ticket also gets you into the **Lake Superior Railroad Museum,** housed at the lowest level, where the old rails run. In addition to plenty of rail cars to clamber through, the history of the rails is on display, from the earliest of engines used in the area to specialty designs like huge rotary snowplows, converted autos that could run on tracks, and an odd-looking log loader that was important for the logging industry throughout the Upper Midwest. Recreated dining cars, model railroads, and an actual train operation simulator round out a fine afternoon.

Two rail tours also leave from the depot. From Memorial Day to Labor Day, the **North Shore Scenic Railroad** (218/722-1273, www.northshorescenicrailroad.org, $12 adults, $5.50 children) runs two 90-minute round-trips a day up the North Shore to the Lester River, at 12:30 and 3 P.M., with an additional trip Fridays and Saturdays at 10 A.M. Tours continue from Labor Day to mid-October but are limited to Fridays, Saturdays, and Sundays at 12:30 and 3 P.M. There are also a number of specialty trips, including an occasional pizza dinner on the train.

The **St. Louis River Railroad** (218/624-7549, www.lsmrr.org, $10 adults, $6 children) heads south from the depot, also for 90 minutes. On nice days, the open safari car is the place to be, as the tracks run through the Duluth area's varied terrain. Trains run from mid-June to early October, Sat.–Sun. 10:30 A.M. and 1:30 P.M.

Other Sights

On the campus of the University of Minnesota Duluth, the **Tweed Museum of Art** (1201 Ordean Ct., Duluth, 218/726-8222, www.d.umn.edu/tma, Tues. 9 A.M.–8 P.M., Wed.–Fri. 9 A.M.–4:30 P.M., Sat.–Sun. 1–5 P.M., $5 suggested donation) houses more than 6,000 works of art in its own dedicated building. Its core is a collection of 600 works of early-20th-century American art donated by a Duluth couple in 1950. The permanent collection now reaches across eras and cultures.

With a primary location in the Depot, the **Duluth Art Institute** (in the Depot 506 Michigan St. W., Duluth, 218/733-7560 and 2229 2nd St. W., Duluth, 218/723-1310, www.duluthartinstitute.org, Memorial Day–Labor Day daily 9:30 A.M.–6 P.M., Labor Day–Memorial Day Mon.–Sat. 10 A.M.–5 P.M., Sun. 1–5 P.M.) is a quintessentially accessible contemporary art museum. Its family programming and hands-on training for artists make it an important part of the local arts community. The rooms are small and friendly, showcasing artists from Duluth and Minnesota's Arrowhead region in changing exhibitions.

RESTAURANTS

Grandma's is an unavoidable institution in Duluth, a Canal Park empire including Grandma's Saloon and Grill, Grandma's Sports Garden, Bellisio's, and Little Angie's Cantina and Grill, all within a block of each other. **Grandma's Saloon and Grill** (522 Lake Ave. S., Duluth, 218/727-4192, daily 11 A.M.–1 A.M.) is the sort of authentic good-feeling place fast-casual restaurants should model themselves after, with towering burgers and mountainous fries, along with enough beer to fill Lake Superior and a large variety of shakes and malts. **Grandma's Sports Garden** (425 Lake Ave. S., Duluth, 218/722-4724, Memorial Day–Labor Day daily 11:30 A.M.–1 A.M.) is more of the same, with more television, even more beer, and live music or a DJ nearly every

FITGER'S

You could wander into the deceptively compact Fitger's complex (600 Superior St. E., Duluth, www.fitgers.com, shops open Mon.-Sat. 10 A.M.-9 P.M., Sun. 11 A.M.-5 P.M.) and wander out blurry-eyed hours – or even days – later, fully satisfied. The former brewery, which operated on this site from 1859 to 1972, now houses four restaurants, a hotel, modern lounge, museum, wine shop, brewing shop, bookstore, fitness center, and more than a half dozen high-end clothing and gift shops. They even roast their own brand of coffee. And, oh yeah – since 1995, beer is again being made in the historic brewery. The whole thing is right on a beautiful patch of the Lakewalk, overlooking Lake Superior, with a high platform for watching the sailboats, the aerial lift bridge, and the trains that run along the lake.

The **Brewhouse** (218/279-2739, www .brewhouse.net, Mon.-Fri. 11 A.M.-10 P.M., SAT.-SUN. 11 A.M.-11 P.M.) is a great place to grab a burger in a classic brewpub atmosphere. Across the hallway, **Red Star** (218/723-7827, www.redstarclub.com, Tues.-Sat. 7 P.M.-2 A.M.) offers music, dancing, and high-end mixed drinks. In the cellar, **Midi** (218/727-4880, www.midi-estaurant.com, Sun.-Thurs. 7 A.M.-10 P.M., Fri.-Sat. 7 A.M.-11 P.M.) serves breakfast, lunch, and dinner in a formal atmosphere. Classic entrées like pepper steak and pan-fried walleye run $13-28. **Baja Billy's** (218/740-2300, www.bajabillys .com, Sun.-Wed. 11 A.M.-1 A.M., Thurs.-Sat. 11 A.M.-2 A.M.), a sprawling bar and Tex-Mex restaurant, offers standard tacos and fajitas and stunning views of the lake.

St. E., 218/727-6117, daily 11 A.M.–1 A.M.) is young, south-of-the-border fun, heavy on the fajitas and margaritas.

Two fantastic Duluth eateries have their roots in the Twin Cities. **Pizza Luce** (11 Superior St. E., Duluth, 218/727-7400, www .pizzaluce.com, Mon.–Thurs. 7 A.M.–1:30 A.M., Fri. 7 A.M.–2:30 A.M., Sat. 8 A.M.–2:30 A.M., Sun. 8 A.M.–1:30 A.M.) serves the same quirky, thick crust pizza you can get in Minneapolis and St. Paul (topped with mashed potatoes or mock duck, if you like). But it also serves breakfast: pesto Benedict, Cajun hash browns, vegan sausage, and more. A pizza serving 3–5 people is about $20; breakfast is around $8–9.

Hell's Kitchen (310 Lake Ave. S., Duluth, 218/727-1620, www.hellskitcheninc.com, Mon.–Fri. 7 A.M.–10 P.M., Sat.–Sun. 7 A.M.–midnight), known to Twin Citians for unbeatable breakfast and brunch, adds dinner and late-night snacks in Duluth. The lemon-ricotta pancakes ($10, served all day, along with all their breakfast favorites) and the walleye BLT ($14) are must-tries.

The best dining by far in Duluth is actually about eight miles north of town. The 🄲 **New Scenic Café** (5461 North Shore Dr., Duluth, 218/525-6274, www.sceniccafe.com, 11 A.M.–10 P.M.) is a critics' darling and a destination for those seeking an up-to-date take on fresh, local cuisine. The restaurant itself is unaffected, comfortable, and subtly elegant, as is the menu, which changes seasonally and will likely include herbs from the garden out front. Expect to spend about $20 for an entrée or $10 for a sandwich.

But on a sunny day, why go inside to eat? **Crabby Bill's** (open for lunch and dinner), in a converted boat at the south end of Canal Park Drive, serves smoked fish, fried fish, brats, cheese curds, and even a Minnesota shore lunch. Grab the single picnic table, or make yourself comfortable on the boulders.

RECREATION

If a brisk walk on the **Lakewalk** isn't enough for you, the **Hartley Nature Center** (3001

night. **Bellisio's** (405 Lake Ave. S., Duluth, 218/727-4921, daily lunch 11:30 A.M.–2 P.M., dinner 5–9 P.M., Fri.–Sat. dinner until 10 P.M.) brings white-tablecloth Italian with entrées like chicken marsala and fennel-roasted rack of pork (about $20) to the mix. And **Little Angie's Cantina and Grill** (11 Buchanan

Woodland Ave., Duluth, 218/724-6735, www .hartleynature.org, Mon.–Fri. 9 A.M.–4 P.M., Sat. 10 A.M.–5 P.M., Sun. noon–5 P.M.) is a great place to satisfy a craving for nature and recreation. The urban park, with a wide variety of natural environments and about a mile across at its widest point, has trails for hiking, biking, cross-country skiing, and snowshoeing, as well as docks for canoeing and fishing. The beautiful modern park building is also a model of sustainable building techniques and houses a small exhibit on green building.

During the winter, downhill skiers can get their fix on the dozen ski and snowboard trails at **Spirit Mountain** (9500 Spirit Mountain Pl., Duluth, 800/642-6377, www .spiritmt.com, Sun.–Thurs. 9 A.M.–8 P.M., Fri.–Sat. 9 A.M.–9 P.M.). There's also a network of groomed cross-country trails.

With up to seven departures a day, **Vista Fleet** (DECC Dock and Harbor Dr., 218/722-6218, www.vistafleet.com, $14–37) makes it easy to get out on the water and see Duluth's beautiful shoreline from the same vantage point as the shipping vessels that built the city. Sightseeing cruises run 90 minutes, while some meal cruises—including brunch, lunch, pizza, or dinner—run the same or a little longer. The fleet includes three boats, from 66 to 92 feet long, with capacities from 80 to 300 passengers. All three have both open observation decks and enclosed seating areas.

PERFORMING ARTS

Duluth has a reputation as an arts-loving community and supports several theaters and musical groups. The **Duluth Playhouse** (506 Michigan Ave. W., Duluth, 218/733-7555, www.duluthplayhouse.org) was among the first community theaters in the United States when it was founded in 1914 and among the first to include children's productions in its season. It moved to its current home in the Union Depot in 1977. The year-round season includes about seven plays for all generations, heavy on the musicals, and three children's productions. The Playhouse is also responsible for **The Play Ground** (11 Superior St. E., 218/733-7555,

www.duluthplayground.org), a 70-seat alternative arts space where performers in all disciplines—theater, dance, music, poetry, art, and film—can present their work.

The **Duluth Symphony Orchestra** (506 W. Michigan St., 218/733-7579, www.dsso .com) performs at the **Duluth Entertainment and Convention Center,** on the harbor. The season, which runs September through May, mixes well-known classical music and pops, including an annual performance by the youth orchestra and a popular December holiday concert.

FESTIVALS AND EVENTS

Unless you're a runner with a room booked a year in advance, the third weekend of June is not the time to visit Duluth. That's when more than 9,000 runners come to run **Grandma's Marathon** (www.grandmasmarathon.com), named for the restaurant, which was a major sponsor when the race started in 1977. Runners start near Two Harbors and continue along Scenic Route 61, finishing in Canal Park, outside the namesake restaurant—you can see the finish line year-round. The race, a Boston Marathon qualifier, registers runners on a first-come, first-served basis. The men's record is 2:09:37 and the women's is 2:27:05.

A slightly smaller crowd—an estimated 4,000 spectators—converges on Duluth on the last Sunday in January for the **John Beargrease Sled Dog Marathon** (218/722-7631, www.beargrease.com). Run since 1981, the marathon is the longest sled dog race in the lower 48 and is an Iditarod qualifier race. Mushers race north from Duluth almost to the Canadian border and back. The mid-distance race, about 100 miles, starts in Duluth and finishes on the shore of Lake Superior in Tofte. The race is named for the son of an Ojibwe chief who helped the communities of the North Shore survive and grow by delivering mail by dogsled in the late 19th century.

SHOPS

A wander through the Canal Park area will turn up plenty of touristy T-shirt shops. For

EXCURSIONS

a sure-fire coming-home present, head to **Grandma's Marketplace** (501 Lake Ave. S., 218/727-5885, www.grandmasrestaurants .com, daily 11 A.M.–6 P.M.), where you'll find a classier collection of Duluth-themed gear, Thymes-brand soaps and lotions (a Minnesota company), and whole sections devoted to moose and black bears. Souvenirs of a different kind can be found at the **Lake Superior Magazine Outlet Store** (310 Superior St. E., 888/244-5253, www.lakesuperior.com, Mon.– Fri. 8:30 A.M.–5:30 P.M.), which sells wall maps, nautical maps, books, gear, and furnishings all related to the lake.

The excellent **Northern Lights Books and Gifts** (307 Canal Park Dr., Duluth, 800/868-8904, www.norlightsbooksense.com, Mon.– Sat. 9 A.M.–9 P.M., Sun. 10 A.M.–6 P.M.) also attracts more thoughtful souvenir-seekers with its broad selection of regional books, from history to fiction to children's books. While that section takes up a good portion of the small store, there's still room left over for several carefully chosen shelves of general works.

A "Duluth Pack," in regional parlance, is a heavy-duty rectangular canvas backpack with a fold-over top. The original 1882 design was known as a "Poirier pack," after the inventor. **Duluth Pack** still makes the bags, along with school bags and heavy-duty luggage, and sells them and at their only retail outlet (365 Canal Park Dr., Duluth, 218/722-1707, www.dulu-thpack.com, Mon.–Sat. 10 A.M.–8 P.M., Sun. 10 A.M.–6 P.M.) along with other high-quality outdoor gear.

For one-stop, less Duluth-oriented shopping, head to the **Dewitt-Seitz Building** in Canal Park (394 Lake Ave. S., Duluth, 218/722-0047, www.dewitt-seitz.com, Mon.– Fri. 10 A.M.–9 P.M., Sat. 10 A.M.–8 P.M., Sun. 11 A.M.–5 P.M.). The renovated warehouse is home to the excellent toy shop **J. Skylark** (218/722-3794), **Hepzibah's Sweet Shoppe** (218/722-5049), and—for an unforgettable and perhaps untransportable souvenir—**Northern Waters Smokehaus** (218/724-7307), which sells smoked lake fish to take with you or

enjoy on the spot. Across the street, **Waters of Superior** (395 Lake Ave. S., Duluth, 218/786-0233, www.watersofsuperior.com, daily 10 A.M.–9 P.M.) combines high-end, contemporary women's clothing with Scandinavian-influenced art in a spare gallery setting.

A little piece of a particular era in Minnesota musical history—when the Minneapolis sound was on the rise in the 1980s—can be found at **Electric Fetus** (12 Superior St. E., Duluth, 218/722-9970, Mon.–Fri. 9 A.M.–8 P.M., Sat.– Sun. 11 A.M.–6 P.M.), a sister store to the original in Minneapolis, selling music, clothing, books, and candles.

For edible goodies, the chocolate counter at **Northwoods Confections and Gifts** (361 Canal Park Dr., Duluth, 218/727-4140, daily 11 A.M.–5 P.M.) can't be beat. The store also offers a good selection of taffy, toys, and regional books. **Torke Weihnachten** (37 Superior St. E., Duluth, 218/723-1225, Mon.–Sat. 10 A.M.–5 P.M.) offers European-style treats, as well as a few sit-down tables where you can enjoy tortes and espresso. The back of the store is taken over by an impressive collection of old-world Christmas tree ornaments.

HOTELS

Duluth is a popular getaway for Minnesotans as well as visitors from farther afield, so its 4,500 hotel rooms fill up fast and reservations are always recommended. The downtown business district offers plenty of convenient chain options, but the mansion district east of downtown, where shipping and railroad tycoons once built grand homes, offers a different taste of Duluth. Eight of these Victorian homes are now beautiful bed-and-breakfasts (find them all at www.duluthbandb .com), with 5–7 rooms each and both romantic and practical details. The neighborhood itself, a quiet area inviting leisurely walks, is a perk. **Ellery House** (28 S. 21st Ave., Duluth, 218/724-7639, www.elleryhouse .com, $129–169 d) is one of these hospitable homes, with a broad porch, delicious breakfast, and welcoming, unobtrusive hosts.

In Canal Park, four large hotels line the Lakewalk, overlooking Lake Superior. **Canal Park Lodge** (250 Canal Park Dr., Duluth, 218/279-6000, www.canalparklodge.com, $149–279 d) is charmingly rustic with a resort-like atmosphere and a high-ceilinged, comfortable lounge in the lobby. Breakfast and high-quality coffee are included in the cost of the rooms, which feature large HD TVs and—if you're lucky—balconies facing the lake.

Two doors down, also on the Lakewalk, **The Inn on Lake Superior** (350 Canal Park Dr., Duluth, 218/668-4352, www.theinnonlakesuperior.com, $183–273 d) is a little older and less flashy, but no less comfortable. The inn focuses on making families comfortable—from a long, leisurely breakfast café to evening storytime and s'mores on the lakeside patio. In a nice Minnesota touch, a large sauna is available for guests to use.

Arguably the most elegant hotel in Duluth is located in a brewery. Well, the building was built in 1885 as a brewery, and now, after handsome renovations, it houses not only a much smaller brewing operation but also—along with a host of other businesses—**Fitger's Inn** (600 Superior St. E., Duluth, 218/722-8826, www.fitgers.com $149–299 d). The 62 rooms (including 20 suites) are, like all of the Fitger's complex's many charms, carved creatively out of the old brewery space. Many have exposed brick walls, raised separate seating areas, and other touches to remind you of the building's history. Luxury suites have fireplaces, balconies, and whirlpools. Be sure to request a lakeside room.

PRACTICALITIES
Tourist Office
The **Visit Duluth tourist information center** (ground floor, 21 Superior St. W., 218/722-4011, www.visitduluth.com, Mon.–Fri. 8:30 A.M.–5 P.M., Sat. 10 A.M.–2 P.M. (summer only), Sun. closed) is operated by the Duluth Convention and Visitors Bureau. You can also pick up brochures from a well-stocked rack in **The Depot.**

Media
Duluth's daily newspaper is the **Duluth News Tribune** (www.duluthnewstribune.com), which delves deeply into local and occasionally statewide news. The *Minneapolis Star Tribune, St. Paul Pioneer Press,* and *New York Times* are all fairly easy to find for more Minnesota and national news. The local alternative weekly, the **Reader Weekly** (www.myspace.com/readerweekly), is published on Thursdays and offers a peek into Duluth's cultural scene, but not much reporting.

Getting There
From the Twin Cities, take I-35 straight north for 150 miles and you will find yourself in the middle of downtown Duluth. Northwest Airlines schedules several flights a day between **Duluth International Airport** (www.duluthairport.com) and Minneapolis-St. Paul (and to Detroit as well), but the cost of these tickets almost never compares favorably to a rental car and a tank of gas. Two **Greyhound buses** a day run between the Twin Cities and Duluth, dropping passengers at three locations in the city: the Greyhound bus terminal (4426 Grand Ave., 218/722-5591), Kenwood Hall at the College of St. Scholastica (1200 Kenwood Ave., 218/723-6000), and Kirby Student Center at the University of Minnesota Duluth (1120 Kirby Dr., 218/726-7286).

Getting Around
If you plan to stay in downtown Duluth and forgo exploring the coast, it's possible to get by without your own car. The city is very walkable: The stretch of Superior Street where you're likely to spend the most time, from Fitger's to The Depot, is only about 1.5 miles long. The **skywalk** system (Mon. 7 A.M.–8:30 P.M., Tues.–Fri. 7 A.M.–7 P.M., Sat. 8 A.M.–7 P.M., Sun. closed) helps pedestrians when the weather's bad and makes it easier to get across I-35, which cuts the lakefront off from downtown. The skywalks are sadly underused compared to the lively Minneapolis-St. Paul systems.

EXCURSIONS

From June through Labor Day, the **Port Town Trolley** carries passengers in a loop through Canal Park and downtown Duluth, running along Lake Avenue and Superior Street. Pick up the trolley at eight locations (the Holiday Center, Radisson Hotel, Depot Museum, Great Lakes Aquarium, Excursion Dock, SS *William A. Irvin,* Lake Superior Maritime Visitor Center, Fitger's Brewery Complex) once every 30 minutes 11:30 A.M.–7 P.M. and ride for just $0.50.

The Duluth Transit Authority runs 20 city bus routes, which run every 10 minutes to every hour during the day, with reduced service on the weekends. Route 5 runs between downtown and the bus station and airport. Route 8 runs up and down Superior, stopping at the Fitger's complex. Pick up schedules (and any bus) at the **Duluth Transit Center** (214 Superior St. W., 218/722-7283). Fares are $1.25 during peak hours (Mon.–Fri. 7–9 A.M. and 2:30–6 P.M.) and $0.60 otherwise.

BACKGROUND

The Setting

"Out there on the edge of the prairie" is how radio host Garrison Keillor describes his fictional hometown, Lake Wobegon, in his weekly radio variety show, *A Prairie Home Companion*. And when the hundreds of thousands of listeners, in Minnesota and around the country, hear those familiar words broadcast each week from St. Paul, they must also picture a city "on the edge"—not quite within the great American Heartland, but opening the door to it.

The Twin Cities sit where the last bit of eastern deciduous forest touches the edge of the great tallgrass prairie that sweeps south and west. Minneapolis is known as the "first city of the West" and St. Paul as the "last city of the East." The Mississippi River, which divides the two, does not do so cleanly. Instead, its north–south course makes a giant sideways S as it passes through the area, cradling neighborhoods of St. Paul that are bounded by the river on three sides. It also divides both cities and the suburbs into rough north and south areas, with much of the wealth and professional opportunities concentrated on the south.

GEOGRAPHY

The Twin Cities are located almost precisely in the middle between the East and West Coasts and also lie right on top of the 45th parallel, exactly halfway between the North Pole and the

Equator. A plaque in Minneapolis's Theodore Wirth Park (look for it near the intersection of Wirth Parkway and Golden Valley Road) marks this point.

True to their flatland reputation, Minneapolis sits 830 feet above sea level and St. Paul 702 feet.

Three rivers pass through the Twin Cities. The Minnesota River meets the Mississippi just south of St. Paul at Fort Snelling, and the St. Croix River flows south from Lake Superior, forming the border with Wisconsin for much of its length, before meeting the Mississippi southeast of the cities, near Hastings.

Retreating glaciers left the area a tremendous gift: nearly 1,000 lakes within the metropolitan area. And when Lake Agassiz, the massive glacial lake that covered much of northern Minnesota and the Dakotas, drained about 13,000 years ago, the water spilling out of it cut the Minnesota River and St. Croix Valleys even deeper.

Historically, the Twin Cities' most important geologic feature is St. Anthony Falls,

the only waterfall along the length of the Mississippi River. The falls originated well downstream of its present location near downtown Minneapolis and moved upstream, first slowly then more quickly, as the soft underlying sandstone eroded and the limestone overlayer collapsed. The waterfall was fixed in place in the late 1800s when, after the city had come to rely on its considerable waterpower, engineers built a massive wood apron (later replaced by concrete) to protect it. Had it moved a short distance farther upstream, the falls would have disappeared altogether.

CLIMATE

Minnesota's climate is characterized by warm, wet summers and cold, dry winters, with some of the greatest temperature variations in the country. While the Twin Cities have the coldest average annual temperature of any major U.S. metropolitan area (45°F), they also on occasion see record-setting temperatures even higher than those in far more southerly parts of the country.

During the summer, the annual butterfly exhibit at the Minnesota Zoo is a great family outing.

© TRICIA CORNELL

The Twin Cities are usually just a smidge warmer than the rest of the state, thanks to the warming effect off all those paved streets and tall buildings trapping heat. January is the coldest month, with an average high of 22°F, and July is the warmest, with an average high of 83°F. The first frost tends to come in early October, the last frost in early May. Below-zero temperatures have been seen in the Twin Cities as early as November 4, on one record-setting occasion in 1991, although that is not common at all.

During the winter, especially, Twin Cities temperatures can swing wildly. On one memorable day in 1996 in the Twin Cities the low temperature was -32°F. A week later, the high was 39°F.

Snow does fly in October and November, but it rarely sticks on the ground. A "permanent" winter snow cover of an inch or more tends to form in December and lasts, on average, three months.

An average year sees about 60 inches of snow. To the surprise of some out-of-towners who associate March with spring, March is the snowiest month, averaging 13.5 inches—and damp, heavy stuff at that. (The explanation locals will give for this strikes fear in the hearts of many: January and February are often just "too cold to snow." Meteorologists quibble, saying it's never actually too cold for snow to form, but colder air does hold less water vapor than warmer air, making large snowfalls less likely.)

The infamous Halloween Blizzard of 1991 set the record for the largest single snowfall, with 28.4 inches falling on the Twin Cities over the course of two days.

The Twin Cities get about two-thirds of their annual precipitation in the summer, with much of it coming in the form of torrential summer storms, rather than slow drizzles. June, the rainiest month with 4.34 inches of rain, sees on average as many as eight days of thunderstorms. Total average rainfall is about 30 inches a year.

History

Although they were not the first humans to inhabit the area that is now the Twin Cities, people of the Hopewell Tradition, a flourishing culture that spread across much of eastern North America between 200 B.C. and A.D. 500, left the most visible mark on the area: clusters of massive burial mounds that now make up Indian Mounds Park near downtown St. Paul.

The Hopewell peoples disappeared, but the Dakota people, who were here when the first European settlers arrived, are very likely the descendants of another ancient culture, the Mississippian, which reached into the southeast corner of what is now Minnesota.

The Dakota are also sometimes known as the "Sioux," a shortened form of the Ojibwe word *nadouessioux,* meaning "poisonous snake." The Dakota and Ojibwe have been fierce rivals, often fighting bloody battles, since the Ojibwe (sometimes known as "Chippewa") first began arriving in the area around 1700. European settlers' westward expansion pushed the Ojibwe out of their homes in the east. The rough and volatile line dividing the territories of the two groups settled more or less across the present-day Twin Cities, and the area saw its share of skirmishes.

What is now St. Anthony Falls, in downtown Minneapolis, was an important landmark for both the Dakota and Ojibwe people. Because they had to portage their canoes there as they came up or downstream, it was a natural spot for a campground. The Dakota called the falls *mnirara* or "curling waters," and the Ojibwe called it *kakabikah,* or "severed rock."

The first European to see the falls was Father Louis Hennepin in 1680. Hennepin, a

Belgian-born Franciscan priest, had been dispatched along with a band of explorers to seek out the headwaters of the Mississippi by the French government. (Many others would be sent on this errand before the American geographer Henry Schoolcraft fixed the source of the river at modern-day Itasca, well northwest of the Twin Cities, in 1832.) Hennepin was captured by the Dakota and spent several months with them before escaping. He headed downriver and came upon the waterfall he named after his patron saint, St. Anthony of Padua. While the waterfall was indeed impressive—about 16 feet—in his enthusiasm he exaggerated its size to a massive 40 or 50 feet high.

Word of the falls spread, attracting explorers and even early tourists, but the United States government didn't show much interest in the area until well after the Revolutionary War. After the Louisiana Purchase brought what is now Minnesota—along with all the land from the Mississippi River to the Rocky Mountains—into United States territory in 1803, the U.S. government sent Army lieutenant Zebulon Pike out to explore the northern reaches of it. Pike himself identified the promontory at the junction of the Minnesota and Mississippi Rivers, just south of the two present-day downtowns, as the perfect spot for a military fort. Pike bought a large tract of land from the Dakota in exchange for promises of better prices on furs, 60 gallons of whiskey, and $200 in trade goods.

In 1819, looking for a way to protect the upper Mississippi River area from British and French fur traders, the U.S. Army ordered a fort built on the spot Pike had chosen. Soldiers and their families arrived to build Fort Snelling, a limestone fortress high above the Mississippi. Out in the hinterlands, far from the cities of the East Coast, the new settlers were largely on their own when it came to meeting their basic needs. They built the first sawmills and cultivated fields alongside the Mississippi.

By August of 1848, fewer than 4,000 Europeans lived in what is now Minnesota, far below what the law required for territorial status. But the lumber companies were

MINNESOTA STATE SYMBOLS

- **State bird:** Common loon (*Gavia immer*)
- **State butterfly:** Monarch (*Danaus plexippus*)
- **State drink:** Milk
- **State fish:** Walleye (*Sander vitreus*)
- **State flower:** Pink-and-white lady's slipper (*Cypripedium reginae*)
- **State fruit:** Honeycrisp apple
- **State gemstone:** Lake Superior agate
- **State grain:** Wild rice (*Zizania aquatica*)
- **State motto:** L'Etoile du Nord (Star of the North)
- **State muffin:** Blueberry
- **State mushroom:** Morel (*Morchella esculenta*)
- **State photo:** "Grace," by Eric Enstrom, 1918
- **State song:** "Hail Minnesota"
- **State tree:** Red or Norway pine (*Pinus resinosa*)

eager for Minnesota to have some sort of official status after Wisconsin had achieved statehood and left them in limbo, no longer part of the Wisconsin Territory. A group of settlers met in Stillwater, chose Henry Sibley as their representative, and sent him off to Congress, essentially with their fingers crossed that he would be seated. He was, and in March 1849, President Zachary Taylor named Alexander Ramsey the first territorial governor.

Minnesota would become a state in very short order, but in the meantime, affairs needed to be settled with the large Native American tribes in the area. The Treaty of Traverse des Sioux in 1851 would be one of the darker days in the history of Minnesota's native peoples. At a gathering place in the southwest corner of the present-day metropolitan area, 35 chiefs signed a treaty giving up 24 million acres to the United States. Immediately after signing, each sat down at a separate table and signed another paper giving up the rights to the annuity payments they had just been promised to repay debts to white traders. The tribes would get little or nothing in return for their land.

STATEHOOD

When Minnesota became a territory, St. Paul was named as its capital. In 1857, there was a drive to move the capital to the town of St. Peter, which was a little more centrally located. The law passed the territorial legislature and only needed the governor's signature. But an opposing legislator, Joseph Rolette, decided to take matters into his own hands. He absconded with the bill and then hid in a hotel drinking and playing cards until the clock ran out on the legislative session and the bill expired, leaving the capital in St. Paul.

Minnesota became a state in 1858 and quickly found itself embroiled in two wars. When the Civil War broke out in 1861, Governor Alexander Ramsey happened to be in Washington, D.C., at the time and responded immediately to President Lincoln's call for troops. Thanks to some new technology—the telegraph—the nation's first volunteers were lined up at Fort Snelling within days. About one in ten Minnesota men fought in the Civil War, in battles from Bull Run to Gettysburg.

Within the year, Minnesota had another war on its hands, this time right at home. The harvests had been bad for several years and the U.S. government had not been paying its annuities to the Dakota. Unrest grew and the situation exploded in the summer of 1862, when four young Dakota men killed a farming family. Brutal battles raged for two months, with horrors committed on both sides. After the Dakota surrendered, thousands of men, women, and children were imprisoned in a camp outside Fort Snelling, where nearly all perished from disease or starvation. More than 300 men were sentenced to hang. President Lincoln personally reviewed the cases and reduced most of the sentences, but the settlers were calling out for blood and 39 Dakota men were hanged.

THE MINNESOTA MIRACLE

After the Civil War, the nation looked westward again and the Twin Cities boomed. It became a center for the lumber industry and then the flour industry, connected to the rest of the country by "the Empire Builder" James J. Hill's railroads. All this growth was fueled by immigration not just from the rest of the country, but from Scandinavia, Germany, Ireland, and Eastern Europe as well. By the late 1870s, well more than one-third of Minnesota's population had been born in another country.

Minneapolis rode the milling wave until 1930, when production dropped off sharply and the city of Buffalo took over as the leading producer. But by that time, other industries were already on the rise. Minnesota Mining and Manufacturing (3M) introduced a wide range of industrial, military, and consumer products (including Scotch tape) that helped it thrive through the war years. Medtronic rose to the top of the biotech field with the first implantable pacemaker. And a number of growing companies in a variety of fields kept Minnesota's diversified economy strong: Honeywell in defense manufacturing, Cargill in grain trading, Control Data and IBM in computers, and General Mills and Land O'Lakes in food production. An enterprising developer built the nation's first indoor shopping mall, Southdale, in the first-ring suburb of Edina in 1956.

By the 1970s, Minnesota had a reputation for a sound economy, a strong education, and a high quality of life. *Time* magazine featured Minnesota governor Wendell Anderson—grinning and holding a walleye on a fishing hook—on the cover in 1973, under the title "The Good Life in Minnesota." Anderson is largely credited with the successful restructuring of funding for municipalities and public schools that helped bring about the Minnesota Miracle.

Anderson, however, left the governor's office in 1976 when he appointed himself to fill the U.S. Senate seat vacated by Walter Mondale, who had been elected vice president. This didn't go over well with Minnesotans, who punished the Democratic-Farmer-Labor Party in subsequent elections and helped usher in an era of moderate Republican leadership in Minnesota, including governors Al Quie and Arne Carlson, U.S. Senator Dave Durenburger, and, later, U.S. Representative Jim Ramstad.

The governor most famous to those outside of Minnesota was surely Jesse Ventura, who was elected on a wave of disgust with the two major parties (or, possibly, in a massive public game of chicken) in 1999. Ventura made himself a reputation for antagonizing both the press and Minnesota's bicameral legislature—and

for governing fairly effectively simply by getting out of the way. He left office in 2003 and was replaced by Republican Tim Pawlenty, a more conservative model of Republican than previous Minnesota leaders. Pawlenty is up for reelection in 2010.

In recent years, Minnesota (and the Twin Cities in particular) has been shaped by new waves of immigrants, as the Latin American, South Asian, and East African communities have grown. St. Paul sent the nation's first Hmong American to a state legislature in 2002, when Mee Moua was elected to the Minnesota Senate. Although the percentage of foreign-born citizens is at 7 percent, rather than around 40 percent as it was in the late 1800s, there are shades of that earlier turbulent time of change and growth.

Government and Economy

GOVERNMENT

Both Minneapolis and St. Paul are strongholds of the Democratic Party—or the Democratic-Farmer-Labor Party, as it is known here. Minneapolis has not elected a Republican mayor since 1973, and St. Paul hasn't since 1952 (although current U.S. Senator Norm Coleman switched to the Republican Party in the middle of his term as St. Paul mayor in 1996). Both the 13-member Minneapolis City Council and the seven-member St. Paul City Council are typically made up almost entirely of DFLers, with a Green Party member or independent or two thrown in for variety.

Another characteristic the cities share is strong neighborhood control. St. Paul's 17 districts are governed by independent district councils. Each has control over its own budget and has a say in vital land-use questions. Minneapolis's neighborhood councils also control significant budgets, used for neighborhood revitalization programs,

Minneapolis City Hall

© TRICIA CORNELL

from housing to scholarships to landscaping and more.

Metropolitan Council

With two major cities sitting cheek by jowl, not to mention the surrounding suburban areas, there's bound to be some redundancy in government functions. In the seven-county Minneapolis-St. Paul metropolitan area (including Hennepin County, which contains Minneapolis, and Ramsey County, which contains St. Paul) there are as many as 188 cities, from tiny New Trier, population 110, to Minneapolis, population 388,000.

The Minnesota State Legislature foresaw the problems this could cause, as disparities grew and municipalities battled for ever scarcer resources, as early as 1967. Lawmakers created the Metropolitan Council to centralize planning and coordinating powers in one body. The council is charged with creating an evolving framework for growth and vetting the growth plans of member communities to be sure they fit that framework.

Today the powerful Met Council (390 Robert St. N., St. Paul, 651/602-1000, www.metropolitancouncil.org) has an annual budget of about $700 million and a staff of 3,700. It is governed by a board of 17 members appointed by the governor and approved by the Minnesota Senate. Each member represents a geographic district within the seven-county area.

In its four-decade history, the council has taken on operating responsibilities beyond its original role as a planner and coordinator. It operates the Metro Transit bus system, serving Minneapolis, St. Paul, and the surrounding communities, as well as the light rail system between the Mall of America and downtown Minneapolis. It also operates the sewer and wastewater treatment programs for 100 communities and funds a system of 49 regional parks.

While the bulk of the council's budget comes from legislative funding, sewer treatment fees, and transit fares, it also serves another important function in the area: redistributing the wealth. Communities give the council 40 percent of the growth in their commercial-industrial tax base since 1971. That money is then redistributed to member communities based on population and the market value of homes.

Democratic-Farmer-Labor Party

One of Minnesota's most telling political quirks is the existence of the Democratic-Farmer-Labor Party, the DFL. That's right, Minnesota doesn't have just any old Democratic Party, it has its very own. The DFL was formed in 1944, when Minnesota's Democrats merged with the Farmer-Labor Party. The Farmer-Labor Party had a presence in other states but had been particularly strong in Minnesota, producing three governors and four U.S. Senators between its founding in 1918 and the merger. Two national Democratic nominees for president—Hubert H. Humphrey in 1968 and Walter Mondale in 1984—have been DFLers, though both lost to their Republican opponents.

ECONOMY

The Mississippi River drove the early economic development of Minneapolis and St. Paul. Long before the railroad reached the new west, waterways tied the new cities to the whole of the eastern seaboard and the burgeoning frontier. St. Anthony Falls powered two boom times in Minneapolis in particular: From 1848 to 1887, Minneapolis sawmills turned out more boards than in any other city in the nation. And from 1884 to 1930, Minneapolis led the world in flour production.

Today the Twin Cities area is a hub for biotechnology, and Minnesota has more Fortune 500 companies per capita than any other state, with 18 of them in the metro area alone. The metro area had a gross metropolitan product of $172 billion in 2005, the 14th largest metropolitan economy in the United States. In fact, the Twin Cities represent about two-thirds of Minnesota's gross state product (and about the same proportion of the state's population).

The Twin Cities also rank first in the nation among major metropolitan areas in labor force participation (82 percent of working-age adults) and employment (77 percent). Minnesota has the country's highest labor-force participation rate for women (72 percent). Unemployment falls slightly below the national average. Workers enjoy the seventh-highest per capita income ($43,696 in 2006) and the third-shortest average commute time (24 minutes in 2006).

In housing, the Twin Cities ranks sixth among metropolitan areas in housing affordability and first in the rate of homeownership (75 percent in 2006).

These factors—and, of course the cultural amenities—no doubt contributed to *Kiplinger* magazine's decision to place the Twin Cities second on its list of smart places to live in 2008 (and on its list of top cities for those married with children in 2007).

The 17 Fortune 500 companies in the metro area are: Target, UnitedHealth Group, Best Buy, St. Paul Travelers, 3M, Supervalu, US Bancorp, CHS, General Mills, Medtronic, Xcel Energy, Land O'Lakes, Thrivent Financial, CH Robinson Worldwide, Nash Finch, Ecolab, and Mosaic Company.

People and Culture

Minnesota has the fastest-growing population in the Midwest, and much of that growth is happening in the Twin Cities metro area, if not in the central cities themselves. The seven-county metro area had a population of 2.8 million in 2007—that's 60 percent of Minnesota's total population—with 388,000 people in Minneapolis, the state's largest city, and 288,000 in St. Paul, the capital. The metro area includes 186 cities, most of which are growing at a faster rate than both Minneapolis and St. Paul, while the two central cities' share of the region's population continues to shrink rapidly. The Metropolitan Council, which oversees planning for the area, predicts that the population will reach 3.7 million by 2030.

Residents of the Twin Cities are, on average, well-educated middle-class people. Thirty-six percent of adults in the metro area have bachelor's degrees, putting Minneapolis-St. Paul fourth among U.S. metropolitan areas. The metro area ranks first in the percentage of population in the middle-income bracket (at 46 percent).

Minnesota has a reputation as a pretty white

Hmong, Spanish, and Somali have joined English on many municipal signs, reflecting the changing population of the Twin Cities.

place. And, according to statewide statistics, yes, it is. But the picture changes depending on where you look. In the central cities—Minneapolis and St. Paul proper—66 percent of the population is white, while in the first-ring suburbs that number is 89 percent, and in the outer 'burbs it's 95 percent. Seven percent of residents in the metro area are foreign-born. Many visitors are surprised to learn that the Twin Cities are home to large Hmong, Somali, Ethiopian, Eritrean, and Liberian populations.

About 50,000 Hmong live in Minnesota, immigrants and the children and grandchildren of immigrants from Vietnam, Thailand, and Laos. The largest number—more than half—live in St. Paul. Outside of Asia, only California's Hmong population is larger. The Hmong started arriving in Minnesota after the Vietnam War, where many had fought on the U.S. side in the "secret war" against the communists in Laos. The population grew again in 2004 when thousands of Hmong refugees from the Wat Tham Krabok camp in Thailand arrived.

Minnesota's Somali population, the largest in the U.S., is estimated by some at 40,000, by others much higher than that. The population grew explosively in the 1990s, after the civil war in Somalia resulted in the total dissolution of a functioning government there. Most of the Somali population is centered in Minneapolis, where Somali-owned businesses and cultural centers are flourishing.

EDUCATION

The University of Minnesota predates the state of Minnesota itself. It was chartered in 1851 and began enrolling students in 1857, the year before Minnesota became a state. It became a post-secondary institution in 1869. Today, it is the fourth largest in the nation, with more than 50,000 students, and boasts a number of top-ranked graduate programs, including chemical engineering, health-care administration, geography, applied economics, psychology, and more.

The Twin Cities metro area, in fact, is home to about two dozen colleges and universities. St. Paul alone ranks second in the nation in the number of higher-education institutions per capita. A number of them—including the University of Minnesota itself—attract many students from out of state who stick around to join the local workforce after they finish their education.

Minnesota has long had a reputation for excellence and innovation in public education. It was the first state to mandate full interdistrict school choice (any student can enroll in any school anywhere in the state, as long as there's room) and the first to introduce charter schools, in 1991.

The Arts

It goes against all the stereotypes—the hard-working, no-nonsense Scandinavian ancestors; the cold weather; its location smack dab in between two coasts that both view themselves as the center of the universe—but the Twin Cities are a place where serious artists do serious art—on stage, on the page, and in their studios. More importantly, this is a place full of happy amateur artists—those who do for the love of doing, and love living in a culture that supports that.

ARTS, CRAFTS, AND FOLK TRADITIONS

Several organizations are working to keep alive some of the Scandinavian folk art traditions that came to Minnesota over a hundred years ago. The **American Swedish Institute** (www.americanswedishinst.org) hosts exhibits and offers classes in woodcarving, bobbin winding, the traditional painting technique known as rosemaling, and other crafts. **Ingebretsen's** (www.ingebretsens.com) is a store specializing in Scandinavian foods and crafts and a mini cultural center. Look on its website for classes in cooking, knitting, weaving, carving, and other crafts. Enterprising citizens also teach classes in a very wide range of crafts through Minneapolis Community Education (http://commed.mpls.k12.mn.us) and its St. Paul counterpart (www.commed.spps.org).

Another folk tradition that you are likely to see—one newer to the Twin Cities—is *pa ndau,* intricate Hmong appliqué work, characterized by concentric squares, often on purses, wallhangings, and pillow covers. A good place to look for *pa ndau* is at the **Minneapolis Farmers Market.** Keep your eyes out, as well, for the more modern cousin of *pa ndau*: story-cloths, which are appliquéd works of art that tell a story. The style originated in the refugee camps of Thailand in the 1970s.

The **Textile Center** (www.textilecentermn.org) is a national umbrella organization for textile arts of all kinds that span centuries and

> ## MADE IN MINNESOTA
>
> Ever wonder where the Bundt pan came from? Right here in St. Louis Park, Minnesota, a product of local company Nordic Ware. Some other notable Twin Cities inventions (well, Spam comes from a little farther afield, in Hormel, Minnesota): the implantable pacemaker, Magnetic Poetry, the Milky Way candy bar, Post-Its, Rollerblades, Spam, and Zubaz (those wide-legged pants from the 1980s).

cultures, with member organizations dedicated to needlepoint, sewing, spinning, knitting, and more. The center hosts exhibits and has a public library collection. In a similar vein, the **Northern Clay Center** (www.northernclaycenter.org) is a national organization based here in the Twin Cities and supporting ceramicists through grants, exhibitions, publications, and more.

For arts of all sorts, from writing to photography, painting, fabric design, and more, the **Split Rock Arts Center** (http://cce.umn.edu/splitrockarts) at the University of Minnesota hosts summer workshops in the Twin Cities and retreats at its location in Cloquet, in northern Minnesota.

LITERATURE

There's just something in the water here—that's sometimes the only explanation people can come up with to explain the Twin Cities' remarkable literary culture. The two cities regularly appear at the top of the list of America's most literate cities (as ranked by Central Connecticut State University, which tracks these things based on libraries, bookstores, publishers, and so on). In 2007, Minneapolis was number one and St. Paul number three.

But there's more to it than mysterious waterborne substances. A strong history of supporting the arts financially, top-notch educational institutions, and generations of immigrants from book-loving cultures all contribute, along with the snowball effect: A great literary culture attracts more people to contribute to it.

The area is home to a one-of-a-kind literary incubator, **Open Book** (www.openbookmn.org), where you'll find the Minnesota Center for Book Arts (www.mnbookarts.org), The Loft Literary Center (www.loft.org), and one of the country's most successful small nonprofit publishers, Milkweed Editions (www.milkweed.org), all under one roof.

The Twin Cities have also been called a hub of small-scale publishers, comparable to New York's status as the hub for mega-scale publishing. In addition to Milkweed, several other small presses survive and thrive here, including Coffee House Press (www.coffeehousepress.org) and Graywolf Publishing (www.graywolfpress.org).

Other pillars of the literary community in the Twin Cities include the **SASE literary arts program** (now part of Intermedia Arts, www.intermediaarts.org), which makes grants to emerging writers and hosts classes and readings, and *Rain Taxi* (www.raintaxi.com), a scrappy quarterly nonprofit literary journal that reviews books nobody else is reviewing but everybody else should be. The folks behind *Rain Taxi* also organize the annual Twin Cities Book Festival, a very well-attended day of readings, talks, and exhibits.

Another much-anticipated event in the literary calendar is the announcement of the Minnesota Book Awards, which honor Minnesota-related authors and illustrators in eight categories and often feature writers who get attention on the national scene as well.

THEATER

When Sir Tyrone Guthrie had a vision of a new sort of theater—one with a resident, professional company dedicated to the classics—he looked all over the country for a good home for it. And he settled on Minneapolis. That was in 1963. What drew Guthrie to the Twin Cities—the strong cultural community, the many colleges

FAMOUS TWIN CITIANS

These are a few of the famous folks to come out of the Minneapolis and St. Paul area.

- **In literature:** Mary Casanova, Kate DiCamillo, Louise Erdrich, F. Scott Fitzgerald, Thomas Friedman, Garrison Keillor, Chuck Klosterman, Sinclair Lewis, Charles Schulz, August Wilson.

- **In politics:** Kofi Annan (graduated from Macalester College in St. Paul), Al Franken, Hubert H. Humphrey, Eugene McCarthy, Walter Mondale, Paul Wellstone, Jesse Ventura.

- **In sports:** the 1980 Olympic hockey team (11 of the 20 players and coach Herb Brooks), Greg LeMond, John Madden, Kevin McHale, Bronko Nagorski, Alan Page, Kirby Puckett.

- **In movies and television:** Loni Anderson, Richard Dean Anderson, Diablo Cody, Joel and Ethan Coen, Josh Hartnett, Tippi Hedren, Craig Kilborn, Peter Krause, Jessica Lange, Mystery Science Theater 3000, Cheryl Tiegs, Lizz Winstead.

- **In music:** the Andrews Sisters, Atmosphere, Babes in Toyland, Brother Ali, Eddie Cochran, Morris Day and the Time, Bob Dylan, The Jayhawks, Jimmy Jam, Mason Jennings, Bob Mould, Prince, The Replacements, Semisonic, Soul Asylum, The Suburbs.

- **In law:** Harry Blackmun, Warren Burger, Pierce Butler, William Douglas.

- **Explorers:** Ann Bancroft, Dan Buettner, Charles Lindbergh, Will Steger.

- **Fictional characters:** Betty Crocker, Jolly Green Giant, Mary Tyler Moore, Pillsbury Doughboy, Rocky and Bullwinkle.

- **Other:** Norman Borlaug, Jean Paul Getty, Billy Graham, Robert Mondavi, Thorstein Veblen, Roy Wilkins.

and universities, the enthusiasm for theater—is still characteristic of the area today.

Twin Citians are proud of the oft-repeated fact that we have more theater seats per capita than anywhere in the United States outside of New York City. At any given time during the season, there are as many as four dozen shows—professional, high-quality shows, generally, not community theater, although there's plenty of that, too—and several theaters run summer shows or have year-round seasons. And the future looks good for theater in the Twin Cities: Younger generations are well-represented among both audiences and theater movers-and-shakers. The highlight of the year for many adventurous theater-goers, young and old, is the Minnesota Fringe Festival, the largest unjuried theater festival in the United States, with attendance at 160 shows topping 40,000.

In addition to the high-profile Guthrie, the Twin Cities has a reputation for strong support of out-of-the-mainstream theaters. Penumbra Theater is one of only three African American theaters in the United States to produce a full season of plays. Penumbra premiered several of playwright August Wilson's plays when he lived and wrote here in the 1980s. And shows at Mixed Blood Theater, which is dedicated to diversity of all kinds, regularly fill all the seats.

Supporting all this enthusiasm for the theater is another critical component of healthy cultural life: arts criticism. While grousing about the lack of arts criticism is a popular pastime in the Twin Cities, the truth is both major daily newspapers employ full-time theater critics, a good thing in a time of slashed media budgets.

TELEVISION AND FILM

Some might argue that the best television to come out of the Twin Cities is the cult classic *Mystery Science Theater 3000,* which ran on Comedy Central and the Sci-Fi channel for 11 years in the 1980s and '90s, even spawning a feature film. Silhouettes—voiced by local comedians and visible at the bottom of the screen as if they were watching the movie themselves—riffed on science fiction B-movies. The series ended in 1999.

MINNESOTA ONSCREEN

The Twin Cities have served as the backdrop for a number of movies in the past decade or so, including:

· *Mighty Ducks* (1992)
· *Grumpy Old Men* (1993)
· *Mallrats* (1995)
· *Fargo* (1996)
· *Drop Dead Gorgeous* (1999)
· *North Country* (2005)
· *A Prairie Home Companion* (2006)

People of a certain age will also remember that Brandon and Brendan of the 1980s TV hit *Beverly Hills 90210* moved from Minnesota to Beverly Hills at the start of the series. Minnesotans of a certain age will remember that the filmmakers apparently threw a dart at the Midwestern portion of the map, looking for an appropriate foil to the Beverly Hills lifestyle. Most mentions of Minnesota places, including Wayzata and the University of Minnesota, were somehow mangled. That's a big turnaround from the 1970s *The Mary Tyler Moore Show,* in which Minneapolis got to play the part of the big city (see the sidebar *Who Can Turn the World On with Her Smile?* in the *Sights* chapter).

The Twin Cities and Minnesota are often played for laughs in the movies as well. *The Mighty Ducks* and *Grumpy Old Men* series were both set in and around the Twin Cities and partially filmed here. In 1995's *Mallrats,* Eden Prairie Center mall, south of Minneapolis, stood in for the locus of universal teenage ennui. And the Minneapolis-St. Paul International Airport stood in for a Midwestern airport in distress in the filming of the 1970 disaster movie *Airport.* And who could forget how Prince burst onto the scene in the 1984 iconic hit *Purple Rain?* It was filmed almost entirely on location in the Twin Cities and is virtually a cinemagraphic tour of many Minnesotans' young adulthood.

ESSENTIALS

Getting There

Exactly halfway between the two coasts, with the largest airport in the Upper Midwest, Minneapolis is easy to get to and, once you're here, easy to get around.

AIRPORT

Minneapolis-St. Paul Airport (MSP) (612/726-5555, www.mspairport.com, open 24 hours a day) is the world's 16th busiest airport and the country's sixth busiest. It is 16 miles southeast of downtown Minneapolis and 12 miles southwest of downtown St. Paul, in the Fort Snelling unincorporated area. It is owned and operated by the Metropolitan Airport Commission, an independent state government

agency. (Fun trivia: The Minneapolis-St. Paul Airport was the set for parts of the 1970 film *Airport*.)

MSP is home base for formerly Minnesota-based Northwest Airlines, which carried about two-thirds of the passengers arriving and departing from the airport each year. Delta Airlines acquired Northwest in 2008 and is in the process of merging. Delta now dominates most of the gates in the main terminal, the Lindbergh Terminal, while the other carrier that uses MSP as its main hub, Sun Country (www.suncountry.com), takes up much of the much smaller Humphrey Terminal. In all, 11 domestic airlines, three

international airlines, and three regional carriers serve the airport. If you're willing to fly Northwest, it's fairly easy to find a direct flight to any other major international airport in the United States, though Northwest's virtual monopoly keeps prices high. Thanks to the strong presence of Iceland Air (www.icelandair.com), flights to Europe via Reykjavik are shorter and cheaper than they are otherwise via the East Coast.

Make sure you know which terminal you're flying to or from. Your paper ticket or itinerary will often say "Terminal L" for the Lindbergh Terminal and "Terminal H" for Humphrey. If you need to travel between the two terminals, the best way to go is via the light rail, which runs 24 hours and is free of charge on this portion of the track alone. The trains run every 7 to 15 minutes. The light rail station at the Lindbergh Terminal is underground, between the blue and red parking ramps. Get on the free people mover tram one level below the baggage claim and ride it to the light rail station. The light rail station at the Humphrey Terminal is on the north side of the orange parking ramp. Take the skyway from Level 2 and follow the signs.

The light rail is also the easiest way to get into downtown Minneapolis. The comfortable trip takes just 25 minutes. For travel other than between the two terminals, you need to buy a ticket.

Metro Transit buses from the airport serve St. Paul and other parts of Minneapolis. Buses leave from Level 1 of the blue and red parking ramps at Lindbergh Terminal. If you land at Humphrey and need to catch a bus, you have to take the light rail to Lindbergh.

Airport taxis leave from the tram level at Lindbergh Terminal (follow signs to Ground Transportation) and from the Humphrey parking ramp on Level 1. Fares are metered at $2.35 per mile with an additional $2.75 trip fee. Fare to downtown Minneapolis will run between $32 and $44 and to downtown St. Paul between $26 and $33.

TRAIN

Amtrak serves **St. Paul's Midway Station** (730 Transfer Rd., St. Paul, 800/872-7245, www .amtrak.com, 6 A.M.–midnight). The station is almost exactly halfway between the two downtowns, just off University Avenue, a major thoroughfare.

One route, the Empire Builder, passes through here, a single train in each direction. The Empire Builder travels between Chicago and Seattle, arriving in St. Paul at 10:31 P.M. headed westbound and 7:05 A.M. headed east. That is, that is the scheduled time. The train is notoriously unpredictable, often held up by bad weather in the Rocky Mountains or other issues near Chicago.

If you arrive from Chicago late at night and don't have a friend waiting to pick you up, your only choice is to join the long line waiting for taxis (incentive to disembark quickly). If you arrive from Seattle in the morning you can try to catch a cab, or you can walk a quarter mile south down Transfer Road to the intersection with University, where eastbound buses will take you to St. Paul and westbound buses will take you to Minneapolis.

Greyhound buses also stop at the Amtrak station.

BUS

Greyhound buses stop in both Minneapolis and St. Paul. The **Minneapolis Greyhound Station** (950 Hawthorne Ave., Minneapolis, 612/371-3325, www.greyhound.com) is on the western edge of downtown Minneapolis, convenient to many Metro Transit bus routes. While this is hardly the roughest area of Minneapolis, it is one in which you need to use caution.

The **St. Paul Greyhound Station** (166 University Ave. W., St. Paul, 651/222-0507, www.greyhound.com) is immediately west of the State Capitol building and a little less than a mile northwest of downtown St. Paul. Several convenient Metro Transit buses run along University Avenue. This, too, is a neighborhood in which you want to be careful.

Getting Around

PUBLIC TRANSPORTATION

Metro Transit operates city buses and one light rail line within Minneapolis and St. Paul and the surrounding suburbs. The route coverage is good, but anyone planning to rely on public transportation outside of the downtown areas should remember to plan extra time for changing buses and for longer waits during off-peak hours.

Full fare is $2.25 during peak hours (Mon.–Fri. 6–9 A.M. and 3–6:30 P.M.) and $1.75 otherwise, with discounts for seniors and people with disabilities with proper ID. Kids under 6 ride free. Within the designated downtown zones in both Minneapolis and St. Paul the fare is just $0.50. Drop exact change into box. The driver can't make change. If you ask the driver for a transfer as you board, he or she will give you a ticket good on any other bus or train within the next 2.5 hours.

You can buy stored-value cards at most Cub Foods and Rainbow grocery stores. For fare passes, route maps, and any other information, go to Metro Transit stores in downtown Minneapolis (719 Marquette Ave., Minneapolis, Mon.–Fri. 7:30 A.M.–5 P.M., Sat.–Sun. closed), downtown St. Paul (101 5th St. E., skyway level, St. Paul, Mon.–Fri. 7:30 A.M.–4:45 P.M., Sat.–Sun. closed), and at the Mall of America (60 E. Broadway, Bloomington, Tues.–Fri. 3–6:30 P.M., Sat. noon–2 P.M. and 3–6:30 P.M., Sun.–Mon. closed).

There's a fantastically convenient trip planner at www.metrotransit.org: Enter your starting point and destination and the time and the website will generate a handful of itineraries, complete with maps and walking directions.

The Hiawatha light rail line (Metro Transit route 55) runs between downtown Minneapolis and the Mall of America, stopping at the Minneapolis-St. Paul Airport. Fares are the same as on the buses. Buy tickets from the vending kiosks on the platforms (cash and credit cards accepted). Ticketing is on the honor system, but conductors do check frequently and fines are hefty. Trains run from about 4 A.M. to about 1 A.M., with waits 7–8 minutes during peak times and more than half an hour in the wee hours.

DRIVING

If you'd like more flexibility and freedom in your travel than you might get from public transportation, you'll need a car. In theory, navigating the cities is fairly straightforward, as both are laid out primarily in a grid system. But nature throws up enough surprises—from rivers to creeks to lakes and

LIGHT RAIL

In 1954, the last streetcar made its final run on Twin Cities tracks, a day some hailed as necessary for modernization and others rued. Fifty years later, the Twin Cities' first light rail line opened, hailed by rail fans and commuters alike – and sports fans, too: They like the easy access to the Metrodome in downtown Minneapolis.

The single line runs between downtown Minneapolis and the Mall of America, stopping at both terminals of the Minneapolis-St. Paul airport. When Target Stadium, downtown's new baseball stadium, opens in 2010, the light rail tracks will be extended for an additional stop, to reach the stadium.

Ridership on the Hiawatha line, as it is known, has exceeded expectations by nearly 60 percent and brought a needed economic boost to the South Minneapolis neighborhoods along its route. That success has spurred more rail projects, including the Northstar Commuter Rail line, which will open between Minneapolis and St. Cloud in 2009, and a second light rail line – the Central Corridor – projected to open in 2014 between downtown Minneapolis and downtown St. Paul along University and Washington Avenues.

major highways—that you'll want to invest in a good road map. When you're at the bookstore perusing maps, make sure you find one that gives you the level of detail you need. Many map publishers cover the whole metro area but without any detail anywhere except in insets of downtown Minneapolis and St. Paul. The **AAA Headquarters** just south of Minneapolis (5400 Auto Club Way, 952/927-2600, Mon.–Thurs. 8 A.M.–7 P.M., Fri. 8 A.M.–6 P.M., Sat. 9 A.M.–5 P.M., Sun. closed) is a great place to get maps of all sorts.

Every major rental car company has an outlet at the airport. **Avis Rent A Car** has locations in both downtown Minneapolis (829 3rd Ave. S., Minneapolis, 612/332-6321, www.avis .com) and downtown St. Paul (411 Minnesota St., St. Paul, 651/917-9955).

Keep some quarters in the car for parking, as meters are plentiful, especially in downtown St. Paul. Ramps and lots, which are also well-signed and easy to find, cost $8–20 a day. In residential neighborhoods, pay attention to signs sometime restricting parking to a single side of the street. At city parks, watch for signs restricting parking to those with prepurchased parking passes.

TAXIS

Outside of downtown Minneapolis and St. Paul, forget trying to hail a cab. In fact, forget trying to hail a cab downtown, too. Instead, head for the nearest major hotel and look for the taxis parked at the rank outside. Fares are standardized: $2.50 flag drop plus $1.90 per mile. An additional fee of $2.75 is added to airport trips. Trips originating at the airport are metered at $2.35 per mile.

Rather than trying to hail a cab, call one—as far in advance as you can, if possible. There are dozens of small companies; in Minneapolis, try **Yellow Taxi** (800/829-4222) or **Blue & White Taxi** (612/333-3333). St. Paul companies include **City Wide Cab Co.** (651/489-1111) and **Diamond Cab** (651/642-1188). There may be a $5 minimum fare. If you're traveling between downtown Minneapolis and downtown St. Paul, expect to pay about $25; from downtown Minneapolis to the Mall of America it's about $23.

BICYCLING

Both Minneapolis and St. Paul are terrific cities to navigate by bike. In fact, each city maintains well over 100 miles of dedicated bike lanes and paved off-road trails. Bike racks are common throughout the cities.

All Metro Transit buses are equipped with bike racks for use at no extra charge, and bikes are allowed on light rail trains.

Purchase the comprehensive **Twin Cities Bike Map** online at www.bikeverywhere .com. It's compiled by avid local cyclists, updated every three years, and printed on heavy water- and tear-resistant paper. It is also available at bookstores and bike shops in the Twin Cities. Map pdfs are available online from the Metropolitan Council (www.metro-council.org), the City of Minneapolis (www .ci.minneapolis.mn.us/bicycles), and St. Paul (www.stpaul.gov).

DISABLED ACCESS

All Metro Transit buses are equipped with wheelchair lifts. All light rail trains have areas set aside for wheelchair customers and offer step-free access so riders in wheelchairs can roll right on. All platforms are wheelchair accessible. For more information, call 612/373-3333 or ask for an *Accessible Transit* brochure at Metro Transit stores.

Tips for Travelers

HOURS

Minneapolis and St. Paul are both early-to-bed, early-to-rise places. Coffee shops open at 6 or 6:30 A.M. Office workers start their day at 8 or even before. Favorite spots for a leisurely weekend breakfast or brunch start to fill up at the not-so-leisurely hour of 9 A.M. And, having gotten started so early, many people are ready to pack it in early. You're unlikely to get an office worker on the phone after 5 P.M. Dinner at 6 is a common reservation request. And it's hard to find a restaurant still serving after 9 P.M. on weekdays and 10 P.M. on weekends. Last call in Minneapolis and St. Paul bars is 2 A.M.—and even then they don't have to kick a lot of people out the door.

"Summer hours" is another interesting Minnesota phenomenon: Many workplaces shift employees' schedules during the tantalizing months of June, July, and August so that they work an extra hour Monday through Thursday and leave at noon on Friday, presumably to head to the family cabin. Even at workplaces that don't officially observe summer hours, trying to get hold of a professional on a summer Friday afternoon is a fool's errand.

TIPPING

As in most other areas of the United States, 15–20 percent is a standard tip for good service at restaurants, salons, valet parking, and other service establishments. Taxi drivers, too, expect a tip. If you're paying cash, it's easiest to hand over exactly what you'd like to pay in total and say, "No change, thanks!" or to specify the amount of change you'd like back.

Baggers at grocery stores do not work for tips and at some establishments cannot accept them.

Tipping your hotel concierge $5–10 per service is standard, as is, at fancier hotels, leaving $2–10 per day for the housekeeping staff.

At the airport, if you check your bag with a skycap at the curb, be prepared to tip about

---

WHAT TO TAKE

If you're accustomed to looking smart and spiffy, by all means pack those trendy or formal clothes. But if your inclination is toward jeans and casual wear, you'll blend right in here. If you're so inclined, you should absolutely bring walking or running shoes or biking gear. Winter visitors will need a heavy coat, gloves, and a good scarf and hat. A possible exception can be made for business travelers and conventioneers staying in hotels connected to the skyways. In June, July, and August, rainstorms can be sudden and severe, calling for an umbrella and jacket.

$3–5 per bag, plus a little more if they go out of their way for you. The courtesy cart drivers do not expect tips but do appreciate them, especially if they go above and beyond.

SMOKING

Smoking is on the decline in Minnesota, as it is throughout the country. About 18 percent of adult Minnesotans smoke, compared to about 21 of Americans nationwide.

The Freedom to Breathe Act, enacted in 2007, prohibits smoking in any indoor public space. This means all Minnesota restaurants, bars, bowling alleys, coffee shops, and office buildings are entirely smoke-free. Smoking is prohibited in the common areas of hotels, but hotel management may choose to allow it in hotel rooms themselves.

Smoking is also permitted on outdoor patios of bars and restaurants, so long as they aren't closed in under a tent. Both the smoker and the owner of the establishment can be charged with a misdemeanor in case of a violation. The law is enforced on a complaint basis only—which means police officers aren't patrolling bars and restaurants looking for illicit ash trays—but Minnesotans in general are a compliant people and you are unlikely to see anyone violating the ban. Compliant, that is, but also clever: Shortly after the ban was enacted, an astute bar owner noticed that the law exempted smokers in theatrical productions.

So he cast all of his customers in a "play" to be performed nightly right in his establishment. He seemed at first to have found a genuine loophole, until the state courts ruled otherwise.

Health and Safety

Some travelers will remember the "Murderapolis" headlines of the 1990s, when the titillating combination of Minneapolis's high murder rate and its staid Midwestern reputation proved too much for the national media to resist. Those days are past, but Minneapolis's murder rate is still tragically high (47 people were murdered in 2007). As a visitor, especially in the two downtowns and in the residential neighborhoods of Southwest Minneapolis, St. Anthony, and south of I-94 in St. Paul, you are unlikely to experience even a hint of this. Some visitors to downtown Minneapolis, however, are surprised by the number of panhandlers they encounter on Hennepin Avenue and Nicollet Mall. Panhandling is not illegal unless it is "aggressive." The city defines "aggressive panhandling" as asking repetitively for money after a person has said "no," or asking for money in a confined or intimidating place (for example, in a bus shelter or on a bus, near an ATM, or at a sidewalk cafe). If this bothers you, the city advises you to call 911 or tell a cop.

There are a few areas where you want to be careful. Much of the city's crime takes place in North Minneapolis, which is north of downtown and west of the Mississippi River. This is an almost entirely residential area, so there isn't much to attract visitors, in any case. In downtown Minneapolis, stay alert near Block E, the entertainment center on Hennepin Avenue. And keep your eyes out as you bar-hop along 1st Avenue after dark. In South Minneapolis, be cautious and stick with a friend on and around Lake Street in the evenings. The Powderhorn and Phillips neighborhoods, which straddle Lake Street in South Minneapolis, are perfectly lovely places during the day but get sketchier in the evenings.

St. Paul's crime rate is significantly lower than Minneapolis's, but there are caveats here, as well. Downtown St. Paul isn't statistically a dangerous place to be, even after dark, but it is deserted, which is a good signal that you don't want to be wandering about alone. Use the buddy system around the Xcel Energy Center and around the bars along West 7th Street. And University Avenue, especially the east end of it, just northwest of the Capitol building, is a place where you want to keep your wits about you.

HOSPITALS
Both downtown Minneapolis and downtown St. Paul have excellent hospitals. **Hennepin County Medical Center** (701 Park Ave., Minneapolis, 612/873-3000, www.hcmc.org) is in downtown Minneapolis. Also convenient to downtown, in South Minneapolis, are **Abbott Northwestern Hospital** (800 28th St. E., Minneapolis, 612/863-4000, www.abbottnorthwestern.com) and **Children's Hospitals and Clinics** (2525 Chicago Ave. S., Minneapolis, 612/813-6000, www.childrensmn.org).

Clustered around downtown St. Paul, you'll find **Bethesda Hospital** (559 Capitol Blvd., St. Paul, 651/232-2000, www.bethesdahospital.org), **Regions Hospital** (640 Jackson S., St. Paul, 651/254-3456, www.regionshospital.com), **St. Joseph's Hospital** (69 Exchange St. W., St. Paul, 651/232-3000, www.stjosephs-stpaul.org), **United Hospital** (333 Smith Ave. N., St. Paul, 651/241-8000, www.unitedhospital.com), and **Children's Hospitals and Clinics** 345 Smith Ave. N., St. Paul, 651/220-6000, www.childrensmn.org). **Gillette Children's** (200 University Ave. E., St. Paul, 651/291-2848, www.gillettechildrens .org) is also in downtown St. Paul, but it offers specialized pediatric services and wouldn't be your first stop for an emergency.

Roughly halfway between the two downtowns are the two campuses of the University of Minnesota Medical Center: **University of Minnesota Medical Center/Children's Hospital, Fairview Riverside campus** (2450 Riverside Ave., Minneapolis, 612/273-3000, www.university.fairview.org) and **University of Minnesota Medical Center/Children's Hospital, Fairview University campus** (500 Harvard St., Minneapolis, 612/273-3000, www.university.fairview.org).

In the southern suburbs, head to **Fairview Southdale Hospital** (6401 France Ave. S., Edina, 952/924-5000, www.southdale .fairview.org). The most convenient hospital in the western suburbs is **Methodist Hospital** (6500 Excelsior Blvd., St. Louis Park, 952/993-5000, www.parknicollet.com/methodist). In the northern and eastern suburbs, **St. John's Hospital** (1575 Beam Ave., Maplewood, 651/232-7000, www.stjohnshospital-mn.org) is available.

The Twin Cities Veterans Administration hospital is **Minneapolis VA Medical Center** (1 Veterans Dr., Minneapolis, 612/725-2000, www.va.gov/minneapolis).

CLINICS AND PHARMACIES

If the emergency room isn't the appropriate option but you can't wait to get an appointment, try urgent care.

Park Nicollet maintains six urgent care clinics. Two convenient ones in the west metro area are **Park Nicollet Clinic–St. Louis Park** (3800 Park Nicollet Blvd., St. Louis Park, 952/993-1000, www.parknicollet.com, Mon.–Fri. 8 A.M.–8 P.M., Sat.–Sun. 8 A.M.–5 P.M.) and **Park Nicollet**

Clinic–Maple Grove (15800 95th Ave. N., Maple Grove, 952/993-1440, www.parknicollet .com). Approximate wait times are updated in real time on their website.

HealthPartners has eight urgent care clinics. The three in Minneapolis and St. Paul proper are **HealthPartners St. Paul** (205 Wabasha St., St. Paul, 952/853-8800, www .healthpartners.com, Mon.–Fri. 5–9 P.M., Sat.–Sun. 9 A.M.–8 P.M.), **HealthPartners Como** (2500 Como Ave., St. Paul, 952/853-8800, www.healthpartners.com, Mon.–Fri. 1–9 P.M., Sat. 9 A.M.–8 P.M.), and **HealthPartners Riverside** (2220 Riverside Ave., Minneapolis, 952/853-8800, www.healthpartners.com, Mon.–Fri. 5–9 P.M., Sat. 9 A.M.–5 P.M., Sun. noon–5 P.M.).

Several **Target** stores operate clinics for diagnosing and treating common minor ailments such as strep and pinkeye. The Target in downtown Minneapolis (900 Nicollet Mall, Minneapolis, 612/338-0085, www .target.com, Mon.–Fri. 8 A.M.–6 P.M., Sat. 9 A.M.–4 P.M., Sun. closed) and the one in North St. Paul (2199 Hwy. 36E, North St. Paul, 651/779-5986, www.target.com, Mon.–Fri. 8 A.M.–8 P.M., Sat.–Sun. 9 A.M.–4 P.M.) are two that have clinics.

Most Targets also have full-service pharmacies (and you truly can't throw…well, anything you can actually throw…without hitting a Target in the Twin Cities).

EMERGENCY SERVICES

For police and fire emergencies in the Twin Cities, dial 911.

The nonemergency number for the St. Paul Police Department is 651/291-1111.

To report nonemergency crimes in Minneapolis, call 311. This is also the number you use to contact any department in the City of Minneapolis. The helpful folks who answer the phone will connect you to the right people. For information about a crime in Minneapolis, call the Tip Line at 612/692-8477.

Information and Services

TOURIST INFORMATION

Neither Minneapolis nor St. Paul has a dedicated tourist information office, but both have excellent online resources. You can contact **Meet Minneapolis,** the city's convention and visitors association, at 888/676-6757 to request information or go to its very well-organized and attractive website, www.minneapolis.org. The **Minneapolis Convention Center** (1301 2nd Ave. S., Minneapolis, 612/335-6000, www.minneapolisconventioncenter.org) is right on the southern edge of downtown Minneapolis and connected to the skyway system.

Contact the **St. Paul Convention and Visitors Association** at 800/627-6101 or go to its website, www.stpaulcvb.org. St. Paul's convention center is the **RiverCentre** (199 Kellogg Blvd. W., St. Paul, 651/265-4800, www.rivercentre.org).

MEDIA AND COMMUNICATIONS
Phones and Area Codes

Until 1998, the area code for the whole of the Twin Cities was 612. That area has subdivided twice since then. Minneapolis (and a small portion of the southern suburb of Richfield) retained the 612 code. St. Paul and the eastern suburbs got 651. And the northeastern suburbs took 763 and the southeastern suburbs 952. All calls within all four area codes are local calls, as are calls from the Twin Cities to parts of the 507 area code to the south and to parts of the 320 area code to the north. You generally do not need to dial the area code if you are calling from within that code's area.

Internet Services

All **Hennepin County Library** branches (www.hclib.org), which include Minneapolis libraries, and all St. Paul Public Library branches (www.stpaul.lib.mn.us) offer free public wireless Internet access. You do not need to have a library card to bring your own computer and work in the library. Library work stations are

WCCO Radio has been an important source of information for Minnesotans for generations.

© TRICIA CORNELL

reserved for library cardholders. Hennepin County Library does not issue cards to out-of-state residents, and St. Paul Public Library charges non-Minnesotans $45 a year.

Nearly all independent coffee shops in town, including all **Dunn Bros.** locations, offer free Wi-Fi (though they do ask that you be courteous to customers who have come to, you know, drink coffee), and many have terminals for customer use (generally limited to 15 minutes). **Panera Bread** and **Bruegger's Bagels** are two chains that commonly offer free Wi-Fi for unlimited use.

In 2007, the city of Minneapolis launched a citywide wireless initiative with **USI Wireless** (www.usiwireless.com). The network is now completed, except for two large triangles the company calls "challenge areas" around Lake of the Isles and the University of Minnesota's East Bank. A subscription, available at the website, costs $17.95–$39.95 a month, depending on the speed of the connection and the length of the contract.

Mail and Messenger Services

There are five post offices in downtown Minneapolis: the **main post office** (100 1st St. S., Minneapolis, 612/349-4715, Mon.–Fri. 7 A.M.–8 P.M., Sat. 9 A.M.–1 P.M., Sun. closed), inside the **Butler Square** building (100 6th St. N., Ste. 120B, Minneapolis, 612/333-3688, Mon.–Fri. 9 A.M.–1:15 P.M. and 2:30–5 P.M., Sat.–Sun. closed), a few blocks from **Loring Park** (18 12th St. N., 612/333-6213, Mon.–Fri. 8:30 A.M.–5 P.M., Sat. 9 A.M.–1 P.M.), in an office building on the north end of town (307 4th Ave. S., 612/333-3153, Mon.–Fri. 9 A.M.–5 P.M., Sat.–Sun. closed), and in an office building a little to the south (110 8th St. S., Minneapolis, 612/333-2574, Mon.–Fri. 7:30 A.M.–5 P.M., Sat.–Sun. closed).

There are two post offices in downtown St. Paul: the **main post office** (180 Kellogg Blvd. E., St. Paul, 651/293-6035, Mon.–Fri. 8:30 A.M.–5:30 P.M., Sat. 9:30 A.M.–noon, Sun. closed) and the **Uptown branch** (408 St. Peter St., St. Paul, 651/889-2457, Mon.–Fri. 8:30 A.M.–5 P.M., Sat.–Sun. closed).

Go to www.usps.com to find one of the dozens of other post offices in the metro area.

The **UPS Store** is an alternative to the U.S. Postal Service and a good place to pick up packing supplies. There's one in downtown Minneapolis (40 7th St. S., Ste. 212, 612/332-4117, Mon.–Thurs. 7 A.M.–7 P.M., Fri. 7 A.M.–6 P.M., Sat. 10 A.M.–4 P.M., Sun. closed) and—convenient if you've just done a lot of shopping—one on Grand Avenue in St. Paul (1043 Grand Ave., St. Paul, 651/222-2019, Mon.–Fri. 8:30 A.M.–7 P.M., Sat. 9 A.M.–5 P.M., Sun. 11 A.M.–4 P.M.). Go to www.ups.com to find other UPS Stores in the area.

There are FedEx drop boxes all over the central business districts in downtown Minneapolis and St. Paul (check the skyway levels of buildings as well as the lobbies).

To talk to an actual human being when you FedEx your package, you'll have to go to the **FedEx Kinko's** in the IDS Center (80 8th St. S., Ste. 180, Minneapolis, 612/343-8000, open 24 hours), in South Minneapolis (1430 Lake St. W., Minneapolis, 612/822-7700, open 24 hours) or in the Summit-University neighborhood of St. Paul (58 Snelling Ave. S., St. Paul, 651/699-9671, open 24 hours).

If you need to have a package or papers delivered within the Twin Cities right away, there are a number of messenger services to choose from. Two large and well-reputed ones are **Street Fleet** (612/623-9999, www.streetfleet.com) and **Quicksilver Express** (651/484-1111, www.qec.com).

Magazines and Newspapers

Two major daily newspapers serve the Twin Cities. The *Minneapolis Star Tribune* (www.startribune.com) was part of the McClatchy chain until 2006, when McClatchy sold it to a private equity firm with no other media holdings, Avista Capital Partners. The *Strib,* as it is known, gets a lot of guff locally for its supposed liberal leanings, but we will leave that to readers to discern. It has a daily circulation of nearly 350,000. The *Minneapolis Tribune,* one of the two papers that merged to form the Star Tribune, dates back to 1867.

The *St. Paul Pioneer Press* (www.pioneerpress.com) is a descendant of the area's oldest daily newspaper, the *St. Paul Pioneer,* founded in 1849. It is now part of the Knight-Ridder chain and serves the east metro area. (It's fairly easy to find a *Star Tribune* in St. Paul, but not so easy to find a *Pioneer Press* in Minneapolis.) The *PiPress,* as it is known, has a daily circulation of nearly 200,000.

The Twin Cities are now down to one alternative weekly, *City Pages* (www.citypages.com), owned by Village Voice media. *City Pages* and the now-defunct *Twin Cities Reader* egged each other on to scoops and admirable reporting until Stern Publishing (now Village Voice Media) purchased both in 1997 and shut down the *Reader.* Recent years have seen the shuttering of other independent voices in the Twin Cities media, including *Pulse* and the print edition of *The Rake.*

There are, however, a number of robust neighborhood newspapers in the area, including the **Downtown Journal** (www.dtjournal.com), a biweekly freebie serving downtown Minneapolis, and its sister the **Southwest Journal** (www.swjournal.com), serving Southwest Minneapolis. Published monthly, **The Bridge** (www.readthebridge.com) covers the northeastern neighborhoods in South Minneapolis and some neighborhoods across the river. In St. Paul, the biweekly **Villager** (www.myvillager.com) serves the Summit-University neighborhood and, to some extent, downtown St. Paul.

The University of Minnesota's student newspaper, the **Minnesota Daily** (www.mndaily.com), is one of the largest student-run newspapers in the country, with a daily circulation of 24,000. It is published every weekday during the school year and twice weekly during the summer. The paper is entirely student-run and -staffed and is supported largely by (student-sold) advertising. *Daily* alumni can be found in nearly every newsroom in the Twin Cities, if not Minnesota. You can find it free on racks in and around the U of M campus.

On the free racks in your hotel lobby and in the skyways you can also find a number of worthwhile reads: The **Minnesota Women's Press** (www.womenspress.com) is a monthly newspaper focusing on women's issues. **Minnesota Parent** (www.mnparent.com), published monthly, and **Family Times**, (www.familytimesinc.com), published bimonthly, cover local parenting issues. The monthly **Minnesota Good Age** (www.mngoodage.com) and the quarterly **Best of Times** (www.familytimesinc.com) aim to reach an older audience.

Also free to pick up on many newsstands are several papers serving individual ethnic communities in the Twin Cities. **Insight News** (www.insightnews.com) has covered the African American community since 1974. It hits newsstands every Monday. The English-language biweekly **Asian Pages** (www.asianpages.com) is based in the Twin Cities but distributed in seven states across the Midwest. The weekly **Asian American Press** (www.aapress.com) also publishes in English, covering the Asian American and Pacific Islander communities. **La Prensa de Minnesota** (www.laprensademn.com) is published in both English and Spanish (in a single edition), and the weekly **Gente de Minnesota** (www.gentedeminnesota.com) is entirely in Spanish. Latino Communications Network publishes both Spanish-language newspapers and the weekly entertainment tabloid **Vida y Sabor,** aimed at a younger audience.

Free to pick up in churches and some newsstands are **Metro Lutheran** and the **Minnesota Christian Chronicle** (www.mcchronicle.com). **The Catholic Spirit** (www.thecatholicspirit.com) is published biweekly and is available by subscription. **American Jewish World** is published weekly and for sale at many bookstores and available by subscription.

The Twin Cities also have three big, glossy lifestyle magazines. **Mpls.St.Paul Magazine** (www.mspmag.com) and **Minnesota Monthly** (www.minnesotamonthly.com) are the two established publications, with a moneyed, slightly older readership. **Metro** is the upstart, reaching for a younger, urban audience. Tiger Oak Publications puts out **Minnesota Bride** twice yearly.

Twin Cities Business (www.tcbmag.com) and **Minnesota Business** (www.minnesotabusiness.com) are both full-color, glossy monthlies serving the business community, while **Upsize Minnesota** (www.upsizemag.com) aims particularly at smaller businesses. Two monthlies with dreadfully boring names are both actually must-reads for movers and shakers: **Finance and Commerce** (www.finance-commerce.com) and **Minnesota Law and Politics** (www.lawandpolitics.com).

Two more free magazines that are worth picking up are the ubiquitous and remarkably thick biweekly **Lavender** (www.lavendermagazine), serving the GLBT community, and the quarterly literary journal with a national reputation, **Rain Taxi** (www.raintaxi.com).

Radio and TV

Corporate radio has the same stranglehold on the Twin Cities market as it does everywhere else. But, as you spin the dial, a few unique frequencies will stand out. **KNOW 91.1** is the home of Minnesota Public Radio (www.mpr .org), where several nationally syndicated programs originate, including Garrison Keillor's *A Prairie Home Companion*. MPR's music station, **The Current 89.1** (www.mpr.org) plays a truly innovative mix of new and time-tested alternative music. **Cities 97.1** (www.cities97.com) reaches a grown-up audience whose beloved '80s hits are veering toward easy listening.

For slick right-wing talk, tune to **KTLK 1003** (www.ktlkfm.com). For community-access lefty talk (including news from Democracy Now) and world music, tune to **KFAI 90.3** (www.kfai.org). Minneapolis Public School students staff the jazz station **KBEM 88.5** (www.jazz88fm.com) 35 hours a week, with professional announcers and syndicated programming filling out the rest of the schedule. **FM 107.1** (www.fm1071.com) fills the day with chatter geared toward a female audience.

On the AM dial, **WCCO 830** (www.wccoradio.com)—"The Good Neighbor"—has kept Minnesotans informed for generations. **KLBB 1220** (www.klbbradio.com) plays nostalgic hits, heavy on the Frank Sinatra. You never know what you're going to get with student DJs spinning the tunes at the University of Minnesota's **KUOM 770 AM** (http://radiok.cce.umn.edu). It's all sports all the time at **KFAN 1130** (www.kfan.com). **KSTP 1500** (www .am1500.com) covers the waterfront with news and sports, including Twins baseball games. **KTNF 950** broadcasts Air America and other left-wing talk. **AM 1280 The Patriot** covers the other end of the political spectrum. **La Invasora 1400** broadcasts music, news, and talk in Spanish.

All the major television networks have affiliates in the Twin Cities. **Twin Cities Public Television** (www.tpt.org) runs seven channels, including tpt 2, its main channel; tpt 17, primarily for rebroadcasts; tpt kids; tpt MN for Minnesota-focused

original programming; tpt Create for craft- and DIY-focused programs; a high-definition channel; and a weather channel.

There are a number of public access stations in the Twin Cities. **Minneapolis Television Network** (www.mtn.org), **Metro Cable Network** (www.mcn6.org), and **St. Paul Neighborhood Network** (www.spnn.org) are the biggest.

PUBLIC LIBRARIES

A merger in 2007 folded the economically faltering **Minneapolis Public Library** system into the **Hennepin County Library** system (www .hclib.org). **St. Paul Public Library** (www .stpaul.lib.mn.us) operates independently of its west metro neighbors.

Visitors can use all libraries without a card, including browsing the open stacks and taking advantage of the free Wi-Fi. But in both systems you need a library card to access computer work stations and to check out books. You also need a library card to check out the **Museum Adventure Pass,** a fantastic deal that offers free admission (for either two or four people) to two dozen museums around the Twin Cities. Both library systems allow residents of the respective cities to preregister online for a card number or to apply in person at any branch with proof of residency. Minnesota residents who live outside of the metro area can register their home library card at Hennepin County or St. Paul Public Library and use the library services like a regular cardholder. Non-Minnesota residents can pay $45 a year for a St. Paul library card. Hennepin County Library does not issue cards to non-Minnesota residents.

The **Minneapolis Central Library** in downtown Minneapolis (300 Nicollet Mall, 612/630-6000, Tues. and Thurs. 10 A.M.–8 P.M., Wed. and Fri.–Sat. 10 A.M.–6 P.M., Sun. noon–5 P.M.) is a beautiful, welcoming public space, with a Dunn Bros. coffee shop, excellent children's area, genealogical research area, and reading room (see the *Sights* chapter for more). Find information on the other 40 Hennepin County Library locations online at www.hclib.org.

The **St. Paul Central Library** (90 4th
St. W., St. Paul, 651/266-7000, Mon.
11:30 A.M.–8 P.M., Tues.–Fri. 9 A.M.–5:30 P.M.,
Sat. 11 A.M.–4 P.M., Sun. 1–5 P.M.) is an impressive building built in 1917 and filling half
a city block on the edge of Rice Park. It was
fully renovated in 2002, maintaining the high
arched windows and opening the interior.
Cafe Zelda serves coffee and treats Mon.–Fri.
7 A.M.–3 P.M. Find information on the other 12
branches online at www.stpaul.lib.mn.us.

PLACES OF WORSHIP

While, historically, St. Paul is largely Irish and
German Catholic and Minneapolis largely
Scandinavian Lutheran, communities of nearly
every religious background have settled in the
Twin Cities. Eastern Orthodox immigrants
from Eastern Europe have left their mark on
Nordeast in Minneapolis, where there was
once a flourishing Jewish community as well.
Highland Park, in St. Paul, has long been a
center of Jewish culture, as has the first-ring
Minneapolis suburb of St. Louis Park. More
recently, Muslim immigrants from Africa have
formed communities in the Cedar-Riverside
neighborhood of Minneapolis and the near-
northern suburbs.

The seat of the **Archdiocese of St. Paul
and Minneapolis** (www.archspm.org) is at
the **Cathedral of St. Paul,** with the **Basilica
of St. Mary** in Minneapolis as its co-
cathedral. Both hold daily mass. For less traditional Catholic worship, go to the open and
welcoming **St. Joan of Arc Church** (4537 3rd
Ave. S., Minneapolis, 612/823-8205, www
.stjoan.com). To learn more about the Catholic
community in the Twin Cities, pick up a copy
of *The Catholic Spirit* (www.thecatholicspirit.
com) at most Catholic churches.

There are dozens of Lutheran churches
in the Twin Cities, including three on or
very near the campus of the University of
Minnesota alone. Three large churches include
University Lutheran Chapel (1101 University
Ave. SE, Minneapolis, 612/331-2747, www.
ulcmn.org), **Gloria Dei Lutheran Church**

Westminster Presbyterian Church in
downtown Minneapolis sits on the end of
Nicollet Mall.

© TRICIA CORNELL

(700 Snelling Ave. S., St. Paul, 651/699-1378,
www.gloriadeistpaul.org), and **Mount Olive
Lutheran Church** (3045 Chicago Ave. S.,
Minneapolis, 612/827-5919, www.mountol-
ivechurch.org). **Lutherans Concerned Twin
Cities** (www.lctwincities.org) maintains a
website with links to gay- and lesbian-friendly
congregations.

Two large churches serve the Greek
Orthodox community: **St. Mary's Greek
Orthodox Church** (3450 Irving Ave. S.,
Minneapolis, 612/825-9595, www.stmarysgoc
.org) and **St. George Greek Orthodox Church**
(1111 Summit Ave., St. Paul, 651/222-6220,
www.saintgeorge.mn.goarch.org). To find
Eastern Orthodox of other stripes, including Antiochian, Coptic, Eritrian, Ethiopian,
Serbian, Romanian, Ukrainian, and Russian,
visit the website of the **Minnesota Eastern
Orthodox Christian Clergy Association**
(www.meocca.org).

Two centers of Jewish culture serve the

roughly 40,000 Jews living in Minneapolis and St. Paul with arts and community programs, child care, and exercise facilities: the **St. Paul Jewish Community Center** (1375 St. Paul Ave., St. Paul, 651/698-0751, www.stpauljcc.org) and the **Sabes Jewish Community Center** (4330 Cedar Lake Rd. S., Minneapolis, 952/381-3400, www.sabesjcc .org). About two dozen synagogues are active in the metro area, including Reconstructionist, Reform, Conservative, and Orthodox congregations. Two large ones are **Mount Zion** (Reform, 1300 Summit Ave., St. Paul, 651/698-3881, www.mzion.org) and **Temple of Aaron** (Conservative, 616 Mississippi River Blvd. S., St. Paul, 651/698-8874, www.templeofaaron .org). Learn more about the Jewish community in Minnesota from the **Minneapolis Jewish Federation** and the **Jewish Federation of St. Paul,** which share the website www.jewishminnesota.org.

Westminster Presbyterian Church (1200 Marquette Ave., Minneapolis, 612/332-3421, www.ewestminster.org) has been a presence in downtown Minneapolis for more than 150 years and hosts frequent lunchtime lectures, open to the public, with speakers of national prominence.

Minnesota falls in the Prairie Star District of the **Unitarian Universalist Association** (www.psduua.org). There are 11 congregations in the Twin Cities area, including **First Universalist Church of Minneapolis** (3400 Dupont Ave. S., Minneapolis, 612/825-1701, www.firstuniv.org) and **Unity Church** (732 Holly Ave., St. Paul, 651/228-1456, www.unityunitarian.org).

A handful of local Quaker groups hold regular meetings, including the **Twin Cities Friends Meeting** (1725 Grand Ave., St. Paul, 651/699-6995, www.tcfm.org) and the **Minneapolis Friends Meeting** (4401 York Ave. S., Minneapolis, 612/926-6159, www .quaker.org/minnfm).

The Rock (612/339-7625, www.rockthechurch.org) holds Friday night services for those who "want God, not religion" (that's their slogan) in Jefferson Community School (1200 26th St. W., Minneapolis).

There are an estimated 150,000 Muslims living in the metro area. The **Islamic Center of Minnesota** (1401 Gardenia Ave. NE, Fridley, 763/571-5604, www.islamiccentermn .org) and the **Muslim American Society of Minnesota** (4100 66th St. E., Inver Grove Heights, 651/457-7170, www.masmn.org) serve as cultural and religious centers. There are a number of masjids, including: **Ummat Muhammad Islamic Center** (315 Lake St. E., Minneapolis, www.masmn.org) and **Al-Taqwa Islamic Center** (735 Snelling Ave. N., St. Paul, www.masmn.org).

The **Hindu Temple of Minnesota** (10530 Troy Ln. N., Maple Grove, 763/425-9449, www.hindumandirmn.org) was founded in the late 1970s and opened in its own building in 2006.

The **Minnesota Zen Meditation Center** (3343 Calhoun Pkwy. E., Minneapolis, 612/822-5313, www.mnzencenter.org) and **Clouds in Water Zen Center** (308 Prince St., Ste. 120, St. Paul, 65/222-6968, www.cloudsinwater.org) are both Buddhist centers in the Soto Zen tradition and are open regularly for meditation, including many classes.

MAJOR BANKS

The largest banks in the Twin Cities are **Wells Fargo** (www.wellsfargo.com) and **TCF Bank** (www.tcfbank.com). You'll find ATMs for both banks all over town. You'll also encounter **Bank of America** (www.bankofamerica.com), **Bremer Bank** (www.bremer.com), **Franklin Bank** (www.franklinbank.com), and **U.S. Bank** (www.usbank.com).

RELOCATION

Thousands of people each year come to visit and end up sticking around or planning to move to the Twin Cities permanently. Yep, it's just that livable here.

As soon as you land in the area (or even before), contact **Twin Cities Transplants** (www .imnotfromhere.org), a social and support group for people of any age who don't have roots in the area.

The **Minneapolis Chamber of Commerce** has a helpful list of links and information for new and prospective residents at www.minneapolischamber.org/relocation.php. The City of Minneapolis maintains a concise list of links to information that new (and longtime) residents need to know, from schools to garbage collection, at www.ci.minneapolis.mn.us/residents. The **St. Paul Convention and Visitors Authority** (www.stpaulcvb.org) has a similar list (click on "Visitors" and then "Relocation Information").

Finding a Job

Most employers still post jobs in the two major newspapers, the *Minneapolis Star Tribune* (www.startribune.com) and *St. Paul Pioneer Press* (www.pioneerpress.com), both of which publish all their job listings online.

Look for jobs at the **University of Minnesota** (www1.umn.edu/ohr), the **City of St. Paul** (www.stpaul.gov/jobs.asp), the **City of Minneapolis** (www.ci.minneapolis .mn.us/jobs), and the **State of Minnesota** (www.careers.state.mn.us). Minnesota maintains a statewide job bank at www.minnesotaworks.net.

The nonprofit **WomenVenture** (www.womenventure.com) offers low-cost career planning services for both men and women.

Housing

The major newspapers, *Minneapolis Star Tribune* (www.startribune.com) and *St. Paul Pioneer Press* (www.pioneerpress.com), again, are good sources of information on apartments for rent. **Craigslist** (http://minneapolis.craigslist.com) is also well-established in the area. **Apartment Search** (www.apartmentsearch .com) has extensive listings of large, managed properties, but no real database of smaller owner-occupied rentals.

Two of the largest real estate agencies in the Twin Cities are **Edina Realty** (www.edinarealty.com) and **Coldwell Banker Burnet** (www .cbburnet.com). The *Newcomer's Handbook for Moving to and Living in Minneapolis-St. Paul* (by Elizabeth Caperton-Halvorson, First Books Inc.) has excellent, detailed descriptions of every neighborhood in the two cities.

RESOURCES

Suggested Reading

HISTORY AND GENERAL INFORMATION

Atkins, Annette. *Creating Minnesota: A History from the Inside Out.* St. Paul: Minnesota Historical Society Press, 2007. A uniquely textured sort of history book, *Creating Minnesota* pieces together the story of Minnesota and Minnesotans through the eyes of individuals, from a mixed-blood interpreter at Fort Snelling to a state congresswoman. Atkins's writing is both dense and readable.

Diers, John, and Aaron Isaacs. *Twin Cities by Trolley.* Minneapolis: University of Minnesota Press, 2007. The story of the streetcars in the Twin Cities—first used in the late 1800s and finally pulled out of service in the 1950s—is the story of a growing metropolis hungry for modernity and eager to travel faster and farther than ever before. Diers and Isaacs, who have both been instrumental in preserving the history of the streetcars through the Minnesota Streetcar Museum, have put together a very readable and relevant history.

King, Tim, and Alice Tanghe. *The Minnesota Homegrown Cookbook.* Osceola, Wisconsin: Voyageur Press, 2008. Through the stories of dozens of beloved restaurants and chefs and more than 100 recipes, the authors paint a picture of Minnesota's remarkable food landscape. It's not all lutefisk and lefse here!

Koutsky, Kathryn Strand, and Linda Koutsky. *Minnesota State Fair: An Illustrated History.* Minneapolis: Coffee House Press, 2007. This mother-daughter team dug deep to find the history and lore behind this most beloved Minnesota institution, along with a fascinating collection of historical photos. Their previous endeavors, *Minnesota Eats Out* and *Minnesota Vacation Days,* also tell important Minnesota stories with humor and depth.

Roberts, Kate. *Minnesota 150: The People, Places, and Things that Shape Our State.* St. Paul: Minnesota Historical Society Press, 2007. In preparation for Minnesota's sesquicentennial in 2008, the Minnesota Historical Society asked people all over the state to nominate people, places, objects, organizations, and phenomena that were uniquely Minnesotan. The flood of responses was culled to 150 and organized into a uniquely illustrative exhibit at the Minnesota History Center and published in this beautifully written and illustrated book.

Seeley, Mark. *Minnesota Weather Almanac.* St. Paul: Minnesota Historical Society Press, 2006. What's more Minnesotan than talking about the weather? Not much. Climatologist and radio commentator Mark Seeley combines weather lore and history, biographies of weather-related figures in local history, and answers to burning weather questions: What's the record number of consecutive below-freezing days in the Twin Cities? Answer: 66.

Walsh, Jim. *The Replacements: All Over But the Shouting.* Osceola, Wisconsin: Voyageur Press, 2007. When the Replacements crashed their way onto the Minneapolis music scene in the late 1970s, disaffected teens from around the country sat up and took notice—not only of the 'Mats, as they were known—but of Minnesota itself. Jim Walsh was there, opening for the Replacements many times, and has been a fixture in Twin Cities journalism since.

White, Bruce. *We Are at Home: Pictures of the Ojibwe People.* St. Paul: Minnesota Historical Society Press, 2007. Historian Bruce White digs for the stories behind a remarkable collection of photographs of Ojibwe people from the earliest daguerreotypes to prints from the 1950s. The book tells stories not only of the Ojibwe people but also of their interaction with the growing population of whites.

LITERATURE AND FICTION

Bly, Carol. *Letters from the Country.* New York: Harper & Row, 1981. In the 1970s, Carol Bly wrote monthly essays for a Minnesota Public Radio feature called *A Letter from the Country.* Those essays became Bly's first book, to be followed by five more books of essays, five novels, and two books on the craft of writing. While Bly's writing evokes what she, following F. Scott Fitzgerald, called "the lost Swede towns," it reflects the natural world and ethical systems that shaped the cultures of Minnesota's city-dwellers, as well. Carol Bly, who died in 2007 at the age of 77, was married to the poet and men's movement leader Robert Bly.

Erdrich, Louise. *Love Medicine.* New York: Henry Holt & Co., 1984. Minnesotan Louise Erdrich won the National Book Critics' Circle Award for her first novel, *Love Medicine,* which tells a tangle of stories centered around a Native American reservation in North Dakota. While this novel and later ones, including the acclaimed *Tracks,* explore her Ojibwe heritage, Erdrich draws on her German-American side for other novels, including *The Beet Queen* and *The Master Butcher's Singing Club.* Erdrich owns Birch Bark Books in Minneapolis.

Fitzgerald, F. Scott. *The Great Gatsby.* New York: Penguin Popular Classics, 2007. While Fitzgerald's 1925 novel is set in Long Island and Manhattan, the Midwestern values of the narrator, Nick, and of Jay Gatsby's father, Henry Gatz, are a constant presence in the story, as the flip side of the lush and amoral lifestyle of the main characters. Fitzgerald was born in St. Paul's Cathedral Hill neighborhood and raised there and in East Coast boarding schools.

Keillor, Garrison. *Lake Wobegon Days.* New York: Viking, 1985. People around the country and the world know Garrison Keillor's inimitable voice from his long-running radio show *A Prairie Home Companion.* That voice is practically audible right off the page in his droll and meandering stories of small-town Midwestern life in *Lake Wobegon Days* and his later Lake Wobegon novels *Pontoon* and *Liberty.*

Kling, Kevin. *The Dog Says How.* St. Paul: Borealis Books, 2007. Playwright, performer, and essayist Kevin Kling is a gifted storyteller who is often heard on National Public Radio. His tales of growing up in suburban Minnesota and his recovery after a serious motorcycle accident are both uniquely Minnesotan and fascinatingly universal.

Landvik, Lorna. *The View from Mount Joy.* New York: Ballantine, 2007. Minnesotan Lorna Landvik mixes humor and a peculiar knack for plot in her novels, many set in Minnesota. *The View from Mount Joy* takes readers back to high school in Minneapolis circa 1972. Her earlier novels include *Angry Housewives Eating BonBons, Patty Jane's House of Curl, Tall Pine Polka, Your Oasis on Flame Lake,* and *Welcome to the Great Mysterious.*

Lewis, Sinclair. *Babbitt.* New York: Signet Classics, 2007. Sinclair Lewis's satirical take on conformity and boosterism in the Midwest hit especially hard in Minneapolis, where Lewis no doubt drew some of his inspiration (he has said that his city of Zenith could have been any midsized Midwestern city). Lewis's equally well-known earlier novel, *Main Street,* tells the story of a strong-willed Minneapolis woman who marries and moves to the small town of Gopher Prairie, a thinly disguised Sauk Centre, Minnesota, Lewis's home town.

Longfellow, Henry Wadsworth. *Song of Hiawatha.* Minneola, New York: Dover Publications, 2006. Longfellow had never visited Minnesota or seen Minnehaha Falls when he wrote his 1855 epic poem set there, but the work became an instant smash hit in its day and attracted many tourists to the falls. Longfellow based his work on the retellings of Ojibwe legend and history by other writers and explorers. Generations of Minnesota schoolchildren have memorized the lines "By the shores of Gitche Gumee / By the shining Big-Sea-Water / Stood the wigwam of Nokomis."

Rølvaag, Ole Edvart. *Giants in the Earth.* New York: Harper, 1927. Norwegian immigrant O. E. Rølvaag (1876–1931) was the first to chronicle the hardships faced by the pioneers on the prairie, from snowstorms to hunger and loneliness, and even the infamous locust plague of 1873–1877. *Giants in the Earth* is the first in a trilogy, followed by *Peder Victorious* and *Their Father's God.*

Rølvaag graduated from St. Olaf College in Northfield and taught there for many years. The Rølvaag Memorial Library is named in his honor.

CHILDREN'S LITERATURE

Lovelace, Maud Hart. *Betsy-Tacy.* New York: Thomas Y. Crowell Company, 1940. Maud Hart Lovelace told her daughter Merian stories about growing up in Mankato, Minnesota, then wrote them down in a series of beloved children's books. The series began in 1940 with *Betsy-Tacy* and culminated in 1955 with *Betsy's Wedding.*

Wargin, Kathy-Jo. *V is for Viking: A Minnesota Alphabet.* Chelsea, Michigan: Sleeping Bear Press, 2003. G is for gopher. L is for loon. M is for Mall of America, on through all 26 letters of the alphabet in this beautifully illustrated children's book, part of a series that covers all 50 states.

Wilder, Laura Ingalls. *Little House on the Prairie.* New York: Harper Collins, 1953 (revised). Generations of children have grown up reading about the adventures of Laura and Ma and Pa and the rest of the families, but Minnesotans have always felt a special connection to the stories, knowing that the real-life Walnut Grove and Plum Creek are a few miles down the road in southern Minnesota.

Internet Resources

ONLINE NEWS AND CHAT

E-Democracy
www.e-democracy.org

This moderated online forum now has discussion groups for 10 cities in the United States, United Kingdom, and New Zealand, but it started right here in the Twin Cities. Users are required to post under their real, full names and give their neighborhood of residence, a policy that has fostered some of the most thoughtful and civil discourse you'll see on the Internet. They're also limited to two posts a day, so you'll find long, thought-out posts rather than sniping and one-liners. This is a great place to find out what's on the minds of ordinary Twin Citians.

Minnesota Independent
www.minnesotaindependent.com

Sponsored by the left-leaning Center for Independent Media, the Minnesota Independent is open and unapologetic about its slant. It also does reporting of the sort that larger news organizations simply aren't doing any more, with a small but professional and scrappy staff.

MinnPost
www.minnpost.com

After a serious shake-up in Twin Cities journalism in the past few years, respected editor Joel Kramer decided to take excellent journalism online. And many of the cities' best reporters and writers followed him. Three main news stories are posted each work day at 11 A.M. A number of in-depth blog posts, covering arts, financial news, and more, appear throughout the day.

Secrets of the City
www.secretsofthecity.com

While the ambitious monthly magazine *The Rake* met its demise in early 2008, its spirit lives on at Secrets of the City, with coverage of Twin Cities culture—from restaurants to fashion shows to bloggy ramblings of local characters. The site has also subsumed the popular locally focused discussion board, MNSpeak, where users post news items and links. (One of the most common topics is about out-of-towners looking for advice on moving to the Twin Cities.)

Twin Cities Daily Planet
www.tcdailyplanet.net

A consortium of small and specialized news sources in the Twin Cities feed into the Twin Cities Daily Planet, which also includes a few originally reported stories as well. It's a great place to catch the news that the bigger news outlets will overlook.

PHOTOS AND MAPS

John R. Borchert Map Library
http://map.lib.umn.edu

A portion of the University of Minnesota's extensive map collection is online, including historical maps of Minneapolis and St. Paul and plat maps from every county in the state.

The Minneapolis Public Library Photo Collection
www.mplib.org/mphoto.asp

More than 10,000 historical photos are available to search online. Look up trolleys or blizzards or political figures or whatever else interests you. You can also order reproductions.

Minnesota Bookstore
www.comm.media.state.mn.us/bookstore

Want your own copy of the local building codes, the Minnesota state accounting statutes, a Minnesota mug, or a state hiking map? It's all here in this eclectic online store run by the state of Minnesota.

Minnesota Historical Society
www.mnhs.org

The Minnesota Historical Society's rich website offers resources for serious researchers and the casually curious. The society's enormous photo collection is online and fully searchable, as are extensive birth and death certificate databases.

Minnesota Reflections
http://reflections.mndigital.org

More than 75 organizations from around the state have pooled their image and document archives into one online searchable database including almost 20,000 images.

TWIN CITIES' BEST BLOGS

Minneapolis Metblogs
http://minneapolis.metblogs.com

Six bloggers who clearly love Minneapolis and love chronicling life here in its big and small moments maintain Minneapolis's Metroblogging site. (Learn more at www.metblogs.com about these collective, city-focused blogs.)

Minnescraper
www.minnescraper.com

The folks behind Minnescraper are passionate about buildings and development in downtown Minneapolis and beyond. While the blog and forum got their start during the condo boom of the early 2000s, the interest remains high. Find detailed information on Minneapolis building projects, maps, photos, and news updates.

Start Seeing Art
www.startsseeingart.com

Beyond a blog, this database of public art famous and obscure throughout Minneapolis and St. Paul is basically a one-man show, with photographs, maps, and brief histories of each of the works.

Twin Cities Sidewalk
http://tcsidewalks.blogspot.com

You can tell a lot about a city from what's going on on its sidewalks. This quirky blog includes a regular "Guess where?" photo of a sidewalk somewhere in the Twin Cities, updates on street life in both Minneapolis and St. Paul, and some personal asides.

The Uptake
www.theuptake.org

"Will journalism be done by you or to you?" asks The Uptake. This is citizen journalism in the hands of some talented folks with a video camera. Much of the video is uploaded live, as it is being shot.

Index

Restaurants Index

Nightlife Index

Shops Index

Hotels Index

www.moon.com

MOON.COM is all new, and ready to help plan your next trip! Filled with fresh trip ideas and strategies, author interviews, informative blogs, a detailed map library, and descriptions of all the Moon guidebooks, Moon.com is all you need to get out and explore the world—or even places in your own backyard. As always, when you travel with Moon, expect an experience that is uncommon and truly unique.

MAP SYMBOLS

═══	Expressway	█	Highlight	✗	Airfield	⚓	Golf Course
═══	Primary Road	○	City/Town	✈	Airport	🅿	Parking Area
═══	Secondary Road	◉	State Capital	▲	Mountain	⬙	Archaeological Site
▪▪▪▪	Unpaved Road	⊛	National Capital	✛	Unique Natural Feature	♟	Church
------	Trail	★	Point of Interest				
··········	Ferry	•	Accommodation	🙟	Waterfall	⛽	Gas Station
━▪━▪	Railroad	▼	Restaurant/Bar	▲	Park	〰	Glacier
▓▓▓	Pedestrian Walkway	■	Other Location	▣	Trailhead	⬚	Mangrove
⟨⟨⟨⟨	Stairs	⋏	Campground	🎿	Skiing Area	▨	Reef
						⬚	Swamp

CONVERSION TABLES

°C = (°F - 32) / 1.8
°F = (°C x 1.8) + 32
1 inch = 2.54 centimeters (cm)
1 foot = 0.304 meters (m)
1 yard = 0.914 meters
1 mile = 1.6093 kilometers (km)
1 km = 0.6214 miles
1 fathom = 1.8288 m
1 chain = 20.1168 m
1 furlong = 201.168 m
1 acre = 0.4047 hectares
1 sq km = 100 hectares
1 sq mile = 2.59 square km
1 ounce = 28.35 grams
1 pound = 0.4536 kilograms
1 short ton = 0.90718 metric ton
1 short ton = 2,000 pounds
1 long ton = 1.016 metric tons
1 long ton = 2,240 pounds
1 metric ton = 1,000 kilograms
1 quart = 0.94635 liters
1 US gallon = 3.7854 liters
1 Imperial gallon = 4.5459 liters
1 nautical mile = 1.852 km

°FAHRENHEIT	°CELSIUS	
230	110	
220	100	WATER BOILS
210		
200	90	
190		
180	80	
170		
160	70	
150		
140	60	
130		
120	50	
110		
100	40	
90		
80	30	
70	20	
60		
50	10	
40		
30	0	WATER FREEZES
20		
10	-10	
0		
-10	-20	
-20	-30	
-30		
-40	-40	

INCH 0   1   2   3   4

CM 0 1 2 3 4 5 6 7 8 9 10

MOON MINNEAPOLIS & ST. PAUL

Avalon Travel
a member of the Perseus Books Group
1700 Fourth Street
Berkeley, CA 94710, USA
www.moon.com

Editors: Annie M. Blakley, Erin Raber
Series Manager: Erin Raber
Copy Editor: Deana Shields
Graphics Coordinator: Kathryn Osgood
Production Coordinator: Lucie Ericksen
Cover Designer: Sean Bellows
Map Editors: Brice Ticen, Albert Angulo
Cartography Director: Mike Morgenfeld
Cartographers: Chris Markiewicz,
    Lohnes & Wright, Jon Twena

ISBN: 978-1-59880-201-6
ISSN: 1947-4121

Printing History
1st Edition – June 2009
5 4 3 2 1

G CURRENT

…vorite gem you'd like to see included in the next edition, or see anything
…ing, clarification, or correction, please drop us a line. Send your
… to feedback@moon.com, or use the address above.

MAP SYMBOLS

▦	Expressway	◖	Highlight	✈	Airfield	⚷	Golf Course
	Primary Road	○	City/Town	✈	Airport	℗	Parking Area
	Secondary Road	◉	State Capital	▲	Mountain	▰	Archaeological Site
	Unpaved Road	◉	National Capital	✛	Unique Natural Feature		Church
- - - - -	Trail	★	Point of Interest				Gas Station
....	Ferry	•	Accommodation	🗠	Waterfall		Glacier
	Railroad	▾	Restaurant/Bar	▲	Park		Mangrove
	Pedestrian Walkway	▪	Other Location	❶	Trailhead		Reef
))))))))))	Stairs	∆	Campground	⛷	Skiing Area		Swamp

CONVERSION TABLES

$°C = (°F - 32) / 1.8$
$°F = (°C \times 1.8) + 32$
1 inch = 2.54 centimeters (cm)
1 foot = 0.304 meters (m)
1 yard = 0.914 meters
1 mile = 1.6093 kilometers (km)
1 km = 0.6214 miles
1 fathom = 1.8288 m
1 chain = 20.1168 m
1 furlong = 201.168 m
1 acre = 0.4047 hectares
1 sq km = 100 hectares
1 sq mile = 2.59 square km
1 ounce = 28.35 grams
1 pound = 0.4536 kilograms
1 short ton = 0.90718 metric ton
1 short ton = 2,000 pounds
1 long ton = 1.016 metric tons
1 long ton = 2,240 pounds
1 metric ton = 1,000 kilograms
1 quart = 0.94635 liters
1 US gallon = 3.7854 liters
1 Imperial gallon = 4.5459 liters
1 nautical mile = 1.852 km

MOON MINNEAPOLIS & ST. PAUL
Avalon Travel
a member of the Perseus Books Group
1700 Fourth Street
Berkeley, CA 94710, USA
www.moon.com

Editors: Annie M. Blakley, Erin Raber
Series Manager: Erin Raber
Copy Editor: Deana Shields
Graphics Coordinator: Kathryn Osgood
Production Coordinator: Lucie Ericksen
Cover Designer: Sean Bellows
Map Editors: Brice Ticen, Albert Angulo
Cartography Director: Mike Morgenfeld
Cartographers: Chris Markiewicz,
    Lohnes & Wright, Jon Twena

ISBN: 978-1-59880-201-6
ISSN: 1947-4121

Printing History
1st Edition – June 2009
5 4 3 2 1

KEEPING CURRENT

If you have a favorite gem you'd like to see included in the next edition, or see anything
that needs updating, clarification, or correction, please drop us a line. Send your
comments via email to feedback@moon.com, or use the address above.